Language Lessons for a Living Education

10

MasterBooks® Curriculum

Editor-in-Chief:
Laura Welch

Editorial Team:
Craig Froman
Willow Meek
Judy Lewis

Art Director:
Diana Bogardus

Design Team:
Diana Bogardus
Jennifer Bauer

First printing: July 2024

Copyright © 2024 by Sarah Gabel, Kristen Pratt, and Master Books®. All rights reserved. No part of this book may be reproduced, copied, broadcast, stored, or shared in any form whatsoever without written permission from the publisher, except in the case of brief quotations in articles and reviews. For information write:

Master Books, P.O. Box 726, Green Forest, AR 72638
Master Books® is a division of the New Leaf Publishing Group, LLC.

ISBN: 978-1-68344-328-5
ISBN: 978-1-61458-904-4 (digital)

Unless otherwise noted, Scripture quotations are from the ESV® Bible (The Holy Bible, English Standard Version®), © 2001 by Crossway, a publishing ministry of Good News Publishers. Used by permission. All rights reserved. The ESV text may not be quoted in any publication made available to the public by a Creative Commons license. The ESV may not be translated in whole or in part into any other language.

Scripture quotations marked KJV are from the King James Version.

Scriptures taken from the Holy Bible, New International Version®, NIV®. Copyright © 1973, 1978, 1984, 2011 by Biblica, Inc.™ Used by permission of Zondervan. All rights reserved worldwide. www.zondervan.com The "NIV" and "New International Version" are trademarks registered in the United States Patent and Trademark Office by Biblica, Inc.™

Vocabulary terms and definitions are based on words taken from *Life of Washington* by Anna C. Reed, *Gifted Mind* by Raymond Damadian, and *The Summit* by Eric Alexander.

Printed in the United States of America

Please visit our website for other great titles: www.masterbooks.com

Permission is granted for copies of reproducible pages from this text to be made for use with immediate family members living in the same household. However, no part of this book may be reproduced, copied, broadcast, stored, or shared in any form beyond this use. Permission for any other use of the material must be requested by email from the publisher at info@nlpg.com.

About the Authors

Sarah Gabel is a home educator with a degree in English and over 20 years of experience in education. She is a mom to five boys and hails from western New York, where she uses her gift of communication in pastoral ministry alongside her husband.

Kristen Pratt served as the Master Books Brand & Curriculum Development Manager, where she developed the Master Books Method. She is a Kingdom-minded entrepreneur and author of the award-winning *Language Lessons for a Living Education* series. She homeschools her children in the beautiful Ozarks.

Table of Contents

Quick Navigation

Course Description 7
Suggested Daily Schedule 11
Exercises 19
Assessments & Grading, Teaching Resources 379
Answer Keys 467

Scope and Sequence

7	**Course Description**	
11	**Suggested Daily Schedule**	
19	**Lesson 1**	*Life of Washington* Introduction 19
		Sentence Basics 21
		Biographies and Autobiographies 23
		Worldview, *Life of Washington (LoW)* pages 5–18 25
		Review 27
29	**Lesson 2**	Picture Study: Moses Viewing the Promised Land 29
		Subjects and Predicates 31
		Biography Notes, Paragraphs, Wisdom Speaks 33
		Literary Analysis: Fiction vs. Nonfiction, *LoW* pages 19–31 ... 35
		Review 37
39	**Lesson 3**	Hymn Study: "Battle Hymn of the Republic" 39
		Verbs: Action and Linking 41
		Citing Sources, Wisdom Speaks 43
		Author's Focus: Character, *LoW* pages 32–45a 45
		Review 47
49	**Lesson 4**	Scripture Study: Psalm 139:1–6 49
		Helping Verbs 51
		Biography Notes, Historical Narrative Essay 53
		Author's Focus: A Secondary Purpose, *LoW* pages 45b–60 ... 55
		Review 57
59	**Lesson 5**	Biography Excerpt: Benjamin Franklin 59
		Verb Tense, Review It! 61
		Descriptive Paragraph, Wisdom Speaks 63
		A New Beginning, *LoW* pages 61–77a 65
		Review 67
69	**Lesson 6**	Picture Study: George Washington 69
		Independent vs. Dependent Clauses, Conjunctions 71
		More on Citations, Taking Notes, Biography Notes 73
		Literary Device: *In Medias Res*, *LoW* pages 77b–94a 75
		Review 77
79	**Lesson 7**	Poem Study: "A Little Boy and a Cherry Tree" 79
		Verb Mood (Indicative, Imperative, Subjunctive), Review It! ... 81
		Reflective Essay, Wisdom Speaks 83
		Literary Device: Imagery, *LoW* pages 94b–107 85
		Review 87

Language Lessons for a Living Education Level 10 — Table of Contents — 3

Lesson 8 — page 89

- Scripture Study: Psalm 139:7–12 89
- Prepositions, Review It! 91
- Finding Items for Citations, Biography Notes 93
- Literary Device: Exposition, *LoW* pages 108–125a 95
- Review 97

Lesson 9 — page 99

- Biography Excerpt: James Madison 99
- Verb Voice: Active vs. Passive, Review It! 101
- Definition Essay, Wisdom Speaks 103
- Author's Focus: Leadership, *LoW* pages 125b–141a 105
- Review 107

Lesson 10 — page 109

- Biography Excerpt: Alexander Hamilton 109
- Quotation Marks, Review It! 111
- Incorporating Quotes, Paraphrases, and Summaries 113
- Literary Device: Foreshadowing, *LoW* pages 141b–153 115
- Review 117

Lesson 11 — page 119

- Picture Study: Arnold Viewing the Destruction of New London 119
- Simple, Compound, and Complex Sentences; Interjections 121
- Biography Notes, Wisdom Speaks 123
- *LoW* pages 154–173a 125
- Review 127

Lesson 12 — page 129

- Hymn Study: "The Liberty Song" 129
- Adjectives, Adverbs, Types of Dependent Clauses: Adjective, Adverb, and Noun 131
- Biography Notes 133
- Literary Device: Anecdote, *LoW* pages 173b–187a 135
- Review 137

Lesson 13 — page 139

- Scripture Study: Psalm 139:13–18 139
- Punctuating Clauses, Review It! 141
- Biography Notes, Wisdom Speaks 143
- Literary Device: Analogy, *LoW* pages 187b–203a 145
- Review 147

Lesson 14 — page 149

- Biography Excerpt: Richard Bassett 149
- Adjectives 151
- Compiling a Works Cited Page 153
- Literary Device: Authorial Intrusion, *LoW* pages 203b–219a 155
- Review 157

Lesson 15 — page 159

- Picture Study: Mount Vernon 159
- Adverbs 161
- The Biography Rough Draft, Literary Devices, Transitions, Wisdom Speaks 163
- *LoW* pages 219b–234a 165
- Review 167

Lesson 16 — page 169

- Poem Study: "Lines Written by a Revolutionary Soldier" ... 169
- Prepositional Phrases Used as Adjectives and Adverbs, Review It! 171
- Rough Draft Due, Biography Cover Design, Works Cited .. 173
- *LoW* pages 234b–250a 175
- Review 177

Lesson 17 — page 179

- Scripture Study: Psalm 139:19–24 179
- Verbal Phrases, Participles, Gerunds 181
- Final Draft Due, Oral Presentation, Converting Your Biography, Wisdom Speaks 183
- Literary Device: Archetype, *LoW* pages 250b–259 185
- Review 187

Lesson 18 — 189

Biography Excerpt: Eldridge [Elbridge] Gerry	189
Verb Phrases: Infinitives, Split Infinitives, Review It!	191
Oral Presentation Due, Oral Presentation Feedback, Biography Feedback	193
LoW pages 260–277	195
Review	197

Lesson 19 — 199

Biblical Autobiography Excerpt: The Apostle Paul, Philippians 3:4–11	199
Pronouns, Review It!	201
Autobiography Assignment, Assignment Details, Wisdom Speaks	203
Gifted Mind: "The Truth" Excerpt	205
Review	207

Lesson 20 — 209

Picture Study: The Damadian Family Photo	209
More on Pronouns, Tricky Pronouns	211
Autobiography Notes: Steps for Writing	213
Gifted Mind: "The Truth" Excerpt	215
Review	217

Lesson 21 — 219

Hymn Study: "A Mighty Fortress Is Our God"	219
Direct Objects, Indirect Objects	221
Autobiography Notes: Memories, Wisdom Speaks	223
Gifted Mind: "The Truth" Excerpt	225
Review	227

Lesson 22 — 229

Scripture Study: Romans 1:18–25	229
Number: Subject-Verb Agreement	231
Autobiography Notes: Anecdotes	233
Gifted Mind: "The Truth" Excerpt	235
Review	237

Lesson 23 — 239

Biblical Autobiography Excerpt: Psalm 3	239
Conjugating Verbs	241
Autobiography Notes: Outline, Wisdom Speaks	243
Gifted Mind: "The Truth" Excerpt	245
Review	247

Lesson 24 — 249

Picture Study: King David Celebrating the Ark of the Covenant	249
Transitive and Intransitive Verbs, Review It!	251
Autobiography Notes: Rough Draft, In Conclusion	253
Gifted Mind: "The Truth" Excerpt	255
Review	257

Lesson 25 — 259

Poem Study: "The Cross"	259
Plural and Singular Nouns	261
Rough Draft Due, Cover Page and Artwork, Oral Presentation, Wisdom Speaks	263
Gifted Mind: "The Truth" Excerpt	265
Review	267

Lesson 26 — 269

Scripture Study: Selections on Truth and Wisdom	269
Possessive Nouns	271
Final Draft Due, Autobiography Reflection, Create an Oral Presentation Plan	273
Gifted Mind: "The Truth" Excerpt	275
Review	277

Lesson 27 — 279

Biblical Autobiography Excerpt: Jesus	279
Forming Possessive Nouns, Colons, Review It!	281
Oral Presentation Due, Wisdom Speaks	283
Gifted Mind: "The Truth" Excerpt	285
Review	287

Lesson 28 — 289
- Excerpt Study: *Evidence for the Bible* 289
- Compound-Complex Sentences, Prefix Study 291
- Summarizing 293
- *The Summit* by Eric Alexander, About the Author 295
- Review 297

Lesson 29 — 299
- Picture Study: Mountain Range with Beautiful Green Landscape 299
- Parallel Items, Suffix Study 301
- Using a Thesaurus, Wisdom Speaks 303
- *The Summit: Deadpoint Reflections* 305
- Review 307

Lesson 30 — 309
- Hymn Study: "Savior, Lead Me Up the Mountain" 309
- Double Negatives, Prefix Study 311
- The Art of Rhetoric, Modes of Persuasion 313
- *The Summit: Deadpoint Reflections* 315
- Review 317

Lesson 31 — 319
- Scripture Study: Mountain Bible Verses 319
- Tricky Words, Suffix Study 321
- Persuasive Essay, Wisdom Speaks 323
- *The Summit: Deadpoint Reflections* 325
- Review 327

Lesson 32 — 329
- Excerpt Study: *Developing a Heart for God* 329
- Misplaced or Dangling Modifiers, Prefix Study 331
- Persuasive Essay Development 333
- *The Summit: Deadpoint Reflections* 335
- Review 337

Lesson 33 — 339
- Picture Study: Climbing Team Success 339
- Irregular Verbs, Suffix Study 341
- Persuasive Essay Rough Draft Due, Wisdom Speaks 343
- *The Summit: Deadpoint Reflections* 345
- Review 347

Lesson 34 — 349
- Poem Study: "The Mountain" 349
- Hyphens, Prefix Study 351
- Persuasion in Advertising 353
- *The Summit: Deadpoint Reflections* 355
- Review 357

Lesson 35 — 359
- Scripture Study: Isaiah 40:9–14 359
- Comma Review, Suffix Study 361
- Oral Presentation, Wisdom Speaks 363
- *The Summit: Deadpoint Reflections* 365
- Review 367

Lesson 36 — 369
- *Answers Magazine* Excerpt: "Making More of the Mountains" 369
- Commonly Misused Words, Prefix/Suffix Review 371
- Etiquette and Communication, Course Self-Evaluation, Oral Presentation Due 373
- *The Summit: Deadpoint Reflections* 375
- Review 377

379 — Assessments & Grading, Teaching Resources

467 — Answer Keys

Using This Course

Course Description

Language Lessons for a Living Education Level 10 equips students to be effective communicators through speaking, writing, and expressing. This course purposefully prepares students to share their faith in a way that impacts their generation and beyond. The biography *Life of Washington* will provide the basis for evaluating the character of one of the most significant men in history. Excerpts from the autobiographies *Gifted Mind* and *The Summit* will give students insight into the minds of two men who served God in very different ways. Students will learn and practice foundational high school–level communication skills through essays, summaries, oral presentations, and through writing a biography and autobiography. Research skills will be strengthened through learning the MLA style of citation. Students will learn how to apply grammar and punctuation rules in their writing. This course employs a variety of features to prepare students for successful high school communication.

Features

	Target Level	High school, Grade 10 and up 1 English credit
	Flexible 180-Day Schedule	Approximately 50 minutes per exercise, five days a week
	Open & Go	Convenient daily schedule, Well-designed lessons
	Engaging Application	Critical thinking, Faith tie-ins, Extension activities
	Assessments	Reviews, Rubrics, Answer Keys

Objectives

▸ Special Features engage students, teaching creativity, spelling, and vocabulary.

▸ Grammar & Punctuation sets up a foundation of high school concepts that are applied through writing.

▸ Students are equipped with biblical application for expression, essay writing, and speaking skills.

▸ Worldview & Literary Analysis teaches literary devices, critical thinking, and biblical worldview application.

▸ Review Days provide reinforcement for all concepts and may be used as assessments.

Companion Books

Required   *Optional*

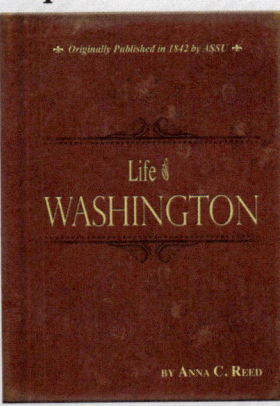

All books available from MasterBooks.com

Placement

Students are ready to begin *Language Lessons for a Living Education* Level 10 when they can write a five-paragraph essay using well-written paragraphs, properly use basic grammar and punctuation, recognize abstract ideas, and are ready to learn high school–level vocabulary.

Supply List

- ☐ 3×5 index cards
- ☐ Notebook
- ☐ Bible
- ☐ Dictionary
- ☐ Thesaurus
- ☐ Independent reading books

Teacher and Course Information

Welcome to *Language Lessons for a Living Education* Level 10! This course offers a biblically-based approach to teaching students about grammar, communication, and worldview analysis while exposing them to works of literature and art. It also offers opportunities to employ the knowledge and skills the students are learning through writing assignments, citing research, literary analysis, grammar exercises, personal evaluation, and oral presentations. The book *Life of Washington* is the foundational text for the first semester. With a focus on the character of George Washington, students will examine his speech and behavior based on biblical truth. We hope that students will desire to emulate the godly character traits they see in others while having the ability to discern ungodly traits as well.

The Grammar & Punctuation exercises are designed to take students deeper into the concepts they have studied in elementary and middle school grammar, using an uncomplicated approach.

Communication exercises teach writing and speaking skills and offer freedom of choice regarding writing topics. Students are challenged to think critically about *what* and *how* they communicate with others through speech and the written word.

Worldview & Literary Analysis exercises expose students to several literary devices to aid them in studying literature and assist them in their writing assignments. Literature is examined in light of biblical truth, and students are challenged to apply these truths to their lives.

Our goal is to come alongside you, the parent, giving you the tools to raise a godly group of world changers who share the good news of the gospel with their generation and impact generations to come. It is exciting to see students progressing through the high school years as they prepare for adulthood!

We pray blessings on you and your family as you educate your students in the wisdom and admonition of the Lord.

In Him,

Sarah Gabel & Kristen Pratt

Course Overview

Exercise 1 of each lesson begins with a special feature, vocabulary and spelling words, and Scripture memory.

Exercise 2 is devoted to grammar and punctuation, including application.

Exercise 3 is all about communication. Students develop their skills in the areas of written, verbal, nonverbal, and technological communication.

Exercise 4 is the worldview and literary analysis day.

Students will study the book *Life of Washington* and excerpts from the books *Gifted Mind* and *The Summit*. They will evaluate worldviews and learn literary devices.

Exercise 5 is a review of what students have learned in the lesson. The review may be used as a quiz or test.

Special Features

The first day of each lesson begins with a special feature that provides a creative and engaging start to the week. The special features rotate between historical excerpts, picture study, hymn study, Scripture study, and poem study.

Excerpts found in the first and second quarters are short historical biographies taken from Tim LaHaye's book *Faith of Our Founding Fathers*. These excerpts give students a glimpse into the lives and worldviews of people who were foundational in the formation of the United States of America and include concepts important to the foundation of any people and society. The third quarter features excerpts from the Bible that are autobiographical in nature, allowing the student to observe how people in the Bible portrayed themselves in writing. The fourth quarter uses excerpts about mountains and how they can be used to teach life lessons.

Picture Study captures the student's imagination and provides visual connections that inspire writing ideas. The pictures presented correspond to the literature from the worldview and literary analysis days, creating a visual connection with the topics studied.

Hymn Study exposes students to classic hymns and traditional writing styles. Students are encouraged to connect with their faith through rewriting verses in their own words, summarizing, and analyzing the views expressed in the hymn.

Scripture Study uses the first semester to walk the student through Psalm 139, with a focus on their importance to the Lord and His thorough knowledge of them. The second semester will examine Scripture related to truth and creation. These studies encourage students to think deeply and apply Scripture to their lives.

Poem Study allows for creative writing along with poetry analysis. Poems are a rich form of communication that can inspire, create images in the mind, and even share the good news of the gospel.

Vocabulary Words are introduced at the start of each weekly lesson and are selected out of the assigned readings from *Life of Washington* and the excerpts included in the curriculum from *Gifted Mind* and *The Summit*. The best way to learn new vocabulary words is in the context of real books. Students will write these vocabulary words along with their definitions on index cards to study throughout the week. They may also be used as spelling words.

Scripture Memory sharpens the mind and strengthens the faith of students. Scripture is alive and sharp. Committing it to memory is an effective method of equipping students for battles they will face throughout their lives.

Grammar & Punctuation

The concepts of grammar and punctuation are taught throughout the entirety of a student's education, and mastery of these concepts is not always achieved. Even educated adults often need to look up grammar or punctuation rules from time to time. However, the more your student can learn and apply the rules of writing, the easier clear communication will become.

This course gives an overview of important grammar and punctuation rules, allowing the student to interact with those rules by recording them on index cards, recognizing them in sample sentences, and applying them in their creative writing. Grammar concepts are also drawn into the vocabulary and communication exercises.

Communication

Communication lessons are birthed out of a belief that communication is important to God. His Word has a lot to say about what and how we communicate. Often, communicating effectively and righteously does not come naturally, but requires awareness and practice. Wisdom Speaks is a biweekly feature that takes an in-depth look at what the Book of Proverbs has to say about our motives, words, and body language. Students will learn that applying these truths to our daily communication — whether verbal, nonverbal, or written — will have a lasting impact on their effectiveness as communicators.

Writing assignments include the following essay types: historical narrative, descriptive, reflective, and definition. Larger writing assignments challenge the student to write a biography about a famous person of their choice during the first semester. The second semester will focus on writing an autobiography. These larger assignments progress slowly, and the student is given detailed instructions and examples. Research is required for some writing assignments, and the MLA style of citation is taught. Two oral presentations give public speaking opportunities, and students are encouraged to use artistic skills in designing cover sheets for writing assignments.

Communication exercises are designed to be personal and to challenge students to think deeply about their communication skills, encouraging them to stretch and grow in how they communicate with God and others.

Course Information

Worldview & Literary Analysis

A biblical worldview lays the foundation for navigating life. During their lifetime, students will be exposed to movies, commercials, books, websites, emails, and texts that will challenge the authority of Scripture. Exercise 4 of this course equips students to recognize and apply a biblical worldview to everything they hear, read, and see.

With *Life of Washington*, a biography of George Washington, as the text for the first semester, students will analyze the worldview of Washington in light of biblical truth and learn about applying that truth to their lives. The second semester features excerpts from *Gifted Mind* and *The Summit*, both autobiographies, in which biblical worldviews will be analyzed as well.

Students will learn to recognize, understand, and use various literary devices, including author focus, secondary purpose, *in medias res*, imagery, exposition, foreshadowing, anecdotes, analogy, and authorial intrusion.

Review Day

Each weekly lesson offers a Review Day that pulls some of the vital topics from the weekly lesson, giving students another chance to interact with the material studied. These reviews can be used as a traditional quiz or can be used open-book style, allowing students access to their index card study tips, the weekly exercises, and the study helps in the back of the book.

There are four sections in each Review Day:

- Vocabulary
- Grammar & Punctuation
- Communication
- Worldview & Literary Analysis

Students should study and correct any questions they got wrong to reap the most benefit from the Review Day.

Rubrics

Rubrics are included for assistance in grading each of the essays, the biography, the autobiography, and the oral presentations. These organizational charts can be very helpful in assessing student performance. Each essay has a slightly different rubric since the essay requirements vary. Rubrics contain categories such as structure, expression, word choice, and grammar/punctuation.

Teaching Resources

Be sure to check out the appendix for additional teaching resources!

- **Independent Reading List:** Use this form to assign and track independent reading books.
- **Recommended Reading Book List:** Suggested Master Books titles to assign as independent reading books.
- **Writing Prompts:** Additional engaging writing assignments for extra practice or just for fun.
- **Worksheets:** Helpful for creating outlines, writing essays, and organizing oral presentations.
- **Spelling and Vocabulary:** Vocabulary study tips, spelling word lists, rules, prefixes, suffixes, and root words.
- **Study Sheets:** Grammar and Communication study sheets reinforce concepts covered in the text.
- **Rubrics:** Guide both the student and the teacher in planning and evaluating writing assignments and oral presentations.
- **List of Revolutionary War Generals:** For use with the book *Life of Washington*.
- **Answer Key:** Provides answers for the numbered questions in the course. A grading guide is included.

Language Lessons Level 10 Daily Schedule

Calendar		Assignment	Due Date	✓	Grade
▶ **First Semester-First Quarter**					
Week 1	Day 1	Lesson 1 • Exercise 1 • Pages 19–20			
	Day 2	Lesson 1 • Exercise 2 • Pages 21–22			
	Day 3	Lesson 1 • Exercise 3 • Pages 23–24			
	Day 4	Lesson 1 • Exercise 4 • Pages 25–26			
	Day 5	Lesson 1 • Exercise 5 • **Review** • Pages 27–28			
Week 2	Day 6	Lesson 2 • Exercise 1 • Pages 29–30			
	Day 7	Lesson 2 • Exercise 2 • Pages 31–32			
	Day 8	Lesson 2 • Exercise 3 • Pages 33–34			
	Day 9	Lesson 2 • Exercise 4 • Pages 35–36			
	Day 10	Lesson 2 • Exercise 5 • **Review** • Pages 37–38			
Week 3	Day 11	Lesson 3 • Exercise 1 • Pages 39–40			
	Day 12	Lesson 3 • Exercise 2 • Pages 41–42			
	Day 13	Lesson 3 • Exercise 3 • Pages 43–44			
	Day 14	Lesson 3 • Exercise 4 • Pages 45–46			
	Day 15	Lesson 3 • Exercise 5 • **Review** • Pages 47–48			
Week 4	Day 16	Lesson 4 • Exercise 1 • Pages 49–50			
	Day 17	Lesson 4 • Exercise 2 • Pages 51–52			
	Day 18	Lesson 4 • Exercise 3 • Pages 53–54			
	Day 19	Lesson 4 • Exercise 4 • Pages 55–56			
	Day 20	Lesson 4 • Exercise 5 • **Review** • Pages 57–58			
Week 5	Day 21	Lesson 5 • Exercise 1 • Pages 59–60			
	Day 22	Lesson 5 • Exercise 2 • Pages 61–62			
	Day 23	Lesson 5 • Exercise 3 • Pages 63–64			
	Day 24	Lesson 5 • Exercise 4 • Pages 65–66			
	Day 25	Lesson 5 • Exercise 5 • **Review** • Pages 67–68			
Week 6	Day 26	Lesson 6 • Exercise 1 • Pages 69–70			
	Day 27	Lesson 6 • Exercise 2 • Pages 71–72			
	Day 28	Lesson 6 • Exercise 3 • Pages 73–74			
	Day 29	Lesson 6 • Exercise 4 • Pages 75–76			
	Day 30	Lesson 6 • Exercise 5 • **Review** • Pages 77–78			

Calendar		Assignment	Due Date	✓	Grade
Week 7	Day 31	Lesson 7 • Exercise 1 • Pages 79–80			
	Day 32	Lesson 7 • Exercise 2 • Pages 81–82			
	Day 33	Lesson 7 • Exercise 3 • Pages 83–84			
	Day 34	Lesson 7 • Exercise 4 • Pages 85–86			
	Day 35	Lesson 7 • Exercise 5 • **Review** • Pages 87–88			
Week 8	Day 36	Lesson 8 • Exercise 1 • Pages 89–90			
	Day 37	Lesson 8 • Exercise 2 • Pages 91–92			
	Day 38	Lesson 8 • Exercise 3 • Pages 93–94			
	Day 39	Lesson 8 • Exercise 4 • Pages 95–96			
	Day 40	Lesson 8 • Exercise 5 • **Review** • Pages 97–98			
Week 9	Day 41	Lesson 9 • Exercise 1 • Pages 99–100			
	Day 42	Lesson 9 • Exercise 2 • Pages 101–102			
	Day 43	Lesson 9 • Exercise 3 • Pages 103–104			
	Day 44	Lesson 9 • Exercise 4 • Pages 105–106			
	Day 45	Lesson 9 • Exercise 5 • **Review** • Pages 107–108			

Language Lessons Level 10 Daily Schedule

Calendar		Assignment	Due Date	✓	Grade
▶ **First Semester-Second Quarter**					
Week 1	Day 46	Lesson 10 • Exercise 1 • Pages 109–110			
	Day 47	Lesson 10 • Exercise 2 • Pages 111–112			
	Day 48	Lesson 10 • Exercise 3 • Pages 113–114			
	Day 49	Lesson 10 • Exercise 4 • Pages 115–116			
	Day 50	Lesson 10 • Exercise 5 • **Review** • Pages 117–118			
Week 2	Day 51	Lesson 11 • Exercise 1 • Pages 119–120			
	Day 52	Lesson 11 • Exercise 2 • Pages 121–122			
	Day 53	Lesson 11 • Exercise 3 • Pages 123–124			
	Day 54	Lesson 11 • Exercise 4 • Pages 125–126			
	Day 55	Lesson 11 • Exercise 5 • **Review** • Pages 127–128			
Week 3	Day 56	Lesson 12 • Exercise 1 • Pages 129–130			
	Day 57	Lesson 12 • Exercise 2 • Pages 131–132			
	Day 58	Lesson 12 • Exercise 3 • Pages 133–134			
	Day 59	Lesson 12 • Exercise 4 • Pages 135–136			
	Day 60	Lesson 12 • Exercise 5 • **Review** • Pages 137–138			
Week 4	Day 61	Lesson 13 • Exercise 1 • Pages 139–140			
	Day 62	Lesson 13 • Exercise 2 • Pages 141–142			
	Day 63	Lesson 13 • Exercise 3 • Pages 143–144			
	Day 64	Lesson 13 • Exercise 4 • Pages 145–146			
	Day 65	Lesson 13 • Exercise 5 • **Review** • Pages 147–148			
Week 5	Day 66	Lesson 14 • Exercise 1 • Pages 149–150			
	Day 67	Lesson 14 • Exercise 2 • Pages 151–152			
	Day 68	Lesson 14 • Exercise 3 • Pages 153–154			
	Day 69	Lesson 14 • Exercise 4 • Pages 155–156			
	Day 70	Lesson 14 • Exercise 5 • **Review** • Pages 157–158			
Week 6	Day 71	Lesson 15 • Exercise 1 • Pages 159–160			
	Day 72	Lesson 15 • Exercise 2 • Pages 161–162			
	Day 73	Lesson 15 • Exercise 3 • Pages 163–164			
	Day 74	Lesson 15 • Exercise 4 • Pages 165–166			
	Day 75	Lesson 15 • Exercise 5 • **Review** • Pages 167–168			

Language Lessons for a Living Education Level 10

Calendar		Assignment	Due Date	✓	Grade
Week 7	Day 76	Lesson 16 • Exercise 1 • Pages 169–170			
	Day 77	Lesson 16 • Exercise 2 • Pages 171–172			
	Day 78	Lesson 16 • Exercise 3 • Pages 173–174			
	Day 79	Lesson 16 • Exercise 4 • Pages 175–176			
	Day 80	Lesson 16 • Exercise 5 • **Review** • Pages 177–178			
Week 8	Day 81	Lesson 17 • Exercise 1 • Pages 179–180			
	Day 82	Lesson 17 • Exercise 2 • Pages 181–182			
	Day 83	Lesson 17 • Exercise 3 • Pages 183–184			
	Day 84	Lesson 17 • Exercise 4 • Pages 185–186			
	Day 85	Lesson 17 • Exercise 5 • **Review** • Pages 187–188			
Week 9	Day 86	Lesson 18 • Exercise 1 • Pages 189–190			
	Day 87	Lesson 18 • Exercise 2 • Pages 191–192			
	Day 88	Lesson 18 • Exercise 3 • Pages 193–194			
	Day 89	Lesson 18 • Exercise 4 • Pages 195–196			
	Day 90	Lesson 18 • Exercise 5 • **Review** • Pages 197–198			
		Mid-Term Grade			

Language Lessons Level 10 Daily Schedule

Calendar		Assignment	Due Date	✓	Grade
▶ Second Semester–Third Quarter					
Week 1	Day 91	Lesson 19 • Exercise 1 • Pages 199–200			
	Day 92	Lesson 19 • Exercise 2 • Pages 201–202			
	Day 93	Lesson 19 • Exercise 3 • Pages 203–204			
	Day 94	Lesson 19 • Exercise 4 • Pages 205–206			
	Day 95	Lesson 19 • Exercise 5 • **Review** • Pages 207–208			
Week 2	Day 96	Lesson 20 • Exercise 1 • Pages 209–210			
	Day 97	Lesson 20 • Exercise 2 • Pages 211–212			
	Day 98	Lesson 20 • Exercise 3 • Pages 213–214			
	Day 99	Lesson 20 • Exercise 4 • Pages 215–216			
	Day 100	Lesson 20 • Exercise 5 • **Review** • Pages 217–218			
Week 3	Day 101	Lesson 21 • Exercise 1 • Pages 219–220			
	Day 102	Lesson 21 • Exercise 2 • Pages 221–222			
	Day 103	Lesson 21 • Exercise 3 • Pages 223–224			
	Day 104	Lesson 21 • Exercise 4 • Pages 225–226			
	Day 105	Lesson 21 • Exercise 5 • **Review** • Pages 227–228			
Week 4	Day 106	Lesson 22 • Exercise 1 • Pages 229–230			
	Day 107	Lesson 22 • Exercise 2 • Pages 231–232			
	Day 108	Lesson 22 • Exercise 3 • Pages 233–234			
	Day 109	Lesson 22 • Exercise 4 • Pages 235–236			
	Day 110	Lesson 22 • Exercise 5 • **Review** • Pages 237–238			
Week 5	Day 111	Lesson 23 • Exercise 1 • Pages 239–240			
	Day 112	Lesson 23 • Exercise 2 • Pages 241–242			
	Day 113	Lesson 23 • Exercise 3 • Pages 243–244			
	Day 114	Lesson 23 • Exercise 4 • Pages 245–246			
	Day 115	Lesson 23 • Exercise 5 • **Review** • Pages 247–248			
Week 6	Day 116	Lesson 24 • Exercise 1 • Pages 249–250			
	Day 117	Lesson 24 • Exercise 2 • Pages 251–252			
	Day 118	Lesson 24 • Exercise 3 • Pages 253–254			
	Day 119	Lesson 24 • Exercise 4 • Pages 255–256			
	Day 120	Lesson 24 • Exercise 5 • **Review** • Pages 257–258			

Calendar		Assignment	Due Date	✓	Grade
Week 7	Day 121	Lesson 25 • Exercise 1 • Pages 259–260			
	Day 122	Lesson 25 • Exercise 2 • Pages 261–262			
	Day 123	Lesson 25 • Exercise 3 • Pages 263–264			
	Day 124	Lesson 25 • Exercise 4 • Pages 265–266			
	Day 125	Lesson 25 • Exercise 5 • **Review** • Pages 267–268			
Week 8	Day 126	Lesson 26 • Exercise 1 • Pages 269–270			
	Day 127	Lesson 26 • Exercise 2 • Pages 271–272			
	Day 128	Lesson 26 • Exercise 3 • Pages 273–274			
	Day 129	Lesson 26 • Exercise 4 • Pages 275–276			
	Day 130	Lesson 26 • Exercise 5 • **Review** • Pages 277–278			
Week 9	Day 131	Lesson 27 • Exercise 1 • Pages 279–280			
	Day 132	Lesson 27 • Exercise 2 • Pages 281–282			
	Day 133	Lesson 27 • Exercise 3 • Pages 283–284			
	Day 134	Lesson 27 • Exercise 4 • Pages 285–286			
	Day 135	Lesson 27 • Exercise 5 • **Review** • Pages 287–288			

Language Lessons Level 10 Daily Schedule

Calendar		Assignment	Due Date	✓	Grade
▶ **Second Semester-Fourth Quarter**					
Week 1	Day 136	Lesson 28 • Exercise 1 • Pages 289–290			
	Day 137	Lesson 28 • Exercise 2 • Pages 291–292			
	Day 138	Lesson 28 • Exercise 3 • Pages 293–294			
	Day 139	Lesson 28 • Exercise 4 • Pages 295–296			
	Day 140	Lesson 28 • Exercise 5 • **Review** • Pages 297–298			
Week 2	Day 141	Lesson 29 • Exercise 1 • Pages 299–300			
	Day 142	Lesson 29 • Exercise 2 • Pages 301–302			
	Day 143	Lesson 29 • Exercise 3 • Pages 303–304			
	Day 144	Lesson 29 • Exercise 4 • Pages 305–306			
	Day 145	Lesson 29 • Exercise 5 • **Review** • Pages 307–308			
Week 3	Day 146	Lesson 30 • Exercise 1 • Pages 309–310			
	Day 147	Lesson 30 • Exercise 2 • Pages 311–312			
	Day 148	Lesson 30 • Exercise 3 • Pages 313–314			
	Day 149	Lesson 30 • Exercise 4 • Pages 315–316			
	Day 150	Lesson 30 • Exercise 5 • **Review** • Pages 317–318			
Week 4	Day 151	Lesson 31 • Exercise 1 • Pages 319–320			
	Day 152	Lesson 31 • Exercise 2 • Pages 321–322			
	Day 153	Lesson 31 • Exercise 3 • Pages 323–324			
	Day 154	Lesson 31 • Exercise 4 • Pages 325–326			
	Day 155	Lesson 31 • Exercise 5 • **Review** • Pages 327–328			
Week 5	Day 156	Lesson 32 • Exercise 1 • Pages 329–330			
	Day 157	Lesson 32 • Exercise 2 • Pages 331–332			
	Day 158	Lesson 32 • Exercise 3 • Pages 333–334			
	Day 159	Lesson 32 • Exercise 4 • Pages 335–336			
	Day 160	Lesson 32 • Exercise 5 • **Review** • Pages 337–338			
Week 6	Day 161	Lesson 33 • Exercise 1 • Pages 339–340			
	Day 162	Lesson 33 • Exercise 2 • Pages 341–342			
	Day 163	Lesson 33 • Exercise 3 • Pages 343–344			
	Day 164	Lesson 33 • Exercise 4 • Pages 345–346			
	Day 165	Lesson 33 • Exercise 5 • **Review** • Pages 347–348			

Calendar		Assignment	Due Date	✓	Grade
Week 7	Day 166	Lesson 34 • Exercise 1 • Pages 349–350			
	Day 167	Lesson 34 • Exercise 2 • Pages 351–352			
	Day 168	Lesson 34 • Exercise 3 • Pages 353–354			
	Day 169	Lesson 34 • Exercise 4 • Pages 355–356			
	Day 170	Lesson 34 • Exercise 5 • **Review** • Pages 357–358			
Week 8	Day 171	Lesson 35 • Exercise 1 • Pages 359–360			
	Day 172	Lesson 35 • Exercise 2 • Pages 361–362			
	Day 173	Lesson 35 • Exercise 3 • Pages 363–364			
	Day 174	Lesson 35 • Exercise 4 • Pages 365–366			
	Day 175	Lesson 35 • Exercise 5 • **Review** • Pages 367–368			
Week 9	Day 176	Lesson 36 • Exercise 1 • Pages 369–370			
	Day 177	Lesson 36 • Exercise 2 • Pages 371–372			
	Day 178	Lesson 36 • Exercise 3 • Pages 373–374			
	Day 179	Lesson 36 • Exercise 4 • Pages 375–376			
	Day 180	Lesson 36 • Exercise 5 • **Review** • Pages 377–378			
		Final Grade			

 **Special Feature**

Lesson 1

As part of this course, we will read the book *Life of Washington* by Anna C. Reed. This book is considered a biography. A **biography** is an account of someone's life written by someone else. A biography often includes the individual's place of birth, date of birth, educational background, religious beliefs, professional experience, areas of expertise, impactful life events, and major achievements. The Gospels are biographies, as they are accounts of Jesus' life written by others.

Anna C. Reed's account of George Washington's life is written in an engaging style that will keep you interested in the life of this extraordinary man who had such an impact on America and, consequently, your life today! From Washington's exciting days as a young boy, his rise through the military, and his eventual presidency, Reed gives the reader a feel for the character and God-given abilities of one of the most prominent names in American history.

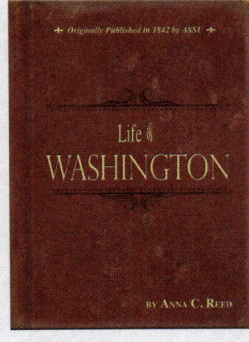

Throughout this lesson, you will read the introduction of this biography. An **introduction** is usually found in a written work about real events and can include a summary of what will be presented, important terms, or background information. In *Life of Washington*, the introduction focuses on another important historical figure, Christopher Columbus. Reed gives a short biography of Columbus because Columbus' vision is foundational to both the beliefs and choices of George Washington. The author is setting the stage for an extraordinary tale: the life and times of the first president of the United States of America.

> A **biography** is an account of someone's life written by someone else.
>
> An **introduction** is usually found in a written work about real events and can include a summary of what will be presented, important terms, or background information.

1. **List** the items a biography often includes.

   _____
   _____
   _____
   _____

Write a 5- to 6-sentence paragraph detailing what you currently know about George Washington.

_____
_____
_____
_____
_____
_____
_____
_____
_____
_____

Special Feature

Lesson 1, Day 1

Name_____ Lesson 1 - Exercise 1 Day 1

Before beginning to read, **study** the vocabulary words listed below.

Vocabulary

amiable	having or displaying a friendly and pleasant manner	**friar**	a member of a religious order of men
caravals (caravels)	small, fast Spanish or Portuguese sailing ships	**hasty**	done or acting with excessive speed or urgency; hurried
charter	a written grant by a country that defines rights and privileges	**lamentations**	passionate expressions of grief or sorrow
convent	a community under monastic vows, especially one of nuns	**province**	an administrative division of certain countries or empires
cultivated	refined and well educated	**reproached**	addressed someone by expressing disapproval or disappointment
desponding	becoming dejected and losing confidence	**resolutely**	in an admirably purposeful, determined, and unwavering manner
disposition	a person's inherent qualities of mind and character	**resolution**	a firm decision to do or not to do something
eloquent	fluent or persuasive in speaking or writing	**toilsome**	involving hard or tedious work
endeavouring (endeavoring)	trying hard to do or achieve something	**tumult**	confusion or disorder

2. **Write** a sentence using the words *convent* and *friar*.

   _____
   _____

3. **Write** a sentence using the word *disposition*.

   _____
   _____

Begin to **read** the introduction to *Life of Washington* on pages 5–18. You will answer questions about the reading assignment on Day 4 of this lesson.

☐ **Use** index cards to **write** each vocabulary word from this lesson on one side and the definition on the other. **Check** the box when complete.

☐ **Copy** the Scripture verse on an index card. **Memorize** it by the end of this lesson. You may choose the Bible translation or use the one given. **Check** the box when complete.

The LORD hath made bare his holy arm in the eyes of all the nations; and all the ends of the earth shall see the salvation of our God. Isaiah 52:10 (KJV)

Name _____ Lesson 1 - Exercise 2 Day 2

Grammar & Punctuation

Why have you studied grammar and punctuation throughout your education? The simple answer: because it's important! Proper use of grammar and punctuation will help you avoid being misunderstood and enable you to communicate clearly. While the rules of grammar may seem extensive, you need not fear them. Repeated exposure and practice will strengthen your skills, allowing you to speak and write with confidence.

The term *grammar* refers to the rules of a language that govern sounds, words, and sentences, as well as how they are combined and understood. The term *punctuation* describes the marks (period, comma, parentheses, etc.) used to separate sentences and their elements to clarify meaning, show emphasis, or express emotion. English grammar is based on eight parts of speech, and learning what they are and how to use them is foundational to understanding grammar. **Study** the chart:

	The Eight Parts of Speech
Noun	names a person, place, or thing
	tree, Jennifer, New York, love
Verb	shows action or state-of-being
	swim, twirl, shout, am, is, were
Adjective	describes a noun or pronoun. Tells what kind, how many, or which one
	blue, kind, ten
Adverb	describes a verb, adjective, or another adverb. Tells when, where, how, or how often.
	slowly, later, above, yesterday
Pronoun	takes the place of a noun
	he, she, it, they, their, him, her
Conjunction	joins words or phrases
	and, yet, although, unless, because, as if
Preposition	describes a relationship between a noun or pronoun and another word that follows
	to, for, with, over, on, between, near, into, at, beneath, in
Interjection	expresses strong feelings or emotions. Often followed by an exclamation point, although sometimes only a comma is needed.
	Hi! Oh no! Yeah! Well,

Each of these parts of speech will be studied in more detail throughout this course. For now, let's look at the basic parts of a sentence.

Sentence Basics

Every sentence needs a subject (noun — the person or thing the sentence is about) and a predicate (verb — what the subject does or is). A sentence that does not contain these two elements is really no sentence at all but rather a sentence fragment. A complete sentence will express a complete thought and end with punctuation.

Name _____ Lesson 1 - Exercise 2 Day 2

Complete sentence	"Columbus was very attentive to the instructions which he received in the few years that he went to school." (p. 5) (contains a subject, *Columbus*, and a predicate, *was attentive*, and expresses a complete thought)
Sentence fragment	"[U]sing every opportunity to gain a knowledge of geography and navigation." (p. 6) (contains the predicate *using* but no subject and does not express a complete thought)

Write a complete sentence describing your hairstyle. Use fun adjectives!

_____

_____

Match the word to the correct definition.

1. _____ interjection
2. _____ pronoun
3. _____ verb
4. _____ noun
5. _____ conjunction
6. _____ adverb
7. _____ adjective
8. _____ preposition

a. describes a noun or pronoun
b. joins words or phrases
c. names a person, place, or thing
d. shows action or state-of-being
e. takes the place of a noun
f. expresses strong feeling or emotion
g. describes a verb, adjective, other adverb
h. describes a relationship between nouns or pronouns and other words

Refer to the Eight Parts of Speech chart to complete the following.

9. **Write** a sentence using a vocabulary word from Day 1 and include an adjective and an adverb.

_____

_____

10. **Write** a sentence about your bedroom that contains a conjunction and an interjection.

_____

_____

Write S for a complete sentence and **F** for a sentence fragment.

11. _____ "He reflected on what he observed in his voyages, and on what he had learned of geography …" (p. 6)
12. _____ "[A]nd being master of his hasty temper …" (p. 7–8)
13. _____ "On Friday, the third day of August, in the year 1492 …" (p. 9)
14. _____ "At the age of fourteen, he went to sea." (p. 6)

☐ **Copy** the definitions for the eight parts of speech with examples of each on index cards for future reference. **Place** a checkmark in the box when completed.

Lesson 1, Day 2 — Language Lessons for a Living Education Level 10

Communication

When learning how to communicate, it is important to understand the many ways there are to relay thoughts and feelings to others. Humans often communicate through writing, speaking, gesturing with hands, moving their bodies, making facial expressions, choosing clothing styles, texting, and designing artwork. Sometimes people communicate a message by not communicating at all. The Book of Proverbs in the Bible has a lot to say about communicating wisely. We will study much of that wisdom throughout this course.

In addition to studying Proverbs, communication lessons will give you an opportunity to:

- Read and write a biography and autobiography.
- Design a front cover for your biography and autobiography.
- Explore multiple essay types.
- Learn skills that will help you polish your writing.
- Be reminded of proper etiquette in all forms of communication.
- Practice your speaking skills.
- Learn how to properly acknowledge researched information.

Biographies and Autobiographies

As you learned on Day 1, a biography is an account of someone's life written by *someone else*. An **autobiography** is an account of a person's life written *by that person*. While there are some similarities between biographies and autobiographies, there are several differences as well.

> An **autobiography** is an account of a person's life written *by that person*.

Study the charts showing the differences and similarities between biographies and autobiographies.

	Differences	
	Biography	**Autobiography**
Authorship	written by someone other than the subject	written by the person the book is about
Point of View	typically written in the third-person point of view (she, her, hers, he, him, his)	typically written in the first-person point of view (I, me, my)
Authorized/ Unauthorized	can be authorized (permission is given by the person the book is about) OR unauthorized (no permission given)	always authorized
Degree of Objectivity	tends to be more objective; the writer gathers research, reviews records, conducts interviews, verifies facts	tends to be less objective, as the author bases content on his or her memories and may be biased

Communication

Lesson 1, Day 3

23

Name _____ Lesson 1 - Exercise 3 Day 3

Similarities	
Primary Purpose	The purpose of both is to give an account of the person's life.
Notable Subjects	The people whose stories are told in these forms tend to be those who are known for their accomplishments, and readers find them interesting.
Nonfiction	Both are works of nonfiction, as they represent real events.

As you read through *Life of Washington*, begin to think of a famous living person or historical figure you would like to write a biography about. The biography assignment is not due until the end of the first semester, in Lesson 18. Over the next several lessons, you will learn about what information belongs in a biography and how to conduct good research. Also, think about what the cover of your biography will look like. You could use your own artwork or, with permission, find some online.

Reading works of nonfiction about the lives of interesting people can be educational, inspiring, entertaining, and motivating. God can use the lives of others as examples of either righteous or evil behavior. There is much to learn from the lives of Christopher Columbus and George Washington.

Study and **copy** the following passage about Christopher Columbus from the introduction in *Life of Washington*.

> He was born about the year 1436, and was the son of a wool-comber, who lived in a city of Italy, called Genoa, and who was too poor to give him much education; but Columbus was very attentive to the instructions which he received in the few years that he went to school. When he was a child, he said he would like to be a sailor, and he was very diligent in using every opportunity to gain a knowledge of geography and navigation. (p. 5–6)

_____
_____
_____
_____
_____
_____
_____
_____

The plans of the diligent lead surely to abundance, but everyone who is hasty comes only to poverty. Proverbs 21:5

Detail of *Dawn of America* by Antonio de Brugada. Naval Museum of Madrid.

Name _____   Lesson 1 - Exercise 4   Day 4

Worldview & Literary Analysis

What is worldview and why is it so important? Our **worldview** is our philosophy about life and is the framework through which we understand the world and our relation to it.[1] A worldview is the result of a person organizing and settling on presupposed ideas they hold to be true.[2] Religion is the foundation we use to build our worldview. It is either based on God's Word or man's word.[3] As we read through biographies, autobiographies, excerpts from books, Scripture, poems, and more, we will be examining the worldviews presented. We will also examine our own thoughts and beliefs and see if they agree with God's Word or man's word.

> Our **worldview** is our philosophy about life and is the framework through which we understand the world and our relation to it.[4]

In this lesson, you started reading the introduction to *Life of Washington*. In this portion of the book, the author, Anna C. Reed, takes us back in time to visit a man who diligently pursued a vision he felt God had given him based on Isaiah 52:10b (KJV): "… all the ends of the earth shall see the salvation of our God." Columbus stated resolutely, "Happen what will, I am determined to persevere, until, by the blessing of God, I shall accomplish the enterprise" (p. 9). Columbus believed there was a world awaiting him on the other side of the ocean, and many years later, George Washington, with the same diligence and determination, would help establish that new land as a world power.

Finish reading the introduction on pages 5–18 and **respond** to the following.

In your own words, **describe** what motivated Columbus to risk his life to find the new world (p. 6).

_____

_____

Read again this quote from Columbus: "Happen what will, I am determined to persevere, until, by the blessing of God, I shall accomplish the enterprise" (p. 9). Columbus had a worldview that recognized the need for God's blessing. This does not mean he always walked in obedience to God, though. A person can acknowledge God in many ways yet still have character flaws. However, through his determination, Columbus had a major impact on the future of the world.

Write a paragraph about a time when you were determined to accomplish something. **Consider** whether you turned to God for strength and gave Him glory for your accomplishment.

_____

_____

_____

_____

_____

_____

_____

---

1 Hodge, Bodie, and Roger Patterson. *World Religions and Cults*, Volume 1. Green Forest, AR: Master Books, 2015, p. 23.
2 Ibid., p. 27.
3 Ibid., p. 11.
4 Ibid., p. 23.

Name _____   Lesson 1 - Exercise 4   Day 4

Fill in the blanks in the following passage, found on page 10.

1. "It was the _____ of Columbus to close each day with an evening _____, for he was a _____ man; and on the evening of that _____ day, on which the staff and thorn stem were seen, he spoke with great _____ to his sailors, and _____ [endeavored] to lead them to be _____ to the mighty _____ of the waves, for his _____ and _____ in guiding them safely to that hour of _____ hope."

On page 10, Reed references the story of Noah and the Ark, comparing Columbus' voyage to Noah's. On page 11, she also likens the sighting of the new land to Moses seeing the Promised Land. **Read** the following paragraph out loud to your instructor using your best reading voice.

> It was the 12th of October, in the year 1492, and the little vessel of Columbus became to him what "the mountain of Nebo," was to the leader of Israel; for as Moses had been led through the dangers of the wilderness, to that mount from which he saw "the promised land," so Columbus had been guided by the same mighty hand over the desert of the ocean, to a spot from which his joyful eyes beheld the unknown land, on which his thoughts and hopes had been for many years engaged. (p. 11)

2. **Discuss** with your instructor any similarities or differences between Columbus seeing the New World and Moses seeing the Promised Land. **List** the similarities and differences. (*Hint:* The account of Moses can be found in the books of Exodus, Leviticus, Deuteronomy, and Numbers.)

   _____
   _____
   _____
   _____
   _____
   _____
   _____
   _____
   _____

3. Columbus' last words were, "Into thy hands, O Lord, I commend my spirit" (p. 14). This is another biblical reference. **Who** spoke these words in the New Testament in Luke 23:46?

   _____

4. Besides Columbus, **list** five other explorers, pioneers, and leaders mentioned in the introduction.

   a. _____   d. _____
   b. _____   e. _____
   c. _____

Name _____   Lesson 1 - Exercise 5   Day 5

 **Review**

☐ **Update** the Reading List chart with books you have read this week.

☐ **Recite** Isaiah 52:10 from memory to your instructor.

Vocabulary Review

Match the words to the correct definition.

1. _____ convent
2. _____ friar
3. _____ endeavouring (endeavoring)
4. _____ toilsome
5. _____ resolution
6. _____ hasty
7. _____ eloquent

a. trying hard to do or achieve something
b. done or made in a hurry or with urgency
c. fluent or persuasive in speaking or writing
d. community, usually of nuns, under religious vows
e. member of a religious order of men
f. involving hard or tedious work
g. firm decision to do or not do something

Using the word bank, **fill in** the correct vocabulary words in the blanks. Not all words are used.

amiable	cultivated	disposition	reproached	tumult
caravals (caravels)	desponding	lamentations	resolutely	

8. "[F]or an order, signed by the king and queen, was given to him to enable him to fit out three _____, or small vessels, for his voyage."

9. "[H]e sailed from Palos, and the friends of the sailors who accompanied him took leave of them with _____, and abuse of Columbus … ."

10. "They were several times disappointed in the same manner, and at length became _____, and _____ Columbus with anger … ."

11. "When the inhabitants heard of his arrival, there was a great _____ … ."

Grammar & Punctuation Review

Define the following parts of speech and give examples.

1. Noun: _____
   Examples: _____
2. Verb: _____
   Examples: _____
3. Adjective: _____
   Examples: _____

Review   Lesson 1, Day 5   27

Name _____   Lesson 1 - Exercise 5   Day 5

4. Conjunction: _____

   Examples: _____

5. **Write** a complete sentence about three positive character traits of Christopher Columbus.
   _____
   _____

Communication Review

1. **List** four of the many ways humans communicate.

   a. _____   c. _____
   b. _____   d. _____

Fill in the blanks about biographies and autobiographies.

2. A biography is written by _____
   _____ .

3. An autobiography is written by _____ .

4. A biography is written from the _____-_____ point of view.

5. An autobiography is written from the _____-_____ point of view.

6. An authorized biography means _____
   _____ .

7. Both biographies and autobiographies are works of _____ .

Worldview & Literary Analysis Review

1. **Define** worldview.
   _____
   _____

2. **Describe** your worldview.
   _____
   _____

3. **Choose** one character trait displayed by Christopher Columbus and **discuss** specific times that trait was evident in his life. Use examples from the introduction to *Life of Washington*. **Write** a complete paragraph of at least five sentences.
   _____
   _____
   _____
   _____
   _____

Special Feature

Lesson 2

Picture Study: Moses Viewing the Promised Land

In Lesson 1, a comparison was made between Moses seeking the Promised Land and Columbus seeking the New World. **Describe** the image with as much detail as you can and then **describe** what you think Moses may be pondering as he looks across the vast land and considers the future of his nation.

_____
_____
_____
_____
_____
_____
_____
_____
_____
_____

Name _____   Lesson 2 - Exercise 1   Day 6

Today you will **begin reading** pages 19–31 in *Life of Washington*. Complete the reading for this section by Exercise 4 of this lesson. Before beginning to read, **study** the vocabulary words listed below.

Vocabulary

adjutant	a military officer acting as an assistant to a senior officer	**imprudent**	not showing care for the consequences of an action; rash
anecdote	a short amusing or interesting story about a real incident or person	**indulgence**	doing something enjoyable even if it has negative consequences
ardently	very enthusiastically or passionately	**intercourse**	communication or dealings between individuals or groups
ascertain	to find something out for certain; make sure of	**regiment**	unit of an army typically commanded by a colonel
connexion (connection)	a relationship in which a person, thing, or idea is associated with something else	**reproof**	an expression of blame or disapproval
constitution*	the composition of something	**requite**	return a favor or respond to love
filial	of or due from a son or daughter		

* Sometimes a word can have several meanings, only discernable based on the context in which it appears in the text.

Write a one-paragraph story using as many of the vocabulary words as you can. Be creative!

_____
_____
_____
_____
_____
_____
_____
_____

☐ **Use** index cards to **write** each vocabulary word from this lesson on one side and the definition on the other. **Check** the box when complete.

☐ **Copy** the Scripture verse on an index card. **Memorize** it by the end of this lesson. You may choose the Bible translation or use the one given. **Check** the box when complete.

Whatever you do, work heartily, as for the Lord and not for men, knowing that from the Lord you will receive the inheritance as your reward. You are serving the Lord Christ.
Colossians 3:23–24

Name _____   Lesson 2 - Exercise 2   Day 7

Grammar & Punctuation

Subjects and Predicates

We learned that a sentence must contain a subject (noun) and a predicate (verb). The **subject** is the *naming part* of the sentence while the **predicate** is the *telling part*. The subject can be a single noun *or* a word or phrase that is functioning as a noun. The predicate always contains a verb. Remember, sentences must begin with a capital letter and end with some sort of punctuation. In the following examples, the **//** separates the subject from the predicate. The verbs are underlined twice.

> The **subject** is the *naming part* of the sentence.
> The **predicate** is the *telling part* of the sentence.

Examples: The small brown fox **//** crept through the cornfield.
Walking a long distance in the heat **//** was not a good idea.
My neighbor's dogs **//** bark continually.

Label the following as either **S** for subject or **P** for predicate, depending on how they would function in a sentence.

1. _____ the loudly chirping bluebirds in the bush outside my window
2. _____ was excitedly telling me about his mother
3. _____ is so tired after a long day at the office
4. _____ an entire heaping plate of cheese and crackers
5. _____ had been reading for over an hour up in his tree house
6. **Create** a predicate for the following subjects. Remember to create a complete sentence and add punctuation.

    The man with the cowboy hat _____ .

    An overjoyed toddler _____ .

    Eating pizza for the third day in a row _____ .

7. **Create** a subject for the following predicates. Remember to begin with a capital letter.

    _____ left me behind at my friend's house.

    _____ was my favorite movie of all time!

    _____ ran up the tree before I knew it.

Grammar & Punctuation   Lesson 2, Day 7   31

Name _____   Lesson 2 - Exercise 2   Day 7

Remember: A noun names a person, place, or thing. A noun can be *common* (any person, place, or thing), or it can be *proper* (a certain person, place, or thing).

8. In the following excerpt from *Life of Washington*, **underline** the common nouns and pronouns and **circle** the proper nouns. (*Hint:* Refer to the eight parts of speech from Lesson 1 if you need to be reminded what a pronoun is.)

> The waters to be crossed were high, and the snow to be waded through, was deep; but persevering resolutely, he arrived at Turtle Creek, where he was told by an Indian trader, that the French commander had died a short time before, and that the French troops had gone into winter quarters. (p. 26)

9. **List** five common nouns. **Separate** them by commas.
   _____

10. **List** five proper nouns. **Separate** them by commas. Remember to capitalize them!
    _____

We always capitalize the names of God. There are so many! Enjoy reading through just some of the names the Bible gives to the Creator. **Copy** them on the lines below. You may use cursive writing to make the names look even more majestic. Which name is your favorite? **Circle** it!

Wonderful	Everlasting God	Adonai	Abba	Holy Spirit
Counselor	Jehovah	Yahweh	Ancient of Days	Lion of Judah
Prince of Peace	Immanuel	Alpha and Omega	Friend of Sinners	Lord God
Jesus	Messiah			

Lesson 2, Day 7   Language Lessons for a Living Education Level 10

Name _____ Lesson 2 - Exercise 3 Day 8

💬 Communication

Biography Notes

As you read the biography of George Washington, begin to think of a person you would like to write a biography about. Observe how the author communicates details about George Washington's life in a way that is logical and interesting. You can learn a lot about writing through reading good literature.

Anna C. Reed opens *Life of Washington* with a paragraph about the hand of the "kind Creator" (p. 19) and His gift of George Washington to America. This is a creative way to begin the biography as opposed to "George Washington was born on February 22nd, 1732, in Virginia." Consider starting your biography with a glimpse at the achievements, impact, or character of the person you are writing about. This will make your readers interested in reading further.

Please choose the subject of your biography in the upcoming week. In Communication Lesson 3, you will identify the person you chose and begin to brainstorm and research. Your biography could be about someone in your family or church. It could also be about a celebrity, historical figure, or Bible figure. It would be beneficial to choose a person you can find enough information on to form a complete story.

Paragraphs

A well-constructed paragraph makes your writing easy to follow and more enjoyable for your readers. A paragraph should consist of a **topic sentence** (briefly explains what the paragraph is about), at least **3–4 supporting sentences** (elaborate on the topic by adding details to explain or support), and a **concluding sentence** (summarizes the topic or presents one final piece of support to round it out). The length of a paragraph can vary depending on the type of writing. **Study** the following paragraph, reading it out loud if possible. The italicized words are old spellings.

> When he was ten years old, his worthy father died, and he became the care of an anxious mother, whose fortune was not sufficient to enable her to give him more than a plain English education. He was very fond of studying mathematics, and applied his mind diligently, in improving all the instruction which he could get in that science. As he grew up to manhood, he was remarkable for the strength and activity of his frame. In running, leaping, and managing a horse, he was unequalled by his companions; and he could with ease climb the heights of his native mountains, to look down alone from some wild crag upon his followers, who were panting from the toils of the rugged way. By these healthful exercises the *vigour* of his constitution was increased, and he gained that hardiness so important to him in the employments designed for him by his Creator. (*Life of Washington*, p. 21–22)

The topic sentence lets us know about Washington's education after his father's death. The supporting sentences fill in the details of his education, interests, and abilities. This paragraph is "rounded out" by showing how these elements worked together to shape who Washington was. You will have a chance to write a paragraph in the next section of this exercise.

Write a sentence that summarizes what you learned about Washington from the example paragraph.

_____

_____

Communication

Name _____   Lesson 2 - Exercise 3   Day 8

Wisdom Speaks

Copy the proverb.

> *The heart of the wise makes his speech judicious and adds persuasiveness to his lips.*
> Proverbs 16:23

_____
_____

Using a dictionary or, with a parent's permission, an online search, **write** the definitions of the following words.

1. judicious: _____
   _____

2. persuasiveness: _____
   _____

Write a sentence using the word *judicious*.

_____
_____

Write a sentence using the word *persuasiveness*.

_____
_____

When our words come from a heart of wisdom, we will not only be able to speak the truth but do it in a way that persuades others to see what is right. **Think** about a time when your words or someone's words to you were both judicious and persuasive. **Write** a paragraph describing this interaction.

_____
_____
_____
_____
_____
_____
_____
_____
_____
_____

Name _____   Lesson 2 - Exercise 4   Day 9

Worldview & Literary Analysis

Literary Analysis: Fiction vs. Nonfiction

A story can be either **fiction** (made up by the author) or **nonfiction** (factually true). In nonfiction, the author needs to be truthful and accurate in presenting the facts for the purpose of educating readers. Examples would include the Bible, textbooks, news articles, biographies, autobiographies, or topical essays. In fiction, the author creates any story they wish using their imagination for the purpose of entertaining readers. Examples would include mystery novels, science fiction, westerns, or fantasy.

List two works of fiction you have read.
_____   _____

List two works of nonfiction you have read.
_____   _____

Finish reading pages 19–31 in *Life of Washington* and **respond** to the following.

Reed opens Chapter I (p. 19) with the following statement: "To give us the delightful assurance, that we are always under the watchful care of our almighty and kind Creator, He has told us that He notices the movements of every little sparrow; and as we are 'of more value than many sparrows,' He will surely ever care for us." Based on this, what do you believe Reed's worldview is regarding the value of human life and God's interaction with it? **Write** 2–3 sentences.

_____
_____
_____
_____

On page 20, we read that Washington's faithful parents taught him the importance of speaking the truth. **List** two reasons mentioned in the text that identify why one may be tempted to "tell a falsehood."

1. _____
2. _____
3. **Write** what the children in Washington's school would say so that it was certain they would be believed. **Think:** Could friends say this of you?

_____
_____

Read the following story from Washington's boyhood found on page 21.

> The story is, that he was playing with a hatchet, and heedlessly struck a favourite fruit-tree in his father's garden. Upon seeing the tree thus mutilated, an inquiry was naturally made for the author of the mischief, when George frankly confessed the deed, and received his father's forgiveness.

Worldview & Literary Analysis

Name _____ Lesson 2 - Exercise 4 Day 9

Although what Washington did was wrong, the way this story is retold is somewhat humorous. The old-fashioned "wordy" style of writing makes this a fun paragraph to read.

Rewrite this paragraph using the common language you are used to. You may need to locate a few words in the dictionary to make sure your sentences stay true to the meaning!

_____
_____
_____
_____
_____
_____
_____

4. **How** old was George Washington when his father passed away? _____

5. **What** did Washington's mother say when he confessed to causing the death of her beloved colt?
_____
_____

6. **Fill in** the blanks from 1 Corinthians 13:6: "it [love] does not _____ at _____ but _____ with the _____."

7. **When** Washington was 15 years old, what was his strong desire?
_____

8. **What** do the following verses teach us about work?

   Proverbs 22:29 – _____
   _____

   Proverbs 16:3 – _____
   _____

9. On page 24, there is a directive given to children in the Word of God: "Let them learn first to show piety at home, and to requite their parents." Washington made decisions based on this command. **Write** the definition of *requite*.
_____
_____

10. At the age of 19, **what** was Washington appointed as?
_____

11. On page 30, we find Washington in a dangerous situation where he falls off a raft into icy waters. **To what or whom** does the author credit Washington's survival?
_____
_____

Name _____ Lesson 2 - Exercise 5   Day 10

Review

☐ **Update** the Reading List chart with books you have read this week.

☐ **Recite** Colossians 3:23–24 from memory to your instructor.

Vocabulary Review

Match the words to the correct definition.

1. _____ indulgence
2. _____ reproof
3. _____ anecdote
4. _____ ascertain
5. _____ connexion (connection)
6. _____ intercourse
7. _____ constitution

a. a usually short narrative of an interesting, amusing, or biographical incident
b. physical makeup of an individual with respect to health, strength, or appearance
c. contextual relation or association
d. criticism for a fault
e. the act of doing/enjoying something as a special treat or pleasure
f. to find out or learn with certainty
g. connection or dealings between persons or groups

Using the word bank below, **write** two sentences, properly using two of the vocabulary words per sentence.

| adjutant | filial | regiment |
| ardently | imprudent | requite |

8. _____
   _____

9. _____
   _____

Grammar & Punctuation Review

Using the symbol **//**, **separate** the subject from the predicate in the following sentences.

1. "The night on which this account was given, was dark and rainy … ."
2. Several of my friends and I enjoyed an ice cream cone at the ball game.
3. "By a firm but mild manner, he gained friends among the inhabitants of the forest … ."
4. "The spot thus described was soon afterwards the site of the French fort Duquesne."

Review   Lesson 2, Day 10   37

Name _____   Lesson 2 - Exercise 5   Day 10

Communication Review

1. **List** the three main parts of a paragraph and how they function.

    a. _____

    b. _____

    c. _____

2. **Fill in** the blanks for the following verse.

    "The _____ of the _____ makes his _____ judicious and adds _____ to his _____." Proverbs 16:23

Worldview & Literary Analysis Review

1. **Describe** the role of an author in the following.

    a. A work of nonfiction:

    _____

    _____

    b. A work of fiction:

    _____

    _____

2. **What** are two reasons a person may want to "tell a falsehood"?

    a. _____

    b. _____

God's hand (His protection and attention) was upon George Washington's life, and Washington gave God the glory for helping him. **Write** about a situation in your life when you saw God's hand intervene and assist you. Give Him thanks and glory!

_____

_____

_____

_____

_____

_____

_____

Special Feature

Lesson 3

Hymn Study: "Battle Hymn of the Republic"
by Julia W. Howe (1819–1910)[1]

Mine eyes have seen the glory of the coming of the Lord;
He is trampling out the vintage where the grapes of wrath are stored;
He hath loosed the fateful lightning of his terrible swift sword:
His truth is marching on.

> *Chorus:*
> *Glory! Glory! Hallelujah!*
> *Glory! Glory! Hallelujah!*
> *Glory! Glory! Hallelujah!*
> *His truth is marching on.*

I have seen him in the watch-fires of a hundred circling camps;
They have builded him an altar in the evening dews and damps;
I can read the righteous sentence by the dim and flaring lamps;
His day is marching on.

He has sounded forth the trumpet that shall never call retreat;
He is sifting out the hearts of all before his judgment seat;
O be swift, my soul, to answer him; be jubilant, my feet!
Our God is marching on.

In the beauty of the lilies Christ was born across the sea,
With a glory in his bosom that transfigures you and me;
As he died to make us holy, let us die that all be free!
While God is marching on.

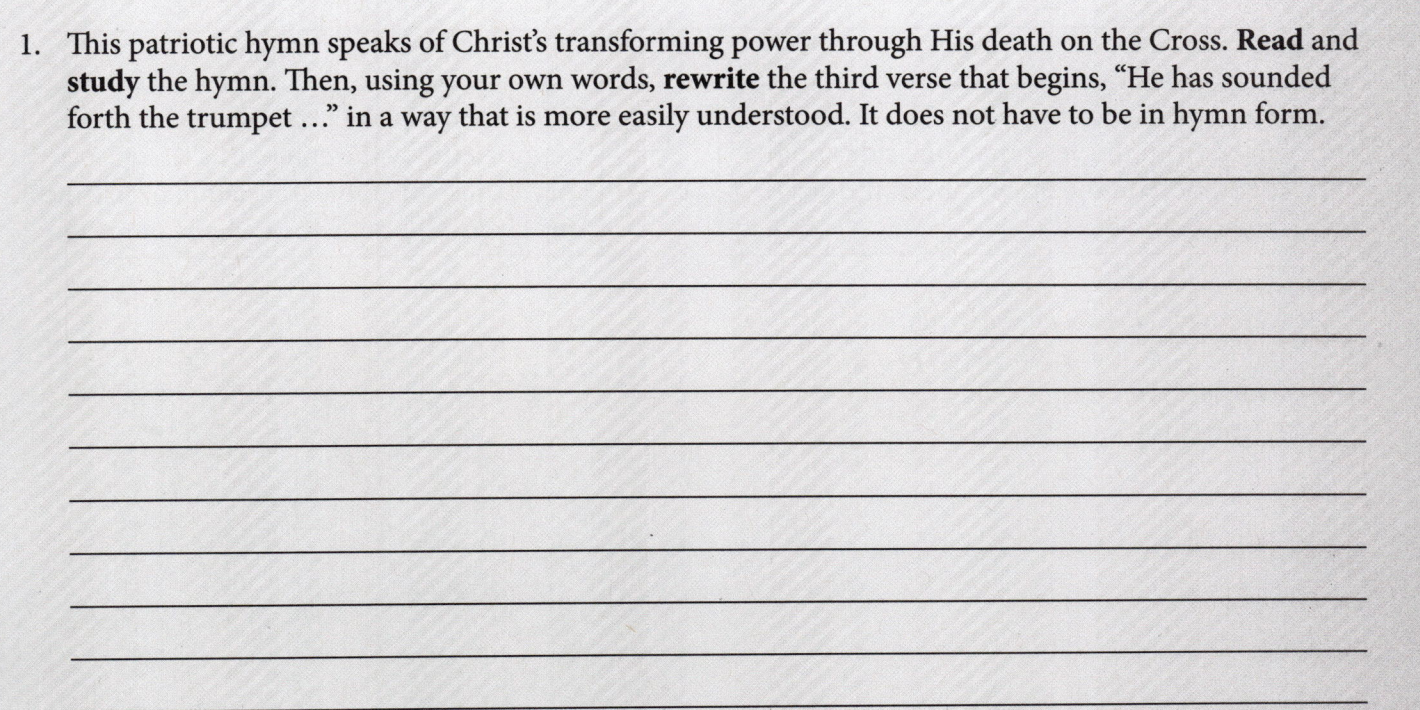

1. This patriotic hymn speaks of Christ's transforming power through His death on the Cross. **Read** and **study** the hymn. Then, using your own words, **rewrite** the third verse that begins, "He has sounded forth the trumpet …" in a way that is more easily understood. It does not have to be in hymn form.

_____
_____
_____
_____
_____
_____
_____
_____
_____
_____

[1] Composer (attributed to): William Steffe, ca. 1830–1911, https://hymnary.org/hymn/BB2020/578.

Name _____   Lesson 3 - Exercise 1   Day 11

Today you will **begin reading** pages 32–45a (end of Chapter I) in *Life of Washington*. Complete the reading for this section by Exercise 4 of this lesson. Before reading, **study** the vocabulary words listed below.

Vocabulary

affable	good-natured, friendly	halt	an abrupt stop
aid-de-camp (aide-de-camp)	assistant to a high-ranking officer	impertinent	disrespectful, rude
approbation	praise or approval	Providence	God's protective care or guidance
cultivation	the preparation of land for crops	suffer	to allow
cumbered	hindered or hampered by someone or something	superintend	to oversee
domestic	relating to home or family	vexation	annoyance, worry, or frustration
engaged	involved in an activity	vigour (vigor)	energy; effort with enthusiasm

2. **Write** a sentence using the words *Providence* and *domestic*.

   _____

   _____

3. **Use** a dictionary or, with parental permission, an online dictionary, and **record** two different meanings for the word *suffer*.

   a. _____

   b. _____

☐ **Use** index cards to **write** each vocabulary word from this lesson on one side and the definition on the other. **Check** the box when complete.

☐ **Copy** the Scripture verse on an index card. **Memorize** it by the end of this lesson. You may choose the Bible translation or use the one given. **Check** the box when complete.

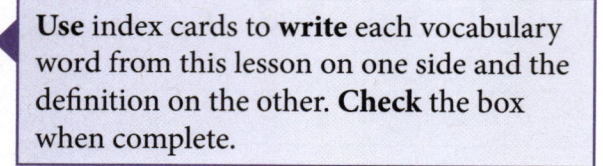

As for you, always be sober-minded, endure suffering, do the work of an evangelist, fulfill your ministry.
2 Timothy 4:5

George Washington and Lord Fairfax on a fox hunt

40   Lesson 3, Day 11   Language Lessons for a Living Education Level 10

Name _____   Lesson 3 - Exercise 2   Day 12

Grammar & Punctuation

Verbs: Action and Linking

Nouns are the *naming* parts of a sentence and verbs are the *telling* parts. **Verbs** appear in the predicate part of a sentence to tell what the subject *does* or who the subject *is*. The predicate portion of a sentence often begins with a verb.

> **Verbs** appear in the predicate part of a sentence to tell what the subject *does* or who the subject *is*.
> A verb is a **linking verb** if it is used to describe the subject.
> If it is an action the subject performs, then it is an **action verb**.

> (SUBJECT)   (PREDICATE)
> *Example:* The mayor of our town, Mr. Reading, // *conducted* the monthly planning board meetings.

Verbs appear in two basic forms: **action verbs** (AV) and **linking verbs** (LV). Within the linking verb category, we find the verb *be*. The verb *be* has eight different forms, and we call these the **state-of-being verbs**. **Study** the chart below.

Verb Type	Function	Examples
Action	What the subject is doing or has done	grab, run, shout, walk, play, sing, cook
State-of-being	Explain the state/condition of the subject	am, is, are, was, were, be, being, been
Linking	Explain the state/condition of the subject	be, become, seem, remain, get, appear

Remember, state-of-being verbs *are* linking verbs. Sometimes a common linking verb can act as an action verb. How do you know the difference between an action verb and a linking verb?

A verb is a **linking verb** if it is used to describe the subject. If it is an action the subject performs, then it is an **action verb**. **Study** this example:

> *Examples:* My friend Quin *appeared* quite distracted at the annual science fair last night.
> (*appeared* is a linking verb describing Quin's condition)
>
> The suspicious man *appeared* from behind the parked car.
> (*appeared* is an action verb telling something the man did)

It is important to memorize the linking verbs. **Study** the chart.

Common Linking Verbs	
Permanent linking verbs	be, become, seem (these verbs are never action verbs)
Sensory linking verbs	appear, feel, look, smell, sound, taste
Conditional linking verbs	act, constitute, come, equal, fall, get, go, grow, keep, prove, remain, stay, turn
State-of-being verbs	am, is, are, was, were, be, being, been

Name _____   Lesson 3 - Exercise 2   Day 12

Underline the verb twice and **label AV** for action verb or **LV** for linking verb. There may be more than one verb in each sentence.

1. A fluffy white cat sits in my neighbor's window every time the sun shines through.
2. The rope came loose on the tree branch, and it fell to the ground with a thud.
3. If you don't keep calm, your heart will beat faster and faster.
4. The dinner looked amazing, and I ate it with a thankful heart!
5. Mandy looked through the car's moon roof at the night sky and contemplated the vastness of the universe.
6. **Write** a sentence using the word *felt* as an action verb.
   _____
   _____
7. **Write** a sentence using the word *felt* as a linking verb.
   _____
   _____

Review It!

Look at the underlined words in the sentence below and decide which part of speech each word represents. Then **write** the word on the line by the correct part of speech. **Refer** to your index cards or the Eight Parts of Speech chart on Day 2.

I <u>watched</u> my sister's <u>science</u> <u>presentation</u>, and <u>she</u> <u>seemed</u> <u>very</u> confident <u>and</u> relaxed. <u>Wow</u>!

8. action verb _____
9. linking verb _____
10. noun _____
11. interjection _____
12. adjective _____
13. pronoun _____
14. adverb _____
15. conjunction _____

Write a sentence that contains an action verb and a linking verb.
_____
_____

☐ **Copy** the Common Linking Verbs chart from this lesson on an index card. **Check** the box when you are done.

Name _____   Lesson 3 - Exercise 3   Day 13

Communication

Citing Sources

When researching information for your writing assignments, it is important to let the reader know the source of your information to avoid plagiarism. **Plagiarism** is the practice of taking someone else's work and passing it off as one's own. Most of the time, citing your sources means listing the author, title, date, and publisher of a book, magazine, or web article where you found information for your writing.

A **citation** is a way to let the reader know that certain material in your writing came from another source. There are two places where citations will appear — in the actual text of your writing and on a separate bibliography (works cited) page attached to the end of your writing. Your biography assignment will require at least *three* outside sources of information.

> **Plagiarism** is the practice of taking someone else's work and passing it off as one's own.
>
> A **citation** is a way to let the reader know that certain material in your writing came from another source.

You have probably noticed citations in books you have read. **Study** the examples below.

Essay text	In his book, *Unveiling the Kings of Israel*, David Down states, "We do not have to look far for evidence that the Flood happened" (Down 27).
Bibliography entry	Down, David. *Unveiling the Kings of Israel*. Master Books, 2012.

Most essays you write in this course will not require you to cite research sources. However, the biography you will be writing in the first semester will need to contain proper citations. Citing sources can become complicated due to the many forms of written and verbal communication. For simplicity's sake, this course will focus on citing books and websites. Therefore, when researching for your biography project, focus on finding books or web articles with your parent's permission.

There are three major styles for citing research designed for different fields of study. In Language Lessons Level 9, the Chicago-Turabian style was taught. In this course, you will learn a style called **MLA (Modern Language Association)**. You will not need to master this information. The details you need to know for this course will be provided for reference as you work through your assignments.

While researching details for your biography, you will gather certain pieces of information. **Study** the chart below showing what items you will need for your citations.

When using a book:	*the book's title, the author's name, the publisher, the publication date, and the page number you are referencing*
When using a website:	*the author's name, the title of the article, the website name, the date of the article, and the URL (The URL is the information in the search bar when you are displaying the researched content. It can be copied and pasted into a word processor or recorded by hand in a notebook.)*

In the back of the book, you will find a Citation Notes Worksheet to help you gather research information for your citations. **Study** this worksheet. You will be using it in future Communication lessons.

Name _____   Lesson 3 - Exercise 3   Day 13

Wisdom Speaks

Copy the proverb.

> *Gracious words are like a honeycomb, sweetness to the soul and health to the body.* Proverbs 16:24

_____

_____

Using a dictionary or, with permission from a parent, an online search, **write** the definitions of the words below.

1. gracious: _____
2. health: _____

Write a sentence using the word *gracious*.

_____

_____

Just like a honeycomb is a container for sweet honey, your words can be containers for a sweetness that ministers to others. When you speak words that are courteous, kind, and pleasant, those words are not only nourishing a person's soul but also impacting their physical health.

When those around us are gracious to us, we feel so much better. We may have increased energy, a more positive outlook, and better rest at night. God made our souls and bodies work together in an amazing way! Because of this, the way we communicate with each other is very important.

Think of a time when someone spoke gracious words to you. Did those words make you happy? Were you able to have a good rest that night? Did you feel more energetic just thinking of those good words? In one paragraph, **describe** your experience.

_____

_____

_____

_____

_____

_____

_____

_____

_____

_____

Name_____ Lesson 3 - Exercise 4 Day 14

Worldview & Literary Analysis

Author's Focus: Character

Reed highlights George Washington's moral character in the situations she records. His courage, endurance, generosity, commitment, prudence, wisdom, bravery, compassion, determination, forgiveness, humility, and dignity all serve as incredible examples of how godly character can shape a nation.

Although Washington was not perfect, as no one is, the character he displayed in tough situations still stands as a testament to what God can do in a life that recognizes His authority. Hopefully you will find inspiration as you read these accounts and that you feel challenged to pursue godly character in your own life.

Finish reading pages 32–45a (end of Chapter I) in *Life of Washington* and **respond** to the following.

1. **What** increased the confidence of his countrymen in Washington's character? (p. 32)
   _____
   _____

2. **Why** did Washington resign his commission? (p. 34)
   _____
   _____
   _____
   _____

3. General Braddock was sent from England to Virginia to help the colonists against the French and Indians. **Why** did he choose Washington to be his aid-de-camp (aide-de-camp)? (p. 34)
   _____
   _____
   _____
   _____
   _____

4. On page 38, a scene is described in which Washington is exposed to extreme danger for three hours. Even his enemies called him "The Spirit-protected man, who would be a chief of nations, for he could not die in battle." **Copy** the quote from the physician who was on the battleground that day.
   _____
   _____
   _____
   _____

Worldview & Literary Analysis

Name _____   Lesson 3 - Exercise 4   Day 14

5. On page 41, Washington states, "I see their situation,—I know their danger, and participate their sufferings, without having the power to give them further relief than uncertain promises. The supplicating tears of the women, and the moving petitions of the men, melt me with deadly sorrow." Washington's heart was moved for the people. Look up Matthew 9:36 and **describe** Jesus' heart toward the crowds.

_____
_____
_____
_____

Describe how you feel when you see others suffering unjustly. Do you have a desire to help?

_____
_____
_____
_____
_____
_____
_____
_____

6. Page 44 describes a scene where Washington buys as much bread as the poor sick people can eat. If you had all the resources to begin a charitable ministry, who would you want to help and how? **Describe** your plan.

_____
_____
_____
_____
_____
_____
_____
_____

7. **Fill in** the blanks in the following passage about Washington found on page 45.

"All his private _____ were as deserving of the _____ of his countrymen, as those of a _____ nature had been of their _____ and _____; and those who were _____ to him, and _____ him best, _____ him most."

Name _____   Lesson 3 - Exercise 5   Day 15

Review

Update the Reading List chart with books you have read this week.

Recite 2 Timothy 4:5 from memory to your instructor.

Vocabulary Review

Match the words to the correct definition.

1. _____ engaged
2. _____ cultivation
3. _____ aid-de-camp (aide-de-camp)
4. _____ cumbered
5. _____ vigour (vigor)
6. _____ halt
7. _____ suffer

a. an abrupt stop
b. hindered or hampered by someone or something
c. energy; effort with enthusiasm
d. to allow
e. involved in an activity
f. the preparation of land for crops
g. an assistant to a high-ranking officer

8. _____ superintend
9. _____ Providence
10. _____ impertinent
11. _____ vexation
12. _____ affable
13. _____ domestic
14. _____ approbation

h. praise or approval
i. good natured, friendly
j. disrespectful, rude
k. relating to home or family
l. annoyance, worry, or frustration
m. God's protective care or guidance
n. to oversee

Grammar & Punctuation Review

1. **Describe** the function of each type of verb.

    a. Action verb: _____

    b. State-of-being verb: _____

2. **List** the four types of common linking verbs.

    a. _____   c. _____

    b. _____   d. _____

Review

Lesson 3, Day 15   47

Name _____ Lesson 3 - Exercise 5 Day 15

Underline the verb twice and **label** it **AV** for action verb and **LV** for linking verb. There may be more than one verb in each sentence.

3. Juan became an important part of our family through a foreign exchange program.
4. When the exam was finally over, I ran outside for some much-needed fresh air.
5. I will remain steadfast when the society around me abandons God's Word.

Communication Review

1. **Define** plagiarism.
   _____
   _____

2. **Explain** what a citation is.
   _____
   _____

3. **List** the items needed when citing a book.
   _____
   _____

4. **List** the items needed when citing a website.
   _____
   _____

Worldview & Literary Analysis Review

1. **What** increased the confidence of his countrymen in Washington's character?
   _____
   _____

2. General Braddock was sent from England to Virginia to help the colonists against the French and Indians. **Why** did he choose Washington to be his aid-de-camp (aide-de-camp)?
   _____
   _____

Copy the quote from a Revolutionary War physician regarding Washington.

> "I expected every moment to see him fall;—his duty, his situation, exposed him to every danger; nothing but the superintending care of Providence could have saved him from the fate of all around him" (p. 38).

_____
_____
_____

Special Feature

Lesson 4

Scripture Study: Psalm 139:1–6

¹O Lord, you have searched me and known me!
²You know when I sit down and when I rise up;
 you discern my thoughts from afar.
³You search out my path and my lying down
 and are acquainted with all my ways.
⁴Even before a word is on my tongue,
 behold, O Lord, you know it altogether.
⁵You hem me in, behind and before,
 and lay your hand upon me.
⁶Such knowledge is too wonderful for me;
 it is high; I cannot attain it.

1. **List** three things God knows about you according to verse 2.

 a. _____

 b. _____

 c. _____

> Charles Spurgeon said about God's unfathomable knowledge concerning us: "I cannot grasp it. I can hardly endure to think of it. The theme overwhelms me. I am amazed and astounded at it. Such knowledge not only surpasses my comprehension, but even my imagination."[1]

Describe how you feel knowing that the God of the universe has complete knowledge about you.
_____
_____

God knows every thought you have and every word you speak. **Describe** how that may affect what you think and say.
_____
_____

2. **Write** the verse from the Scripture study that describes how God protects you.
_____
_____

Sometimes people do not like being watched, so the idea of God watching them may cause discomfort. How does knowing that God loves you very much and wants to spend eternity with you change this concept from one of discomfort to one of comfort? **Write** your thoughts.
_____
_____
_____
_____

---

1 Spurgeon, Charles. *The Treasury of David* Vol. 1. Peabody, MA: Hendrickson Publishers, 1990.

Name _____   Lesson 4 - Exercise 1   Day 16

Today you will **begin reading** pages 45b–60 in *Life of Washington*. Complete the reading for this section by Exercise 4 of this lesson. Before reading, **study** the vocabulary words listed below.

Vocabulary

assail	to violently attack or assault	**oblige**	to constrain with physical or legal force
cordial	warm and friendly	**opulence**	great wealth or luxury
eloquence	persuasive or fluent speaking or writing	**pecuniary**	relating to money
entrenchment	a place of shelter from enemy fire	**repeal**	to annul by an authoritative act
garrison	troops stationed in a location	**stores**	items accumulated for a specific purpose
indulgence	the act of indulging (spoiling)	**unanimity**	agreement by all involved
infantry	soldiers marching on foot	**unostentatiously**	not excessively or in a showy manner
magistrate	civil officer or judge dealing with minor offenses		

Write a sentence using the words *indulgence* and *opulence*. Include two adjectives.
_____
_____

Write a sentence using the word *magistrate*. Include one common noun and one proper noun.
_____
_____

3. **Fill in** the blanks using the vocabulary list. (*Hint*: The quote is found on page 54 of *Life of Washington*.)

"The detachment proceeding to Concord; the commanding officer sent six companies of light _____ to take possession of the bridges which were beyond the town, while the main body were employed in destroying the _____ in Concord."

☐ **Use** index cards to **write** each vocabulary word from this lesson on one side and the definition on the other. **Check** the box when complete.

☐ **Copy** the Scripture verse on an index card. **Memorize** it by the end of this lesson. You may choose the Bible translation or use the one given. **Check** the box when complete.

He who dwells in the shelter of the Most High will abide in the shadow of the Almighty.
Psalm 91:1

Name _____   Lesson 4 - Exercise 2   Day 17

Grammar & Punctuation

Helping Verbs

In the last grammar lesson, you learned about action and linking verbs. Another type of verb is used when the main verb needs a little "help." **Helping verbs**, also called auxiliary verbs, are used with the main verb to form a verb phrase. **Study** the chart.

> **Helping verbs**, also called auxiliary verbs, are used with the main verb to form a verb phrase.
>
> **Modal verbs** are helping verbs that show possibility, intent, ability, or necessity.

The Primary Helping Verbs	
The primary helping verbs are *to be*, *to have*, and *to do*. They can appear in the following forms:	
To be:	*am, is, are, was, were, being, been, will be* (notice these are also state-of-being verbs!)
To have:	*has, have, had, having, will have*
To do:	*does, do, did, will do*
	(*Note*: Negative forms are also helping verbs: *don't, haven't, won't, didn't, doesn't, aren't*, etc.)
Examples:	Mikayla *was writing* her essay even though she had a headache. (*was* is the helping verb) Eliana *had been peeling* apples with her mother all afternoon. (*had been* is the helping verb) Jailyn *does swim* much faster than the other girls. (*does* is the helping verb)

Draw two lines under the entire verb phrase (helping verb + main verb).

1. Micah will be singing the national anthem at the baseball game this weekend.
2. The last brownie in the pan was eaten by my little brother.
3. My mother did call the doctor's office back.
4. I will be sorting through all these photos for hours!

Refer to the Primary Helping Verbs chart to complete the following.

Write a sentence with a *to be* helping verb.

_____

_____

Write a sentence with a *to have* helping verb.

_____

_____

Write a sentence with a *to do* helping verb.

_____

_____

Name _____   Lesson 4 - Exercise 2   Day 17

In addition to the primary helping verbs, there are nine modal helping (auxiliary) verbs. **Modal verbs** are helping verbs that show possibility, intent, ability, or necessity.

Modal Helping Verbs	
Full list: *can, could, will, would, shall, should, may, might,* and *must*	
To show possibility:	*may, might, could, must*
To show intent:	*would, should, will, might, shall*
To show ability:	*can, could, may, might*
To show necessity:	*must (have to, have got to)*
Examples:	Despite the rain, I *might walk* to the park with the dog this afternoon. You *must feel* so rejuvenated after that power nap. I *could have been* a professional athlete with a little hard work.

Draw two lines under the entire verb phrase (modal verb + main verb).

5. I knew I should have gone with my sister on the camping trip.
6. You must believe in the Lord Jesus Christ to be saved, as there is no other way.
7. Isabella might have found the most important clue in the mystery!

Refer to the Modal Helping Verbs chart to complete the following.

Write a sentence with a modal helping verb that shows *possibility*.

_____
_____

Write a sentence with a modal helping verb that shows *intent*.

_____
_____

Write a sentence with a modal helping verb that shows *ability*.

_____
_____

Write a sentence with a modal helping verb that shows *necessity*.

_____
_____

☐ **Copy** the primary and modal helping verbs from this lesson on index cards. **Check** the box when you are done.

Name _____ Lesson 4 - Exercise 3 Day 18

Communication

Biography Notes

In Lesson 2, you were challenged to choose the subject for your biography. Hopefully you have chosen someone you are excited to write about! Remember, you have the entire first semester to complete your biography. You will be guided through the process to create the best writing possible.

Today you will begin gathering basic information about the subject of your biography. You are not writing paragraphs. You are simply jotting down notes to use in the future. Not all information may be available or applicable to your subject, so fill in as much as possible. *Note:* The information you gather today will *not* need to be cited. This is considered general knowledge information. No one "owns" these facts. However, it is a good idea to keep notes about the books or websites you use, as these may be helpful resources when you start writing your biography. See the Citation Notes Worksheet in the back of the book.

Fill in the blanks regarding your subject with the use of books, your own personal knowledge, or an online search with a parent's permission.

Subject's full name: _____

Year and place of birth: _____

Year and place of death (if no longer living): _____

Childhood (where they grew up, who were their parents/siblings, etc.):
_____
_____
_____
_____

Adulthood (where they lived, name any spouse/children, any significant extended family):
_____
_____
_____
_____
_____

Education (where they received an education, areas of brilliance/expertise, talents, interests):
_____
_____
_____

Communication   Lesson 4, Day 18

Name _____ Lesson 4 - Exercise 3 Day 18

Historical Narrative Essay

Today you will be writing a short essay telling a story about a historical figure. A **historical narrative essay** tells a story about a person from history. It is written in the third person (using pronouns like *he*, *she*, or *they*). Your essay will not be a biography; rather, it will focus on an event the person was involved in. Choose a person other than the subject of the biography you will be writing. Perhaps there is a story you have read in your history course you found interesting.

> A **historical narrative essay** tells a story about a person from history.

This type of essay should be entertaining and engaging to read. First, you will present your character, including any information important to the story you are about to tell. Next, you will tell the story from beginning to end, using vivid descriptions of the character and event. Finally, you will conclude the essay with a paragraph that reflects on what the character learned or how they or the story impacted history. You will not need to cite sources for this essay.

Steps for Writing a Historical Narrative Essay
1. Review the Historical Narrative Rubric in the back of this book. This rubric will let you know what is expected in your writing and what your instructor will consider in grading your essay.
2. Choose the subject of your essay and develop a title.
3. Research or review the information you know about the person and the event you will write about.
4. Create an outline to guide you as you write. Use the Historical Narrative Essay Outline provided in the back of this book.
5. Write your five-paragraph essay using the Historical Narrative Essay Worksheet in the back of the book, or you may type your essay using a 12-point font and double spacing.
6. Create a cover sheet for your essay that includes your name, the date, the assignment (Historical Narrative Essay), and the title of your essay. Optional: You may wish to include artwork on the cover sheet that represents your historical figure or event.

Subject/title of essay: _____

You will have until the Review Day at the end of this lesson to complete this assignment. **Have** your instructor sign below after reviewing your essay using the Historical Narrative Essay Rubric in the back of the book.

Instructor signature:

_____

Washington the Soldier, an 1834 portrait of Washington on horseback during the Battle of the Monongahela

Lesson 4, Day 18

Language Lessons for a Living Education Level 10

Name _____   Lesson 4 - Exercise 4   Day 19

Worldview & Literary Analysis

Author's Focus: A Secondary Purpose

Sometimes a biography will seek to do more than instruct the reader about the life of the subject. The writer may use the subject's character or life events to promote certain ideas. In these situations, the subject of the biography is used as an example of good or bad behavior in such a way as to persuade the reader to accept or reject the principles presented.

In *Life of Washington*, Reed clearly uses the words and actions of George Washington and others in the story to instruct on issues of morality and a God-centered worldview. Remember, a worldview is a philosophy about life and is the framework through which we understand the world and our relation to it.[1] Here are some examples where Reed has highlighted a God-centered worldview:

- Columbus stated he would only accomplish his mission with "the blessing of God." (p. 9)
- Washington's parents taught him the importance of trusting God's Word when it says to obey one's parents. (p. 24)
- Reed credits "the protecting hand of God" on Washington's life. (p. 30)

Reed's use of Washington's life to promote moral character and a focus on God's hand in the lives of mankind are abundant throughout the biography. Keep an eye out for more of them as you read. Do not miss the all-important "secondary purpose" of this book!

Finish reading pages 45b–60 in *Life of Washington* and **respond** to the following.

Reed begins Chapter II (p. 45) with this statement: "The desire to possess power, and the ill use of it when possessed, have caused much misery in nations, societies, and families; and even children show the evil effects in overbearing conduct to each other, and in delighting to crush the feeble worm which crawls at their feet. But if that love which fulfils [fulfills] the law of God were in every heart, the precept of our divine Redeemer, 'All things whatsoever ye would that men should do to you, do ye even so to them,' would be the rule of all actions; then families, societies, and nations, would be ever peaceful."

In this statement, the author suggests that following the Golden Rule, which is to do unto others as you would have them do unto you, would prevent all sorts of misery in the world. Do you agree? **Discuss** your thoughts with your instructor.

1. The English government had unjustly used its power over the colonists by trying to get them to pay for expenses incurred during the French and Indian War. **List** two reasons given as to why the Americans refused to pay extra taxes. (p. 46)

   a. _____
   _____

   b. _____
   _____

---
[1] Hodge and Patterson. *World Religions and Cults*, Volume 1, p. 23.

Worldview & Literary Analysis   Lesson 4, Day 19

Name _____   Lesson 4 - Exercise 4   Day 19

2. On page 47, we see two opposing viewpoints. Mr. Greenville wants the Americans to help pay for the French and Indian War, but Colonel Barre has strong opposing words for Mr. Greenville. **Study** these two points of view and **summarize** the argument between them.

   _____
   _____
   _____
   _____
   _____
   _____

3. **What** day was appointed as a day of fasting, humiliation, and prayer? (p. 50) _____

4. According to the final paragraph on page 50, **describe** the author's worldview when it comes to prayer and its effect on the fight for freedom.

   _____
   _____
   _____
   _____

5. Mr. Thompson tells a gentleman how to spot Washington during a session of Congress. **What** does he tell the gentleman to look for? (p. 51)

   _____
   _____

6. **List** three reasons why Americans "took up arms." (p. 56–57)

   a. _____
   b. _____
   c. _____

7. On page 59, Reed expresses, "There is so much cause for sorrow connected with a victory in battle …" After carefully reading her comments about war on this same page, **summarize** her beliefs.

   _____
   _____
   _____
   _____
   _____

8. **List** the three reasons Washington was chosen as Commander. (p. 60)

   a. _____
   b. _____
   c. _____

Name _____   Lesson 4 - Exercise 5   Day 20

Review

☐ **Update** the Reading List chart with books you have read this week.

☐ **Recite** Psalm 91:1 from memory to your instructor.

Vocabulary Review

Match the words to the correct definition.

1. _____ oblige
2. _____ indulgence
3. _____ opulence
4. _____ eloquence
5. _____ repeal
6. _____ magistrate
7. _____ unanimity
8. _____ unostentatiously

a. great wealth or luxury
b. agreement by all involved
c. not excessively or in a showy manner
d. the act of indulging (spoiling)
e. to constrain with physical or legal force
f. to annul by an authoritative act
g. civil officer or judge dealing with minor offenses
h. persuasive or fluent speaking or writing

9. _____ infantry
10. _____ stores
11. _____ assail
12. _____ garrison
13. _____ entrenchment
14. _____ cordial
15. _____ pecuniary

i. soldiers marching on foot
j. to violently attack or assault
k. troops stationed in a location
l. relating to money
m. a place of shelter from enemy fire
n. items accumulated for a specific purpose
o. warm and friendly

Grammar & Punctuation Review

1. **Fill in** the blank: Helping verbs are also called _____ verbs.

2. **List** two types of helping verbs.

   a. _____   b. _____

Draw two lines under the verb or verb phrase (primary or modal helping verb + main verb). There may be more than one verb or verb phrase in each sentence.

3. We have been having the best summer weather I can remember.

4. He doesn't think he will be able to come over after the concert tonight.

5. Melanie might compete in the pie-baking contest, but she needs more practice first.

Review   Lesson 4, Day 20   57

Name _____   Lesson 4 - Exercise 5   Day 20

6. **Write** a sentence that contains a modal helping verb that shows possibility.
   _____
   _____

Communication Review

1. **Describe** a historical narrative essay.
   _____
   _____

2. **Write** a one-paragraph summary of the historical narrative you wrote on Day 18.
   _____
   _____
   _____
   _____
   _____
   _____
   _____
   _____

Worldview & Literary Analysis Review

1. **Describe** what is meant by a "secondary purpose" in a biography.
   _____
   _____

2. **List** two examples of Reed highlighting a God-centered worldview in *Life of Washington*.
   a. _____
      _____
   b. _____
      _____

3. Mr. Thompson tells a gentleman how to spot Washington during a session of Congress. **Record** what he tells the gentleman to look for.
   _____
   _____
   _____
   _____

Special Feature

Lesson 5

Biography Excerpt: Benjamin Franklin (1706–1790) by Tim LaHaye

Benjamin Franklin was easily one of the most renowned men of the colonies, and certainly the most outstanding personality in Pennsylvania. He was the 15th child in a family of 17 children. His godly parents hoped he would become a minister, but they lacked the funds from their candle-making business to pay for his formal education.

Franklin became a printer early in life, having begun his apprenticeship at age 12, and moved from his home in Boston to Philadelphia. There, despite his youth, he distinguished himself as a literary genius with a rare, practical outlook on life. He received wide acclaim from his annual writing and publication of *Poor Richard's Almanac* (from 1732 through 1757), second in popularity only to the Bible throughout the colonies.

His intellectual gifts are obvious in that while he had only two years of formal schooling at best, he taught himself five languages and became a great inventor and scientist, which earned him the reputation as "the Newton of his age." His practical, philosophical, and scientific writings were translated and used in many languages, granting him worldwide acclaim. Several foreign universities awarded him honorary degrees, earning him the title "Doctor Franklin." He was famous for the stove that bears his name, the discovery of electricity through his famous kite experiment, and his subsequent invention of the lightning rod — which has no doubt spared many families from tragedy.[1]

1. **Why** was Benjamin Franklin at a disadvantage when it came to money for his education?
   _____
   _____

2. **List** two titles/nicknames Franklin was given.
   a. _____ b. _____

3. **Describe** Franklin's education and **compare** it to your own education.
   _____
   _____
   _____
   _____

Franklin came from a large family. **Write** a short paragraph describing what it would be like to be part of a family with 17 children. Use your imagination and be descriptive!
_____
_____
_____
_____
_____

---

[1] LaHaye, Tim. *Faith of Our Founding Fathers*. Master Books, 2022, p. 105–106.

Name _____   Lesson 5 - Exercise 1   Day 21

Today you will **begin reading** pages 61–77a (ending at "Staten Island") in *Life of Washington*. Complete the reading for this section by Exercise 4 of this lesson. Before reading, **study** the vocabulary words listed below.

Vocabulary

animate	to bring to life	**riotous**	involving public disorder
bade	to speak a greeting or farewell	**scantily**	in a way that is insufficient
defray	to provide money for an expense	**siege**	compelling surrender by cutting off supplies
frigate	a warship	**temperate**	self-restrained; moderate
melancholy	feeling of sadness; pensive	**truce**	agreement between enemies to suspend fighting
provincial	concerning a province, empire, or country	**veneration**	respect or reverence
prudent	showing thought for the future		

Write a fun story in which you "drop" yourself into any moment in American history. **Use** at least six of the vocabulary words. Have fun and remember to use proper grammar and punctuation!

_____
_____
_____
_____
_____
_____
_____
_____
_____
_____

☐ **Use** index cards to **write** each vocabulary word from this lesson on one side and the definition on the other. **Check** the box when complete.

☐ **Copy** the Scripture verse on an index card. **Memorize** it by the end of this lesson. You may choose the Bible translation or use the one given. **Check** the box when complete.

The simple believes everything, but the prudent gives thought to his steps. Proverbs 14:15

Name _____ Lesson 5 - Exercise 2   Day 22

Grammar & Punctuation

Verb Tense

In the last grammar lesson, you learned about helping, or auxiliary, verbs. These verbs help express the main verb's tense. **Verb tense** refers to when the action takes place in a sentence — whether it happened in the past, is happening in the present, or will happen in the future. **Study** the examples.

> **Verb tense** refers to when the action takes place in a sentence — whether it happened in the past, is happening in the present, or will happen in the future.

PAST	PRESENT	FUTURE
Cody *slept* all afternoon.	Cody *is sleeping* on the couch.	Cody *will sleep* after the game.

The three main tenses are *past, present,* and *future*. However, there are additional aspects that give more detail, such as the length of time the action occurred, where a past action has an impact on the present, and which actions happened first. These additional aspects are the *simple tense, perfect tense, continuous tense,* and *perfect continuous tense*. **Study** the charts.

Verb Tenses

	Past	Present	Future
Simple	I *walked* to town.	I *walk* to town.	I *will walk* to town.
Perfect	I *had walked* to town.	I *have walked* to town already.	I *will have walked* to town.
Continuous	I *was walking* to town.	I *am walking* to town.	I *will be walking* to town.
Perfect Continuous	I *had been walking*.	I *have been walking* all day.	I *will have been walking*.

Tense Construction

	Past	Present	Future
Simple	suffix *-ed*	simple verb	*will* + simple verb
Perfect	*had* + suffix *-ed*	*have* + suffix *-ed*	*will have* + suffix *-ed*
Continuous	*was* + suffix *-ing*	*am* + suffix *-ing*	*will be* + suffix *-ing*
Perfect Continuous	*had been* + suffix *-ing*	*have been* + suffix *-ing*	*will have been* + suffix *-ing*

Refer to the Tense Construction chart to complete the following.

1. **Write** a sentence using the verb *laugh* in the past perfect continuous tense.

   _____

   _____

Grammar & Punctuation   Lesson 5, Day 22   61

Name _____ Lesson 5 - Exercise 2 Day 22

2. **Write** a sentence using the verb *fumble* in the future simple tense.
   _____
   _____

3. **Write** a sentence using the verb *scribble* in the present perfect tense.
   _____
   _____

4. **Write** a sentence using the verb *flow* in the future continuous tense.
   _____
   _____

5. **Write** a sentence using the verb *instruct* in the past simple tense.
   _____
   _____

Review It!

Underline the subject(s) and **circle** the verbs in the following sentences. (Day 7) (*Hint*: There may be more than one subject and verb.)

6. Apparently, Justin and Jamie are camping this weekend whether it rains or not.
7. Abigail unloads trucks at the local food pantry every Thursday afternoon.
8. I have been praying about which college to attend this fall, but I feel intimidated.

On the line, **indicate** whether the underlined verb is action or linking. (Day 12)

9. _____ All my problems <u>seem</u> so small compared to issues like world hunger.
10. _____ After all these years, my grandfather finally <u>received</u> an award for his military service.
11. _____ My mother says that the older I get, the more I <u>look</u> like my father.

Underline the primary and modal helping verbs and **circle** the main verb and any other verbs. (Day 17)

12. Janner could have eaten the entire pizza, but his self-control restrained him.
13. We were passionately singing our hearts out at the Christmas Eve service last night.
14. Amazingly, we will have been living in our home for 20 years this coming April.
15. Aunt Sue should be making the apple pies for the bake sale again this year.

☐ **Copy** the Tense Construction chart on an index card. It may take more than one card. **Check** the box when you are done.

Name _____   Lesson 5 - Exercise 3   Day 23

Communication

Descriptive Paragraph

Today you will write a descriptive paragraph. A **descriptive paragraph** creates a scene that vividly describes a person, place, or thing. This type of paragraph describes the way something looks, sounds, tastes, smells, or feels. It should be a written experience the reader can almost "see." You could describe an object, place, person, animal, etc.

> A **descriptive paragraph** creates a scene that vividly describes a person, place, or thing.

A well-written descriptive paragraph will use figurative language to paint a picture in the reader's mind. **Review** these five figures of speech and **include** at least two of them in your paragraph.

Figures of Speech	
Simile	compares two different things using the words *like* or *as*
	Last night I was so exhausted that I slept like a log.
Metaphor	compares two things without using the words *like* or *as*
	God will turn your heart of stone into a heart of flesh.
Personification	attributes human qualities to something nonhuman
	The wind was screaming in my face as I turned the corner.
Oxymoron	joins two opposite words to create a unique effect and is both true and false at the same time
	There is such sweet sorrow when a friend passes away.
Hyperbole	uses exaggeration for emphasis, effect, or impact and is not to be interpreted literally
	I am so hungry I could eat an elephant!

1. **Write** a descriptive paragraph. Describe something you find interesting!

   Subject/title of paragraph: _____

   _____
   _____
   _____
   _____
   _____
   _____
   _____
   _____
   _____

   Instructor **sign here** after reviewing the paragraph: _____

Communication

Wisdom Speaks

Copy the proverb.

> *Fine speech is not becoming to a fool; still less is false speech to a prince.* Proverbs 17:7

_____

_____

Using a dictionary or online search with parental permission, **write** the definitions of the words below.

2. fine (adjective form): _____

   _____

3. becoming (adjective form): _____

Write a sentence using the words *fine* and *becoming* as defined above.

_____

_____

In this proverb, a comparison is made. Fine speech does not suit a fool because it is inconsistent with the character of a fool. Even worse, false speech does not suit a prince, as it does not match what is expected from royalty.

This reminds us of a truth Jesus spoke in Luke 6:44. Jesus said,

> "… for each tree is known by its own fruit. For figs are not gathered from thornbushes, nor are grapes picked from a bramble bush."

It would be odd to see an apple tree growing bananas, wouldn't it? In the same way, fine speech does not fit with a fool and neither does false speech with a prince. The bottom line is, we should all sound like what we claim to be!

Write a sentence describing traits a "fool" does not typically possess.

_____

_____

Write a sentence describing actions a good prince would typically not engage in.

_____

_____

Name _____   Lesson 5 - Exercise 4   Day 24

Worldview & Literary Analysis

A New Beginning

Washington was chosen as the commander-in-chief of the army, refusing pay, and humbly declaring "… I do not think myself equal to the command I am honoured [honored] with" (p. 60). Although he did not feel like he was good enough for this challenge, he trusted God to equip him. He was about to face events that would challenge him to the core of his being, tempt his areas of weakness, and develop his skills as a leader.

This lesson's reading opens with the following statement: "The peaceful enjoyments of his comfortable home were to be given up, but no selfish desire of ease ever caused him to shrink from the performance of a duty which was to benefit others" (p. 61). As he gave up his home life for army life, Washington would learn to lean into God's wisdom and trust His guidance more than ever.

Finish reading pages 61–77a (ending at "Staten Island") in *Life of Washington* and **respond** to the following.

1. **For what** two reasons would Washington draw the sword and act as a soldier? (p. 61)
   _____
   _____

2. Washington had a hard time training men for the army. **Explain** how he was able to hold his anger in check during this frustrating time. (p. 62)
   _____
   _____

3. Washington showed respect for the customs of other cultures and religions (p. 63). Is it possible to do this without compromising one's faith? **Look up** 1 Peter 3:15 in a Bible of your choice and **write** a response of 2–3 full sentences.
   _____
   _____
   _____
   _____
   _____

4. In one battle, the English lost 200 men and the Americans lost 10. This reminds us of a "David and Goliath" situation. **Copy** the quote from King Asa found on page 67.
   _____
   _____

5. **Why** did Washington need patience? (p. 67)
   _____
   _____

Name _____   Lesson 5 - Exercise 4   Day 24

6. **Give** evidence that the author believes God rules the weather. (p. 68)
   _____
   _____

7. On page 69, we see that the goal of the war changed for the Americans. **How** did it change and why?
   _____
   _____
   _____
   _____
   _____
   _____
   _____

8. Regarding the Declaration of Independence and its signers, Reed states, "So great is the estimation in which those persons are held who signed this paper, that an account of the life of each of them has been published, and the document is held in the highest veneration by every American" (p. 71). Is this still true today? **Discuss** this question with your instructor and **respond** with 2–3 full sentences.
   _____
   _____
   _____
   _____
   _____
   _____

9. Washington didn't let power and admiration place him above the law. He saw himself as a servant to the people. **Why** do you think this characteristic makes a good leader? (p. 73)
   _____
   _____

10. Washington made sure all the troops were safe before he considered himself (p. 76). **Read** Philippians 2:3–4 in the Bible translation of your choice and **copy** it.
    _____
    _____

11. **Did** Washington view the war as an offensive or defensive campaign? (p. 77)
    _____
    _____

Name _____   Lesson 5 - Exercise 5   Day 25

Review

☐ **Update** the Reading List chart with books you have read this week.

☐ **Recite** Proverbs 14:15 from memory to your instructor.

Vocabulary Review

Match the words to the correct definition.

1. _____ defray
2. _____ bade
3. _____ scantily
4. _____ truce
5. _____ siege
6. _____ provincial
7. _____ prudent

a. to speak a greeting or farewell
b. in a way that is insufficient
c. compelling surrender by cutting off supplies
d. concerning a province, empire, or country
e. to provide money for an expense
f. agreement between enemies to suspend fighting
g. showing thought for the future

8. _____ frigate
9. _____ veneration
10. _____ riotous
11. _____ temperate
12. _____ melancholy
13. _____ animate

h. feeling of sadness; pensive
i. self-restrained; moderate
j. to bring to life
k. a warship
l. respect or reverence
m. involving public disorder

Grammar & Punctuation Review

1. **Define** verb tense.
   _____
   _____

2. **Write** a sentence using the verb *wiggle* in the past perfect continuous tense.
   _____
   _____

3. **Write** a sentence using the verb *paint* in the future perfect tense.
   _____
   _____

4. **List** the helping verb and suffix that are added to form the present continuous tense.
   _____

Name _____   Lesson 5 - Exercise 5   Day 25

Communication Review

1. **Define** a descriptive paragraph.
   _____
   _____

2. **Write** a simile.
   _____

3. **Write** a metaphor.
   _____

4. **Write** an example of personification.
   _____

5. **Create** an oxymoron.
   _____

6. **Use** hyperbole.
   _____

Worldview & Literary Analysis Review

Fill in the blanks from the quote found on Day 24.

1. "The _____ enjoyments of his _____ home were to be _____ _____, but no selfish _____ of ease ever caused him to _____ from the performance of a _____ which was to benefit _____."

2. For **what** two reasons would Washington draw the sword and act as a soldier?
   _____
   _____

3. Washington had a hard time training men for the army. **Explain** how he was able to hold his anger in check during this frustrating time.
   _____
   _____

4. Washington made sure all the troops were safe before he considered himself. **Read** Philippians 2:3–4 in the Bible translation of your choice and **copy** it.
   _____
   _____

Special Feature

Lesson 6

Picture Study: George Washington

Study the picture and **write** a descriptive paragraph. **Describe** the colors, the weather, the mood, the location, and any other points of interest you can think of.

_____
_____
_____
_____
_____
_____
_____
_____

Special Feature · Lesson 6, Day 26

Name _____   Lesson 6 - Exercise 1   Day 26

Today you will **begin reading** pages 77b–94a (ending at "General Prescot") in *Life of Washington*. Have this section read by Exercise 4 of this lesson. Before reading, **study** the vocabulary words listed below.

Vocabulary

adhere	to believe in and follow a certain practice	**inoculation**	to immunize against disease
candour (candor)	open and honest expression	**mortification**	sense of shame or humiliation
convey	to carry or transport an object or idea	**peculiar**	special or distinctive
dispersed	spread out over an area	**preceding**	coming before
fording	crossing a shallow body of water by wading	**presumption**	idea or belief not known for certain
implore	to beg someone to do something	**sundry**	various kinds or several
imputation	a charge of wrongdoing		

1. Use the vocabulary list to **fill in** the blanks from the quote found on page 78 of *Life of Washington*.

   "From the hours allotted to sleep, I will borrow a few moments to _____ my thoughts on _____ important matters to Congress. I shall offer them with that sincerity which ought to characterize a man of _____ [candor], and with the freedom which may be used in giving useful information, without incurring the _____ of _____."

2. To show your grasp of the vocabulary words, **rewrite** Washington's quote in your own words.

   _____
   _____
   _____
   _____

☐ **Use** index cards to **write** each vocabulary word from this lesson on one side and the definition on the other. **Check** the box when complete.

☐ **Copy** the Scripture verse on an index card. **Memorize** it by the end of this lesson. You may choose the Bible translation or use the one given. **Check** the box when complete.

Then I turned my face to the Lord God, seeking him by prayer and pleas for mercy with fasting and sackcloth and ashes. Daniel 9:3

Name _____   Lesson 6 - Exercise 2   Day 27

Grammar & Punctuation

Independent vs. Dependent Clauses

A **clause** is a group of related words that contains a subject (noun) and a predicate (verb). An **independent clause** conveys a complete thought and can stand alone as a sentence. A **dependent clause** does *not* contain a complete thought and therefore cannot stand alone as a sentence.

A dependent clause "depends" on more information to make sense. An independent clause is referred to as the *main clause*, while the independent clause is called the *subordinate clause*. The term **subordinate** means the clause is of "lesser importance." **Study** these examples.

A **clause** is a group of related words that contains a subject (noun) and a predicate (verb).
An **independent clause** conveys a complete thought and can stand alone as a sentence.
A **dependent clause** does *not* contain a complete thought and therefore cannot stand alone as a sentence.
The term **subordinate** means the clause is of "lesser importance."

Independent clause	I knew we would be great friends.
Dependent clause	When she first introduced herself
Independent clause with a dependent clause	I knew we would be great friends when she first introduced herself.

Identify whether the underlined clause is independent or dependent by **writing IND** or **DP** above the clause.

1. The police officer easily spotted the criminal, <u>who was frantically running through the alley in a vain attempt to escape.</u>
2. <u>Above the tops of trees</u>, I noticed a huge flock of geese approaching, likely wanting to land on the pond.
3. I have a lot of energy for my schoolwork today <u>since I slept like a log last night!</u>
4. <u>Unfortunately, we will need to miss church today</u> because four feet of snow fell in our region overnight.
5. Before I can go to the lake, <u>I really need to get my laundry done or I won't have anything to wear.</u>

Write a sentence that contains both an independent and a dependent clause. Include a helping verb. (Day 17)

_____

_____

Write a sentence with one independent clause that contains a state-of-being verb. (Day 12)

_____

_____

Name _____ Lesson 6 - Exercise 2 Day 27

Conjunctions

When a sentence has more than one clause, we need a word to help link them together. **Conjunctions** are words used to connect clauses or sentences. They can also coordinate words within the same clause. When a sentence contains a conjunction, we usually see multiple verbs as well. We will study three types of conjunctions.

> **Conjunctions** are words used to connect clauses or sentences. They can also coordinate words within the same clause.

Three Types of Conjunctions	
Coordinating conjunctions	*for, and, nor, but, or, yet, so* (remember them with the acronym FANBOYS) Used to join sentence elements of the same type.
	I want to go to the fair, *but* I'm so tired.
Correlative conjunctions	*either-or, neither-nor, both-and, not only-but also, no sooner-than, rather-than* Used to join equal sentence parts and occur in pairs.
	Either go with mom *or* stay at home.
Subordinating conjunctions	*after, although, as, because, before, if, once, since, that, unless, until, when, where, while, as if, even though, so that* Used to join dependent clauses to independent clauses.
	I will stay in the car *until* the rain stops.

Underline the conjunction and **write CD** for coordinating, **CL** for correlative, or **SB** for subordinating.

6. My brother is not only my sibling, but also my best friend.
7. Fall is one of the most beautiful seasons of the year, and I always try to soak up every minute of the beauty before winter sets in.
8. Until I experienced white water rafting for the first time, I had no idea the adventure I was missing out on.
9. While sunsets can be stunning, staring at the sun is very bad for your eyes.
10. The laws in the United States are based on a biblical worldview, yet so many in our country have turned their hearts away from biblical values.
11. **Write** a sentence containing an independent and a dependent clause. Include a subordinating conjunction and an action verb. (Day 12)

    _____
    _____

12. **Write** a sentence that includes a correlative conjunction and a primary helping verb. (Day 17)

    _____
    _____

Name _____   Lesson 6 - Exercise 3   Day 28

Communication

More on Citations

A **citation** is required when you quote or paraphrase someone's words or refer to a source substantially. However, it is *not always* necessary to cite or document information from your research. **Study** the chart below that shows three instances where citation is not required.

> A **citation** is required when you quote or paraphrase someone's words or refer to a source substantially.

Citation Not Required	
Common knowledge	Information widely available in reference works, such as dates and locations of historical events, biographical facts about famous people, or circumstances surrounding major historical events.
	The attack on Pearl Harbor occurred in Honolulu, Hawaii, on December 7, 1941.
Allusions	Alluding to a well-known passage to create an effect.
	My brother is the *Einstein* in the class. "*To be or not to be*" is the question I was asking!
Passing mentions	Mentioning an author or work in passing when you have not referred to any aspect of it specifically.
	My favorite storybook growing up was *The 10-Minute Bible Journey*, as it really helped me understand the Bible better.

There are three main ways to incorporate citable material into your writing. **Study** the chart below.

Three Ways to Incorporate Citable Material	
Direct quote	Use the exact words of another person where it fits into your writing.
Paraphrase	Use your own words to retell the information yet include all the important details the source gives.
Summarize	Use your own words to condense a lengthy source so it fits with your topic and space.

On Day 48, you will be given details about "plugging" this information into the text of your biography in the MLA style of formatting. For now, simply keep track of where you found the information so you can easily locate it when you begin writing.

Taking Notes

As you begin your research, it is important to keep notes on where you found the information and what parts of it you want to use. If you see a quote or a section to paraphrase or summarize, record a portion of it along with its location. The Citation Notes Worksheets in the back of this book are designed to help you keep track of your research. Keep this worksheet nearby as you research your subject. Gathering this information as you go along will make creating a works cited page much easier and will help you incorporate important information into your biography.

Day 38 contains a chart showing where you typically find the author, title, publisher, publication date, article title, and other items associated with the source. You may reference the chart if you need help locating these items.

Name_____   Lesson 6 - Exercise 3   Day 28

Biography Notes

In recent lessons, you learned to write a narrative essay and a descriptive paragraph for the purpose of practicing the writing skills needed for your biography. Practicing storytelling and descriptive writing will help build your skills as you work on your biography, so keep those in mind.

Today you will gather more information about your biography subject. Remember, not all information may be available or applicable to your subject, so fill in as much as you can. You are not writing paragraphs. You are simply jotting down notes to use in the future. Refer to Days 13 and 28 if you need to review documenting research material.

Record the following information about your subject with the use of books, your own personal knowledge, or an online search with a parent's permission. **Use** the Citation Notes Worksheets found in the back of the book to fill in information for citing sources.

Accomplishments (discoveries, achievements, inventions, creations, notable actions, etc.):
_____
_____
_____
_____

Impact and legacy (their effect on the world/others, what they are remembered most for, etc.):
_____
_____
_____
_____

Difficulties overcome (obstacles such as financial, cultural, educational, physical, character issues, etc.):
_____
_____
_____
_____

Character traits (positive traits such as determination, compassion, etc.; negative traits such as stubbornness, impatience, etc.):
_____
_____
_____
_____

Name _____   Lesson 6 - Exercise 4   Day 29

Worldview & Literary Analysis

Literary Device: *In Medias Res*

A **literary device** is a technique used to help an author achieve a certain purpose in their writing. We will study several literary devices as we continue to read through *Life of Washington* and prepare to write a biography.

What if a biography doesn't start at the beginning of the subject's life?

Reed uses a literary technique called *in medias res* in the introduction to *Life of Washington*. *In medias res* is a Latin term meaning "in the midst of things." **In medias res** is used to "pull the reader in" by instantly plunging them into the middle of an important or dramatic event in the story. The introduction, a short biography of Columbus, opens with, "In the year 1486, a foot traveller [traveler], holding a boy by the hand, stopped at the gate of a convent in Spain, to ask for some bread and water for his wearied child" (p. 5). Reed doesn't mention the name of Columbus or his birthplace and year until the second half of the first page.

> A **literary device** is a technique used to help an author achieve a certain purpose in their writing.
>
> ***In medias res*** is used to "pull the reader in" by instantly plunging them into the middle of an important or dramatic event in the story.

In length, this literary device could be as short as a paragraph or even take up the first chapter. It could be taken from early in the story, the climax, or even after the resolution as characters are sorting through the events that occurred.

This is a technique you could use as you plan out the biography you are writing. However, a word of caution is necessary. Using *in medias res* can sometimes be confusing for the reader who is not yet familiar with the setting or characters in your story, so make sure to use it in a way that is clearly understandable.

Finish reading pages 77b–94a (ending at "General Prescot") in *Life of Washington* and **respond** to the following.

1. **What** was it that was "very distressing" to Washington when the troops were stationed at King's Bridge? (p. 77)

   _____
   _____

2. On page 79, we see a comparison between the appearance of the British (English) soldiers and the American soldiers. **Describe** the differences between the two armies.

   _____
   _____
   _____

3. The American troops faced extreme physical hardship. **Explain**, according to the account on page 82, how and why they were able to endure such difficulties.

   _____
   _____
   _____
   _____

Name _____   Lesson 6 – Exercise 4   Day 29

4. We see Washington in a very dangerous situation, and Reed makes the statement, "Wisdom to plan, strength to act, were given to him by the mighty God of armies" (p. 85). **Describe** a time in your life when you needed "[w]isdom to plan, and strength to act."

   _____
   _____
   _____
   _____
   _____
   _____

5. Washington was given "[w]isdom to plan, and strength to act" as he ordered his troops to light fires along the edge of the creek (p. 85). **What** advantage did these fires give the American troops?

   _____
   _____
   _____

6. The Bible is full of commands to parents about passing down accounts of the works of God. **Fill in** the blanks of this description of a father sharing a story found on page 86.

   "… [I]n after years, many a _____ _____, seated in his comfortable home, and surrounded by the _____ for whose rights he had that night been struggling, delighted, with _____ _____, to tell them, how the _____ _____ _____ _____ were commanded by their great _____, to aid a people struggling for their _____."

7. Washington placed himself between enemy and troops, showing bravery and leadership. **Finish** the following line from page 87.

   "He was between the fires of the two armies, but the _____
   _____."

8. An unnamed officer had high praise for General Washington. **Read** his quote at the top of page 88 and **describe** what he meant by "He is surely Heaven's peculiar care."

   _____
   _____
   _____

9. Congress "advised each state to appoint a day of humiliation and prayer, to implore God to forgive their sins as a people, and assist them by his favour in their day of trouble" (p. 90). **What** does this say about the worldview of men in Congress at this point in history?

   _____
   _____

Name _____   Lesson 6 - Exercise 5   Day 30

Review

☐ **Update** the Reading List chart with books you have read this week.

☐ **Recite** Daniel 9:3 from memory to your instructor.

Vocabulary Review

Match the words to the correct definition.

1. _____ convey
2. _____ sundry
3. _____ candour (candor)
4. _____ imputation
5. _____ presumption
6. _____ mortification
7. _____ fording

a. a charge of wrongdoing
b. open and honest expression
c. sense of shame or humiliation
d. idea or belief not known for certain
e. to cross a shallow body of water by wading
f. to carry or transport an object or idea
g. various kinds or several

8. _____ dispersed
9. _____ preceding
10. _____ peculiar
11. _____ inoculation
12. _____ adhere
13. _____ implore

h. spread out over an area
i. to immunize against disease
j. coming before
k. to beg someone to do something
l. special or distinctive
m. to believe in and follow a certain practice

Grammar & Punctuation Review

1. **Define** an independent clause.
   _____
   _____

2. **Define** a dependent clause.
   _____
   _____

Identify whether the underlined clause is independent or dependent by **writing IND** or **DP** above the clause.

3. <u>The Psalms are my favorite verses to read</u>, yet <u>I love reading the Gospels as well</u>.

4. <u>Even though my church is only one block from my house</u>, <u>my family is occasionally late for services</u>!

5. <u>We are going on a cruise in the spring</u> or <u>spending a week at my aunt's cabin in Canada</u>.

Review   Lesson 6, Day 30   77

Name _____   Lesson 6 – Exercise 5   Day 30

6. **List** the coordinating conjunctions. (*Hint*: FANBOYS)
   _____

7. **List** two sets of correlative conjunctions.
   a. _____   b. _____

8. **List** four subordinating conjunctions.
   a. _____   c. _____
   b. _____   d. _____

Communication Review

1. **Describe** when a citation is needed in writing.
   _____
   _____

2. **List** the three instances when a citation is *not* required.
   a. _____   c. _____
   b. _____

3. **List** three ways to incorporate citable material into your writing.
   a. _____   c. _____
   b. _____

Worldview & Literary Analysis Review

1. **What** does the Latin term *in medias res* mean?
   _____
   _____

2. **Describe** how *in medias res* is used as a literary device.
   _____
   _____

3. **Describe** how Reed uses *in medias res* in the introduction to *Life of Washington*.
   _____
   _____

Special Feature

Poem Study: "A Little Boy and a Cherry Tree"
by Annette Wynne

A little boy and a cherry tree,
A strong young man who proved to be
A worker with his brain and hand,
A soldier for his well-loved land,
A statesman answering the call
Of home and country, over all,
A glorious patriot, noble son,
A soldier—President—a man!
Was Washington!

Read the poem out loud by yourself three times and then **read it out loud** to your instructor.

Choose a godly character trait you see Washington exemplifying in this poem and **write** a paragraph about how his life may have been different if he *did not* possess this trait.

_____
_____
_____
_____
_____
_____
_____
_____

Write a short poem describing your character, abilities, and accomplishments. **Remember** to give God the glory for who you are!

_____
_____
_____
_____
_____
_____
_____
_____

Name _____ Lesson 7 - Exercise 1 Day 31

Today you will **begin reading** pages 94b–107 in *Life of Washington*. Complete this reading by Exercise 4 of this lesson. Before reading, **study** the vocabulary words listed below.

Vocabulary

avert	to ward off	**obstructions**	obstacles or blockages
capitulation	the action of surrendering or ceasing to resist	**profusion**	great quantity; lavish display
disposed	inclined toward something	**rash**	having a lack of caution
flotilla	a fleet of ships or boats	**redoubt**	small, temporary fortification
Hessians	German forces serving the British	**sanguinary**	involving much bloodshed
intelligence	information concerning an enemy	**surmounting**	overcoming
marquis	a nobleman of Europe	**tories**	American colonists supporting the British side

1. **Write** a sentence using the word *sanguinary* and include an abstract noun.
   _____
   _____

2. **Write** a sentence using the words *surmounting* and *obstructions*. Include an adverb.
   _____
   _____

The word "rash" refers to acting without caution. **Think** of a time that you may have acted rashly and **describe** it. Also, include how the outcome may have changed had your actions been more cautious.
_____
_____
_____
_____
_____
_____

☐ **Use** index cards to **write** each vocabulary word from this lesson on one side and the definition on the other. **Check** the box when complete.

☐ **Copy** the Scripture verse on an index card. **Memorize** it by the end of this lesson. You may choose the Bible translation or use the one given. **Check** the box when complete.

Do not rejoice when your enemy falls, and let not your heart be glad when he stumbles, lest the LORD *see it and be displeased, and turn away his anger from him.* Proverbs 24:17–18

Name _____ Lesson 7 - Exercise 2 Day 32

Grammar & Punctuation

Verb Mood

Verb mood reveals how the verb is to be regarded, whether as a fact, a command, an uncertainty, a wish, etc. It reveals the intention of the writer or speaker. There are three main types of verb mood: indicative, imperative, and subjunctive.

> **Verb mood** reveals how the verb is to be regarded, whether as a fact, a command, an uncertainty, a wish, etc.
> The **indicative mood** expresses a fact.
> The **imperative mood** makes a direct request or a demand.
> The **subjunctive mood** expresses a condition that is hypothetical, doubtful, wishful, or not factual.

Indicative Mood

The **indicative mood** expresses a fact. Most sentences are written in the indicative mood. In these sentences, the verb will express some sort of action as a statement of fact.

> *Examples:* Ashton *travels* down south with his family every winter.
> I *enjoy* worship music.
> Joshua *walks* his dog after school.
> Riley *plays* the guitar at church.

Imperative Mood

The **imperative mood** makes a direct request or a demand. The verb expresses a direct call to action. Sometimes the subject "you" will be understood; other times the subject will be clearly addressed.

> *Examples:* *Stop talking* that way.
> When you get home from work, *put* the clothes in the dryer.
> *Love* your neighbor.
> Gabriel, *take* the chicken out of the oven.

Subjunctive Mood

The **subjunctive mood** expresses a condition that is hypothetical, doubtful, wishful, or not factual. The verb will show action but may not be factual. Sentences in this mood often include the phrase, "If I were."

> *Examples:* If I *were* in your shoes, I *wouldn't* hesitate.
> Jill *suggested* that Angela *walk* to school.
> The pastor *requires* that all band members *be* on time.
> I *propose* you *start* your work soon.

On the line, **indicate** whether the verb mood is indicative, imperative, or subjunctive.

1. _____ If my dad was here, he could have started the lawnmower for us.
2. _____ Jessica, go help your sister with her math flashcards.
3. _____ I doubt the rain will hold off until we have finished setting up camp.
4. _____ Conner is an excellent public speaker.

Name _____ Lesson 7 - Exercise 2 Day 32

5. _____ Every house on this street is made of brick.
6. _____ Take out the trash since tomorrow is our trash pick-up day.

Write a sentence using the subjunctive mood and include a proper noun. (Day 7)
_____
_____

Write a sentence using the imperative mood and include a common noun. (Day 7)
_____
_____

Write a sentence using the indicative mood and include a linking verb. (Day 12)
_____
_____

Review It!

Look at the underlined words in the sentence and decide which part of speech each word represents. Then **write** the word on the line by the correct part of speech. (*Hint*: Some parts of speech will have more than one word.) **Refer** to your index cards or the Eight Parts of Speech chart on Day 2.

The <u>sun</u> <u>was setting</u> <u>over</u> the <u>horizon</u> <u>and</u> the <u>most beautiful pink</u> <u>hue</u> <u>was cast</u> <u>on</u> the <u>clouds</u>.

7. action verb(s) _____
8. adjective(s) _____
9. noun(s) _____
10. helping verb(s) _____
11. preposition(s) _____
12. conjunction(s) _____
13. **Write** a sentence containing two independent clauses connected by a coordinating conjunction. Include an adverb and an adjective. (Day 2)
_____
_____

☐ **Copy** the three types of verb mood from this lesson on your index cards. Give examples of each. **Check** the box when you are done.

82 Lesson 7, Day 32   Language Lessons for a Living Education Level 10

Name _____   Lesson 7 - Exercise 3   Day 33

Communication

Reflective Essay

A **reflective essay** explores a concept, idea, or observation from the writer's point of view. This is the first-person point of view and uses the pronouns *I, me, we,* and *us*. A reflective essay can include emotions, humor, and opinions while revealing a lot about the writer as they share their perspective on a subject. Examples could include a memorable family vacation, getting fit, a lesson you learned, a journal entry, being homeschooled, etc.

> A **reflective essay** explores a concept, idea, or observation from the writer's point of view.

A reflective essay does not need to tell a complete story, although it may. Its focus is on the writer's experience and opinions regarding a subject or event. First, introduce your essay with a thesis statement. Remember, a thesis statement is a sentence that expresses the main idea you want to get across. Next, reflect on the topic you chose by sharing in detail, giving the reader enough information to understand your topic and your opinion. Finally, close your essay with a conclusion that restates your thesis (in a slightly different way) and gives solid reasons for your opinion or reflection on the subject matter.

Steps for Writing a Reflective Essay
1. Review the Reflective Essay Rubric in the back of this book. This rubric will let you know what is expected in your writing and what your instructor will consider in grading your essay.
2. Choose the subject of your essay and develop a title.
3. Develop a thesis statement, the main point you want to make in your reflection.
4. Create an outline to guide you as you write. Use the Reflective Essay Outline Worksheet provided in the back of this book.
5. Write your five-paragraph essay using the Reflective Essay Worksheet or you may type your essay using a 12-point font and double spacing.
6. Create a cover sheet that includes your name, the date, the assignment (Reflective Essay), and the title of your essay. Optional: You may wish to include artwork on the cover sheet that represents the subject you are reflecting on.

Subject/title of essay: _____
Thesis statement: _____
_____
_____
_____
_____

You will have until the Review Day at the end of this lesson to complete this assignment. **Have** your instructor sign below after reviewing your essay using the Reflective Essay Rubric in the back of the book.

Instructor signature: _____

Communication

Name _____ Lesson 7 - Exercise 3 Day 33

Wisdom Speaks

Copy the proverb.

> *Whoever restrains his words has knowledge, and he who has a cool spirit is a man of understanding.* Proverbs 17:27

_____
_____

Using a dictionary or online search with a parent's permission, **write** the definitions of the words below.

1. restrain: _____
_____

2. cool (as related to emotion): _____
_____

Paraphrase Proverbs 17:27.

_____
_____

Have you ever had a difficult time restraining your words? Often while communicating with others, we may think of words that would be hurtful, unnecessary, or disrespectful. Sometimes our thoughts might be true (your hair is a huge mess today!) but unwise to speak out loud. This proverb teaches that having knowledge helps us to know what *not* to say. As you learn more about proper communication, your knowledge will increase and the words you should *not* speak will lessen. This is God's work in you!

Write about a time you had a "cool spirit," showing that you had understanding in a situation.

_____
_____
_____
_____
_____
_____
_____
_____
_____
_____
_____

Name _____   Lesson 7 - Exercise 4   Day 34

Worldview & Literary Analysis

Literary Device: Imagery

Imagery is a literary device that uses vivid descriptions to paint a picture in the mind of the reader. These "pictures" are meant to portray the emotional or sensational experience going on in the text. The aim is for the reader to feel like they are within the experience being described. By using descriptive language and figures of speech, a writer can appeal to the reader's five senses as well as their emotions. The imagery is not limited to mental pictures but can include sensations and emotions as well.

> **Imagery** is a literary device that uses vivid descriptions to paint a picture in the mind of the reader.

Reed uses imagery in *Life of Washington* in several places. On page 88, she describes Washington's troops in this way: "His wearied troops had been one night, and some of them two, with out sleep. The march had been fatiguing and painful to the soldiers, whose bare feet left traces of blood to mark their path, and the cold was piercing to those who were thinly clad."

We all understand what it is to feel cold and tired. In our minds we can understand what that must have felt like, and we can picture the bloodstains on the ground from the soldiers' feet. We can emotionally connect the misery they must have felt.

Reed effectively transports the reader to the scene with her use of imagery. **Search** through this lesson's reading assignment for another example of imagery. **Copy** it here.

_____
_____
_____
_____
_____
_____

Finish reading pages 94b–107 (end of Chapter IV) of *Life of Washington* and **respond** to the following.

1. When he knew the American army in the north was a feeble one, **how** did Washington prove the patriotism of his feelings? (p. 94)
   _____
   _____

2. **What** was the motive that always ruled Washington's actions as an officer? (p. 94)
   _____
   _____

3. **Why** did Washington receive the thanks of Congress? (p. 97)
   _____
   _____

Name _____   Lesson 7 - Exercise 4   Day 34

4. On page 97, an American officer was dying and asked a woman for prayer. The author states, "Thus in that hour, when the soul feels what it truly is, and that soon it must be in the presence of its holy Creator and just Judge, the duty and the value of *prayer* is owned; and on almost every bed of death is fulfilled the words of Scripture, 'O Thou that hearest prayer, unto Thee shall all flesh come'" (Psalm 65:2; KJV). In your own words, **summarize** the author's statement including the verse.

_____
_____
_____
_____
_____

5. Washington's good friend, the marquis Lafayette, was injured at the battle of Brandywine. Reed then gives a sort of "mini-biography" of Lafayette on pages 98–99. **Write** a paragraph of at least four sentences describing the character and motives of Lafayette regarding America and its cause.

_____
_____
_____
_____
_____

6. General St. Clair had ordered the American troops to withdraw quietly and set nothing on fire. This order was disobeyed. **What** was the result? (p. 101)

_____
_____

7. **Think** of a time when you disobeyed, and it resulted in a poor outcome. **Write** it here.

_____
_____
_____

8. When relating a great victory against the English, the author did not rejoice in defeating the enemy. **Fill in** the blanks in the following statement found on page 103.

"These _____ battles are not recited to fill the mind with a _____ of _____ which should strike us with _____, at the dreadful result produced by _____ _____. They are facts, however, connected with our country's _____ _____ _____; and, no doubt, such signal success _____ greatly the hearts of those who stood up for its _____ [defense]."

9. Specific intelligence was given to Washington that greatly aided his decision-making. **Name** the woman who bravely passed this information on. (p. 106)

_____

Lesson 7, Day 34   Language Lessons for a Living Education Level 10

Name _____   Lesson 7 - Exercise 5   Day 35

Review

☐ **Update** the Reading List chart with books you have read this week.

☐ **Recite** Proverbs 24:17–18 from memory to your instructor.

Vocabulary Review

Match the words to the correct definition.

1. _____ tories
2. _____ profusion
3. _____ obstructions
4. _____ redoubt
5. _____ Hessians
6. _____ marquis
7. _____ avert

a. to ward off
b. small, temporary fortification
c. great quantity; lavish display
d. German forces serving the British
e. a nobleman of Europe
f. obstacles or blockages
g. American colonists on the British side

8. _____ flotilla
9. _____ sanguinary
10. _____ disposed
11. _____ surmounting
12. _____ capitulation
13. _____ rash
14. _____ intelligence

h. inclined toward something
i. overcoming
j. having a lack of caution
k. information concerning an enemy
l. the action of surrendering or ceasing to resist
m. involving much bloodshed
n. a fleet of ships or boats

Grammar & Punctuation Review

1. **List** the three main types of verb mood.

   a. _____   b. _____   c. _____

2. **Describe** the indicative mood.
   _____
   _____

3. **Describe** the imperative mood.
   _____
   _____

4. **Describe** the subjunctive mood.
   _____
   _____

Name _____ Lesson 7 - Exercise 5 Day 35

On the line, **indicate** whether the verb mood is indicative, imperative, or subjunctive.

5. _____ If I had finished school on time, I could have gone to the lake with Dad.

6. _____ Ella, go to the garage and find my hammer, please.

7. _____ I believe the study of creation is such a fascinating topic to research.

Communication Review

1. **Describe** a reflective essay.
   _____
   _____

2. **Write** a one-paragraph summary of the reflective essay you wrote on Day 33.
   _____
   _____
   _____
   _____
   _____
   _____
   _____
   _____

Worldview & Literary Analysis Review

1. **Define** "imagery" as a literary device.
   _____
   _____

2. **Describe** the aim of using imagery in writing.
   _____
   _____

3. **What** was the motive that always ruled Washington's actions as an officer?
   _____
   _____

4. **Who** was Lydia Darrah?
   _____
   _____

Special Feature

Scripture Study: Psalm 139:7–12

⁷Where shall I go from your Spirit?
  Or where shall I flee from your presence?
⁸If I ascend to heaven, you are there!
  If I make my bed in Sheol, you are there!
⁹If I take the wings of the morning
  and dwell in the uttermost parts of the sea,
¹⁰even there your hand shall lead me,
  and your right hand shall hold me.
¹¹If I say, "Surely the darkness shall cover me,
  and the light about me be night,"
¹²even the darkness is not dark to you;
  the night is bright as the day,
  for darkness is as light with you.

King David wrote this psalm, and he was in awe of God's presence in his life. Have you ever thought deeply about God's presence being with you? If so, **write** your thoughts about that in complete sentences.

_____
_____
_____
_____
_____
_____

1. **List** the four places the psalmist describes as being places where God is present.

    a. _____   c. _____
    b. _____   d. _____

David knew that no matter where he went, "even there your hand shall lead me." Do you feel that God is leading your life through His Word and those in authority over you? **Explain** your answer.

_____
_____
_____
_____

2. David knew that not even the grave could separate him from God's love. In Romans 8:38–39, Paul expounds on this idea. **Look up** the verses and **copy** them here.

_____
_____
_____

Name _____   Lesson 8 – Exercise 1   Day 36

Today you will **begin reading** pages 108–125a (ending at "restored") in *Life of Washington*. Have this section read by Exercise 4 of this lesson. Before reading, **study** the vocabulary words listed below.

Vocabulary

alliance	a union formed for mutual benefit	**insinuations**	hints or suggestions of something bad
busybodies	people who meddle in other's affairs	**miscreant**	a person behaving criminally
campaign	a series of military operations with a goal in mind	**mutiny**	open rebellion against authority, especially by soldiers or sailors
censure	to disapprove, especially in a formal statement	**procure**	to obtain by effort
dispersion	distribution of items or people over an area	**reconciliation**	restoration of relationship
diverted	caused to change course	**render**	to do a service for another
fidelity	faithfulness to a person, belief, or cause	**sentiment**	a view, attitude, or opinion
idle	avoiding work	**specimen**	an example that is typical of its kind
inclinations	tendencies toward a particular way		

3. **Write** a sentence using the words *alliance* and *campaign*. Include at least two adjectives.

   _____
   _____

4. **Write** a sentence using the word *busybodies*. Include a possessive pronoun.

   _____
   _____

5. **Write** a sentence using the word *mutiny*. Include a proper noun.

   _____
   _____

☐ **Use** index cards to **write** each vocabulary word from this lesson on one side and the definition on the other. **Check** the box when complete.

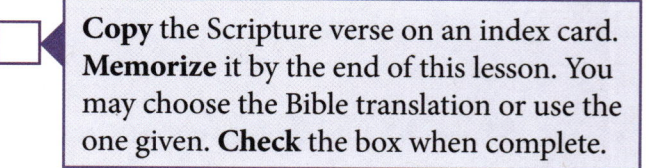

☐ **Copy** the Scripture verse on an index card. **Memorize** it by the end of this lesson. You may choose the Bible translation or use the one given. **Check** the box when complete.

"[A]nd call upon me in the day of trouble; I will deliver you, and you shall glorify me." Psalm 50:15

Grammar & Punctuation

Prepositions

A **preposition** is a word that shows a relationship between its object, usually a noun or pronoun, and another word in the sentence. A preposition is used before a noun or pronoun to show location, time, association, direction, means, cause, opposition, or exception.

> A **preposition** is a word that shows a relationship between its object, usually a noun or pronoun, and another word in the sentence.

> *Example:* We saw a show *at* the theater.
> (The preposition *at* connects the show to *where* we saw it.)

The **object of the preposition** is a noun or pronoun that follows the preposition. In the example, the noun *theater* would be the object of the preposition.

A **prepositional phrase** is a group of words consisting of the proposition, its object, and any other words that modify the object. In the example, the words *at the theater* would be the prepositional phrase.

This chart arranges the prepositions by category. Notice some prepositions fit into more than one category and some contain more than one word. **Study** the chart.

Preposition Chart	
Location	above, across, against, around, at, behind, below, beneath, beside, between, beyond, by, in, in front of, inside, on, outside, over, past, toward, under, upon, within
Time	after, at, before, between, by, during, for, in, on, past, since, until, till, up to
Association	about, according to, along with, among, around, as for, besides, for, like, of, with
Direction	down, from, into, off, onto, out, out of, through, to, up
Means	by, by means of, with
Cause	because of, due to, in view of, on account of
Opposition or Exception	against, apart from, but, despite, except, except for, in spite of, instead of, without

Place parentheses around the prepositional phrases and **underline** the objects of the preposition. There may be more than one in each sentence.

> *Example:* Marie glanced (across the <u>room</u>) and noticed Jonathan speaking (with a <u>friend</u>).

1. Over the hill and beyond the next valley lies a village known for its cheesemaking.
2. The frightened kitten quickly climbed up the tree as the ferocious dog came around the corner.
3. Against all odds, the American patriots fought for the cause of freedom with great determination.
4. I was hoping we would have time to stop at the library after soccer practice.
5. Because the forecasted storm was looming, we cut short our picnic at the park.
6. According to the latest polls, fewer Americans are identifying themselves with a church.
7. Not very many students in my class have ever traveled outside the United States.
8. Sometimes in the winter, our temperatures drop below zero.

Name _____   Lesson 8 - Exercise 2   Day 37

9. **Write** a sentence containing a prepositional phrase regarding location. Include two adjectives. (Day 2)
   _____
   _____

10. **Write** a sentence containing a prepositional phrase regarding cause. Include an adverb. (Day 2)
    _____
    _____

11. **Write** a sentence containing a prepositional phrase regarding opposition or exception. Include a helping verb. (Day 17)
    _____
    _____

12. **Write** a sentence containing a prepositional phrase regarding direction. Include a conjunction. (Day 27)
    _____
    _____

Review It!

Underline the subject once and any verb(s) twice. **Circle** any conjunctions. (Day 27)

13. Reese left rehearsal early but was late for her doctor's appointment anyway.
14. We rarely cook broccoli since some family members dislike it.
15. Jonathan not only built his kids an amazing treehouse but also added a climbing net.
16. **Write** a sentence containing a permanent linking verb. (Day 12)
    _____
    _____

17. **Write** a sentence containing a sensory linking verb. (Day 12)
    _____
    _____

18. **Write** a sentence containing a conditional linking verb. (Day 12)
    _____
    _____

☐ **Copy** the preposition chart on an index card. **Work on memorizing** the prepositions. **Check** the box when you are done.

Name _____   Lesson 8 - Exercise 3   Day 38

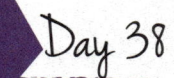

Communication

Finding Items for Citations

It is helpful to know where to search for the items you will need for your citations. **Study** the chart below and use it as a reference when taking research notes.

For a Book	
Author	**The primary creator of the work you are citing.** If there is more than one author, record both names in your notes. The author's name is usually found near the title of the book.
Title	**The name of the book you are referencing.** Usually prominently displayed on the cover.
Publisher	**The entity responsible for producing the work.** The name of the publisher is often located on the title page or the copyright page.
Date	**The date this version of the work was published.** It is located on either the title page or the copyright page. Use the most recent date listed.
Location	**The actual page number or numbers you are referencing.**

For a Website	
Author	**The creator of the web article.** The author's name is usually located near the title. If no author is listed, skip this item and move on to the title.
Title of article	**The name of the article contained within the website.** It is usually in a prominent location.
Website name	**The exact name of the website you are referencing.**
Date of article	**The date the article was written.** If no date is listed, record the date you referenced it.
URL	**The address of any given resource on the Web.** At the top of your browser, click the address bar to select the entire URL. It can be copied into a word processing document or handwritten into your notes.

As you progress through writing your biography, you will be given details regarding the placement of the citation information you are gathering. The important thing for now is that you record each item as you go along. It never hurts to have extra information, so when in doubt, write it out!

Study the examples of citations as they would appear in a bibliography (works cited page) for books and websites in the MLA style.

> Reed, Anna C. *Life of Washington*. Attic Books, 2013.

> Ham, Ken. "New Dinosaur Tracks Unearthed in Texas' Paluxy River." *Ken Ham Blog*, 11 Sept. 2023, https://answersingenesis.org/dinosaurs/footprints/new-dinosaur-tracks-unearthed-texas-paluxy-river/.

Communication   Lesson 8, Day 38

Name _____ Lesson 8 - Exercise 3 Day 38

Biography Notes

Today you will answer questions about your biography subject. Your answers can be your own opinion, but "sprinkling in" some quotes by the person themselves or from the commentary of others would certainly make your claims more credible. Using the Citation Notes Worksheets in the back of this book, **record** the sources of any information that requires a citation. Remember, throughout the biography, you will need to cite at least *three* sources you have gathered researched information from.

Answer the questions regarding your subject using complete sentences. You may use books, your own personal knowledge, or an online search with a parent's permission.

What lasting impact has this person had on the world?

_____
_____
_____
_____
_____
_____
_____
_____

Is this person a positive or negative role model? Explain.

_____
_____
_____
_____
_____
_____
_____
_____

Why did you choose this person as the subject of your biography?

_____
_____
_____
_____
_____
_____
_____
_____

Name _____ Lesson 8 - Exercise 4 Day 39

Worldview & Literary Analysis

Literary Device: Exposition

Exposition is a literary device that introduces background information important to the story. It may concern real or fictional characters, settings, events, historical facts, or environmental details. Its purpose is to help the reader better understand what is going on.

> **Exposition** is a literary device that introduces background information important to the story.

Too much exposition may become boring to a reader, so it is important to mix it in with other devices like imagery and dialogue. The writer needs to find a balance between giving too little detail and sharing too much detail. This is why it is helpful to have a parent or friend read a sample of your writing and share their opinion.

Reed uses exposition extensively in her narrative of Washington's life. His life is one filled with many important historical events, and although you may think her book is loaded with them, there is much she had to leave out for the sake of length.

On page 114, Reed states, "Several letters were addressed to some members of Congress, by commissioners authorized by the British government, assuring them of honours [honors] and reward, if they would procure a reconciliation on the terms they offered—that is, to remain colonies." This is a historical fact inserted to let the reader know what was happening, giving the reader insight as to why the Americans were acting and feeling as they were.

Search the pages of *Life of Washington* you have read already and find a short example of exposition and **record** it here.

_____
_____
_____

Finish reading pages 108-125a (ending at "restored") in *Life of Washington* and **respond** to the following.

1. **What** literary device is being used in the following phrase? (p. 108)

   "… many naked, bleeding feet, on the frozen earth."

   _____

2. Chapter V (p. 108) opens with a lengthy description of the suffering endured by Washington's troops. In a Bible translation of your choice, look up Romans 5:3–4 and Romans 8:18. **Study** these Scriptures and **write** about how you think they can be applied in situations involving suffering.

   _____
   _____
   _____
   _____
   _____
   _____

Name _____ Lesson 8 - Exercise 4 Day 39

3. On pages 108–109, Reed contrasts the scene of the suffering troops with future Americans who are celebrating a "free and prosperous land." **Write** a paragraph of 6–7 sentences comparing these two scenes and conclude it with your opinion regarding Reed's decision to fast forward to this celebratory scene.

   _____
   _____
   _____
   _____
   _____
   _____
   _____
   _____

4. Washington's wife played a major role in uplifting her husband in some of his darkest hours. (p. 110) **Fill in** the blanks of this excerpt.

   "When it was _____, she was with him to share his _____,

   and endeavour [endeavor] to contribute to _____ his sad _____,

   by her attentions and expressions of _____, firm _____, that

   _____ _____ would soon come."

5. The King of England offered Congress member Joseph Reed a high position and lots of money if he could get the American Congress to submit to the wishes of the king (p. 114). He replied by saying the king was "not rich enough to do it" (p. 115). **What** did Reed mean by this?

   _____
   _____

6. Washington found himself in a spot where he was being lied about, but to defend himself, he would have had to reveal secrets that would put his country in danger. **Copy** the words of Washington from the top of page 117 regarding this situation.

   _____
   _____
   _____

7. Washington used to go a short distance from the military camp to pray. In a Bible translation of your choice, read Matthew 14:23 and Hebrews 5:7. **Describe** why you think Washington went off by himself to pray and how Jesus is an example we should follow in prayer.

   _____
   _____
   _____
   _____

Name _____ Lesson 8 - Exercise 5 Day 40

Review

- **Update** the Reading List chart with books you have read this week.
- **Recite** Psalm 50:15 from memory to your instructor.

Vocabulary Review

Match the words to the correct definition.

1. _____ censure   a. avoiding work
2. _____ busybodies   b. caused to change course
3. _____ sentiment   c. people who meddle in others' affairs
4. _____ specimen   d. a series of military operations with a goal in mind
5. _____ campaign   e. a view, attitude, or opinion
6. _____ idle   f. a union formed for mutual benefit
7. _____ reconciliation   g. to disapprove, especially in a formal statement
8. _____ alliance   h. an example that is typical of its kind
9. _____ diverted   i. restoration of a relationship

10. _____ procure   j. to do a service for another
11. _____ inclinations   k. distribution of items or people over an area
12. _____ miscreant   l. open rebellion against authority, especially by soldiers or sailors
13. _____ render   m. to obtain by effort
14. _____ insinuations   n. faithfulness to a person, belief, or cause
15. _____ fidelity   o. hints or suggestions of something bad
16. _____ mutiny   p. a person behaving criminally
17. _____ dispersion   q. tendencies toward a particular way

Grammar & Punctuation Review

1. **Define** a preposition.
   _____
   _____

2. **Define** the object of the preposition.
   _____
   _____

Name _____ Lesson 8 - Exercise 5 Day 40

Place parentheses around the prepositional phrases and **underline** the objects of the preposition. There may be more than one in each sentence.

3. With renewed enthusiasm, Jason tried climbing to the top of the rock wall again.
4. Into the depths of the ocean the submarine plunged and set out on its maiden voyage.
5. Without any knowledge of edible plants, the lost hikers were in danger of starvation.
6. The moon shone outside our cabin and cast a gorgeous glow on the snow around us.
7. **Write** a sentence containing a prepositional phrase regarding location.

_____
_____

Communication Review

1. **Define** the following citation items for a book.
    a. Author: _____
    b. Title: _____
    c. Publisher: _____
    e. Date: _____
    f. Location: _____

Worldview & Literary Analysis Review

1. **Define** "exposition" as a literary device.

_____
_____

2. **Describe** how a writer can avoid making literary exposition boring for the reader.

_____
_____

3. **Write** a paragraph sharing your opinion on the exposition present in *Life of Washington*. Tell whether you think the author does a good job of sharing important details without overdoing it.

_____
_____
_____
_____
_____
_____
_____

Special Feature

Biography Excerpt: James Madison (1751–1836) by Tim LaHaye

James Madison is referred to by most historians as "the Father of the Constitution." No man was better prepared to be one of the Founding Fathers in temperament, intellect, background, education, and commitment.

On March 16, 1751, he was born into the devout home of James and Molly Conway Madison in Port Conway, Virginia. His father was a wealthy plantation owner and member of the Episcopal (or state) Church, in which he was baptized on the 21st day of his life. He was homeschooled by his godly mother and grandmother, and two tutors came to his residence to give instruction, one of whom was an Episcopalian minister. These men taught him Latin, Greek, arithmetic, literature, French, and Spanish. They also established a broad and diverse reading schedule.

Due to what his parents considered heretical views, which they felt had crept into the local college of William and Mary (probably the early waves of French skepticism), they sent him to Princeton, where he studied for the ministry. Here he fell under the influence of the Reverend John Witherspoon, one of the nation's leading theologians and legal scholars. This helped to establish a theological base for Madison's thinking, and it never left him. He also developed lifetime friends, some of whom went into the ministry. Chief among them were William Bradford, who after his divinity studies went into law, and Samuel Stanhope Smith, who became a Presbyterian minister and was later Witherspoon's successor at Princeton. …

Long after he returned to Virginia, young Madison continued to pursue his theological studies. It may have been at this period in his life, while out walking with his father one day that he entered into a life-molding experience. We don't know exactly when it took place, but an incident in his youth that made a deep impression on him was his standing with his father outside the jail in the village of Orange and listening to several Baptists preach from the window of the cell in which they were confined because of their religious opinions.[1]

Respond to the following.

1. **Name** four people who had a positive impact on young John Madison.

   a. _____   c. _____

   b. _____   d. _____

2. **Name** four people who have had a positive impact on your life.

   a. _____   c. _____

   b. _____   d. _____

---

[1] Endnote from excerpt: Gaillard Hunt, *James Madison and Religious Liberty* (Washington, DC: American Historical Association, Government Printing Office, 1902), p. 167. Biography excerpt from: LaHaye, Tim. *Faith of Our Founding Fathers*. Master Books, 2022, p. 117–118.

Name _____   Lesson 9 - Exercise 1   Day 41

Today you will **begin reading** pages 125b–141a (ending at "September") in *Life of Washington*. Have this section read by Exercise 4 of this lesson. Before reading, **study** the vocabulary words listed below.

Vocabulary

banishment	driven out from home or country	impious	lacking respect or reverence
barbarous	cruel, savage, and brutal	imprecations	cursing
bayonet	a blade fixed to the muzzle of a rifle	infidel	a non-Christian or one who opposes Christianity
consoled	comforted someone in time of grief	profane	to abuse something sacred
conspicuous	clearly visible, standing out	suppress	to put down forcibly
desertion	the abandonment of a person or cause	vice	an immoral behavior
hostilities	acts of war	wanton	unprovoked
imminent	about to happen		

3. **Write** a sentence using the words *banishment* and *infidel*. Include a conjunction. (Day 37)

   _____
   _____

4. Using the vocabulary list, **fill in** the blanks in this quote found on page 126.

   "… but I have beheld no day since the commencement of _____, when I have thought her liberties in such _____ danger as at present."

5. **Write** a paragraph of 5–6 sentences using one of the vocabulary words in each sentence.

   _____
   _____
   _____
   _____
   _____
   _____

☐ **Use** index cards to **write** each vocabulary word from this lesson on one side and the definition on the other. **Check** the box when complete.

☐ **Copy** the Scripture verse on an index card. **Memorize** it by the end of this lesson. You may choose the Bible translation or use the one given. **Check** the box when complete.

And they shall teach my people the difference between the holy and profane, and cause them to discern between the unclean and the clean. Ezekiel 44:23 (KJV)

Name _____ Lesson 9 - Exercise 2 Day 42

Grammar & Punctuation

Verb Voice: Active vs. Passive

The **verb voice** tells whether the subject is acting or being acted upon. In the **active voice**, the subject is doing the action. In the **passive voice**, the action is happening to the subject.

> The **verb voice** tells whether the subject is acting or being acted upon.
> In the **active voice**, the subject is doing the action.
> In the **passive voice**, the action is happening to the subject.

> **ACTIVE VOICE** | **PASSIVE VOICE**
> *Example*: The baby shark ate the fish. | The fish was eaten by the baby shark.

Active Voice

Use the active voice when you want the reader to focus on the subject and the action it is doing, and *not* the target of the action. Regardless of what verb is used, a sentence structured so the subject performs the verb is using the active voice. The active voice is more direct than the passive voice, so most of the writing you do in school and relationally (like in a text) is best written in the active voice.

> *Examples*: Shantel runs five miles every Saturday morning just to keep up her stamina.
> I humbly request your presence at my graduation ceremony next month.

Write a sentence using the active voice. Include a helping verb. (Day 17)

_____

_____

Passive Voice

Use the passive voice when you want the reader to focus on the action being described or the action's target, and *not* on who or what is performing the action. The passive voice is often used in scientific writing and news reports. It gives attention to the action that occurred or the object receiving the action.

> *Examples*: A house was burned to the ground by arsonists on the west side of the city last night.
> The weary horse is given a bucket of water by the farmer.

Write a sentence using the passive voice. Include a prepositional phrase. (Day 37)

_____

_____

A passive-voice sentence can be changed to active voice with a little restructuring.

> *Examples*: Skydiving is loved by many outdoor enthusiasts. (passive voice)
> Many outdoor enthusiasts love skydiving. (active voice)

1. **Rewrite** this passive voice sentence to make it active.

   The building was sold by the government.

   _____

Grammar & Punctuation   Lesson 9, Day 42   101

Name _____   Lesson 9 - Exercise 2   Day 42

2. **Rewrite** this active voice sentence to make it passive.

   My teacher took the class to the museum.

   _____

Sometimes in the passive voice, the doer of the action is not mentioned but only implied.

   Examples: The batter was mixed vigorously. (passive — the "doer" is implied)
   The chef mixed the batter vigorously. (active — the "doer" is clearly stated)

3. **Rewrite** this passive voice sentence into the active voice by creating a "doer" of the action.

   The giant oak tree in the park was cut down.

   _____

Write active or passive on the line to indicate the voice of the verb.

4. _____ The lawn at the college was mowed by a group of student volunteers.
5. _____ Twenty loaves of banana bread were sold by the youth group at church.
6. _____ The football coach led his team to the state championship game last fall.
7. _____ Corn was the only food eaten by the lab rats during the experiment.
8. _____ Truck drivers work long hours and need to get plenty of rest to stay alert.
9. _____ My cousin Leah travels all over as a nanny for her missionary aunt and uncle.

Review It!

10. **Fill in** the verb tense chart using the verb "jump." (Day 22)

	Past	Present	Future
Simple	I _____	I _____	I _____
Perfect	I _____	I _____	I _____
Continuous	I _____	I _____	I _____
Perfect Continuous	I _____	I _____	I _____

☐ **Copy** the definitions of active and passive voice on an index card and include examples of each. **Check** the box when you are done.

Name _____   Lesson 9 - Exercise 3   Day 43

Communication

Definition Essay

A **definition essay** defines a term or an idea, such as a vocabulary word, abstract concept, historical word, technical term, or any idea that can be defined. This is a unique type of essay because it not only defines a term or idea by teaching about it, but can also reveal little-known facts, the word's origins, or its implications. It can be argumentative if the writer has a stance to defend regarding the term. Ideas for a definition essay could include: "What does *liberty* mean?" "How the word *evolution* can be used," "Defining the concept of *friendship*," "What is the *American dream*?"

> A **definition essay** defines a term or an idea, such as a vocabulary word, abstract concept, historical word, technical term, or any idea that can be defined.

To begin your essay, introduce the word, term, or concept and provide a definition as well as a thesis statement (main point). Next, elaborate on your thesis statement by making points about what you are defining. Lastly, conclude with a strong statement showing how your points support your thesis.

> **Steps for Writing a Definition Essay**
> 1. Review the Definition Essay Rubric in the back of this book. This rubric will let you know what is expected in your writing and what your instructor will consider in grading your essay.
> 2. Choose the term or idea you will be defining and write a basic definition. This could be taken directly from a dictionary, or you may create your own definition that you are prepared to defend or elaborate on.
> 3. Develop your thesis statement. This is the main point you want to express regarding the term or idea you have chosen.
> 4. Create an outline to guide you as you write. Use the Definition Essay Outline provided in the back of the book.
> 5. Write your five-paragraph essay using the Definition Essay Worksheet or you may type your essay using a 12-point font and double spacing.
> 6. Create a cover sheet that includes your name, the date, the assignment (Definition Essay), and the title of your essay. Optional: You may wish to include artwork on the cover sheet that represents the idea or term you are defining.

Term/idea: _____
Definition: _____
_____
_____

You will have until the Review Day at the end of this lesson to complete this assignment. **Have** your instructor sign below after reviewing your essay using the Definition Essay Rubric in the back of the book.

Instructor signature: _____

Name _____   Lesson 9 - Exercise 3   Day 43

Wisdom Speaks

Copy the proverb.

> *Even a fool who keeps silent is considered wise; when he closes his lips, he is deemed intelligent.* Proverbs 17:28

_____
_____

Using a dictionary or online search with a parent's permission, **write** the definitions of the words below.

1. wise: _____
   _____

2. intelligence: _____
   _____

A person can have an appearance of wisdom by simply staying quiet. Why is this? In Matthew 12:34b, Jesus says,

> *"For out of the abundance of the heart the mouth speaks."*

When a fool opens his mouth, foolishness comes out because his heart is not right. Even a fool who stays quiet can appear more intelligent!

Copy the quote from Jesus about the heart in Matthew 12:34b.

_____
_____

3. So, if a foolish person can "appear" intelligent or wise by keeping their mouth closed, how can we know the difference between a wise person and a fool? What signs should you look for? **Look up** James 3:13 and **write** the answer in a complete paragraph.

   _____
   _____
   _____
   _____
   _____
   _____
   _____

Name _____   Lesson 9 - Exercise 4   Day 44

Worldview & Literary Analysis

Author's Focus: Leadership

Reed chooses many accounts of Washington that show his skill as a leader. First, he recognized God as his leader and gave Him the glory in all types of situations. Secondly, Reed highlights Washington's concern for his troops, showing that he was willing to give up his life for them. Lastly, she shows Washington's willingness to bring correction to his troops when needed.

All these qualities made him one of the most respected leaders in American history. As you study this lesson's reading selection, search for times when Washington displayed leadership.

Finish reading pages 125b–141a (ending at "September") and **respond** to the following.

1. When referring to the war, Washington makes this statement. **Fill in** the blanks. (p. 126)

   "The hand of _____ is so _____ in all this, that he must be worse than an _____ that lacks _____, and more than _____, that has not _____ to acknowledge his obligations."

2. Washington felt strongly that the hand of God was heavy upon the cause of freedom the colonists were fighting for. **What** do you think made him feel so strongly? **Answer** in 2–3 sentences.

   _____
   _____
   _____
   _____

3. The following statement is found on pages 126–127: "The Indians on the frontiers of the states had been practising [practicing] their barbarous warfare, in connexion [connection] with some of the equally barbarous white settlers." In 2–3 sentences, **evaluate** Reed's worldview regarding race. **Does** this statement reveal an unbiased attitude?

   _____
   _____
   _____
   _____

4. A good leader should encourage and praise those under him or her when they perform nobly. On page 127, we see a letter written by Washington to his troops. The Bible teaches us to give honor and praise when praise is due. **Copy** Romans 13:7 from a Bible translation of your choice.

   _____
   _____
   _____
   _____
   _____

Name _____ Lesson 9 - Exercise 4   Day 44

5. While there are times a leader needs to praise and encourage, there are also times a leader needs to bring correction or rebuke. Reed records, "It was in the summer of this year, that General Washington took measures to suppress the habit of profane swearing which prevailed in the army. The following general order is sufficiently illustrative of his views of that most vulgar and impious practice" (p. 129). **Read** the order about swearing and **summarize** it.

_____
_____
_____
_____
_____

6. The English army under General Cornwallis was having great success in Carolina and offered terms to the residents in the area if they would submit. Reed states that "many of the richest inhabitants gave up their property and went into banishment from their homes, rather than remain upon the terms offered to them." Imagine how difficult it would be to give up your home for the cause of your country's freedom. **Write** 2–3 sentences telling what decision you might make and how you would feel about it.

_____
_____
_____
_____
_____

7. The American army had many times when they needed food, clothing, shelter, and weaponry. This was a great concern of Washington's. On page 137, we read, "The state of his army caused him distress and vexation. He felt for the officers …" Using a dictionary or online source with a parent's permission, look up the words *distress* and *vexation*. **Write** 3–4 sentences explaining your opinion on whether Washington was justified in feeling this way. Were these times when distress and vexation were called for?

_____
_____
_____
_____
_____
_____
_____

Lesson 9, Day 44

Language Lessons for a Living Education Level 10

Name _____   Lesson 9 - Exercise 5   Day 45

Review

☐ **Update** the Reading List chart with books you have read this week.

☐ **Recite** Ezekiel 44:23 from memory to your instructor.

Vocabulary Review

Match the words to the correct definition.

1. _____ hostilities   a. the abandonment of a person or cause
2. _____ imminent   b. cruel, savage, and brutal
3. _____ conspicuous   c. acts of war
4. _____ infidel   d. clearly visible, standing out
5. _____ barbarous   e. to put down forcibly
6. _____ consoled   f. about to happen
7. _____ desertion   g. a non-Christian or one who opposes Christianity
8. _____ suppress   h. comforted someone in time of grief

9. _____ profane   i. to abuse something sacred
10. _____ impious   j. unprovoked
11. _____ imprecations   k. driven out from home or country
12. _____ wanton   l. a blade fixed to the muzzle of a rifle
13. _____ vice   m. cursing
14. _____ bayonet   n. lacking respect or reverence
15. _____ banishment   o. an immoral behavior

Grammar & Punctuation Review

1. **Describe** the active voice.
   _____
   _____

2. **Describe** the passive voice.
   _____
   _____

Write active or passive on the line to indicate the voice of the verb.

3. _____ Our lawn was mowed by a landscaping service this past summer.

4. _____ The elephant lifted its trunk high in the air and then slapped it on the water.

Name _____   Lesson 9 - Exercise 5   Day 45

5. _____ Old hymns were sung each Sunday at my grandmother's church.

6. _____ My mail carrier drives her own vehicle instead of a postal service vehicle.

7. **Rewrite** this active voice sentence to make it passive.

> The garbage man left our garbage bins lying in the middle of the street.

_____
_____

Communication Review

1. **Define** a definition essay.

_____
_____

2. **Write** a one-paragraph summary of the definition essay you wrote on Day 43.

_____
_____
_____
_____
_____
_____
_____

Worldview & Literary Analysis Review

1. **List** three ways the author of *Life of Washington* shows Washington's skills as a leader.

   a. _____
   _____

   b. _____
   _____

   c. _____
   _____

Fill in the blanks.

2. When referring to the war, Washington makes this statement.

   "The hand of _____ is so _____ in all this, that he must be worse than an _____ that lacks _____, and more than _____, that has not _____ to acknowledge his obligations."

Special Feature

Lesson 10

Biography Excerpt: Alexander Hamilton (1757–1804) by Tim LaHaye

Alexander Hamilton was one of those brilliant, dedicated patriots without whose help it is doubtful the Constitution would have been completed, and it is probable that without his support, it would not have been ratified — particularly by the important state of New York, for all its other delegates left the convention in disgust before it was completed.[1]

Hamilton, a prolific writer, inspired the *Federalist Papers* that were circulated throughout the colonies, 51 of which he wrote. While Madison is termed "the Father of the Constitution," it isn't an exaggeration to call Hamilton "the Ratifier of the Constitution." It was his tireless and brilliant energy that secured ratification from more than the required two-thirds of the states, most of which passed it on the first vote.

During the Revolutionary War, the young Hamilton distinguished himself in battle and with the pen, which drew him to the attention of General George Washington, who appointed him his aide-de-camp and staff lawyer. He served in this capacity for four years and was promoted to Lieutenant Colonel. As secretary of the treasury, he distinguished himself in what is popularly called "Hamiltonianism." After the Constitution was ratified, he founded the *New York Post* and one of the state's first banks.[2]

A **summary** pulls out the most important parts of a piece of writing and concisely condenses those parts using one's own words. A summary does not copy word for word but rather restructures the information in a more concise way to communicate the main point.

> **Ratified** means gave formal consent to; signed and made official (usually a treaty or official document).
>
> A **summary** pulls out the most important parts of a piece of writing and concisely condenses those parts using one's own words.

1. **Write** a summary of this excerpt about Alexander Hamilton.

---

1 Endnote from excerpt: M.E. Bradford, *A Worthy Company* (Marlborough, NH: Plymouth Rock Foundation, 1982), p. 91.
2 Biography excerpt from: LaHaye, Tim. *Faith of Our Founding Fathers*. Master Books, 2022, p. 127.

Name _____ Lesson 10 - Exercise 1 Day 46

Today you will **begin reading** pages 141b–153 in *Life of Washington*. Have this section read by Exercise 4 of this lesson. Before reading, **study** the vocabulary words listed below.

Vocabulary

delusive	giving a misleading or false impression	**perilous**	full of danger or risk
depraved	wicked; morally corrupt	**rectitude**	moral behavior or thinking; righteousness
dissipation	squandering energy or resources	**sloop of war**	a warship with one gun deck
feeble	lacking strength; weakness	**timid**	easily frightened; lacking courage
feigned	insincere; pretended	**traitor**	a person who betrays their country, friend, etc.
indignation	anger provoked by perceived unfairness	**treason**	the crime of betraying one's country
ingenuous	innocent and unsuspecting	**vice**	an immoral or wicked behavior
insolence	rude or disrespectful actions		

Write a paragraph using as many vocabulary words as you can. **Circle** each vocabulary word once you finish. (*Hint:* Many of these words can be used as adjectives to describe nouns in your paragraph.)

_____
_____
_____
_____
_____
_____
_____
_____
_____

☐ **Use** index cards to **write** each vocabulary word from this lesson on one side and the definition on the other. **Check** the box when complete.

☐ **Copy** the Scripture verse on an index card. **Memorize** it by the end of this lesson. You may choose the Bible translation or use the one given. **Check** the box when complete.

Enter by the narrow gate. For the gate is wide and the way is easy that leads to destruction, and those who enter by it are many. For the gate is narrow and the way is hard that leads to life, and those who find it are few. Matthew 7:13–14

Grammar & Punctuation

Quotation Marks

Quotation marks are used frequently in all sorts of writing. It is important to know when and how to use them to avoid miscommunication about who is speaking. Here are some of the ways they are used.

When to Use Quotation Marks	
Direct Quotations	Quotation marks are used to indicate the exact words of a writer or speaker. Do not use them if you are paraphrasing or summarizing someone else's words.
	Alyssa commented, "I know God has a greater purpose for my life."
Dialogue	Dialogue is a conversation between two or more people and often occurs in books, plays, and movies. Use quotation marks to enclose the words of the speakers and begin a new paragraph whenever the speaker changes.
	"I'm going to run down to the post office to drop off this package," Dad said. "Oh, do you mind," Jesse asked, "if I go with you?"
Titles of Short Works	Use quotation marks to enclose the titles of short works like essays, stories, songs, articles, chapters of a book, individual episodes of radio or television programs, and most poems. Quotation marks are not needed for chapters of the Bible.
	The best chapter in that book was "Overnight Voyage."
Special Words	Sometimes a word, phrase, or expression may need to be set off from the rest of the sentence to emphasize it for purposes like impact, skepticism, a twist of meaning, etc.
	Sometimes "experts" miss the mark. The word "blue" can refer to a color or a mood.

Rules for Quotation Marks and Other Sentence Punctuation	
Commas and periods appear *before* ending quotation marks.	
	"I want to know God's Word better," Sarah expressed. David replied, "So do I."
Colons and semicolons appear *after* ending quotation marks.	
	Maggie answered, "I need all the help I can get"; then she proceeded to ignore my advice.
Question marks and exclamation points may appear inside or outside the quotation marks. If the quotation itself is a question or exclamation, the punctuation goes *inside* the quotation marks. If the quotation did not include these marks originally, the punctuation comes *after* the quotation marks.	
	"What a beautiful day!" exclaimed Austin. I can't believe he said, "The tickets are free"!

Name _____   Lesson 10 – Exercise 2   Day 47

Place quotation marks, commas, periods, question marks, and exclamation points where needed in the following sentences.

1. My friend Rachel asked Will your family be at the homeschool picnic this Saturday
2. Just as I was falling asleep my mom questioned Did you finish the dishes
3. Look out yelled my dad as the ball whipped past my head
4. The word see could refer to a person's eyesight or to the act of understanding a concept
5. The chapter Relevant for Today contained a lot of interesting information
6. **Write** a sentence containing a person's exact words in which you are asking a question, yet their quote is not a question.
   _____
   _____

7. **Write** a sentence that contains a special word that would need to be set off with quotation marks.
   _____
   _____

8. **Write** a sentence that includes a song title and your opinion about it.
   _____
   _____

Review It!

Place parentheses around the prepositional phrases and **underline** the objects of the preposition (Day 37). There may be more than one in each sentence.

9. Be careful playing in the backyard because ticks are hiding under the leaves.
10. In view of the circumstances, let's wait until Monday.
11. With no clear-cut directions, assembling the desk was difficult.

Circle the prepositional phrase that completes each sentence.

12. There were several large bats clinging to the beams _____ .
    a. while sleeping   b. under the bridge   c. quietly
13. The best place to set up your tent is _____ .
    a. anywhere you feel comfortable   b. beside the trees   c. where there is shade
14. _____ the roof on my aunt's house has needed to be fixed.
    a. I have been telling you   b. It's pretty obvious that   c. For over ten years,

112 Lesson 10, Day 47   Language Lessons for a Living Education Level 10

Name _____   Lesson 10 - Exercise 3   Day 48

Communication

Incorporating Quotes, Paraphrases, and Summaries

On Day 38, you learned that "sprinkling" in some quotes from outside sources about the subject of your biography would add credibility to your writing. Today you will learn how to add direct quotes, paraphrases, and summaries. You do not need to master this material but should become familiar with it and use this lesson as a reference while writing your biography. Here are three ways to "plug" research information into your writing.

	Incorporating Research from a Book in MLA Style
Direct Quote	**Use the exact words found in your research.** There are three ways to use a quote:
	1. A quote of four or fewer lines can be set off with quotation marks and included in a sentence. If the author's name is mentioned in the sentence, do not include it in parentheses at the end. If not mentioned, it must be included along with the page number in parentheses at the end of the quote.
	As LaHaye points out, "With his roots deeply entrenched in the Pennsylvania Quaker faith, John Dickinson was anything but a sectarian or unbeliever" (141).
	It is said of Dickinson, "With his roots deeply entrenched in the Pennsylvania Quaker faith, John Dickinson was anything but a sectarian or unbeliever" (LaHaye 141).
	2. A quote of four or more lines can be set in a block quotation apart from the text. The indent should be ½ inch from the left margin, and no quotation marks are needed.
	In his book *Faith of Our Founding Fathers*, Tim LaHaye states: Dickinson was an intellectual activist, yet he refused to sign the Declaration of Independence because no union of government was ready to take the place of the old. He did fight in the war, however, and was later recognized by both Delaware and Pennsylvania, where he served as president of the supreme Executive Council. He founded Dickinson College in Carlisle, Pennsylvania, in 1773. (141)
	3. A full or partial quote can be integrated into your own sentence using quotation marks. The parenthetical citation belongs directly after the quote.
	The idea that "Dickinson was anything but a sectarian or unbeliever" (LaHaye 141) has historical support.
Paraphrase	**Use your own words yet include all the important information the source gives.** Leave out what does not apply to the point you are trying to make.
	Original: "James McHenry was a refined gentleman who studied medicine under the famous Dr. Rush of Philadelphia (a dedicated Christian). He was an ardent patriot with a pronounced hostility toward England (quite typical of the Irish)" (LaHaye 154).
	Paraphrase: James McHenry was a gentleman who studied medicine under the famous Dr. Rush and was also a patriot with hostile feelings toward England (LaHaye 154).
Summary	**Use your own words to condense a lengthy source so it fits with your topic and space.**

Communication   Lesson 10, Day 48   113

Name _____   Lesson 10 - Exercise 3   Day 48

> *Original:* "When war broke out, he volunteered and served with distinction on the medical staff under Washington and Lafayette. Fort McHenry, birthplace of our national anthem, was named in his honor. He said little during the Constitutional Convention, but his presence made Maryland's majority vote favor the strong federal government advocated by Washington, Madison, and Randolph" (LaHaye 154).
>
> *Summary:* McHenry volunteered on the medical staff under Washington and Lafayette, and Fort McHenry was named in his honor. Although he did not speak much during the Constitutional Convention, his presence was certainly felt regarding a strong federal government (LaHaye 154).

Incorporating Research from a Website in MLA Style

When citing a website, list the author's last name in parentheses. If no author is listed, use the article title. No page number or URL is required in-text. These items would only appear on the works cited page. If you use two separate articles written by the same author, both the author's name and article title should be included in the parenthetical citation.

> We do not need to find human and dinosaur tracks together to know that the Bible is true (Ham).

If you include the information's location in your sentence, you do *not* need to do a parenthetical citation, although you would still need the works cited entry.

> In his article "New Dinosaur Tracks Unearthed in Texas' Paluxy River," Ken Ham argues that we do not need to find human and dinosaur tracks in the same place to know the Bible is true.

Additional Notes on MLA Style

All pages in MLA style should be double spaced. If writing by hand, skip every other line.

All punctuation should be placed *after* the parenthetical citation unless it's a question mark or exclamation point that belongs to the quote *or* if using a block quote.

> *Example of question mark within the quoted words:* LaHaye reasons, "This leads a normal person to ask, 'Where did today's scholars get their information?' " (13).
>
> *Example of an exclamation point as a part of your sentence:* I was astonished to learn that "the religious history of America had been systematically stolen from our nation's texts" (LaHaye 9)!

The first time you refer to a source, use the author's full name. If you mention the source again, use only the person's last name.

> "Tim LaHaye writes …" The next mention would say, "LaHaye writes …"

If you want to add a word or words to a quotation, place brackets around the information you are adding to differentiate it from the person you are quoting.

> LaHaye points out, "Secularism is taught in those same textbooks [which is not surprising], a life and worldview for children and young people that little resembles the one taught in this nation for the first 150 years of its history" (9).

If you want to omit a word or words from a quotation, indicate the deleted information by using ellipses, which are three periods separated by spaces (…) with a space before and after.

> LaHaye points out, "Secularism is taught … a life and worldview … that little resembles the one taught in this nation for the first 150 years of its history" (9).

Name _____   Lesson 10 - Exercise 4   Day 49

Worldview & Literary Analysis

Literary Device: Foreshadowing

Foreshadowing is a literary device used to hint at events yet to come in a story. It can create tension or suspense by giving the reader just enough information to make them curious about what is to come.

> **Foreshadowing** is a literary device used to hint at events yet to come in a story.

At the very beginning of this lesson's reading assignment, we see an example of foreshadowing. Reed states, "While he was absent, the fierce but artful passion of revenge was busy in the heart of an American, forming a plot of treason" (p. 141). At this point, the reader does not know who the traitor might be, but this little glimpse into future events creates a curiosity and desire to find out!

As you work along on the biography you are writing, consider the use of foreshadowing to create suspense. Think about an event in the life of your character that you could give your readers a clue about before actually relating the event.

The tempter and the traitor - the treason of Arnold on the night of September 21, 1780

Finish reading pages 141b–153 in *Life of Washington* and **respond** to the following.

1. Reed uses foreshadowing to introduce the story of General Benedict Arnold with the statement, "… the fierce but artful passion of revenge was busy in the heart of an American, forming a plot of treason" (p. 141). **Was** this foreshadowing effective in rousing your curiosity? **Explain** your answer.

   _____
   _____

2. **Fill in** the blanks in this character assessment of General Arnold found on page 141.

   "His _____ _____ was soon restored; but the _____ of his mind was _____: and he who had endured _____ with _____, and had been a hero in battle, was overcome by the _____ of ease, and became a _____ in the resistance of _____ to the practice of _____."

3. **Look up** Matthew 7:13–14 in the Bible translation of your choice and **share** why you think it is easier for human beings to follow the "broad way that leadeth to destruction" (p. 141).

   _____
   _____

Name _____ Lesson 10 - Exercise 4   Day 49

Rewrite the following statement about Benedict Arnold's response to Washington's reproof in your own words.

> "He received reproof from stern virtue with feelings of bitter resentment. Vice had so hardened his heart, that the consciousness of deserving punishment had not the effect of softening it to repentance; and to plan for revenge against the officers who had sentenced him, and the upright and noble man who had reproved him, became the employment of his thoughts" (p. 142).

_____
_____
_____
_____
_____
_____

4. Benedict Arnold's heart was being drawn into sin, and it was going to cost him. **Look up** James 1:14–15 and **describe** what it teaches about how sin starts.

_____
_____

5. General Arnold uses a helper in his plot of treason named Major André. **Explain** why the foundation of André's principles was the wrong one. (p. 144)

_____
_____

6. It was said that Major André's heart "could no longer willingly practise [practice] deception," and he confessed his crimes (p. 151). **Finish** this sentence regarding the reaction to the coming punishment of André.

   "Universal sorrow was _____
   _____."

7. The treasonous plot of Arnold* was uncovered and thus it failed; ironically, it worked to the benefit of the Americans. Reed expresses her worldview regarding the "workings of Divine power" in these circumstances. **Fill in** the blanks from her statement on page 152.

   "We are so ready to forget how _____ and _____ the power of God is, that we think and speak of events, which we consider _____, as if they were not _____ by him; but to say that any event happens '_____ _____,' or '_____ _____,' has no meaning, unless chance and accident are used as names for the _____ workings of _____ power, which overrules the _____ occurrence as certainly as the _____ event."

*To this day, someone considered a traitor is often referred to as a "Benedict Arnold."

Name _____   Lesson 10 - Exercise 5   Day 50

Review

☐ **Update** the Reading List chart with books you have read this week.

☐ **Recite** Matthew 7:13–14 from memory to your instructor.

Vocabulary Review

Match each word to the correct definition.

a. delusive	d. feeble	g. ingenuous	j. rectitude	m. traitor
b. depraved	e. feigned	h. insolence	k. sloop of war	n. treason
c. dissipation	f. indignation	i. perilous	l. timid	o. vice

1. _____ warship with one gun deck
2. _____ crime of betraying one's country
3. _____ lacking strength; weakness
4. _____ immoral or wicked behavior
5. _____ full of danger or risk
6. _____ insincere; pretended
7. _____ squandering energy, resources
8. _____ giving misleading or false impression
9. _____ wicked; morally corrupt
10. _____ easily frightened; lacking courage
11. _____ innocent and unsuspecting
12. _____ rude or disrespectful actions
13. _____ betrays country or friend
14. _____ moral behavior; righteousness
15. _____ anger provoked by perceived unfairness

Grammar & Punctuation Review

Place quotation marks, commas, periods, question marks, and exclamation points where needed.

1. Jared looked at me and exclaimed I could not be happier to call you my brother
2. With all we have going on this week said Erica I don't see us having time to finish our project
3. Do you remember the song With My Eyes Looking Up that we used to sing at church
4. The word cool has so many different meanings
5. Were you surprised when the announcer said The concert is canceled

Review

Lesson 10, Day 50   117

Name _____   Lesson 10 - Exercise 5   Day 50

Communication Review

1. **List** the three ways to incorporate a quote from research in MLA style.

   a. _____

   _____

   b. _____

   _____

   c. _____

   _____

2. **Explain** what it means to paraphrase researched information.

   _____

   _____

3. **Explain** what it means to summarize researched information.

   _____

   _____

4. **Fill in** the blanks.

   The first time you refer to a source, use the author's _____ _____. If you mention the source again, use only the author's _____ _____.

Worldview & Literary Analysis Review

1. **Define** foreshadowing.

   _____

   _____

2. **Write** a paragraph explaining how a person's heart can be deceived and drawn into sin, as Benedict Arnold's was.

   _____

   _____

   _____

   _____

   _____

   _____

   _____

   _____

Special Feature

Lesson 11

Picture Study: Arnold Viewing the Destruction of New London

Examine the picture and the expression on Benedict Arnold's face. **Imagine** what might be going on in his thoughts. **Study** the words of Anna C. Reed in her description of what happened in the heart of Benedict Arnold (p. 141–143). **Rewrite** this passage in your own words.

_____
_____
_____
_____
_____
_____
_____
_____
_____
_____

Name _____ Lesson 11 - Exercise 1 Day 51

Today you will **begin reading** pages 154–173a (ending at "fought and bled") in *Life of Washington*. Have this section read by Exercise 4 of this lesson. Before reading, **study** the vocabulary words listed below.

Vocabulary

abate	to cause to become smaller or less intense	musket	light gun with a long barrel
approbation	approval or praise	mutineer	soldier or sailor rebelling against authority
discharge	to fire a weapon, such as a gun	powder horn	horn of an ox or cow used to hold gunpowder
disperse	spread over a large area	scorn	contempt
drolly	in a curious or unusual way	standard	military or ceremonial flag carried on a pole
fortitude	courage in pain or difficulty	stinted	supplied in an inadequate way
homespun	made or created on a spinning wheel at home	trifling	trivial or unimportant
ignorant	lacking knowledge or awareness	vanquished	defeated thoroughly
mountaineers	people living in mountainous areas		

1. **Write** a sentence using the words *musket* and *discharge*. Include a proper noun.
   _____
   _____

2. **Write** a sentence using the words *mountaineers* and *powder horn*. Include three adjectives. (Day 2)
   _____
   _____

3. **Write** a sentence using the words *mutineer* and *scorn*. Include an adverb. (Day 2)
   _____
   _____

☐ **Use** index cards to **write** each vocabulary word from this lesson on one side and the definition on the other. **Check** the box when complete.

☐ **Copy** the Scripture verse on an index card. **Memorize** it by the end of this lesson. You may choose the Bible translation or use the one given. **Check** the box when complete.

Count it all joy, my brothers, when you meet trials of various kinds, for you know that the testing of your faith produces steadfastness. James 1:2–3

Name _____ Lesson 11 - Exercise 2 Day 52

Grammar & Punctuation

Simple, Compound, and Complex Sentences

Review dependent clauses, independent clauses, and conjunctions taught on Day 27.

A **simple sentence** contains one independent clause. It has no dependent clause and expresses only one idea. It isn't the length of the sentence that makes it simple, but the content.

> A **simple sentence** contains one independent clause.
> A **compound sentence** contains two independent clauses connected by a coordinating conjunction and a comma.
> A **complex sentence** has one independent clause and one dependent clause.
> An **interjection** is a word or phrase used to express a feeling, make a request, or give a command.

INDEPENDENT CLAUSE
Example: Our entire family worked hard raking leaves all afternoon.

A **compound sentence** contains two independent clauses connected by a coordinating conjunction and a comma.

INDEPENDENT CLAUSE — **INDEPENDENT CLAUSE**
Example: Our entire family worked hard raking leaves all afternoon, so we ordered a pizza for dinner.

A **complex sentence** has one independent clause and one dependent clause. The dependent clause may function as an adjective, adverb, or noun clause.

DEPENDENT CLAUSE — **INDEPENDENT CLAUSE**
Example: After sleeping in until 10 o'clock, our entire family worked hard raking leaves all afternoon.

Label the sentences as simple, compound, or complex.

1. _____ Natalie and Carrie rode their new bikes to the grocery store yesterday.
2. _____ Although I really enjoy playing the piano, I just can't find the time to practice adequately.
3. _____ George Washington loved his country, and he proved it through his words and actions.

Write a complex sentence that contains a prepositional phrase. (Day 37)

_____

_____

Write a compound sentence in the active voice. (Day 42)

_____

_____

Name _____   Lesson 11 - Exercise 2   Day 52

Write a simple sentence that includes a helping verb. (Day 17)

_____
_____

Interjections

An **interjection** is a word or phrase used to express a feeling, make a request, or give a command. It is typically a short, abrupt remark and is often followed by an exclamation point. Sometimes a comma or period is used. **Study** the examples.

> *Examples: Dear me!* I nearly missed getting off the right exit!
> *Well,* I should have known we would have been late.
> I left my favorite pen at church. *Oh well.*
> You can come to my party. *Sweet!*

Interjections are used most often in conversation, whether written or spoken. They can be used in informal writing like texts to friends, diary entries, or conversations in works of fiction. Formal writing, such as school essays or academic resources, requires factual and impartial language, so most interjections would be too "relaxed" to use in these settings.

An interjection can appear anywhere in a sentence and requires some sort of punctuation to set it off. If an interjection appears in the middle of a sentence, use commas to enclose it.

> *Examples: Indeed!* I could not agree more. (beginning)
> I feel, *wow,* like I don't know which one to pick! (middle)
> So you forgot to bring your sleeping bag, *huh?* (end)

How you punctuate an interjection has a major effect on its meaning. Be careful to choose the punctuation necessary to properly communicate your meaning. **Study** the examples.

> *Examples:* You finished writing your biography. *Really?*
> *Really,* I did finish writing my biography.
> *Really!* I finished writing my biography today!

Write a sentence using an interjection with an exclamation point.

_____
_____

Write a sentence using an interjection in the middle of the sentence (enclose it with commas).

_____
_____

Write a sentence using an interjection with a question mark.

_____
_____

Name _____ Lesson 11 - Exercise 3 Day 53

Communication

Biography Notes

In the last Communication lesson, you were taught ways to incorporate researched material into your biography. It is important to know *how* to introduce that material in your writing. Some of the examples given were "LaHaye *states* ..." or "LaHaye *points out* ..." A **signal verb** is a verb used to indicate how someone is expressing their ideas. Become familiar with the signal verbs in the chart below. It is good to have a variety of them in mind to avoid using the same introduction to quotes, paraphrases, and summaries.

> A **signal verb** is a verb used to indicate how someone is expressing their ideas.

Signal Verbs	
To introduce a fact/statement	*states, writes, mentions, adds, points out, notes, comments, finds, observes, discusses, expresses, considers, explores, illustrates*
To introduce a claim	*claims, argues, posits, reasons, asserts, proposes*
To introduce what the author focuses on or excludes	*emphasizes, stresses, highlights, focuses on, centers their argument around, overlooks, ignores, downplays, omits, excludes*

Search some of your biography research sources and practice introducing a quote, paraphrase, or summary using some of the signal verbs from the chart. **Write** three examples using three different signal verbs. A variety of lines are provided for shorter or longer references. You will want to use these examples in your biography, so be sure to save them for later.

_____
_____
_____
_____
_____
_____
_____
_____
_____
_____
_____
_____
_____
_____

Communication

Name_____   Lesson 11 - Exercise 3   Day 53

Wisdom Speaks

Copy the proverb.

> *A fool takes no pleasure in understanding, but only in expressing his opinion.* Proverbs 18:2

_____

_____

Using a dictionary or an online search with a parent's permission, **write** the definitions of the words below.

1. fool: _____

   _____

2. opinion: _____

   _____

Write a sentence expressing Proverbs 18:2 in your own words.

_____

_____

Fools worship their own opinions and perhaps don't believe anyone else can contribute to their understanding. They don't believe they need anyone's insight but their own and are focused on self instead of God. How can you avoid being foolish in this way? How can you be a person who takes pleasure in understanding? **Write** your answer in a paragraph.

_____
_____
_____
_____
_____
_____
_____
_____
_____

Name_____   Lesson 11 - Exercise 4   Day 54

Worldview & Literary Analysis

George Washington, his generals, and his troops were not the only Americans sacrificing a great deal in the fight for freedom. Men, women, and children all throughout the colonies met with various trials that proved their commitment to the cause.

We will examine some of these stories, and I hope you are able to appreciate the sacrifices made by these courageous individuals whose pain and suffering led to the peace and freedom you live in today.

Finish reading pages 154–173a (ending at "fought and bled") in *Life of Washington* and **respond** to the following.

1. General Cornwallis considered South Carolina a conquered state, and any efforts to resist him by the citizens he called "acts of rebellion" (p. 155). **What** orders did he give regarding these "rebels"?
   _____
   _____

   Describe how you would feel if your family lived in South Carolina at this time.
   _____
   _____
   _____
   _____

2. **Describe** what Officer Marion and his brave men would do to assist their countrymen. (p. 157)
   _____
   _____

3. On pages 157–159, an anecdote about Marion and his men is shared in which they invite an English officer to eat with them. **What** food did they prepare and how did they eat it?
   _____
   _____

4. The English officer was astounded by the way the American troops lived. On page 158, Marion gives a response beginning with, "I would rather …" **Write** his full response.
   _____
   _____
   _____

5. The English officer returned to his commander looking so defeated the commander was alarmed. **Fill in** the blanks in the officer's response to the commander. (p. 159)

   "I have seen an American general and his men without _____, and almost _____ _____, living upon _____, and drinking water, and all for _____.

   What _____ have we against such men?"

Worldview & Literary Analysis   Lesson 11, Day 54   125

Name_____   Lesson 11 - Exercise 4   Day 54

6. In contrast to the deep commitment seen in the Americans' hearts, some of the English lacked courage, bravery, and even commitment to their own. **What** did English General Tarlton do regarding his own men? (p. 160)

   _____
   _____

7. **Why** was desertion by his troops not feared by General Sumpter? (p. 160)

   _____
   _____

8. On page 163, we find "a young lad, who was too small to hold a sword." **What** did this young boy do in aid of General Washington?

   _____
   _____

9. On page 168, we meet the very determined Mrs. Heyward. The English are trying to make her illuminate her house, and she defies their orders at the risk of losing everything. **Fill in** the blanks of her final statement to the officer.

   "You have the _____ … and seem _____ to use it, but you _____

   _____ my _____, and I will _____ illuminate" (p. 169).

10. **Why** was the name Tarlton heard with dread by the Americans? (p. 169)

    _____
    _____

11. **Summarize** the story of the young man who deserted the American cause under English pressure but then "repented" and wanted to return, including the acts done by his sister. (p. 170)

    _____
    _____
    _____
    _____
    _____
    _____
    _____
    _____
    _____
    _____
    _____

Name _____   Lesson 11 - Exercise 5   Day 55

Review

☐ **Update** the Reading List chart with books you have read this week.

☐ **Recite** James 1:2–3 from memory to your instructor.

Vocabulary Review

Match each word to the correct definition.

a. abate	e. drolly	i. mountaineers	m. scorn	q. vanquished
b. approbation	f. fortitude	j. musket	n. standard	
c. discharge	g. homespun	k. mutineer	o. stinted	
d. disperse	h. ignorant	l. powder horn	p. trifling	

1. _____ approval or praise
2. _____ trivial or unimportant
3. _____ contempt
4. _____ light gun with a long barrel
5. _____ made or spun at home
6. _____ courage in pain or difficulty
7. _____ to fire a weapon, such as a gun
8. _____ soldier or sailor rebelling
9. _____ horn of an ox or cow used to hold gunpowder
10. _____ in a curious or unusual way
11. _____ supplied in an inadequate way
12. _____ military or ceremonial flag on a pole
13. _____ cause to become smaller, less intense
14. _____ lacking knowledge or awareness
15. _____ people living in mountains
16. _____ defeated thoroughly
17. _____ spread over a large area

Grammar & Punctuation Review

1. **Define** a compound sentence. **Write** a compound sentence.

   _____
   _____
   _____
   _____

2. **Define** a complex sentence. **Write** a complex sentence.

   _____
   _____
   _____
   _____

Review   Lesson 11, Day 55   127

Name _____ Lesson 11 - Exercise 5 Day 55

3. **Write** a sentence containing an interjection.

   _____
   _____

Communication Review

1. **Define** a signal verb.

   _____
   _____

2. **List** any six of the signal verbs meant to introduce a fact or statement.

   a. _____   d. _____
   b. _____   e. _____
   c. _____   f. _____

Worldview & Literary Analysis Review

1. **Fill in** the blanks.

   a. General Cornwallis called any efforts to resist him "_____ _____ _____."

   b. Officer Marion said, "I would rather _____ to obtain the blessing of _____ for my country, and feed on _____, than desert the _____, and gain by doing so, all the _____ that _____ owned."

3. In this lesson's reading, we saw a young lad come to the aid of General Washington and a determined woman who refused to illuminate her house for the English. **Choose** one of these characters and **write** a paragraph about what they did and what you admire about them.

   _____
   _____
   _____
   _____
   _____
   _____
   _____
   _____
   _____
   _____
   _____
   _____
   _____
   _____

Special Feature

Hymn Study: "The Liberty Song" by John Dickinson (1768)

Summarize the main points of each verse and the chorus of Dickinson's hymn in your own words.

Come join hand in hand brave Americans all,
And rouse your bold hearts at fair Liberty's call;
No tyrannous acts shall suppress your just claim,
Or stain with dishonour [dishonor] America's name.

> *Chorus:*
> In Freedom we're born and in Freedom we'll live,
> Our purses are ready,
> Steady, Friends, Steady.
> Not as slaves, but as Freemen our money we'll give.

Our worthy Forefathers - Let's give them a cheer
To climates unknown did courageously steer;
Thro' Oceans, to deserts, for freedom they came,
And dying bequeath'd us their freedom and Fame.

Their generous bosoms all dangers despis'd,
So highly, so wisely, their Birthrights they priz'd;
We'll keep what they gave, we will piously keep,
Nor frustrate their toils on the land and the deep.

The Tree their own hands had to Liberty rear'd;
They liv'd to behold growing strong and rever'd;
With transport they cry'd, "Now our wishes we gain
For our children shall gather the fruits of our pain."

Swarms of placemen and pensioners soon will appear
Like locusts deforming the charms of the year;
Suns vainly will rise, Showers vainly descend,
If we are to drudge for what others shall spend.

Then join hand in hand brave Americans all,
By uniting we stand, by dividing we fall;
In so Righteous a cause let us hope to succeed,
For Heaven approves of each generous deed.

All ages shall speak with amaze and applause,
Of the courage we'll show in support of our laws;
To die we can bear - but to serve we disdain,
For shame is to freedom more dreadful than pain.

This bumper I crown for our Sovereign's health
And this for Britannia's glory and wealth;
That wealth and that glory immortal may be,
If she is but just - and if we are but Free.

Name _____   Lesson 12 – Exercise 1   Day 56

Today you will **begin reading** pages 173b–187a (ending at "great rapidity") in *Life of Washington*. Have this section read by Exercise 4 of this lesson. Before reading, **study** the vocabulary words listed below.

Vocabulary

artillery	large guns used in land warfare	**eminence**	fame; recognized superiority in a certain field
batteries	a fortified place for heavy guns	**fortifications**	defensive walls or reinforcements against attack
candid	straightforward, truthful	**hasty**	hurried; acting with excessive speed
confederation	organization of groups united in alliance or league	**impropriety**	improper act or remark
conflagration	a large fire causing great destruction	**industrious**	being diligent, hardworking
defrayed	provided money to pay an expense	**piety**	the quality of being reverent; religious
desertions	the actions of forsaking a person or cause	**procure**	to obtain with effort
effectual	successful at producing a desired or intended result	**rapidity**	movement or reaction with speed

Write a paragraph using as many vocabulary words as you can. **Circle** each vocabulary word once you finish.

_____
_____
_____
_____
_____
_____
_____
_____

☐ **Use** index cards to **write** each vocabulary word from this lesson on one side and the definition on the other. **Check** the box when complete.

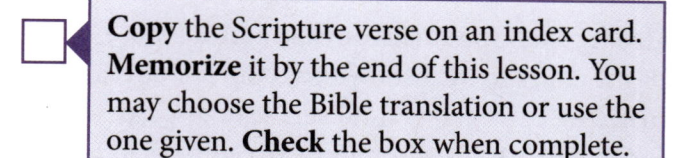

☐ **Copy** the Scripture verse on an index card. **Memorize** it by the end of this lesson. You may choose the Bible translation or use the one given. **Check** the box when complete.

*Have I not commanded you? Be strong and courageous. Do not be frightened, and do not be dismayed, for the L*ORD *your God is with you wherever you go.* Joshua 1:9

Name _____ Lesson 12 - Exercise 2 Day 57

Grammar & Punctuation

Adjectives

An **adjective** describes or modifies a noun and answers questions like *which one*, *what kind*, or *how many*. **Articles**, the words *a*, *an*, and *the*, are considered adjectives as well. Adjectives usually precede the noun or pronoun they modify.

> An **adjective** describes or modifies a noun and answers questions like *which one*, *what kind*, or *how many*.
> An **adverb** describes a verb, adjective, or other adverb and answers questions like *how much*, *how often*, *when*, *why*, *where*, or *to what extent*.

> *Example:* Racing through *the muddy* field on *my new white* bike was probably *a bad* idea.

Underline the adjectives, including articles, in the following sentences.

1. An ice-cold blueberry smoothie on a hot summer afternoon quenches my thirst like nothing else.
2. The smell of sizzling bacon wafted through the entire campground early in the chilly morning.
3. My favorite school subjects are American history, British literature, and creative writing.

Adverbs

An **adverb** describes a verb, adjective, or other adverb and answers questions like *how much*, *how often*, *when*, *why*, *where*, or *to what extent*. An adverb can come before or after the word it modifies and be anywhere in the sentence.

> *Example:* My father *always* gives too many hints about our Christmas gifts!
>
> The adverb *always* tells how often my father gives too many hints. In this sentence, the adverb is modifying the verb *gives*.

Many adverbs end in *-ly*, such as *quickly*, *sweetly*, *quietly*, *humbly*, etc. Adverbs can tell where (*above*, *below*, *inside*). They can tell when (*earlier*, *lately*, *soon*, *today*). The word *not* is also an adverb. To see a larger list of adverbs, look at the chart on Day 72.

Underline the adverbs. There may be more than one per sentence.

4. Yesterday, my pet iguana escaped from its cage and got lost in my bedroom!
5. I crept through the garage quietly, trying not to scare the sleeping dog.
6. I only forget to do my laundry occasionally.
7. After we get the pool cleaned out, we will be able to properly winterize it.

You will learn more details about adjectives and adverbs in Lessons 14 and 15.

Name _____ Lesson 12 - Exercise 2 Day 57

Types of Dependent Clauses: Adjective, Adverb, and Noun

> An **adjective clause** is a dependent clause that acts as an adjective by modifying a noun or pronoun in another clause.
>
> An **adverb clause** is a dependent clause that functions as an adverb by modifying the verb, adjective, or adverb in the sentence.
>
> A **noun clause** is a dependent clause that functions as a noun.

Sometimes a dependent clause can function as an adjective, adverb, or noun.

An **adjective clause** is a dependent clause that acts as an adjective by modifying a noun or pronoun in another clause. Typically, an adjective is one word, but an adjective clause is a dependent clause that functions as an adjective in the sentence.

Examples: The Revolutionary War soldier, who was honored by his countrymen, gave glory to God. I love traveling out West, where the climate is warm and dry.

The underlined portions describe *The Revolutionary War soldier* and *West*. They describe the main noun in the sentence, so they function as adjectives.

An **adverb clause** is a dependent clause that functions as an adverb by modifying the verb, adjective, or adverb in the sentence. Remember, adverbs describe or modify verbs, adjectives, or other adverbs and answer questions like *how, when, why, where, to what extent,* or *under what conditions*. Adverb clauses are introduced by subordinating conjunctions. Refer to Day 27 or your index cards for the list of subordinating conjunctions.

Examples: Since I have no energy left today, I would rather sit and watch a movie than do yard work. After years of juggling practice, my brother finally won a competition.

The underlined portions begin with subordinating conjunctions and function as adverbs. The clause in the first example describes *why* I would rather sit and watch. The clause in the second example describes *when* my brother won.

A **noun clause** is a dependent clause that functions as a noun. Remember, nouns name a person, place, or thing. Most noun clauses begin with the subordinating conjunction *that*. Other noun clauses can begin with the word *whether*.

Examples: That houses sell better in the summer is an agreed-upon fact in the real estate business. The Smiths wondered whether their house would sell at all.

The underlined portions function as nouns in these sentences. If the clause can answer the question "What?" it is likely a noun clause. In the example, you can ask the question, "The Smiths wondered what?"

Underline the dependent clause in each sentence and **write** on the line **ADJ** for adjective clause, **ADV** for adverb clause, or **N** for noun clause.

8. _____ The football player, whose contract expired in March, contacted his agent for advice.

9. _____ While not everybody loves to cook, most people can at least make themselves a sandwich.

10. _____ Alex knew that racing against Jake would not be an easy win.

11. _____ Once he saw the ball headed his way, he instantly jumped to his feet and ran toward it.

12. _____ Whether I should go on the missions trip to Europe has become a big question in my house.

Name _____ Lesson 12 - Exercise 3 Day 58

Communication

Biography Notes

Today you will write an introductory paragraph for your biography. The introduction needs to captivate the reader's attention, and there are several ways to do this. Below are some ideas.

> A **thesis statement** expresses the main idea you are trying to get across about your subject.

- Begin with a quote either by or about your subject (something that reveals the essence of who they are or what others appreciate about them).
- Describe their greatest accomplishment.
- Relate a fascinating anecdote about them.
- Give interesting information about the subject without revealing their name yet.

The introductory paragraph could include the person's full name and the time in which they lived. This information could also be held until the second paragraph, depending on your choice to use any of the introduction styles listed above. The first paragraph will conclude with a thesis statement. Remember, a **thesis statement** expresses the main idea you are trying to get across about your subject. It will signify to the reader the direction your writing is taking. **Study** the introductory paragraph example.

"My first wish is to see the whole world in peace, and the inhabitants of it as a band of brothers, striving who should contribute most to the happiness of mankind." These words of George Washington encapsulate his lifelong effort to establish and maintain peace in his own country and across the world. Little did anyone know that a boy born in Bridges Creek, Virginia, on the 22nd of February in 1732, would play a major role in a nation's fight for freedom, setting that nation up as a world power for centuries to come. Anna C. Reed expressed, "His history is as a shining light upon the path of virtue; for he 'acknowledged God in all his ways' " (19). George Washington spoke words of peace from his heart before God and mankind and validated them with his actions both in public and in private.

This sample paragraph opened with a quote, chosen because it supports the thesis statement located at the *end* of the paragraph. If you open with a quote, be sure it is closely related to the main idea you will present in your thesis statement. You do not need to begin with a quote. This is just one of many possibilities.

Works Cited

Reed, Anna C. *Life of Washington*. Attic Books, 2013.

The thesis statement about Washington in the example sets up the expectation that the paper will center around Washington's desire for peace and how his actions confirmed his intentions. The stories, facts, and quotes presented in the rest of the biography should support this thesis statement. You will begin by writing your thesis statement, which will help guide you in introducing your subject. Remember, for the purposes of this assignment, the thesis statement will be the *last* sentence in your opening paragraph.

Name _____ Lesson 12 - Exercise 3 Day 58

Write your thesis statement.
_____
_____

Write your opening sentence.
_____
_____

Now it is time to put it all together! **Rewrite** your opening sentence, add three to five supporting sentences, and conclude with your thesis statement.

Write your introductory paragraph.
_____
_____
_____
_____
_____
_____
_____
_____
_____
_____
_____

Did you notice the sample in-text citation in the paragraph about Washington? The page number (19) is located after the quote by Reed, and a works cited reference is included in the example. If you used researched material in your paragraph, **practice writing** a works cited entry here. (Days 13 and 38)
_____
_____
_____
_____

Have your instructor read your opening paragraph, checking it over using the rubric in the back of the book, and sign below.

Instructor signature: _____

> **Remember!** Your biography needs to be 4–5 pages typed and double spaced, or 6–7 pages handwritten, skipping every other line.

Name _____   Lesson 12 - Exercise 4   Day 59

Worldview & Literary Analysis

Literary Device: Anecdote

An **anecdote** is like a short story within a story that usually focuses on a single character. Most anecdotes are simple stories that can be true or fictional and are used by the author to underscore a certain aspect or trait of the character that they wish to emphasize. In *Life of Washington*, Reed uses several anecdotes to reveal Washington's character in specific situations. Keep an eye out for these anecdotes and how they are used.

> An **anecdote** is like a short story within a story that usually focuses on a single character.

As you write your biography, think of places you can insert anecdotes that highlight the qualities of your subject. Choose stories that are interesting and concise and match the main ideas you are trying to portray.

Finish reading pages 173b–187a (ending at "great rapidity") in *Life of Washington* and **respond** to the following.

1. **Why** were efforts made in each state to contribute to the relief of the troops? (p. 173)
   _____
   _____

   Do you feel it is important to appeal to others' emotions on behalf of those in need? **Explain**.
   _____
   _____
   _____
   _____

2. Cornwallis insulted Lafayette by referring to him as "the boy" (p. 175). **Why** was the enemy (Cornwallis) convinced he could not overtake Lafayette?
   _____
   _____

3. On page 177, Reed shares an anecdote about the caretaker of Washington's property, who bends under threats from the English to burn down Washington's house. After reading Washington's response to this incident, **share** what you believe the author wants us to know about Washington's character based on this anecdote.
   _____
   _____
   _____

4. When others became sad and fearful, **how** did Washington stay courageous? (p. 178)
   _____
   _____

Name _____   Lesson 12 - Exercise 4   Day 59

Copy this quote from pages 179–180.

> "Every one, who with piety notices the providences of God, can know that our best blessings are often hid beneath our disappointments, as sweet flowers are concealed in bitter buds."

_____
_____
_____

Have you ever had a blessing come out of a situation that seemed disappointing at first? **Explain**.

_____
_____
_____
_____
_____
_____

5. On page 180, we see Washington responding to a disappointment that caused his natural tendency toward anger to erupt. Mr. Peters observed how Washington dealt with his anger. **Summarize** what Mr. Peters observed.

_____
_____
_____
_____

6. Mrs. Motte was a dedicated and selfless woman whose home had to be sacrificed for the cause of freedom. She made a statement about the sacrifice of her property that is found on page 183. **Record** her response.

_____
_____

Do you believe most Americans could make this type of sacrifice today? **Explain** your answer.

_____
_____
_____
_____
_____
_____
_____

Name _____   Lesson 12 - Exercise 5   Day 60

Review

☐ **Update** the Reading List chart with books you have read this week.

☐ **Recite** Joshua 1:9 from memory to your instructor.

Vocabulary Review

Match each word to the correct definition.

a. artillery	e. conflagration	i. eminence	m. industrious
b. batteries	f. defrayed	j. fortifications	n. piety
c. candid	g. desertions	k. hasty	o. procure
d. confederation	h. effectual	l. impropriety	p. rapidity

1. _____ large fire causing great destruction
2. _____ movement or reaction with speed
3. _____ a fortified place for heavy guns
4. _____ to obtain with effort
5. _____ fame; recognized superiority in field
6. _____ provided money to pay an expense
7. _____ large guns used in land warfare
8. _____ defensive walls; reinforcements against attack
9. _____ straightforward, truthful
10. _____ improper act or remark
11. _____ quality of being reverent
12. _____ hurried; excessive speed
13. _____ successful at producing a desired result
14. _____ actions of forsaking a person or cause
15. _____ diligent, hardworking
16. _____ organization of groups united in alliance

Grammar & Punctuation Review

1. **List** the questions adjectives answer.

   a. _____   c. _____

   b. _____

2. **List** the questions adverbs answer.

   a. _____   d. _____

   b. _____   e. _____

   c. _____   f. _____

Underline the adjectives and adverbs.

3. Suspiciously, the large red fox slithered into the chicken coop for a surprise attack.
4. We must patiently wait until tomorrow to eat those delicious cookies!

Review

Name _____ Lesson 12 - Exercise 5 Day 60

Write adjective, adverb, or noun to indicate the function of the underlined clause.

5. _____ Whenever <u>that dog with the brown spots</u> sees a car, he barks like crazy!

6. _____ The last day <u>that the sun was this bright</u>, I got sunburned so badly.

7. _____ <u>Although I truly love construction work</u>, I feel led to enter ministry full time.

8. _____ I realized that, <u>while not everyone knows what career they want</u>, most people know what they love to do.

Communication Review

1. **List** four ways an introduction can captivate a reader regarding a biography subject.

   a. _____
   b. _____
   c. _____
   d. _____

2. **Describe** a thesis statement.
   _____
   _____

Worldview & Literary Analysis Review

1. **Define** an anecdote.
   _____
   _____

2. **Fill in** the blanks.

   Most _____ are simple stories that can be _____ or _____ and are used by the author to _____ a certain aspect or _____ of the character that they wish to _____.

3. **Choose** an anecdote from *Life of Washington* and **summarize** it in one paragraph.
   _____
   _____
   _____
   _____
   _____
   _____
   _____
   _____

138 Lesson 12, Day 60 Language Lessons for a Living Education Level 10

Special Feature

Lesson 13

Scripture Study: Psalm 139:13–18

¹³ For you formed my inward parts;
   you knitted me together in my mother's womb.
¹⁴ I praise you, for I am fearfully and wonderfully made.
Wonderful are your works;
   my soul knows it very well.

¹⁵ My frame was not hidden from you,
when I was being made in secret,
   intricately woven in the depths of the earth.
¹⁶ Your eyes saw my unformed substance;
in your book were written, every one of them,
   the days that were formed for me,
   when as yet there was none of them.

¹⁷ How precious to me are your thoughts, O God!
   How vast is the sum of them!
¹⁸ If I would count them, they are more than the sand.
   I awake, and I am still with you.

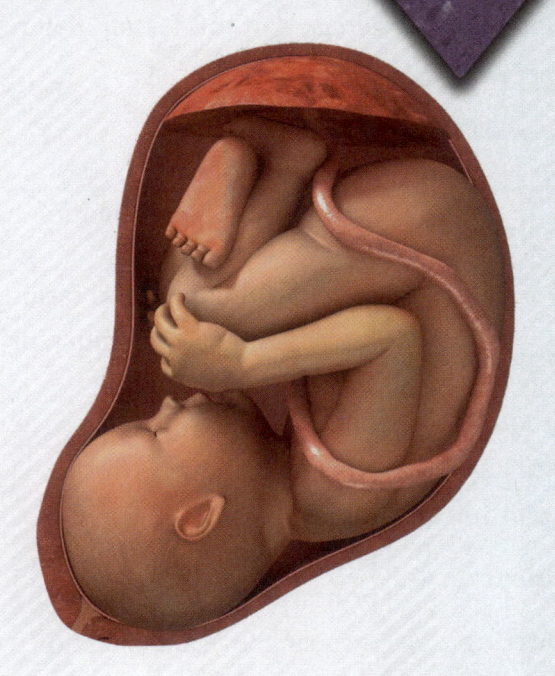

The psalmist, King David, is intimately aware of God's direct involvement with every aspect of the human body and soul. He knows that the God of all creation personally formed him in his mother's womb, intricately weaving him together in the darkness. David describes God's thoughts toward him as "precious" and "vast," declaring them uncountable.

Think deeply about how God formed you in your mother's womb. He chose everything about your physical makeup and personality. He has seen every one of your days before they even came to be. **Write** a paragraph describing how this makes you feel and express your awe and appreciation of what God has done in creating you. Be unafraid! Express your heart.

Special Feature   Lesson 13, Day 61

Name _____   Lesson 13 - Exercise 1   Day 61

Today you will **begin reading** pages 187b–203a (ending at "assembled") in *Life of Washington*. Have this section read by Exercise 4 of this lesson. Before reading, **study** the vocabulary words listed below.

Vocabulary

adjourned	took a break with intention to resume later	**imbitter** (embitter)	cause to feel bitterness or resentment
bosom	center of thoughts and feelings	**ingratitude**	lack of gratitude
compensation	repayment for loss, injury, or suffering	**interposition**	intervention or interference
delinquency	neglect of duty	**pacific**	peaceful in character
deportment	a person's manners or behavior	**posterity**	future generations of people
detestation	intense dislike	**renown**	fame; being known by many
eminent	famous or respected within a profession	**sentinels**	soldiers or guards who keep watch
endearing	inspiring love and affection	**solemn**	formal, dignified, serious
felicity	happiness	**subsistence**	minimum level necessary for support
harbinger	person or thing announcing the approach of another		

1. **Write** a sentence using the words *ingratitude* and *eminent*. Include a prepositional phrase. (Day 37)

_____

_____

2. **Write** a sentence using the words *solemn* and *posterity*. Include a helping verb. (Day 17)

_____

_____

☐ **Use** index cards to **write** each vocabulary word from this lesson on one side and the definition on the other. **Check** the box when complete.

☐ **Copy** the Scripture verse on an index card. **Memorize** it by the end of this lesson. You may choose the Bible translation or use the one given. **Check** the box when complete.

Little children, let us not love in word or talk but in deed and in truth. 1 John 3:18

Name _____   Lesson 13 - Exercise 2   Day 62

Grammar & Punctuation

Punctuating Clauses

There are some rules to remember when determining when and where commas are used to separate clauses. **Study** the chart.

Commas and Clauses
Nonessential clauses are set off with commas. One way to determine if a comma is necessary is to ask whether the clause is essential or nonessential to the meaning of the sentence.
I left my sweater, <u>which was a gift from my aunt</u>, in the shopping cart at the grocery store.
The phrase *which was a gift from my aunt* is not essential to the meaning of the sentence. It is an adjective clause that tells us more about *my sweater*.
Use commas to separate two independent clauses connected by a conjunction. These clauses can both stand alone as a sentence and are connected by a conjunction, so a comma is placed after the first clause.
<u>The army set up camp in the dark</u>, yet <u>they did it with perfection</u>.
Three or more short independent clauses need a comma separating them.
<u>The flowers bloomed</u>, <u>the grass grew</u>, and <u>the trees budded</u>.
A comma is needed after a long (five words or more) introductory prepositional phrase.
<u>With a great deal of joy in their hearts</u>, the children opened their presents.
A comma is needed after an introductory adverb clause.
<u>Before I am able to give my honest opinion</u>, I will need to review the entire document.
Use a comma after any introductory element that modifies the sentence.
<u>To put it simply</u>, I really need more time to practice before I am able to teach someone else.

Place commas where necessary.

1. Next Wednesday which happens to be the first day of the month is the day I plan to start my new workout routine.
2. The Constitution describes the executive legislative and judicial branches of our government.
3. The church picnic was over but no one felt like leaving.
4. Behind the parking lot at the school the teachers set up the field day events.
5. Yesterday was our first day of school so my mother took us out to the library and then out to lunch.
6. Well let's just hope for the best in every situation.
7. Usually I wake up early on Sunday mornings but today I overslept and was late for church!
8. Communicating well helps our relationship with family our interactions with friends and our prayer life with the Lord.
9. Mount Everest the world's tallest mountain can fit inside the Mariana Trench the deepest part of the ocean.

Name _____ Lesson 13 - Exercise 2 Day 62

10. **Write** a sentence using Rule 1 from the Commas and Clauses chart.
_____
_____

11. **Write** a sentence using Rule 3 from the Commas and Clauses chart.
_____
_____

12. **Write** a sentence using Rule 6 from the Commas and Clauses chart.
_____
_____

Review It!

Underline the adjectives (the articles *a*, *an*, and *the* are also considered adjectives). (Days 2 and 52)

13. The light rain was falling from the gray sky so gently that one could barely notice it.
14. The rough tree bark snagged my favorite green sweater as I walked by.
15. A beam of soft moonlight fell onto my bed through the tiny slit in my curtains.
16. The crisp autumn sky was ablaze with magnificent color, and a chill filled the frosty air.

Name _____   Lesson 13 - Exercise 3   Day 63

Communication

Biography Notes

Today you will set up a structure for your biography by writing an outline. An **outline** is an organizational plan for your writing. You may wonder why you are writing an outline *after* you have written your introductory paragraph. This is because, in some situations, it's helpful to first establish your thesis so you have a clear direction for your writing. Your outline should come together much easier now that you have an introduction to inspire the structure. A basic topical outline is sufficient for your biography. Use Roman numerals to introduce each paragraph and letters for supporting points. **Study** the outline example based on the sample paragraph from Day 58.

> An **outline** is an organizational plan for your writing.

Topic Outline: Uses Words or Phrases	
I. Quote by Washington	II. (Second paragraph topic)
a. Encapsulate lifelong effort	a. (supporting idea/fact)
b. Birthdate and place	b. (supporting idea/fact)
c. Major role in fight for freedom	c. (supporting idea/fact)
d. Quote by Reed from page 19	III. (Third paragraph topic)
e. Thesis statement	a. (supporting idea/fact) … and so on

Look over the notes you have gathered about your subject and **write** an outline for your biography. You can use a notebook to brainstorm first. You may also use the Biography Outline found in the back of this book.

Name _____ Lesson 13 - Exercise 3   Day 63

Wisdom Speaks

Copy the proverb.

> *A fool's lips walk into a fight, and his mouth invites a beating.*
> *A fool's mouth is his ruin, and his lips are a snare to his soul.*
> Proverbs 18:6–7

_____
_____
_____

Using a dictionary or an online search with a parent's permission, **write** the definitions of the words below.

1. ruin: _____
   _____

2. snare: _____
   _____

Write a sentence expressing Proverbs 18:6–7 in your own words.

_____
_____
_____

It is the nature of a fool to argue with others, and sometimes this can even lead to physical violence or correction. Sadly, foolish words hurt the fool the most. The fool walks in pride and is consumed with self-focus. However, the fool's very words become a trap for his soul and lead to destruction.

3. **Write** the portion of today's verse that would be considered personification. (Day 23)

   _____
   _____
   _____

4. **Write** the portion of today's verse that would be considered a metaphor. (Day 23)

   _____
   _____

Lesson 13, Day 63   Language Lessons for a Living Education Level 10

Name _____   Lesson 13 - Exercise 4   Day 64

Worldview & Literary Analysis

Literary Device: Analogy

An **analogy** is a literary device that connects two seemingly unrelated concepts to show their similarities in a way that expands on a thought or idea. Analogies take a comparison much further than metaphors and similes do. They are used to support a claim rather than just provide imagery. They provide a new or deeper meaning to the concepts presented by explaining or indicating a larger point.

> An **analogy** is a literary device that connects two seemingly unrelated concepts to show their similarities in a way that expands on a thought or idea.

In this lesson's reading, the author compares freedom to a seed sown in weakness and guarded with toil. She takes the concept of a seed, something small yet full of potential, and compares it to the idea of freedom surrounded by toil. This seed of freedom eventually grows into victory and produces independence and peace. Seeds must die before they can produce a harvest, and so must the Americans die to themselves — and some physically — before freedom can be harvested.

Finish reading pages 187b–203a (ending at "assembled") in *Life of Washington* and **respond** to the following.

1. In this lesson's reading, we finally come to the end of the Revolutionary War. The English are defeated by surrendering. **What** did Washington say to his troops as the defeated English army marched out of town? (p. 189)

   _____
   _____
   _____

2. Luke 6:27–28 states, "But I say to you who hear, Love your enemies, do good to those who hate you, bless those who curse you, pray for those who abuse you." According to this verse, **how** should we treat our enemies? **Explain**.

   _____
   _____

3. When Congress heard of the English surrender, they went to a church to thank God for their deliverance. They also issued a proclamation (p. 190). **Record** it here.

   _____
   _____

4. The author shares an anecdote that reveals the special relationship between Washington and his mother. **Describe** their relationship and their dedication to one another. (p. 191–192)

   _____
   _____
   _____
   _____

Name _____ Lesson 13 - Exercise 4 Day 64

5. With the war finally over, it was time for the troops to get paid by their government. This was not so easily done, and Washington had to plead on their behalf (p. 196–197). **Fill in** the blanks from part of Washington's letter to Congress regarding troop pay.

"[I]f … the _____ of the army are to be the only _____ by this revolution; if retiring from the field they are to grow old in _____, _____ and _____, and owe the miserable _____ of that life to _____, which has hitherto been spent in honour [honor], then shall I have learned what _____ is; then shall I have realized a tale which will _____ [embitter] every moment of my _____ _____."

Copy the analogy made by Reed regarding freedom. (p. 199)

> "The seeds of freedom which had been sown in weakness, and guarded with toil through eight years, produced a rich harvest in the blessings of *independence* and *peace*, which spread quickly over the United States …"

_____
_____
_____
_____

6. On page 202, Washington gives advice to a young man who promised to do something for him but did not follow through. **Record** Washington's advice to the young man.

_____
_____

The final farewell between Washington and his troops is a very sad one. **Summarize** this emotional scene in your own words. (p. 202–203)

_____
_____
_____
_____
_____
_____
_____
_____
_____

Name _____   Lesson 13 - Exercise 5   Day 65

Review

☐ **Update** the Reading List chart with books you have read this week.

☐ **Recite** 1 John 3:18 from memory to your instructor.

Vocabulary Review

Match each word to the correct definition.

a. adjourned	e. detestation	i. felicity	m. interposition	q. sentinels
b. bosom	f. deportment	j. harbinger	n. pacific	r. solemn
c. compensation	g. eminent	k. imbitter (embitter)	o. posterity	s. subsistence
d. delinquency	h. endearing	l. ingratitude	p. renown	

1. _____ neglect of duty
2. _____ peaceful in character
3. _____ happiness
4. _____ intense dislike
5. _____ future generations
6. _____ a person's manners or behavior
7. _____ center of thoughts and feelings
8. _____ soldiers or guards keeping watch
9. _____ fame; being known
10. _____ person or thing announcing the approach of another
11. _____ famous or respected within profession
12. _____ lack of gratitude
13. _____ cause to feel bitterness
14. _____ minimum necessary for support
15. _____ repayment for loss
16. _____ inspiring love and affection
17. _____ intervention or interference
18. _____ took a break with intention to resume
19. _____ formal, dignified, serious

Grammar & Punctuation Review

Place commas where necessary.

1. The house on the right the one my aunt used to live in was just sold to a young family from Texas.
2. In the Rocky Mountains the cliffs are steep the trees are huge and the rivers run clear.
3. Assuming the cloud cover remains it may be okay that you forgot your sunblock.
4. Over the past three days we have seen an abundance of much-needed rain in our community.
5. The Bible study group prayed together for they were of one mind concerning the lost.
6. **Write** a sentence with an introductory prepositional phrase of five or more words. Make sure to punctuate it correctly.

_____
_____

Review   Lesson 13, Day 65   147

Name _____   Lesson 13 - Exercise 5   Day 65

Communication Review

1. **Define** an outline.

   _____
   _____

2. **Fill in** the blanks regarding an outline.

   Use _____ _____ to introduce each _____ and _____ for supporting _____.

3. **Read** the verse.

   > *A fool's lips walk into a fight, and his mouth invites a beating. A fool's mouth is his ruin, and his lips are a snare to his soul.* Proverbs 18:6–7

   a. **Write** the portion of the verse considered to be personification.

   _____
   _____

   b. **Write** the portion of the verse considered to be a metaphor.

   _____
   _____

Worldview & Literary Analysis Review

1. **Define** an analogy.

   _____
   _____

2. **Fill in** the blanks regarding an analogy.

   Analogies take a _____ much further than _____ and similes do. They are used to support a claim rather than just provide imagery. They provide a new or deeper _____ to the concepts presented by explaining or indicating a _____ _____.

3. **List** the four ways Luke 6:27–28 instructs us to treat our enemies.

   a. _____
   b. _____
   c. _____
   d. _____

Special Feature

Lesson 14

Biography Excerpt: Richard Bassett (1745–1815) by Tim LaHaye

After working with Richard Bassett at the Constitutional Convention for several months, [William] Pierce described him as "a religious enthusiast, lately turned Methodist, who serves his country because it is the will of the people that he should do so. He is a man of plain sense, and has modesty enough to hold his tongue. He is a gentlemanly man, and is in high estimation among the Methodists."[1]

Historian M.E. Bradford concurs with this description.

Richard Bassett was one of the most devout of the Framers. He was converted to Methodism during the revolution and became a close personal friend of Bishop Francis Asbury, who held meetings on his plantation. Bassett freed his slaves and then employed them as hired labor. But he was no egalitarian or champion of radical change. Rather, he should be remembered as one of the pillars of the old order in Delaware.... He is best remembered for his contributions to the life of his chosen church, his generosity toward what he saw as the work of God.[2]

Although he was born of a tavern-keeper who abandoned him and his mother, Bassett was adopted by a relative named Peter Lawson, who provided him a Christian environment and training, which may account for his deep commitment to Christ and His church. It is said that he contributed half the cost for building the First Methodist Church in Dover.[3]

1. **List** eight of Bassett's good character traits, actions, or commendations by others that are highlighted by LaHaye in this excerpt. The first one has been done for you.

    a. He "serves his country because it is the will of the people that he should do so."
    b. _____
    c. _____
    d. _____
    e. _____
    f. _____
    g. _____
    h. _____

---

1 Endnote from excerpt: W. Cleon Skousen, *The Making of America* (Washington, DC: The National Center for Constitutional Studies, 1985), p. xv.
2 Endnote from excerpt: M.E. Bradford, *A Worthy Company* (Marlborough, NH: Plymouth Rock Foundation, 1982), p. 214.
3 Biography excerpt from: LaHaye, Tim. *Faith of Our Founding Fathers*. Master Books, 2022, p. 136.

Name _____ Lesson 14 - Exercise 1 Day 66

Today you will **begin reading** pages 203b–219a (ending at "Mary, the Mother of Washington") in *Life of Washington*. Have this section read by Exercise 4 of this lesson. Before reading, **study** the vocabulary words listed below.

A. Vocabulary

agriculture	the practice of farming crops or animals	**haven**	place of safety; a refuge
august	respected and impressive	**illustrious**	well-known, respected, admired for achievement
beseech	to ask urgently	**minuteness**	being very small in size
condescended	showed feelings of superiority	**navigation**	process of planning and following a route
confounded	emphasized anger or annoyance	**patronage**	support given by a patron or sponsor
consolation	comfort after disappointment or loss	**profuse**	plentiful, abundant
diffidence	shyness due to a lack of confidence	**sanguine**	positive or optimistic in a bad situation
dissolution	dismissal of an assembly or official body	**superseded**	took the place of
economical	good value for the price	**venerable**	respect due to age, character, or wisdom

2. Use the word bank to **fill in** the blanks from this portion of Washington's resignation letter found on page 205. Notice that some of the vocabulary words are from previous lessons.

arduous	interposition	Providence	sanguine
diffidence	patronage	rectitude	superseded

"I resign with satisfaction the appointment I accepted with _____; a diffidence in my abilities to accomplish so _____ a task, which, however, was _____ by a confidence in the _____ of our cause, the support of the supreme power of the union and the _____ of heaven. The successful termination of the war has verified the most _____ expectations; and my gratitude for the _____ of _____, and the assistance I have received from my countrymen, increases with every review of the momentous contest."

☐ **Use** index cards to **write** each vocabulary word from this lesson on one side and the definition on the other. **Check** the box when complete.

☐ **Copy** the Scripture verse on an index card. **Memorize** it by the end of this lesson. You may choose the Bible translation or use the one given. **Check** the box when complete.

Do not rejoice when your enemy falls, and let not your heart be glad when he stumbles, lest the LORD *see it and be displeased, and turn away his anger from him.* Proverbs 24:17–18

Name _____   Lesson 14 - Exercise 2   Day 67

Grammar & Punctuation

Adjectives

You have learned that an adjective describes or modifies a noun and answers questions like *which one*, *what kind*, or *how many*. Today we will look at seven different types of adjectives. **Study** the chart.

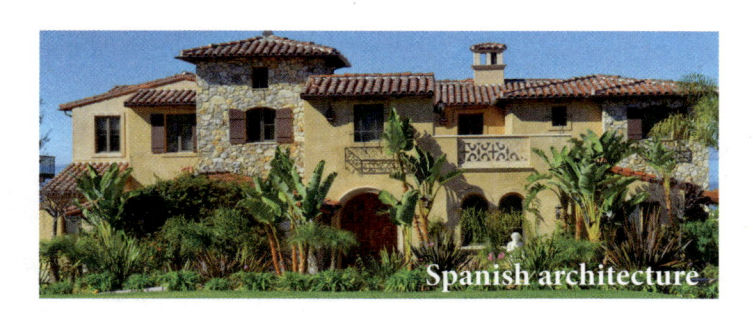

Spanish architecture

Seven Types of Adjectives	
Descriptive Adjective	names a quality of the noun or pronoun that it modifies
	yellow flower, *larger* fish, *soft* rabbit, *sad* expression
Proper Adjective	derived from a proper noun. These include words for nationalities, languages, and ethnicities.
	Spanish architecture, *European* lifestyle, *French* class, *American* diet
Limiting Adjective	restricts the meaning of the word it modifies
	this book, *that* house, *the* car
Interrogative Adjective	used to ask a question
	Whose hat is this? *Which* book belongs to you?
Coordinate Adjective	consists of two or more adjectives separated by a comma instead of a coordinating conjunction
	a *large*, *sharp* knife; the *warm*, *scented* fabric; the *constant*, *monotonous* noise
To understand if two or more adjectives should be connected by commas, see if the order of the adjectives can be reversed. If they can be reversed, a comma can be used to separate them.	
	The boy ate a *crisp*, *shiny* apple. OR The boy ate a *shiny*, *crisp* apple. Reversing *crisp* and *shiny* does not change the meaning; therefore, a comma is placed in between. These are coordinate adjectives.
	The boy ate *two shiny* apples. OR The boy ate *shiny two* apples. Reversing *two* and *shiny* does change the meaning; therefore, a comma should not be used. These are *not* coordinate adjectives.
Compound Adjectives	consist of two or more words that function as a single unit. Depending on its position within the sentence, the compound adjective is punctuated with a hyphen. When the compound adjective comes *before* the noun it modifies, use a hyphen. When it *follows* the noun it modifies, do not use a hyphen.
	The item at the museum was a *seventeenth-century* vase. (hyphen used) The vase at the museum was from the *seventeenth century*. (no hyphen)

Name _____   Lesson 14 - Exercise 2   Day 67

Determiners as Adjectives	Determiners, like articles (*a, an, the*), numbers, and pronouns, can function as adjectives. Determiners are like limiting adjectives because they restrict the nouns they modify. Determiners functioning as adjectives tell *which one, how many*, and *whose*.
	Articles (*a, an, the*)
	Possessive pronouns (*my, our, your, his, her, its, their*)
	Relative pronouns (*whose, which, whichever, what, whatever*)
	Demonstratives (*this, these, that, those*)
	Indefinite pronouns (*any, each, other, some*, etc.)
	Cardinal numbers (*one, two, three*, etc.)
	Ordinal numbers (*first, last, second*, etc.)
	Possessive proper nouns (*Levi's, John's*)
	John's truck broke down *five* miles from *his* house.

Underline the adjectives, including all articles.

1. The basket contained two chocolate muffins and a large tin of gourmet coffee.
2. I bought a birthday gift for my best friend at the Polish pottery shop in the nearby village.
3. This book has been the best source of encouragement for homeschool families!
4. A biblical worldview is essential to maintaining one's walk with Christ.
5. **Write** a sentence containing a proper adjective and a limiting adjective.
   _____
   _____

6. **Write** a sentence containing coordinate adjectives. (Make sure to use a comma if necessary!)
   _____
   _____

7. **Write** a sentence containing a compound adjective. (*Examples:* short-term, grass-fed, ice-cold, etc.)
   _____
   _____

8. **Write** a sentence containing an interrogative adjective and two descriptive adjectives.
   _____
   _____

Name _____ Lesson 14 - Exercise 3 Day 68

Communication

Compiling a Works Cited Page

Review the portions of Days 13, 28, and 38 that relate to citing research.

Sometimes the terms "works cited" and "bibliography" are used interchangeably, but they are not the same. A works cited page lists only sources you have actually referred to and cited in your paper. A bibliography lists all the sources you have consulted, whether you referred to and cited the source or not. For our purposes, we will create a works cited page. **Study** the example.

Works Cited

Down, David. *Unveiling the Kings of Israel*. New Leaf Publishing Group, LLC, 2012.

Ham, Ken. "New Dinosaur Tracks Unearthed in Texas' Paluxy River." *Ken Ham Blog*, 11 Sept. 2023, answersingenesis.org/dinosaurs/footprints/new-dinosaur-tracks-unearthed-texas-paluxy-river/.

Lambert, John C. *Adventures of Missionary Heroism*. New Leaf Publishing Group, LLC, 2017.

Reed, Anna C. *Life of Washington*. Attic Books, 2013.

Ross, Dr. Marcus. "*T. rex*—Fashioned To Be Fearless." *Answers Magazine*, 10 Mar. 2019, answersingenesis.org/dinosaurs/types/t-rex-fashioned-to-be-fearless/.

Formatting a Works Cited Page in MLA Style

Authors are listed by last name first and placed in alphabetical order.
Books, magazines, and blogs are italicized.
Periods are used after the author's name, a book or article title, and at the very end of the citation.
Commas are used after the publisher, blog title, and any other elements, such as volume numbers.
All lines are double spaced, and any second lines in a single citation are indented ½ inch. Page margins should be one inch.
Dates are listed in the day, month, and year format (27 Oct. 2024). If no date is given for a web source, record the date you accessed the information (Accessed 10 Dec. 2023).
If a source has two authors, list them in alphabetical order separated by the word "and." Only the first author would be listed by last name. (Gabel, Sarah, and Kristen Pratt.)
The URL identifying a web source should be copied and pasted onto the works cited page. Omit the beginning of the URL that reads, "https://."

Name _____   Lesson 14 - Exercise 3   Day 68

1. **Practice** creating a works cited page for the following references. Use slanted letters to indicate italics, and remember to put the sources in alphabetical order.

   A book titled *Geology by Design: Interpreting Rocks and Their Catastrophic Record*, written by Carl Froede, Jr. This book was published by New Leaf Publishing Group, LLC, in 2017. (*Hint*: The "Jr." should be added after the author's first name and preceded by a comma.)

   A book titled *Wonders of Creation: Design in a Fallen World*, written by Stuart Burgess and Andy McIntosh. This book was published by New Leaf Publishing Group, LLC, in 2018.

   An entry in the Ken Ham Blog entitled "Did an Empire Rule North America Before Europeans Arrived?" The date of this article is October 17, 2023. The URL is https://answersingenesis.org/blogs/ken-ham/2023/10/17/did-empire-rule-north-america-before-europeans/.

   Works Cited

Name _____ Lesson 14 - Exercise 4 Day 69

Worldview & Literary Analysis

Literary Device: Authorial Intrusion

Authorial intrusion is a literary device in which the author directly addresses the reader by interrupting the story. The author momentarily steps out of the story to address the reader, offering an explanation, commentary, or personal opinion.

> **Authorial intrusion** is a literary device in which the author directly addresses the reader by interrupting the story.

In this lesson's reading, Reed suddenly and directly addresses the readers as "Young Americans!" (p. 211). She issues a warning to her audience about wishing to be free from the just and righteous laws of the Creator. She will use this technique a few more times before the end of this book. Keep an eye out for authorial intrusion and consider its effectiveness in persuading the reader.

Finish reading pages 203b–219a (ending at "Mary, the Mother of Washington") in *Life of Washington* and **respond** to the following.

1. What "proved that [Washington] had a right to the noble title of *an honest man*"? (p. 204)

   _____
   _____
   _____
   _____
   _____
   _____
   _____
   _____

2. Washington made a speech before Congress to resign as Commander of the Army. **To what** did he commend the interests of the country? (p. 205)

   _____
   _____

3. Washington was so happy to finally be back home on his farm. **Fill in** the blanks from a letter he wrote to his good friend Lafayette. (p. 207)

   "At length I have become a _____ _____, on the banks of the Potomac, and under the shade of my 'own _____ and my own _____-_____' and free from the bustle of a _____ and the busy cares of _____ _____. I have not only retired from all public _____, but am retiring within _____, and shall be able to view the _____ walk, and tread the _____ of _____ _____, with heartfelt _____."

Worldview & Literary Analysis   Lesson 14, Day 69   155

Name _____   Lesson 14 - Exercise 4   Day 69

4. On page 208, the author states, "When the English ceased to act as enemies of his country, Washington did not cherish against them feelings of resentment." Based on the rest of this paragraph and on Washington's past actions, **explain** why you believe Washington was able to walk in forgiveness when the English had done his country so much harm.

_____
_____
_____
_____

5. Lafayette's heart is grieved because his home country of France had thrown off moral restraint. **What** were the consequences of this? (p. 211)

_____
_____

What do you feel the author is pointing out about a nation like France that did not fear God or regard His commandments?

_____
_____

6. On page 211, the literary device called authorial intrusion appears. Beginning with the phrase "Young Americans!" **summarize** the author's direct address to her readers.

_____
_____

This lesson's reading ends with a very sad goodbye between Washington and his dear mother. Have you ever lost to death someone you were close to? In two or three sentences, **explain** why Christians can find comfort in these moments.

_____
_____
_____
_____

George Washington on his death bed, attended by family and friends. By Junius Brutus Stearns, c. 1853.

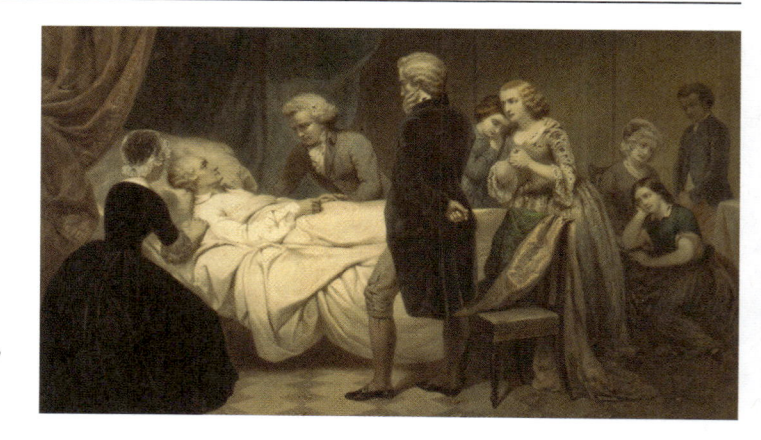

156   Lesson 14, Day 69   *Language Lessons for a Living Education* Level 10

Name _____   Lesson 14 - Exercise 5   Day 70

Review

☐ **Update** the Reading List chart with books you have read this week.

☐ **Recite** Proverbs 24:17–18 from memory to your instructor.

Vocabulary Review

Match each word to the correct definition.

a. agriculture	e. confounded	i. economical	m. navigation	q. superseded
b. august	f. consolation	j. haven	n. patronage	r. venerable
c. beseech	g. diffidence	k. illustrious	o. profuse	
d. condescended	h. dissolution	l. minuteness	p. sanguine	

1. _____ being very small in size
2. _____ good value for the price
3. _____ to ask urgently
4. _____ took the place of
5. _____ support given by a patron or sponsor
6. _____ respected and impressive
7. _____ plentiful, abundant
8. _____ place of safety; a refuge
9. _____ emphasizing anger or annoyance
10. _____ respect due to age, character, or wisdom
11. _____ process of planning and following a route
12. _____ shyness due to lack of confidence
13. _____ practice of farming crops or animals
14. _____ positive or optimistic in a bad situation
15. _____ comfort after disappointment or loss
16. _____ showed feelings of superiority
17. _____ dismissal of an assembly or official body
18. _____ well-known or respected for achievement

Grammar & Punctuation Review

Match the type of adjective to the example given.

1. _____ proper adjective
2. _____ descriptive adjective
3. _____ limiting adjective
4. _____ interrogative adjective
5. _____ coordinate adjective
6. _____ compound adjective

a. he had a *surprised* expression
b. *whose* job is that?
c. the *soft, black* cat
d. *that* fish was huge
e. the *African* sunset
f. the *high-powered* saw

Underline the adjectives, including articles. There may be more than one per sentence.

7. Scuba diving requires a person to have excellent health and good swimming skills.
8. Tropical rainforests are the most biologically diverse terrestrial ecosystems on the planet.
9. Canada's Pacific coast climate is relatively mild, yet the Prairie Provinces have greater weather extremes.

Name _____ Lesson 14 – Exercise 5 Day 70

Communication Review

1. **Explain** the difference between a works cited page and a bibliography.
   _____
   _____

2. Use the following information to **construct** a works cited entry for the following two sources.

   A book titled *The Summit*, written by Eric Alexander and published by New Leaf Publishing Group, LLC, in 2016.

   A blog by Ken Ham with the title "Did an Empire Rule North America Before Europeans Arrived?" The URL for this article is https://answersingenesis.org/blogs/ken-ham/2023/10/17/did-empire-rule-north-america-before-europeans/. The date of this article was October 17, 2023.

   _____
   _____
   _____
   _____
   _____
   _____
   _____

Worldview & Literary Analysis Review

1. **Define** authorial intrusion.
   _____
   _____

2. **Write** the phrase Reed uses to introduce her authorial intrusion in *Life of Washington* on page 211.
   _____

3. **List** two entities Washington commended the interests of his country to.
   a. _____
   b. _____

4. Lafayette grieves that his home country of France has thrown off moral constraint. **List** the three consequences of his country's behavior.
   a. _____
   b. _____
   c. _____

Special Feature

Lesson 15

Picture Study: Mount Vernon

Study the picture of George Washington's home, Mount Vernon. **Imagine** the colors you would see and the sounds you would hear if you were sitting on a picnic blanket in the soft grass. **Write** a descriptive paragraph of 6–8 sentences about this scene. Include a simile and a metaphor. Use lively adjectives and adverbs. **Read** your paragraph to your instructor.

Name _____   Lesson 15 - Exercise 1   Day 71

Today you will **begin reading** pages 219b–234a (ending at "so highly") in *Life of Washington*. Have this section read by Exercise 4 of this lesson. Before reading, **study** the vocabulary words listed below.

Vocabulary

adieu	goodbye	**homage**	honor or respect shown publicly
agency	organization overseeing transactions between parties	**impute**	to lay blame, often falsely
benediction	bestowing of a blessing	**judicious**	good judgment or sense
beneficent	generous or doing good	**meritorious**	deserving of praise or reward
benign	gentle and kindly	**pardon**	the action of forgiving or being forgiven for an offense
concourse	a crowd or assembly of people	**punctuality**	quality of being on time
consecrate	to make or declare as sacred	**supplication**	the action of asking or begging humbly
conspicuous	standing out; clearly visible	**tenor**	general course or tendency
ferry	ship or boat where people or items are carried across a small body of water	**treaty**	an agreement made by negotiations

Write a paragraph using as many vocabulary words as you can. **Circle** each vocabulary word once you finish.

_____
_____
_____
_____
_____
_____
_____
_____
_____

☐ **Use** index cards to **write** each vocabulary word from this lesson on one side and the definition on the other. **Check** the box when complete.

☐ **Copy** the Scripture verse on an index card. **Memorize** it by the end of this lesson. You may choose the Bible translation or use the one given. **Check** the box when complete.

And he made from one man every nation of mankind to live on all the face of the earth, having determined allotted periods and the boundaries of their dwelling place. Acts 17:26

Name _____ Lesson 15 - Exercise 2   Day 72

Grammar & Punctuation

Adverbs

You have learned that adverbs are words that modify verbs, adjectives, or other adverbs. They answer questions like *how, when, why, where, to what extent,* or *under what conditions*. As you learned in a previous lesson, adverbs can modify more than just one word; they can modify phrases, clauses, and entire sentences.

> *Examples:* The pastor had to speak *loudly* over the crowd noise. (*loudly* modifies the verb *speak*)
> The dog was *really* dirty after a run through the field. (*really* modifies the adjective *dirty*)
> *Clearly*, the directions were not specific enough. (*Clearly* modifies the entire sentence)
> The ice fisherman stepped *very* gently onto the ice. (*very* modifies the adverb *gently*)
> That cardinal is *still* under the birdfeeder. (*still* modifies the phrase *under the birdfeeder*)

There are different types of adverbs to be aware of. **Study** the adverb chart.

Seven Types of Adverbs	
Adverbs of Manner	An adverb of manner answers the question *how?*
	badly, beautifully, happily, cheerfully, hard, quickly, adequately, healthy, fast, well, better, courageously, etc.
Adverbs of Place	An adverb of place answers the question *where?*
	below, inside, there, up, down, outside, inside, near, far, above, away, etc.
Adverbs of Time	An adverb of time answers the question *when?*
	after, before, during, always, later, early, now, often, yesterday, rarely, recently, sometimes, then, today, tomorrow, usually, never, soon, etc.
Adverbs of Degree	An adverb of degree answers the question *how much?*
	almost, completely, enough, entirely, extremely, hardly, nearly, just, little, much, quite, rather, too, very, etc.
Adverbs of Frequency	An adverb of frequency answers the question *how often?*
	always, never, usually, seldom, sometimes, occasionally, frequently, every now and then, etc.
Interrogative Adverbs	**An interrogative adverb introduces a question.** They are usually placed at the beginning of the sentence.
	how, when, why, and *where*
Conjunctive Adverbs	**Conjunctive adverbs act as transitional words that join and relate to independent clauses.**
	accordingly, certainly, finally, nevertheless, moreover, previously, therefore, also, alternatively, consequently, etc.

Name _____   Lesson 15 - Exercise 2   Day 72

The word *not* is also an adverb. Therefore, contractions with the word *not* (*haven't, couldn't, wouldn't*, etc.) are also used as adverbs.

> *Examples:* You do *not* need to finish your dinner. You *don't* need to finish your dinner.
> I have *not* taken the dog out today. I *haven't* taken the dog out today.

Underline the adverbs. **Circle** the word or words they modify. There may be more than one adverb per sentence. (*Hint:* Some adverbs may be underlined AND circled, and some may modify the entire sentence.)

1. The hungry lion ravenously attacked his fresh kill.
2. At Thanksgiving dinner, Aaron ate the pumpkin pie rather greedily.
3. Every child at the piano recital completed their piece beautifully.
4. You need to play outside.
5. I am very excited about this flight to Europe!
6. How do you plan to finish that entire puzzle by yourself?
7. Consequently, there was not enough paint left over to paint the shed.

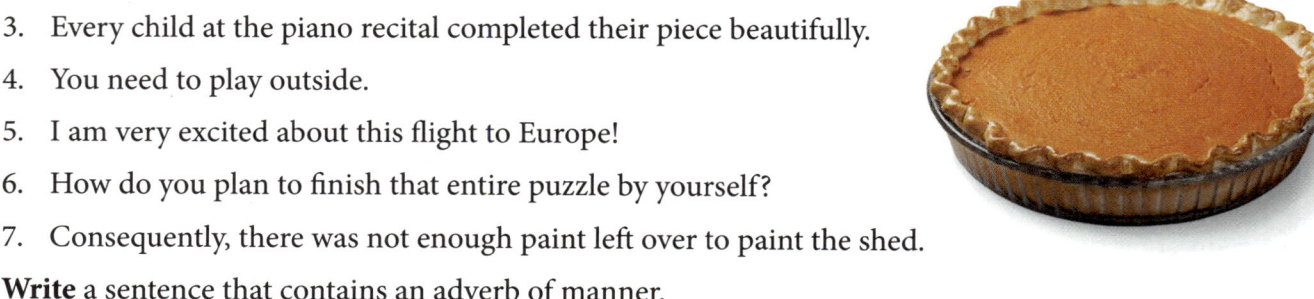

Write a sentence that contains an adverb of manner.

_____

_____

Write a sentence that contains an adverb of time.

_____

_____

Write a sentence that contains a conjunctive adverb.

_____

_____

8. **Fill in** the blanks with adverbs from the Seven Types of Adverbs chart.

_____, we _____ enjoyed a walk in the park _____ of town. We had _____ done this before. Young children _____ played on the swings, mothers _____ chatted on the benches, and older couples _____ strolled _____ the winding path. It was _____ pleasant. I _____ hope we do this _____!

Name _____   Lesson 15 - Exercise 3   Day 73

Communication

The Biography Rough Draft

It is time to put it all together and write your biography rough draft! A **rough draft** is the first version of a piece of writing that needs editing and rewriting. A **final draft** is the final version of a piece of writing that has been edited and rewritten.

> A **rough draft** is the first version of a piece of writing that needs editing and rewriting.
>
> A **final draft** is the final version of a piece of writing that has been edited and rewritten.

You gathered information about your biography subject under the Biography Notes section on Days 18, 28, 38, 53, and 58. Your outline was written on Day 63, and the works cited practice page is on Day 68. Look over all these notes and construct paragraphs based on your outline. Before beginning to write, let's look at a couple of tools to assist you in your writing.

Literary Devices

Choose two literary devices to incorporate into your biography. Here is a list of devices and the days they are taught.

In medias res (Day 29)	Anecdote (Day 59)	Imagery (Day 34)	Analogy (Day 64)
Exposition (Day 39)	Authorial intrusion (Day 69)	Foreshadowing (Day 49)	Archetype (Day 84)

Transitions

It is important that your biography flows from one paragraph to the next. Sometimes it is helpful to use a transitional word or phrase to connect paragraphs. **Study** the chart below and keep these transitions in mind when beginning a new paragraph.

Transitional Words and Phrases Show:			
Emphasis	**Addition**	**Contrast**	**Order**
Undoubtedly	Along with	Unlike	Following
Unquestionably	Apart from this	Nevertheless	At this time
Obviously	Moreover	On the other hand	Previously
Particularly/in particular	Furthermore	Nonetheless	First/firstly
Especially	Also	Despite/in spite of	Second/secondly
Clearly	Too	In contrast to	Third/thirdly
Importantly	As well as that	Contrary to	Finally
Absolutely	Besides	Alternatively	Subsequently
Definitely	In addition	Conversely	Above all
Without a doubt	Not only … but also	Even so	Before
Indeed	Additionally	Differing from	First and foremost

Communication

Name _____   Lesson 15 - Exercise 3   Day 73

Start writing your rough draft. It will be due in Exercise 3 of the next lesson (Day 78). Remember to keep your story in chronological order unless using a literary device like *in medias res*. Also, you can enhance your biography's impact by adding personal insights and opinions about your subject. Be sure to stay in the third person (avoid the pronoun *I*).

Your biography needs to be 4–5 pages typed (double spaced) or 6–7 pages handwritten in a notebook (every other line). This page total does not include a cover sheet or works cited page, which you will put together in the next lesson. Be sure to reference the Biography Rubric in the back of the book so you understand the expectations. Happy writing!

Wisdom Speaks

Copy the proverb.

> *If one gives an answer before he hears, it is his folly and shame.* Proverbs 18:13

_____
_____

Using a dictionary or an online search with a parent's permission, **write** the definitions of the words below.

1. folly: _____
_____

2. shame: _____
_____

Write a sentence expressing Proverbs 18:13 in your own words.
_____
_____

Good communication is not only about how we express ourselves but also about how well we listen. If we are too quick to answer without fully hearing the other person, we may find ourselves in an embarrassing situation.

Write a sentence containing the word *folly* based on the definition you wrote.
_____
_____

Write a sentence containing the word *shame* based on the definition you wrote.
_____
_____

As you go about your day, **pay attention** to how well you are listening to others before you respond to them. **Pray** and ask God to help you be a better listener.

Name _____   Lesson 15 - Exercise 4   Day 74

Worldview & Literary Analysis

Today's reading opens with Washington's difficult departure from his beloved farm where he had hoped to spend his remaining days. Yet because his character demanded the placement of others' needs before his own, he responded to the request of his country to serve them as their first president.

He lacked confidence in himself to meet his country's expectations, but his fervent desire to serve and his unshakable faith in God gave him the strength to accept the position of the first president of the United States of America.

Finish reading pages 219b–234a (ending at "so highly") in *Life of Washington* and **respond** to the following.

1. Washington's enjoyment of solitude in his own home was disrupted by his country's call for him to be their first president. **Record** the journal entry made by Washington at the close of the day he left Mt. Vernon on his way to become President Washington. (p. 219)

   _____
   _____
   _____
   _____
   _____
   _____

   Why do you think Washington was feeling what he described in his journal?

   _____
   _____
   _____

2. As Washington's neighbors said goodbye, they lamented the loss they would all feel on their own level (p. 220). **Fill in** the blanks.

   "Our aged must lose their _____,—our youth, their _____,—our agriculture, its _____,—our commerce, its _____,—our academy, its _____,—our poor, their _____."

3. Every town Washington went through on his way to New York to accept the presidency had planned to greet him with parades and signs. Yet, we read he wished the journey to be private. **What** character trait does this show?

   _____

4. **What** happened when the Chancellor proclaimed that George Washington was the president of the United States? (p. 222)

   _____
   _____

Worldview & Literary Analysis   Lesson 15, Day 74   165

Name _____   Lesson 15 - Exercise 4   Day 74

5. In his first address, Washington speaks to the American people, saying, "No people can be bound to acknowledge and adore the invisible hand which conducts the affairs of men, more than the people of the United States" (p. 223). **What** reason does he give for this statement?

   _____
   _____
   _____

6. While president, Washington set rules that governed his own family (p. 224–226). **List** three of the rules he set up for his own home.

   a. _____
   b. _____
   c. _____

7. Washington made the following statement to a visitor who arrived late to his home: "Our cook never asks if the company has come, but if the hour has come" (p. 225). **What** did he mean by this?

   _____
   _____

8. Moravian missionaries preached the gospel of Jesus Christ to some of the Indians (Native Americans). Some believed and lived in the blessings of God. However, many continued to attack the settlers along the frontier. Washington wanted peace with the Indians and not war (p. 229–231). **What** were some ways he tried to make peace while also defending families on the frontier?

   _____
   _____
   _____
   _____

9. Washington had a desire to "cultivate peace with all the world," and therefore did not allow America to get involved in the "general war" going on in the world (p. 232-233). **What** did he secure for his country in doing so?

   _____

10. While the war raged amongst other nations, **what** was happening in America and **how** did it benefit other nations? (p. 233)

    _____
    _____
    _____
    _____

Name _____ Lesson 15 - Exercise 5 Day 75

Review

☐ **Update** the Reading List chart with books you have read this week.

☐ **Recite** Acts 17:26 from memory to your instructor.

Vocabulary Review

Match each word to the correct definition.

a. adieu	e. benign	i. ferry	m. meritorious	q. tenor
b. agency	f. concourse	j. homage	n. pardon	r. treaty
c. benediction	g. consecrate	k. impute	o. punctuality	
d. beneficent	h. conspicuous	l. judicious	p. supplication	

1. _____ goodbye
2. _____ gentle and kindly
3. _____ generous or doing good
4. _____ good judgment or sense
5. _____ to lay blame, often falsely
6. _____ general course or tendency
7. _____ quality of being on time
8. _____ standing out; clearly visible
9. _____ ship or boat where people or animals are carried across water
10. _____ a crowd or assembly of people
11. _____ action of asking or begging humbly
12. _____ bestowing a blessing
13. _____ to make or declare as sacred
14. _____ honor or respect shown publicly
15. _____ organization overseeing party transactions
16. _____ an agreement made by negotiation
17. _____ deserving of praise or reward
18. _____ the action of forgiving or being forgiven for offense

Grammar & Punctuation Review

Match the type of adverb with the example given.

1. _____ adverb of manner
2. _____ adverb of place
3. _____ adverb of time
4. _____ adverb of degree
5. _____ adverb of frequency
6. _____ interrogative adverb
7. _____ conjunctive adverb

a. always, never, usually, seldom, occasionally
b. how, when, why, where
c. almost, completely, entirely, hardly, nearly
d. badly, happily, cheerfully, quickly, hard, well, better,
e. after, before, during, always, never, soon
f. accordingly, certainly, finally, therefore, also
g. below, down, inside, up, outside, inside, near, far

Name _____   Lesson 15 - Exercise 5   Day 75

Underline the adverbs. There may be more than one per sentence.
8. My dog River greedily consumed the plate of chicken scraps I left in his bowl.
9. Yesterday we had a flat tire, and Dad quite easily changed it while we waited in the car.
10. Unfortunately, my average fell below the rest of the class, and I needed to study diligently to make up for it.
11. How often do you read Scripture?

Communication Review

1. **Explain** the difference between a rough draft and a final draft of a paper.
   _____
   _____

2. **Write** a sentence using a transitional word of emphasis.
   _____
   _____

3. **Write** a sentence using a transitional word of order.
   _____
   _____

Copy the proverb.

> *If one gives an answer before he hears, it is his folly and shame.* Proverbs 18:13

_____
_____

Worldview & Literary Analysis Review

1. **List** three rules Washington set to govern his own family.
   a. _____
   b. _____
   c. _____

2. **List** three rules your family abides by.
   a. _____
   b. _____
   c. _____

Special Feature

Lesson 16

Poem Study: "Lines Written by a Revolutionary Soldier"
(author unknown)

Read the poem to your instructor. **Discuss** the concepts of suffering, freedom, and thanksgiving regarding those who fight for the benefit of others. (*Note:* At the time this poem was written, some writers omitted letters for style or in cases where the letter is silent.)

On the cold earth I oft have lain,
Oppress'd with hunger toil and pain,
While storms and tempests roar'd around,
And frost and snow had cloth'd the ground
The British troops, did us assail,
In storms of snow, and rattling hail,
All this with patience long we bore,
Until that sanguine war was o'er.
And Independence made secure,
For which we did those toils endure,
Our hostile foes then left our shore,
Retired for to return no more,—
Fair freedom now her laurels spread
O'er hostile fields where warriors bled;
No more we hear the din of war,
Nor thund'ring annon from a far,
Here peace spreads o'er our fertile plains,
No tyrants shake their galling chains,
Our ships safe o'er the ocean glide,
And waft in wealth with ev'ry tide,
My friends remember us who bled,
When on the sanguine fields you tread,
Nor spurn us if of you we crave,
Some aid while tot'ring o'er the grave.
Our fleeting days will shortly end,
Then with our native dust we blend.
Death soon will close our languid eyes,
And all our cares beneath the skies:
Columbia's sons who us survive,

And in this land of freedom live,
Revere that Providential hand,
That long has blest your happy land—
Your Constitution ever prize,
Your tow'ring frame will reach the skies,
And while you all in Union blend,
It will from war your shores defend—
Daily improvements here are made
For agriculture and for trade,
Here tow'ring manufacturers rise
Where'er you turn your wand'ring eyes;
Your treasuries now with gold o'erflow,
Riches abound where'er you go,
No hostile banners you alarm,
You sit at home free from all harm—
Long may your happy land be blest,
And you enjoy both peace and rest;
Look back and see what we have done,
Generations yet to come,
Shall find a lasting peaceful home.
Extol the victories we have won,
And when we all in dust shall sleep,
To our memories will long vigils keep,
And o'er our heads will trophies raise,
With lasting songs of joy and praise.
And now my friends a long adieu,
Our fleeting days are short and few,
We soon must leave this trying shore.
And land where time shall be no more.

Name _____ Lesson 16 - Exercise 1 Day 76

Today you will **begin reading** pages 234b–250a (ending at "a Christian") in *Life of Washington*. Have this section read by Exercise 4 of this lesson. Before reading, **study** the vocabulary words listed below.

Vocabulary

ambassador	an official representative sent to another country	insurrection	violent uprising against authority
arbiter	person who settles a dispute	omit	to leave out or exclude, intentionally or forgetfully
clamour (clamor)	loud, confusing noise, usually that of people	perpetual	never ending or changing
clemency	mercy or lenience	privateer	privately owned armed ship
conferred	granted or bestowed upon	quell	to put an end to
exemplary	the best of its kind	restitution	restoration of something lost or stolen
indigent	poor and needy	tyrant	cruel, oppressive ruler
indispensable	something that is absolutely necessary	unremitted	never ceased
insolent	rude; arrogant lack of respect	zeal	great enthusiasm for a cause or object

1. **Write** a sentence using the words *quelled* and *insurrection*. Use an infinitive as an adverb. (Day 62)

   _____

   _____

Fill in the blanks in these excerpts from *Life of Washington* using this lesson's vocabulary words.

2. "Washington was just, and would not yield to the _____ [clamor] which was raised against the English. He was of the opinion, that 'peace ought to be pursued with _____ _____ …' " (p. 236).

3. "I cannot _____ the occasion to repeat my fervent supplications to the Supreme Ruler of the universe and sovereign _____ of nations …" (p. 241).

☐ **Use** index cards to **write** each vocabulary word from this lesson on one side and the definition on the other. **Check** the box when complete.

☐ **Copy** the Scripture verse on an index card. **Memorize** it by the end of this lesson. You may choose the Bible translation or use the one given. **Check** the box when complete.

Blessed are the peacemakers, for they shall be called sons of God. Matthew 5:9

Name _____   Lesson 16 - Exercise 2   Day 77

Grammar & Punctuation

Prepositional Phrases Used as Adjectives and Adverbs

Review prepositions on Day 37.

An **adjective prepositional phrase** modifies a noun and functions as an adjective in the sentence. Remember, adjectives tell *which one*, *what kind*, or *how many* and describe or modify a noun in the sentence. Unlike adjectives, which usually come *before* the noun they modify, adjective prepositional phrases come *after* the noun.

> An **adjective prepositional phrase** modifies a noun and functions as an adjective in the sentence.
>
> An **adverb prepositional phrase** modifies a verb, adjective, or other adverb and functions as an adverb in the sentence.

ADJECTIVE
Examples: The horse (with the black mane) belongs to Amber.
(The prepositional phrase *with the black mane* functions as an adjective since it describes or modifies the noun *horse*.)

ADJECTIVE
Her favorite show (on television) was canceled due to poor ratings.
(The prepositional phrase *on television* functions as an adjective because it describes the noun *show*.)

An **adverb prepositional phrase** modifies a verb, adjective, or other adverb and functions as an adverb in the sentence. Remember, adverbs tell *how*, *when*, *why*, *where*, *to what extent*, or *under what conditions*. Adverb prepositional phrases that modify adjectives and adverbs must go *after* the words they modify. If they modify a verb, they can be found *anywhere* in the sentence.

ADVERB
Examples: Whales are the largest mammals that live (on the earth).
(The prepositional phrase *on the earth* functions as an adverb phrase by telling us *where* whales live.)

ADVERB
My little cousins behave (with the utmost respect).
(The prepositional phrase *with the utmost respect* modifies the verb *behave* by telling us *how* the cousins behave.)

Prepositions that function as prepositional adverbs include: *about, above, across, after, along, around, before, behind, below, between, beyond, by, down, in, inside, near, on, opposite, out, outside, over, past, round, since, through, throughout, under, up, within,* and *without*.

Place parentheses around the adjective prepositional phrases and **write** the word they modify.

1. _____ The first chapter is the very best chapter in the book.
2. _____ The house by the field has been abandoned.
3. _____ A large black cat with white paws keeps sneaking around.

Grammar & Punctuation   Lesson 16, Day 77   171

Name _____   Lesson 16 - Exercise 2   Day 77

Place parentheses around the adverb prepositional phrases and **write** the word or words they modify. (*Hint:* Remember to ask *how, when, why, where, to what extent,* or *under what conditions.*)

4. _____ I can run extremely fast in my new soccer cleats.
5. _____ We will tour Alaska by plane.
6. _____ The snake slithered around the tree.

Complete the sentences with an adjective prepositional phrase.

7. The elderly man _____ sat down by me on the park bench.
8. I chose to sit under the tree _____ so I could enjoy the cool shade.
9. Dear Lord, we especially thank You for all the food _____ .

Complete the sentences with an adverb prepositional phrase.

10. When I approached the door, my puppy jumped up _____ .
11. To know the answers to life's biggest questions, look _____ .
12. I have always been a little bit afraid to swim _____ .

Review It!

Match the terms to the correct definition. (*Hint:* Study the chart on Day 2.)

13. _____ pronoun   a. expresses a feeling, makes a request, or gives a command
14. _____ action verb   b. describes or modifies a noun or pronoun
15. _____ conjunction   c. takes the place of a noun (*he, she, it, they,* etc.)
16. _____ noun   d. joins words or phrases
17. _____ adjective   e. names a person, place, or thing
18. _____ adverb   f. indicates state (*am, is, are, was, were, be, being, been*)
19. _____ state-of-being verb   g. describes the relationship between a noun and another word
20. _____ interjection   h. verb expressing action (*laugh, talk, run,* etc.)
21. _____ preposition   i. describes or modifies a verb, adjective, or other adverb

Write a sentence using a helping verb. (Day 17)

_____
_____

Name _____   Lesson 16 - Exercise 3   Day 78

Communication

Rough Draft Due

Turn in your rough draft to your instructor. Using the Biography Rubric found in the back of the book, **have** your instructor evaluate your rough draft, noting needed corrections and making suggestions. You will make your corrections, take your instructor's suggestions, and **rewrite** your rough draft, creating a final draft of your biography. The final draft is due in the next lesson on Day 83. Ask your instructor to sign below after evaluating your rough draft.

Instructor's signature: _____

Biography Cover Design

Today you can get creative! You will **design** a cover sheet for your biography that will include the artwork you design, the title of your biography, your name as the author, the title of this course, and the date. These items should be centered on the page (either at the top or bottom) and in the order listed here. Remember to use proper capitalization and punctuation in your titles.

Your artwork should reflect the character, personality, and life of the subject you chose. If you love to draw, this artwork could be done by hand. If you prefer to use computer images or digital drawing programs, you may do so with permission from a parent.

The cover page will be attached to the front of the final draft of your biography. On the second page of this exercise, you will find an area to "sketch" out or plan your design. This will be the rough draft of your cover page.

Works Cited

If you haven't already done so, it is time to type or write your works cited page. Make sure you follow the formatting instructions found on Day 68. You should have at least three different sources of research information for your paper. If you are citing a source that does not seem to fit the simplified instructions in this course, you may do an online search for MLA citations with a parent's permission. **Have** your instructor sign below after reviewing your cover page and works cited page.

Instructor's signature: _____

Communication

Name_____ Lesson 16 - Exercise 3 Day 78

Name _____   Lesson 16 - Exercise 4   Day 79

Worldview & Literary Analysis

With the use of authorial intrusion, Reed takes an example from history and uses it to warn young people of the "evil effects" of indulging in "*strong drink*" (p. 235). She is not only writing a biography about a famous person's life, but she is also using the events of that life to drive home several moral lessons.

As you near the end of *Life of Washington*, pay close attention to the moral lessons and overarching theme the author is trying to convey to the reader.

Finish reading pages 234b–250a (ending at "a Christian") in *Life of Washington* and **respond** to the following.

1. In another example of authorial intrusion, Reed addresses "Young Americans" and warns them against **what** "powerful foe"? (p. 235)

   _____

2. **Identify** this statement as either a simile or metaphor: "… *strong drink* is a tyrant which chains the body in disgrace and poverty." (p. 235)

   _____

3. **How** did some of the inhabitants of western Pennsylvania become a disgraceful example? (p. 235)

   _____
   _____

4. On page 236, **for what** two reasons were Washington's cares perhaps greater than at any other period of his administration?

   a. _____
   _____

   b. _____
   _____

5. Throughout his life, Washington sought peace whenever possible. He believed "peace ought to be pursued with unremitted zeal" (p. 236). **Fill in** the blanks from Matthew 5:9.

   "_____ are the _____, for they shall be called _____ _____."

6. On page 237, we are given more insight into Washington's views about the Indians (Native Americans). While there is much controversy about these topics from history, and there is good and evil on both sides, **summarize** what you believe Washington's attitude to be regarding the Indians.

   _____
   _____
   _____
   _____
   _____

Name _____ Lesson 16 - Exercise 4 Day 79

7. On pages 238–240, we read an anecdote about Lafayette's imprisonment by the French. A couple of men try to free him from prison, but their plan fails, and they end up before a judge. The judge states, "If ever I need a friend, I hope that friend may be an American" (p. 240). **Why** do you think the judge says this?

_____
_____
_____
_____

Regarding his retirement from the presidency and public life, Washington wrote the following to a friend. **Copy** his statement found on page 242:

> "To the wearied traveller [traveler], who sees a resting place, and is bending his body to lean thereon, I now compare myself."

_____
_____

Washington left his countrymen with many instructions about morality. **Copy** the following quotes.

> "Of all the dispositions and habits which lead to political prosperity, religion and morality are indispensable supports" (p. 246).

_____
_____

> "… [W]ithout an humble imitation of the example of the divine Author of our blessed religion, we cannot hope to be a happy nation" (p. 247).

_____
_____

8. In 1826, Washington's nephew, Bushrod Washington, was elected **what**? (p. 249)

_____
_____

9. Chief-Justice Hale of England gave **what** reason for the behavior of those convicted of capital crimes? (p. 250)

_____
_____

Name _____ Lesson 16 - Exercise 5 Day 80

Review

☐ **Update** the Reading List chart with books you have read this week.

☐ **Recite** Matthew 5:9 from memory to your instructor.

Vocabulary Review

Match each word to the correct definition.

a. ambassador	e. conferred	i. insolent	m. privateer	q. unremitted
b. arbiter	f. exemplary	j. insurrection	n. quell	r. zeal
c. clamour (clamor)	g. indigent	k. omit	o. restitution	
d. clemency	h. indispensable	l. perpetual	p. tyrant	

1. _____ to put an end to
2. _____ cruel, oppressive ruler
3. _____ never ceased
4. _____ mercy or lenience
5. _____ the best of its kind
6. _____ poor and needy
7. _____ granted or bestowed upon
8. _____ never ending or changing
9. _____ privately owned armed ship
10. _____ violent uprising against authority
11. _____ loud, confusing noise, usually by people
12. _____ great enthusiasm for a cause or object
13. _____ representative sent to another country
14. _____ rude; arrogant lack of respect
15. _____ leave out or exclude
16. _____ person who settles a dispute
17. _____ something absolutely necessary
18. _____ restoration of something lost or stolen

Grammar & Punctuation Review

Fill in the blanks.

1. Unlike adjectives, which usually come _____ the noun they modify, adjective prepositional phrases come _____ the noun.

2. Adverb prepositional phrases that modify _____ and _____ must go _____ the words they modify. If they modify a _____, they can be found _____ in the sentence.

Place parentheses around the adjective prepositional phrases and **write** the word or words they modify.

3. _____ The police officer with the service dog helped my mother and me.
4. _____ The shed beside the house needed to be power washed.
5. _____ Put the cat outside, or he will eat the food on the table.

Review

Name _____ Lesson 16 - Exercise 5   Day 80

Place parentheses around the adverb propositional phrases and **write** the word or words they modify.

6. _____ The student stood up and spoke with great passion.
7. _____ We usually go Christmas shopping after Thanksgiving.
8. _____ I swam beside the dock, hoping to find my goggles.

Communication Review

1. **Describe** how you feel about the subject of your biography after having researched their life. Do you have a different perspective now? **Write** a paragraph of 5–6 sentences.

_____
_____
_____
_____
_____
_____
_____
_____
_____
_____
_____
_____
_____

Worldview & Literary Analysis Review

1. **Name** the "powerful foe" Reed warns "Young Americans" about.

_____

Fill in the blanks in these quotes by Washington.

2. "Of all the dispositions and _____ which lead to _____ _____, religion and _____ are _____ supports."

3. "… [W]ithout an _____ imitation of the example of the _____ Author of our blessed _____, we cannot hope to be a happy _____."

Special Feature

Lesson 17

Scripture Study: Psalm 139:19–24

¹⁹ Oh that you would slay the wicked, O God!
   O men of blood, depart from me!

²⁰ They speak against you with malicious intent;
   your enemies take your name in vain.

²¹ Do I not hate those who hate you, O Lord?
   And do I not loathe those who rise up against you?

²² I hate them with complete hatred;
   I count them my enemies.

²³ Search me, O God, and know my heart!
   Try me and know my thoughts!

²⁴ And see if there be any grievous way in me,
   and lead me in the way everlasting!

Early in this psalm, David expresses his awe for God's creation and wisdom and then suddenly switches to a focus on the wicked and his disdain for them. He even says he hates them! This is because David is consumed with love and zeal for God and His commands. When he sees the wicked hating God, he desires to defend God's honor.

1. David mentions four ways the wicked are offensive to God. **List** them.

   a. _____
   b. _____
   c. _____
   d. _____

David wraps up Psalm 139 with an admission that God knows him better than he knows himself, acknowledging that his Creator understands him at the deepest level. With a humble heart and a desire for holiness, David asks God to show him his own sin. He doesn't want to be held back from "the way everlasting" and miss out on walking closely with his Father God. You can have this attitude as well!

Pray and ask your Father God to reveal the truth about you. Thank Him for creating you and showing His love and concern for you. **Write** your prayer.

_____
_____
_____
_____
_____
_____
_____

Name _____ Lesson 17 - Exercise 1 Day 81

Today you will **begin reading** pages 250b–259 in *Life of Washington*. Have this section read by Exercise 4 of this lesson. Before reading, **study** the vocabulary words listed below.

Vocabulary

ague	illness involving fever and shivering	incision	surgical cut made to the flesh
assent	expression of agreement; approval	intelligibly	in a way that is clear and understood
bleed	to draw blood as medical treatment	intered* (interred)	placed in a grave or tomb
blister of flies	ointment for blistering the skin in order to draw out toxins	oration	a formal speech given at a ceremony
calomel	a white powder used medically to purge toxins	orifice	an opening in the body
convulsed	suffered involuntary muscle contractions	pavilion	outdoor shelter
divert	draw attention from something	sal volatile	a scented solution used as a smelling salt
expired	died	tartar emetic	substance used to induce vomiting
frank	open, honest, and direct		

*Likely a misspelling in the book *Life of Washington*.

Write a paragraph using as many vocabulary words as you can. **Circle** each vocabulary word once you finish.

_____
_____
_____
_____
_____
_____
_____

☐ **Use** index cards to **write** each vocabulary word from this lesson on one side and the definition on the other. **Check** the box when complete.

☐ **Copy** the Scripture verse on an index card. **Memorize** it by the end of this lesson. You may choose the Bible translation or use the one given. **Check** the box when complete.

Jesus said to her, "I am the resurrection and the life. Whoever believes in me, though he die, yet shall he live." John 11:25

Name _____   Lesson 17 - Exercise 2   Day 82

Grammar & Punctuation

Verbal Phrases

A **verbal phrase** functions as a noun, adjective, or adverb and *not* as a verb. It may look like a verb, but it's not a verb, as it has a different function in the sentence.

> *Examples:* The *dreaming* dog was quivering on the sofa. (*dreaming* is used as an adjective to describe *dog*)
> The dog was *dreaming*, and so he quivered. (*dreaming* is the action verb)

Today we will study two types of verbal phrases: **participles** and **gerunds**.

> A **verbal phrase** functions as a noun, adjective, or adverb and *not* as a verb.
>
> A **participle** is a verb that functions as an adjective.
>
> A **participial phrase** is a phrase that includes the participle and any words that modify or complement the participle.

Participles

A **participle** is a verb that functions as an adjective. A **participial phrase** is a phrase that includes the participle and any words that modify or complement the participle.

> *Example:* <u>Training after school each day</u>, the soccer team greatly improved. (*Training* is the participle, and the other words complement the participle. The phrase serves as an adjective, telling us more about the soccer team.)

There are three forms of participles.

- The **present participle** describes a condition that is happening at the same time as the action in the sentence. It is formed by adding the **suffix -*ing***.
- The **past participle** describes a condition that happened before the action in the sentence. It is formed by adding the **suffix -*ed***.
- The **perfect participle** describes an action that has already finished. It is formed by using the word ***having***.

Study the following chart and **fill in** the missing words.

Present Participle (-*ing*) (action same time as verb)	Past Participle (-*ed*) (action before the verb)	Perfect Participle (*having*) (action already finished)
training	trained	having trained
1.	2.	having laughed
creating	3.	4.
5.	submerged	6.

Grammar & Punctuation   Lesson 17, Day 82   181

Name _____ Lesson 17 - Exercise 2 Day 82

Write a sentence for each type of participle.

Past participle:

_____
_____

Perfect participle:

_____
_____

Identify the underlined participial phrases by writing present, past, or perfect on the line. **Circle** the word the participial phrase describes or modifies.

7. _____ The students <u>sitting by the stage</u> are awaiting their turn to receive their diplomas.

8. _____ <u>Drenched by the unforeseen thunderstorm</u>, the hikers sought shelter under the entrance to a cave.

9. _____ My mother, <u>having worked all day in the garden</u>, slumped into her favorite chair and asked for a glass of water.

Gerunds

A **gerund** is a verbal phrase that functions as a noun and is formed with the **suffix -ing**. Present participles also use the suffix -ing, but they function as adjectives, whereas gerunds function as a noun. Identifying the verb in the sentence will help you know whether a phrase is used as a noun or an adjective. A gerund usually comes just before or after the main verb. **Study** the examples to see the difference between a gerund and a present participle.

> A **gerund** is a verbal phrase that functions as a noun and is formed with the **suffix -ing**.

> *Examples:* <u>Jogging along the winding path</u> was exhilarating for the athlete. (gerund phrase, functions as a noun – notice this phrase comes right before the verb *was*)
> <u>Jogging along the winding path</u>, the athlete suddenly came across a fallen tree. (participial phrase, functions as an adjective describing the athlete)

Underline the verbal phrase and **write** present, past, or perfect on the line to identify a participial phrase (adjective). **Write** gerund to identify a noun phrase.

10. _____ My sister really enjoys reading for hours every day.

11. _____ Having said all that I could to explain my point, I needed to leave the conclusions to those around me.

12. _____ Excited about our trip out West, I worked diligently to book all our overnight stays ahead of time.

13. _____ Sewing my own clothing has always been something I've longed to learn how to do.

14. _____ Leaning on the shovel, the construction worker sipped some ice water.

Name _____ Lesson 17 - Exercise 3 Day 83

Communication

Final Draft Due

The **final draft** of your biography is due today. I hope you are proud of the effort you have put in and that you and your instructor have enjoyed reading it.

Before printing or handwriting your final copy, read over the rough draft one last time, thinking of ways you could improve it based on the expectations found in the Biography Rubric. When you are satisfied with your writing, staple the cover page, biography, and works cited page together and give it to your instructor for a final review.

Instructor's signature: _____

Oral Presentation

While the written word comprises a portion of our daily communication, the spoken word is a far larger portion. The term *oral* means by word of mouth. It refers to something that is spoken rather than written. When you write something, such as an essay, you have a chance to make corrections and polish your writing before giving it to someone to read. However, when presenting something orally, you don't have the luxury of deleting a mistake. Perhaps this is why a lot of people are uncomfortable with an oral presentation.

Don't be intimidated! With practice, you can become comfortable speaking in front of others. The good news is that your oral presentation will be based on the biography you just wrote, so you are already very familiar with what you will speak about. You and your instructor will determine the audience you will present to. Some possibilities are as follows: homeschool co-op group, immediate family, group of friends, youth group, Sunday school class, grandparents, or instructor only.

Determine your audience and **plan** to present your biography orally *before* the next communication lesson on Day 88. Your instructor should use the Oral Presentation Rubric for grading.

Audience: _____

Date and time: _____

Converting Your Biography

When presenting your biography, avoid simply reading off the paper. You should know the stories (anecdotes) about your subject well enough to recall them from memory. It is okay to use your paper as a guide, but maintain eye contact with your audience and be aware of your facial expressions, keeping an upbeat attitude and expressing excitement regarding your subject. Use the Oral Presentation Worksheet to help you plan.

If you would like to add visual aids, you may consider displaying a photo of your subject, perhaps a book they have written, or some other item associated with them. This is an opportunity to show others the hard work you put into your biography. Have fun with it!

Communication

Name _____ Lesson 17 - Exercise 3 Day 83

Wisdom Speaks

Copy the proverb.

> *Listen to advice and accept instruction, that you may gain wisdom in the future.* Proverbs 19:20

_____
_____

Using a dictionary or an online search with a parent's permission, **write** the definitions of the words below.

1. advice: _____
   _____

2. instruction: _____
   _____

Write a sentence expressing Proverbs 19:20 in your own words.

_____
_____

A wise person always wants more wisdom. They are willing to be corrected because their deepest desire is to be right with God. A teachable person is one who is willing to listen to advice and receive instruction, not letting pride stand in the way.

It is interesting that this verse mentions the future because by listening to sound instruction *now*, you are setting yourself up to be a person who can increase in wisdom your whole life. What a wonderful system the Lord set up — that the younger can learn from the older and avoid foolish mistakes.

Write a paragraph praising God for providing you with advice and instruction through His Word and through the wisdom of those who instruct you.

_____
_____
_____
_____
_____
_____
_____
_____
_____
_____

Name _____   Lesson 17 - Exercise 4   Day 84

Worldview & Literary Analysis

Literary Device: Archetype

An **archetype** is a literary device that refers to a universal symbol or pattern that recurs in stories and other forms of literature across different cultures and time periods. When the author sets up an archetype, it is for the purpose of connecting the reader with a character, situation, or symbol. Archetypes are universally recognized and therefore allow for greater understanding by most readers.

> An **archetype** is a literary device that refers to a universal symbol or pattern that recurs in stories and other forms of literature across different cultures and time periods.

Three main categories of archetypes are *character*, *situational*, and *symbolic*. **Study** the examples.

Archetypes	
Character Archetype	the hero, the villain, the mother or father figure, the creator, the jester
Situational Archetype	a lost love, an orphan destined for greatness, death/rebirth, a fall from greatness, a quest, light vs. darkness
Symbolic Archetype	trees (nature or life), fire (destruction or creativity), darkness (evil or despair), a garden (love or fertility), an island (isolation or loneliness)

Reed uses *character archetypes* by linking her characters to the hero, the villain, the savior, etc. We also observe situations like the struggle between good and evil (light and darkness). *Situational archetypes* are evident in stories of friends sacrificing for each other, the apparently weak Americans overcoming the more powerful English, and evil plans being thwarted. *Symbolic archetypes* are used many times with references to biblical accounts and by the mention of Washington's spring — the idea of pure, clean, and refreshing water symbolizes what Washington brought to his countrymen.

Finish reading pages 250b–259 in *Life of Washington* and **respond** to the following.

1. "But his Creator was soon about to call him from all earthy duties" (p. 251) is an example of **what** literary device?

   _____

2. **What** one word does the author use to describe the task of giving an account of Washington's final days? _____

3. One of Washington's attendants, Tobias Lear, wrote a statement regarding Washington's final days. **Summarize** what happened on Thursday and Friday from his account. (p. 251–252)

   _____
   _____
   _____
   _____
   _____
   _____

Name _____   Lesson 17 - Exercise 4   Day 84

4. **List** three of the medical treatments Washington received during his brief illness. (p. 253–256)

   a. _____

   b. _____

   c. _____

5. Considering the entire account of Tobias Lear, in a paragraph, **describe** his relationship with Washington. **Give** direct quotes or examples from the text. (p. 251–257)

   _____
   _____
   _____
   _____
   _____
   _____
   _____
   _____

6. **Where** was Washington's wife as he expired (passed away)? (p. 257)

   _____
   _____

7. In a letter from the Senate to President John Adams regarding Washington's death, we see the statement, "Our country mourns a father" (p. 258). **What** category of archetype would this fall under?

   _____

8. **What** is written over the tomb of George Washington? (p. 259)

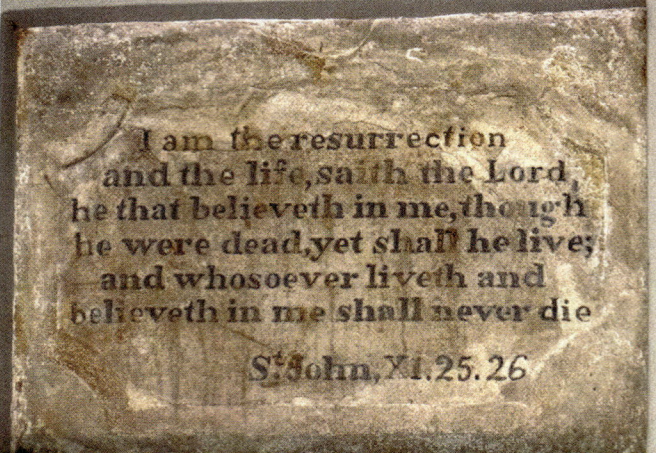

   _____
   _____

Language Lessons for a Living Education Level 10

Name _____   Lesson 17 – Exercise 5   Day 85

Review

☐ **Update** the Reading List chart with books you have read this week.

☐ **Recite** John 11:25 from memory to your instructor.

Vocabulary Review

Match each word to the correct definition.

a. ague	e. calomel	i. frank	m. oration	q. tartar emetic
b. assent	f. convulsed	j. incision	n. orifice	
c. bleed	g. divert	k. intelligibly	o. pavilion	
d. blister of flies	h. expired	l. intered (interred)	p. sal volatile	

1. _____ died
2. _____ placed in a grave or tomb
3. _____ open, honest, and direct
4. _____ an opening in the body
5. _____ outdoor shelter
6. _____ draw attention from something
7. _____ surgical cut made to the flesh
8. _____ expression of agreement; approval
9. _____ ointment for blistering the skin in order to draw out toxins
10. _____ substance used to induce vomiting
11. _____ white powder used to purge toxins
12. _____ scented solution used as smelling salt
13. _____ suffered involuntary muscle contractions
14. _____ in a way that is clear and understood
15. _____ illness involving fever, shivering
16. _____ to draw blood as a medical treatment
17. _____ a formal speech given at a ceremony

Grammar & Punctuation Review

1. **Define** verbal phrase.

   _____

   _____

Match the verbal phrase to the example given.

2. _____ perfect participle   a. same time as sentence action; formed by adding -ing
3. _____ present participle   b. action has already finished; formed by using the word *having*
4. _____ past participle   c. happened before sentence action; formed by adding -ed
5. _____ gerund   d. functions as a noun; formed by adding -ing

Name _____ Lesson 17 - Exercise 5 Day 85

Underline the verbal phrase and **write** present, past, or perfect on the line to identify a participial phrase (adjective), or **write** gerund to identify a noun phrase.

6. _____ The women running in the race were running for a cause that was dear to their hearts.

7. _____ Preparing our property for winter is something my entire family participates in.

8. _____ Erin, thrilled for the chance to participate in the choir, practiced every evening in her bedroom.

9. _____ The plan, having been thought through for many months, was finally put into place.

10. _____ The rabbit who hopped out of the cage was quickly caught by the little boy.

Communication Review

1. **List** three aspects of writing that you feel you have improved while writing your biography.

    a. _____

    b. _____

    c. _____

Worldview & Literary Analysis Review

1. **Define** an archetype.

    _____
    _____

2. **List** two examples for each archetype.

    a. Character archetype: _____

    b. Situational archetype: _____

    c. Symbolic archetype: _____

3. **Record** what is written over Washington's tomb.

    _____
    _____

Special Feature

Lesson 18

Biography Excerpt: Eldridge* Gerry (1744–1814) by Tim LaHaye

Said M.E. Bradford of Gerry, "Few Americans of his generation had so much to do with the nation's history, performed on so large a stage, and yet retained so intense an identity with their provincial origins as did Eldridge Gerry."[1] He never lost sight of his mission to represent the state of Massachusetts. Although he refused to sign the Constitution because it did not contain a bill of rights, he was nevertheless very influential in its formation. He gave 119 speeches during the Convention, offered several motions and seconds, and successfully modified many of the provisions from the original Virginia Plan.

"No one in that Philadelphia meeting spoke more forcefully for the Bill of Rights than did Eldgridge [sic] Gerry."[2] He considered a bill of rights necessary to restrain the federal government's authority. While Gerry recognized that total democracy leads to anarchy, he also realized that a limited government was essential. If he could see our present government of over three million bureaucrats and employees, he would probably be tempted to proclaim, "I told you so!" However, all our Founding Fathers would probably say the same.[3]

*The name "Eldridge" is a misspelling. The correct spelling is "Elbridge."

1. **Record** the reason Gerry did not sign the Constitution.
   _____
   _____

2. Use a dictionary or online search with a parent's permission and **define** the following words.
   a. democracy: _____
   _____

   b. anarchy: _____
   _____

3. **Write** a one-paragraph response sharing your opinion regarding Gerry's refusal to sign the Constitution. **Discuss** your response with your parent or instructor.
   _____
   _____
   _____
   _____
   _____
   _____
   _____

---

1 Endnote from excerpt: M.E. Bradford, *A Worthy Company* (Marlborough, NH: Plymouth Rock Foundation, 1982), p. 181.
2 Endnote from excerpt: Ibid., p. 9.
3 Biography excerpt from: LaHaye, Tim. *Faith of Our Founding Fathers*. Master Books, 2022, p. 206–207.

Name _____ Lesson 18 – Exercise 1 Day 86

Today you will **begin reading** pages 260–277 (the conclusion) in *Life of Washington*. Have this section read by Exercise 4 of this lesson. Before reading, **study** the vocabulary words listed below.

Vocabulary

assiduity	close attention to one's behavior	**maxims**	short statements expressing a truth
canon	general law or principle used to judge	**quires**	collections of paper, usually 24 sheets
choler	anger	**partiality**	unfair bias; favoritism
culpable	deserving of blame	**pensive**	engaged in deep thought
disparagement	unkind remarks showing disrespect	**precept**	a rule to regulate behavior or thought
folio	piece of paper, numbered on the front side	**solicitude**	care or concern about someone or something
fraternal	like brothers; brotherly	**sublime**	excellence or beauty that inspires admiration
imbibing	absorbing or assimilating	**tractable**	easy to influence or control
inculcated	instilled by constant instruction	**vestryman**	an assistant within the church
logarithm	the power to which a number must be raised to get another number	**vitiate**	spoil or impair the quality of

4. **Write** a sentence using the words *pensive* and *fraternal*. Include a prepositional phrase used as an adjective. (Day 72)

_____

_____

5. **Write** a sentence using the words *vestryman* and *canon*. Include a prepositional phrase used as an adverb. (Day 72)

_____

_____

☐ **Use** index cards to **write** each vocabulary word from this lesson on one side and the definition on the other. **Check** the box when complete.

☐ **Copy** the Scripture verse on an index card. **Memorize** it by the end of this lesson. You may choose the Bible translation or use the one given. **Check** the box when complete.

Blessed is the man who walks not in the counsel of the wicked, nor stands in the way of sinners, nor sits in the seat of scoffers; but his delight is in the law of the Lord, and on his law he meditates day and night. Psalm 1:1–2

Lesson 18, Day 86 Language Lessons for a Living Education Level 10

Name _____ Lesson 18 – Exercise 2 Day 87

Grammar & Punctuation

Verb Phrases: Infinitives

In the last grammar lesson, you learned that participles and gerunds look like verbs, but they function as adjectives and nouns. An **infinitive** is a verbal phrase that can function as a noun, adjective, or adverb. Infinitives consist of the word *to* plus a verb form (*to* + verb). An **infinitive phrase** includes the infinitive plus any modifiers or objects. **Study** the chart.

> An **infinitive** is a verbal phrase that can function as a noun, adjective, or adverb.

Infinitive Functions	
Infinitive as a noun	*To conquer my fears* was the main reason for the climb. (serves as a subject noun)
Infinitive as an adjective	The teacher gave out several verses *to be memorized*. (describes verses)
Infinitive as an adverb	We work hard *to bring honor to God*. (tells *why*)
Prepositional phrase, *not* an infinitive	After swimming, we went *to the grocery store*. (The word *to* followed by a noun, not a verb, means this is a prepositional phrase, not an infinitive.)

Infinitives as nouns are easier to spot if you identify the main verb in the sentence because the noun infinitive will usually come directly *before* or directly *after* the verb.

> *Example:* Our aim is *to improve*. OR *To improve* is our aim. (As a noun, the infinitive can come right before or right after the verb *is*.)

Infinitives as adjectives can be identified because they usually follow a noun in the sentence.

> *Example:* The place *to eat pizza* is Big Al's. (As an adjective, the infinitive comes after the noun *place*.)

Infinitives as adverbs can be identified by asking the adverb questions: *how, when, why, where*.

> *Example:* We pray over our dinner *to thank God*. (As an adverb, the infinitive tells *why* we pray.)

Identify the underlined phrase as a noun, adjective, or adverb if it is an infinitive, OR **label** it as a prepositional phrase.

1. _____ In my opinion, the best apples <u>to bake</u> are Granny Smith.
2. _____ <u>To do well at sports</u>, you must practice a lot.
3. _____ <u>To enjoy winter</u> is my goal this year!
4. _____ <u>To fear the Lord</u> is the wisest decision you could make.
5. _____ We enjoyed eating dinner and then went <u>to the ice cream shop</u>.
6. _____ Jessica is the person <u>to ask about jewelry making</u>.
7. _____ Rianna is excited <u>to meet her pen pal</u>.

Name _____   Lesson 18 – Exercise 2   Day 87

8. **Write** a sentence using an infinitive as a noun.

   _____
   _____

9. **Write** a sentence using an infinitive as an adjective.

   _____
   _____

10. **Write** a sentence using an infinitive as an adverb.

    _____
    _____

Split Infinitives

When a word or phrase appears between *to* and the verb, it is called a **split infinitive**. These are considered by some to be improper and should be avoided. It is possible to fix a split infinitive by restructuring the sentence.

> *Examples:* This is the kind of horse I hope *to someday buy*. (incorrect: *someday* is between *to* and *buy*)
> This is the kind of horse I hope *to buy someday*. (correct: split is fixed by moving *someday*)
> Eric tried *to quietly walk* across the floor. (incorrect: *quietly* is between *to* and *walk*)
> Eric *quietly walked* across the floor. (correct: split is fixed by rewording the sentence)

Fix these split infinitives by rewording the sentences.

11. My dad began to quickly pick up the shards of glass off the floor.

    _____
    _____

12. Melanie promised to always feed the dog on time.

    _____
    _____

13. We expected to easily profit enough money for our missions trip.

    _____
    _____

Review It!

First, **place** parentheses around the prepositional phrases (Day 37), then **underline** any adjectives.

14. Over the course of three hours, my friend Angela sewed ten Christmas ornaments.
15. Despite the heat, the exhausted boys completed the treacherous hike up the steep mountain.
16. My Aunt Rachel was the fancy, older lady with the dog.

Name _____ Lesson 18 - Exercise 3 Day 88

💬 Communication

Oral Presentation Due

When you have completed the oral presentation of your biography, **have** your instructor sign below.

Instructor's signature: _____

Oral Presentation Feedback

Expressing yourself verbally (orally) in a way that others can understand is something you will need to improve on throughout your life. "Finding the words" to share your thoughts and opinions is a skill that needs to be practiced. Sometimes this will be in a more formal setting, like a presentation at work, and sometimes in an informal setting, such as a family meeting about chores not getting done. Whatever the setting, communication skills are vital. Let's look at how you communicated in your presentation.

Write a paragraph describing how you felt before making your oral biography presentation. Were you nervous? Confident? Excited?

_____
_____
_____
_____
_____
_____
_____
_____
_____

Write a paragraph describing the presentation. Who was in your audience? Did you use visual aids? Did you communicate everything you wanted to? Did you forget anything? Did your words flow smoothly, or did you find that you were losing your place? Did your audience give feedback?

_____
_____
_____
_____
_____
_____
_____
_____
_____

Communication

Name _____ Lesson 18 - Exercise 3 Day 88

Biography Feedback

Write a three-paragraph response describing your biography writing experience. In the first paragraph, explain what drew you to choose your subject. In the second paragraph, relate something you discovered about your subject that surprised you. And finally, in your third paragraph, share your opinion about the biography writing experience. Describe what you enjoyed about the process, what you found challenging, and what was most rewarding.

Have your instructor read your response, discuss it with you, and sign below.

Instructor's signature: _____

Name _____   Lesson 18 - Exercise 4   Day 89

Worldview & Literary Analysis

You have reached the conclusion to *Life of Washington*! I hope you have enjoyed looking back into the rich history of the United States through the life of one of its greatest benefactors. The author, Anna C. Reed, clearly wanted this book not only to relate a story but also to inspire moral character and a worldview that places God in the center.

When George Washington was a young teenager, he compiled a list of rules referred to as *The Rules of Civility and Decent Behaviour [Behavior] in Company and Conversation*. This is often shortened to *Washington's Rules of Civility*. It is believed that Washington was inspired by a list of behaviors originally written by French Jesuits (priests and missionaries) in the 1500s. George wrote these 110 rules and used them to guide his personal behavior and interactions with others.

Finish reading the conclusion on pages 260–277 in *Life of Washington* and **respond** to the following.

Reed includes a few selections from *The Rules of Civility* to show the reader "their general character" (p. 260). **Rewrite** the following rules in your own words. You may also "modernize" them to fit today's world.

"Play not the peacock, looking everywhere about you to see if you be well decked, if your shoes fit well, if your stockings sit neatly, and clothes handsomely" (p. 261).

_____
_____
_____
_____

"Be not curious to know the affairs of others; neither approach to those that speak in private" (p. 261).

_____
_____
_____

"Come not near the books or writings of any one so as to read them, unless desired, nor give your opinion of them unasked; also look not nigh when another is writing a letter" (p. 261).

_____
_____
_____

"Read no letters, books, or papers in company; but when there is a necessity for doing it, you must ask leave" (p. 261).

_____
_____

Worldview & Literary Analysis

Name _____   Lesson 18 - Exercise 4   Day 89

On page 264, we see a portion of a letter from Washington to his young nephew who was under his care. Washington states, "Your future character and reputation will depend very much, if not entirely, upon the habits and manners which you contract in the present period of your life." **Share** your opinion about this advice. Do you believe it to be true?

_____
_____
_____

The attitude of Washington's mother was that "the most learned education is useless" without "virtuous principles" (p. 267). **What** do you think she meant by this?

_____
_____
_____

1. At one point, it was proposed to make George Washington a king. **Record** Washington's response to this proposal. (p. 268–269)

   _____
   _____
   _____
   _____

2. Reed shares a letter written by Washington's granddaughter in which she relates the following: "He spoke little, generally never of himself. I never heard him relate a single act of his life during the war" (p. 273). **What** does this observation reveal about Washington's character?

   _____
   _____

3. **Fill in** the blanks from this statement found on page 276.

   "Through all his course of _____ and _____, in adversity

   or prosperity, he was just _____, _____, honest,

   _____, brave, humane, modest,—a real lover of his _____, and an humble

   _____ of God. Was he not worthy of your _____?"

List two aspects of Washington's character you would like to imitate.

a. _____
   _____
   _____

b. _____
   _____
   _____

Name _____   Lesson 18 - Exercise 5   Day 90

Review

Update the Reading List chart with books you have read this week.

Recite Psalm 1:1–2 from memory to your instructor.

Vocabulary Review

Match each word to the correct definition.

a. assiduity	e. disparagement	i. inculcated	m. pensive	q. sublime
b. canon	f. folio	j. logarithm	n. precept	r. tractable
c. choler	g. fraternal	k. maxims	o. quires	s. vestryman
d. culpable	h. imbibing	l. partiality	p. solicitude	t. vitiate

1. _____ easy to influence or control
2. _____ deserving of blame
3. _____ spoil or impair the quality of
4. _____ like brothers; brotherly
5. _____ unfair bias; favoritism
6. _____ assistant within the church
7. _____ engaged in deep thought
8. _____ absorbing or assimilating
9. _____ anger
10. _____ excellence or beauty that inspires admiration
11. _____ care or concern about someone or something
12. _____ general law or principle used to judge
13. _____ collections of paper, usually 24 sheets
14. _____ short statements expressing truth
15. _____ rule to regulate behavior or thought
16. _____ instilled by constant instruction
17. _____ unkind remarks showing disrespect
18. _____ close attention to one's behavior
19. _____ piece of paper numbered on front
20. _____ power a number must be raised to get another number

Grammar & Punctuation Review

1. **Define** infinitive.

   _____
   _____

2. **Explain** what an infinitive consists of.

   _____
   _____

3. **Explain** the difference between an infinitive and a prepositional phrase that begins with the word *to*.

   _____
   _____

Review   Lesson 18, Day 90   197

Name _____ Lesson 18 - Exercise 5 Day 90

Identify the underlined phrase as a noun, adjective, or adverb if it is an infinitive phrase, OR **write** preposition if it is a prepositional phrase.

4. _____ <u>To live in a free country</u> should not be taken for granted.
5. _____ Jesus is coming <u>to take his Bride</u>, the Church, to heaven with Him.
6. _____ Without a doubt, the town park is the best place <u>to ride my skateboard</u>.
7. _____ So often when we go <u>to church</u>, I find myself realizing how thankful I am for my brothers and sisters in Christ.

8. **Rewrite** the sentence to fix the split infinitive.

> The state championships were something I hoped to someday attend.

_____
_____

Communication Review

In the last lesson, you made an oral presentation. Did you know that the Apostles gave oral presentations frequently as they shared the gospel? Sometimes their oral presentations were before hostile crowds. **Read** Acts 2:14–41.

1. In 2–3 sentences, **describe** the result of Peter's oral presentation.

_____
_____
_____
_____

Worldview & Literary Analysis Review

Copy the following *Washington's Rules of Civility*.

> "When you speak of God or His attributes, let it be seriously and with reverence."

_____
_____

> "Speak not evil of the absent, for it is unjust."

_____
_____

Special Feature

Lesson 19

Biblical Autobiography Excerpt: The Apostle Paul, Philippians 3:4–11

Many writers in the Bible speak in the first person and give us a glimpse into their personal lives. The Apostle Paul had much to say about how his life and heart were both dramatically altered after his encounter with Christ. **Read** these selections from Philippians that are autobiographical in nature.

> [T]hough I myself have reason for confidence in the flesh also. If anyone else thinks he has reason for confidence in the flesh, I have more: circumcised on the eighth day, of the people of Israel, of the tribe of Benjamin, a Hebrew of Hebrews; as to the law, a Pharisee; as to zeal, a persecutor of the church; as to righteousness under the law, blameless. (vv. 4–6)

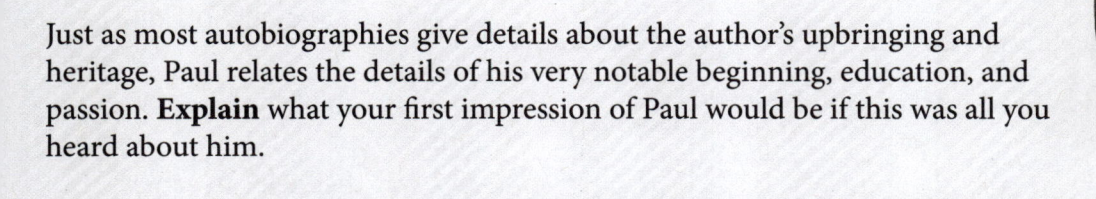

Just as most autobiographies give details about the author's upbringing and heritage, Paul relates the details of his very notable beginning, education, and passion. **Explain** what your first impression of Paul would be if this was all you heard about him.

_____
_____
_____
_____
_____
_____

> But whatever gain I had, I counted as loss for the sake of Christ. Indeed, I count everything as loss because of the surpassing worth of knowing Christ Jesus my Lord. For his sake I have suffered the loss of all things and count them as rubbish, in order that I may gain Christ and be found in him, not having a righteousness of my own that comes from the law, but that which comes through faith in Christ, the righteousness from God that depends on faith—that I may know him and the power of his resurrection, and may share his sufferings, becoming like him in his death, that by any means possible I may attain the resurrection from the dead. (vv. 7–11)

Verses 7–11 sound very different from Paul's opening statement about himself. **Describe** how Paul felt about all his accomplishments once he had come to know Christ.

_____
_____
_____
_____
_____

Name _____ Lesson 19 - Exercise 1 Day 91

The third quarter Worldview & Literary Analysis days will feature excerpts from the chapter "The Truth" in the book *Gifted Mind*, an autobiography of Dr. Raymond Damadian, inventor of the magnetic resonance imaging (MRI) machine. **Study** these words that are bolded in the excerpt you will read on Day 94.

Vocabulary

back-story (backstory)	history or background	**insatiable**	cannot be satisfied
contraption	machine or device with a strange appearance	**local**	belonging to a particular area
embroidery	decorative designs by needlepoint	**MRI**	magnetic resonance imaging; medical scanning
exhilarating	strong feelings of excitement; elation	**perseverance**	persistence despite difficulty or delay
furrowed	face or forehead marked with lines or wrinkles	**ridicule**	making fun of someone or something
genesis	creation or beginning	**strategically**	in a way that helps to achieve a plan
herringbone	pattern with short parallel lines resembling fish bones	**tweed**	rough-surfaced woolen cloth originating in Scotland
industry	processing or manufacturing particular goods in factories	**unique**	only one of its kind; unlike others

1. **Write** a sentence using the words *contraption* and *industry*. Include an action verb (Day 12) and an adverb (Day 72).

   _____

   _____

2. Use the word bank to **fill in** the blanks.

   | contraption | genesis | insatiable | perseverance | ridicule | unique |

   Despite facing _____ over the _____ I had built, I hoped my _____ would pay off. The _____ of my idea came about due to my _____ desire to create something _____.

☐ **Use** index cards to **write** each vocabulary word from this lesson on one side and the definition on the other. **Check** the box when complete.

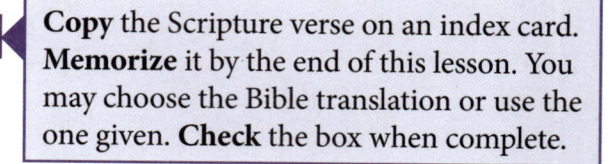

☐ **Copy** the Scripture verse on an index card. **Memorize** it by the end of this lesson. You may choose the Bible translation or use the one given. **Check** the box when complete.

For this reason I bow my knees before the Father, from whom every family in heaven and on earth is named, that according to the riches of his glory he may grant you to be strengthened with power through his Spirit in your inner being. Ephesians 3:14–16

Name _____ Lesson 19 - Exercise 2 Day 92

Grammar & Punctuation

Pronouns

A **pronoun** takes the place of a noun in a sentence to avoid repetition of the noun. It can be singular (referring to one) or plural (referring to more than one). Pronouns are listed as one of the eight parts of speech. There are several types of pronouns, and some categories overlap. Learning how to use them properly will help you communicate more accurately and efficiently.

> A **pronoun** takes the place of a noun in a sentence to avoid repetition of the noun.
>
> The **antecedent** is the noun the pronoun takes the place of.

Examples: Jackson lost his position on the team. Jackson was really upset. (no pronouns used)
Jackson lost his position on the team. *He* was really upset. (pronoun used)

The **antecedent** is the noun the pronoun takes the place of. In the example, the antecedent is *Jackson*. To find the antecedent, look for the noun the pronoun is referring to. There isn't always an antecedent.

Circle the antecedent and **underline** the pronoun.

1. When Eric got a job and moved into a new apartment, he felt very independent.
2. Lacie always loved reading historical fiction. It was her favorite genre by far.

Study the chart showing three types of pronouns.

Subject (Personal) Pronouns	Object Pronouns	Relative Pronouns
Replace the subject	Object of a verb	Connect relative clauses
I, we, you, he, she, it, they	me, us, you, her, him, it, them	that, what, which, who, whom
You are my best friend.	Jane gave *me* a ride home.	The cat *that* napped awoke.
He is my uncle.	The bird belongs to *him*.	The man *who* knocked came in.

Subject pronouns usually appear at the beginning of a sentence, while object pronouns appear later since they are the object of the verb. (*example:* I gave *her* a hug.)

Underline the pronouns. **Circle** any antecedents. **Label** the pronouns as **SP** (subject), **OP** (object), or **RP** (relative). There may be more than one pronoun per sentence.

3. The lumberjack who was injured on the job finally recovered enough to return to work today.
4. I would love to attend the same university that Erica went to.
5. Every time I visit Charlene, she bakes me a different type of pie.
6. The car, which had a flat tire, was stuck on the side of the road for over a week.
7. I would rather go with you to the concert.

Write a sentence containing a subject pronoun and a relative pronoun.

_____

_____

Name _____ Lesson 19 - Exercise 2 Day 92

Study the chart showing three types of pronouns.

Demonstrative Pronouns	Indefinite Pronouns	Reflexive Pronouns
Point to or replace antecedent	Non-specific	Ending in *-self* or *-selves*
that, this, these, those	*one, other, none, some,*	*myself, yourself, himself, herself,*
Great *idea*. **That** will work!	*anybody, everybody, no one*	*itself, oneself, themselves,*
He picked up the *book* and said,	*Nobody* seemed to care.	*yourselves, ourselves*
"**This** is for my wife."	*Everybody* was there today.	She took **herself** out of the game.

Underline the pronouns. **Circle** any antecedents. **Label** the pronouns as **DP** (demonstrative), **IP** (indefinite), **RFP** (reflexive), **SP** (subject), **OP** (object), or **RP** (relative). There may be more than one pronoun per sentence. **Refer** to the two pronoun charts from this lesson.

8. What an incredible idea. That is the best plan anybody has come up with so far!
9. Kristy told the nurse at the office, "Don't blame yourself."
10. If you let yourself sleep in too late, it will be difficult to fall asleep tonight.
11. I knew those were the healthiest-looking chickens in the coop.
12. The horse found itself on the wrong side of that fence once again.

Write a sentence containing a demonstrative pronoun and a reflexive pronoun.
_____
_____

Review It!

Write a complex sentence (Day 52) that includes a subordinating conjunction (Day 27).
_____
_____

Fill in the blanks to define an infinitive. (Day 87)

13. An infinitive is a _____ phrase that can _____ as a _____, _____, or _____. Infinitives consist of the word _____ plus a verb form (*to* + verb).

☐ Using your index cards, **copy** the six types of pronouns taught in this lesson. Include the title and examples for each. **Check** the box when you are done.

Name _____ Lesson 19 - Exercise 3 Day 93

Communication

Autobiography Assignment

In the first semester, you wrote a biography (an account of someone else's life) and read through the biography *Life of Washington* by Anna C. Reed. Throughout the third quarter, you will have an opportunity to write an autobiography (an account of your life) and read the first chapter of *Gifted Mind*, an autobiography of Dr. Raymond Damadian, inventor of the MRI. While this first chapter does not cover the life of Dr. Damadian, it gives a glimpse into the purpose of his autobiography. It will challenge you to consider the purpose of your autobiography and what you want others to "take away" after reading it.

Writing a biography required research and citation as you scoured sources in search of the person's life details. An autobiography will require some research but *not* the type you would look for in a book or online. Since this account is about *you*, asking parents, relatives, and friends for details, opinions, and quotes will enhance your autobiography and give credibility to it. Since most of us cannot remember details of our very early childhood, asking parents or guardians is the best place to start. Some of you may even be adopted or may not be living with your parents. You have a special story all your own, and you can be sure God is working in your life!

When Christians write an autobiography, they consider not only what they want others to know about them, but also what they want to communicate about God. In the chapter "The Truth" in *Gifted Mind*, Dr. Damadian is more concerned about communicating the truth about God than he is about impressing the reader with his life and abilities.

As you work through the details you wish to include in your autobiography, look for a central theme or secondary purpose (Day 19). Besides the details of your life, what is it that you want to teach the reader and encourage them toward? How does your life demonstrate a particular truth or character trait? How does your life prove the goodness or mercy of God? These are just some questions to ask, but there are plenty more. Pray about what God would have you focus on as you write.

Assignment Details

- Your autobiography needs to be 4–6 pages typed with a 12-point font and double spaced or 7–8 pages handwritten, skipping every other line. It will include a cover page with artwork.

- The rough draft is due on Day 123 of Lesson 25. The final draft is due on Day 128 of Lesson 26.

- Throughout the next few lessons, you will gather information and learn autobiography writing skills, then you will put all the pieces together and write your autobiography.

You will answer more questions in future lessons, but today begin by **recording** basic details.

Full name and nickname (if you have one): _____

Date and location of birth: _____

Parents and siblings: _____

_____

Name _____ Lesson 19 - Exercise 3 Day 93

Wisdom Speaks

Copy the proverb.

> *Cease to hear instruction, my son, and you will stray from the words of knowledge.* Proverbs 19:27

_____
_____

Using a dictionary or an online search with a parent's permission, **write** the definitions.

1. cease: _____
   _____

2. stray (verb): _____
   _____

Based on the words you just defined, **paraphrase** Proverbs 19:27 in your own words.

_____
_____

Interestingly, the word "cease" is associated with a gradual ending, not an abrupt one. That implies that ceasing to hear instruction happens gradually. No one wakes up one day and thinks, "I am going to refuse to listen to instructions from now on!" Instead, a person is deceived and slowly strays away from listening to truth and wisdom. It begins with "plugging one's ears" and refusing to actively listen. Remember that listening is a huge part of communication. It is how we receive what is spoken by others and by God. Without the act of listening, there is no communication. However, listening is not just hearing with the ears, but receiving in the heart and mind and then applying it to life.

Write a paragraph about the importance of listening to *and* applying instruction. **Include** a simile.

_____
_____
_____
_____
_____
_____
_____
_____
_____

Worldview & Literary Analysis

Read the following excerpt from the chapter "The Truth" found in *Gifted Mind*.

From where I sit in my Long Island office, I am surrounded by vivid reminders of over 50 years of science and research. Volumes of books, papers, and research are stacked neatly (or sometimes not-so-neatly) on shelves or **strategically** placed on my desk — every one of them with a **unique** story to tell. Across the room, I can see a photograph of me and President Ronald Reagan in which he awarded me the National Medal of Technology. Behind me hangs an **embroidery** depicting the first-ever **MRI** scan of a human being. Looking to my right, I see an entire wall is devoted to pictures of my children and precious grandchildren. Each of these pictures forever captures a moment in time, some memorable snapshot of my life, family, and work.

But one of these photographs tells a particularly interesting story. It's a black and white photo of a mustached man seated inside an odd-looking **contraption** made of wood and canvas. The man is clothed in a thick wool sweater and an equally dense wool overcoat. Leather boots, laced and buckled up over his calves, add a touch of adventure to his outfit. Leather gloves protect his hands from cold weather. What looks like a **herringbone tweed** cap is tightly perched atop his head. And a nearly extinguished hand-rolled cigarette dangles from his mustached mouth.

The **furrowed** brow on the man's face appears to say, "Well, get on with it. Hurry and take the photo and get out of the way."

But there is an interesting **back-story** [backstory] behind this particular picture, and one that affects every one of us today. The picture has its **genesis** in Dayton, Ohio. It's the 1890s, and two **local** brothers have decided to start their own bicycle shop. With hard work and **perseverance**, before long they expanded their bicycle business to some five locations on the west side of Dayton. But with competition rapidly growing in the bicycle **industry** in those days, the brothers decided it wasn't enough just to sell other company's products. So they decided to invent their own brand of bicycle, which they eventually succeeded in doing. Their top-of-the-line model was called the "Van Cleve," which sold for $65, while the less expensive "St. Clair" could be bought for $42.50. Neither of these was considered "minor purchases" in a time when the average American income was just over $300 per year. Today, over a hundred years later, only five of the bicycles manufactured by the brothers' company are known to exist.

But even in the 1800s, cyclists felt the "need for speed," and a brisk bicycle ride was often compared to the **exhilarating** sensations a bird must feel when it flies. This concept sparked an **insatiable** curiosity in the two men, and soon they began setting their sights on creating the first-ever heavier-than-air flying machine. For some six years they tested and re-tested their ideas, and after many failures and trial runs, on December 17, 1903, their previously **ridiculed** idea finally became a reality. On that historic day, Wilbur and Orville Wright successfully made four short flights at Kitty Hawk, North Carolina. The age of flight was officially born.[1]

---

1 Damadian, Raymond. *Gifted Mind*. New Leaf Publishing Group, LLC, 2015, p. 7–8.

Name _____   Lesson 19 - Exercise 4   Day 94

At the beginning of this course, you learned the difference between a biography and an autobiography (Day 3). *Life of Washington* was a biography written by Anna C. Reed in which she focused on the character of Washington and his relationship with God. Today, you read an excerpt from the book *Gifted Mind* by Dr. Raymond Damadian. This book is an autobiography, written with the help of Jeff Kinley. Dr. Damadian writes about his own life, his discoveries about God's truth, and his invention of the MRI. This course will cover the first chapter of *Gifted Mind* throughout the third quarter.

Respond to the following regarding today's reading excerpt.

1. Dr. Damadian opens his biography with a scene of him sitting in his office. **What** items does he describe as having a "unique story to tell"?
   _____

2. **What** does each picture on the wall tell him about?
   _____
   _____

3. Dr. Damadian chooses to open his autobiography not with his birth, but with a "walk down memory lane" in his office after clearly having lived many years. Here he uses the literary device *in medias res* (Day 29). **Why** do you think he chooses to open with this scene?
   _____
   _____
   _____

Dr. Damadian immediately shifts from these "snapshots" of his life into an anecdote about the Wright brothers and their ridiculed pursuit of flight. He uses this anecdote because it relates to his own pursuit of truth and scientific discovery. **Write** a paragraph talking about the many ways the Wright brothers' invention of the airplane has affected your life today. **Think** of the many things that could not happen without air travel.

_____
_____
_____
_____
_____
_____
_____
_____

Lesson 19, Day 94   Language Lessons for a Living Education Level 10

Name _____   Lesson 19 - Exercise 5   Day 95

Review

☐ **Update** the Reading List chart with books you have read this week.

☐ **Recite** Ephesians 3:14–16 from memory to your instructor.

Vocabulary Review

Match each word to the correct definition.

a.	back-story (backstory)	e.	furrowed	i.	insatiable	m.	ridicule
b.	contraption	f.	genesis	j.	local	n.	strategically
c.	embroidery	g.	herringbone	k.	MRI	o.	tweed
d.	exhilarating	h.	industry	l.	perseverance	p.	unique

1. _____ cannot be satisfied
2. _____ belonging to a particular area
3. _____ strong feelings of excitement
4. _____ processing or manufacturing goods
5. _____ only one of its kind
6. _____ magnetic resonance imaging
7. _____ pattern resembling fish bones
8. _____ rough-surfaced woolen cloth
9. _____ make fun of someone or something
10. _____ persistence despite difficulty
11. _____ history or background
12. _____ marked with lines or wrinkles
13. _____ decorative designs by needlepoint
14. _____ machine with strange appearance
15. _____ creation or beginning
16. _____ in a way that helps achieve a plan

Grammar & Punctuation Review

Circle the antecedent and **underline** the pronoun.

1. After hours of studying, Melody finally memorized all the books of the Bible, and she felt so accomplished.
2. The tractor broke down on the side of the road, and it obviously wasn't going to be moved anytime soon.

Underline the pronouns. **Circle** any antecedents. **Label** the pronouns as **SP** (subject), **OP** (object), or **RP** (relative). There may be more than one pronoun per sentence, and some antecedents may be pronouns too.

3. The horses always stay very close to the barn when they hear a thunderstorm coming.
4. We went to the children's museum that features antique toys.
5. When we went to the lake, Mom gave me a surprise picnic lunch!

Name _____ Lesson 19 - Exercise 5 Day 95

Underline the pronouns. **Circle** any antecedents. **Label** the pronouns as **DP** (demonstrative), **IP** (indefinite), **RFP** (reflexive), **SP** (subject), **OP** (object), or **RP** (relative). There may be more than one pronoun per sentence.

6. He gave himself permission to enjoy some cookies.

7. These haybales are soaking wet from all the rain last night.

8. Everybody will notice that rainbow!

Communication Review

1. In your own words, **describe** the type of research an autobiography will need and **how** it differs from the research needed for a biography.

   _____
   _____
   _____
   _____

2. **Describe** what Christians should consider when writing an autobiography.

   _____
   _____

Copy the proverb.

> *Cease to hear instruction, my son, and you will stray from the words of knowledge.*
> Proverbs 19:27

   _____
   _____

Worldview & Literary Analysis Review

Dr. Damadian had photos on his office walls that told a story about his life. If someone only had your family photos, **describe** what impression they may have of you and your life.

   _____
   _____
   _____

If you were to use the literary device *in medias res* to open your autobiography, **describe** the scene in your life would you use.

   _____
   _____

Special Feature

Lesson 20

Picture Study: The Damadian Family Photo

When you write an autobiography, you consider many different aspects of your life from your past, present, and sometimes even your future. This can bring a lot of memories to mind.

Study the Damadian family photo and **describe** in detail what you see. Consider the time period, colors, genders, ages, what the family is doing, facial expressions, and other details. You can share your opinion about what this family might be like.

_____
_____
_____
_____
_____
_____
_____
_____
_____
_____
_____

Name _____   Lesson 20 - Exercise 1   Day 96

Study these vocabulary words that are bolded in the excerpt from "The Truth" that you will read on Day 99.

Vocabulary

attributes	qualities or characteristics of a person or thing	**inquisitiveness**	tending to inquire or investigate
awe	reverential respect with fear; wonder	**philosophers**	people who seek wisdom or enlightenment
combustion	chemical process of reaction causing heat	**theologians**	those who study the nature of God or religion
embedded	fixed firmly or deeply in something	**validate**	to prove the accuracy
fundamental	foundational; basic or essential to something	**verifiable**	able to be proved true

1. **Write** a sentence using the words *inquisitiveness* and *philosophers*. Include a prepositional phrase. (Day 37)

   _____
   _____

2. **Write** a sentence using the words *theologians* and *awe*. Include an adverb. (Day 72)

   _____
   _____

3. **Write** a sentence using the words *verifiable* and *fundamental*. Include quotation marks somewhere in your sentence. (Day 47)

   _____
   _____

☐ **Use** index cards to **write** each vocabulary word from this lesson on one side and the definition on the other. **Check** the box when complete.

☐ **Copy** the Scripture verse on an index card. **Memorize** it by the end of this lesson. You may choose the Bible translation or use the one given. **Check** the box when complete.

Jesus said to him, "I am the way, and the truth, and the life. No one comes to the Father except through me." John 14:6

Name _____ Lesson 20 - Exercise 2 Day 97

Grammar & Punctuation

More on Pronouns

You learned several types of pronouns in the last grammar lesson, and today we will look at a few more categories. **Study** the pronoun chart.

Interrogative Pronouns	Reciprocal Pronouns	Distributive Pronouns
Introduce questions	**Describe mutual relationships**	**Refer to individuals in a group**
who, whose, whom	*each other, one another*	*either, each, neither, any, none*
what, which	Josh and Jen are competing	We all entered the race, but *none* of us won.
What is your name?	with *each other*.	Of the two options, *neither* seemed like
Which one is yours?	My friends love *one another*.	a good choice.

Underline the pronouns. **Circle** any antecedents. **Label** the pronouns as **INT** (interrogative), **RC** (reciprocal), or **DIS** (distributive).

1. Which winter coat belongs to Olivia?
2. Last summer, Matthew and Jackson went camping with each other for the first time.
3. Choosing a winner was difficult because none of the competitors made a mistake.

Write a sentence using a reciprocal pronoun.

_____

_____

Write a sentence using a distributive pronoun.

_____

_____

The next group of pronouns has to do with possession. **Possessive pronouns** show ownership and function as nouns. **Possessive adjectives** are pronouns functioning as adjectives that show ownership. **Study** the chart.

Possessive Pronouns	Possessive (or Pronominal) Adjectives
Designate ownership (possession)	**Appear before the noun to modify it**
mine, yours, ours, his, hers, theirs, its	*my, your, our, his, her, their, its, whose,* etc.
I believe that letter is *mine*.	The bird flew out of *its* cage.
He didn't know the phone was *hers*.	I would love to visit with *your* mother.

Note: By now you have probably observed the overlap within the categories of pronouns, as many of the lists share the same words. Determining which category the pronoun belongs in depends on its function in the sentence.

Grammar & Punctuation

Name _____ Lesson 20 - Exercise 2 Day 97

Label the underlined pronoun with **PP** (possessive pronoun) or **PA** (possessive adjective). **Circle** any antecedents. Remember, there is not always a written antecedent.

4. Eliana was thrilled because her lost luggage was finally returned after over a week of waiting.

5. When Jay met his new coach, he realized the coach's house was just down the street from his!

6. Our first day of summer tradition has always been picnicking with my cousins. It is a favorite tradition of mine.

Write a sentence that contains a prepositional phrase (Day 37) and a possessive adjective.

_____

_____

Tricky Pronouns

Sometimes it can be tricky determining which pronoun to use. **Study** these tips for correct pronoun use.

Tip 1: A lot of writers and speakers get tripped up in deciding when to use *who* and when to use *whom*. *Who* is used as the subject of a sentence, and *whom* is used as the object of a verb or preposition.

> *Examples:* Who wants to go to the zoo? (*Who* is the subject of the sentence)
> God blesses *whom* He will. (*whom* is the object of the verb)

Underline the correct pronoun.

7. I am one (who, whom) loves to decorate for the holidays!

8. To (who, whom) should I offer my gratitude?

9. The teacher will choose (whoever, whomever) she wishes to lead the group.

Tip 2: People are often confused about when to use *me* versus *myself*. Use *myself* only when you are the subject of the sentence (when you have mentioned yourself already). Use *me* only as the object of the sentence (the word affected by the verb).

> *Examples:* I always give *myself* time to think before making a decision.
> (*myself* is used because *I* is the subject)
> Always ask Mom or *me* before walking to town.
> (*me* is used because it is the object of the verb)

Underline the correct pronoun. (*Hint:* Pay attention to the verbs because one of these is tricky!)

10. I couldn't believe that I had allowed (me, myself) to fall for that old trick!

11. You should contact (me, myself) if you have any further questions about the concepts we studied.

12. I felt confident that the class would elect (me, myself) as president.

☐ Using your index cards, **copy** the five types of pronouns from this lesson. Include the titles and examples of each. **Check** the box when you are done.

Name _____ Lesson 20 - Exercise 3 Day 98

Communication

Autobiography Notes: Steps for Writing

Study the chart. We will work through these steps over the course of the autobiography assignment.

> **Steps for Writing an Autobiography**
> 1. **Observe examples:** Read an autobiography that sounds interesting, observe how the author retells their life story, and look for the use of literary devices and themes.
> 2. **Write down your most important memories:** Think of the events in your life that stand out the most, the people who have had the greatest influence on you, and the times God has been very present in situations.
> 3. **Establish a theme:** As you record your most important memories, you should see an overall theme emerge. Perhaps you realized how many times God has provided in moments of great need, how often you were able to overcome great odds with the help of the Lord and family, how certain relationships have molded you, or how you have grown as a person through life experiences.
> 4. **Create a detailed outline:** Outlines can feel like an unnecessary step when you want to get started on writing, but a good outline will help your writing come together much easier.
> 5. **Write a rough draft:** Use your outline to construct a rough draft (making sure to use proper grammar and structure), write concise sentences, and employ some literary devices to make your story interesting. Have someone read it and offer feedback.
> 6. **Write a final draft:** This will be your polished, final piece of writing.

Record the following information about your life. The answers will help you in developing the direction of your autobiography.

Describe yourself using three adjectives.

_____

List your strengths and abilities.

_____
_____
_____
_____

List your weaknesses.

_____
_____
_____
_____

Communication

Name _____   Lesson 20 - Exercise 3   Day 98

Record your greatest achievement(s).
_____
_____
_____

Copy a Scripture verse that has been instrumental in your life.
_____
_____

Copy a famous quote that represents you or speaks to you.
_____
_____
_____

List two people who have been leaders or mentors in your life and what they have taught you.
_____
_____
_____

Share your most important goals.
_____
_____
_____

List some family traditions you have enjoyed and have been impacted by.
_____
_____
_____

Share the biggest challenge(s) you have overcome.
_____
_____
_____

List your hobbies.
_____
_____
_____

Name _____ Lesson 20 - Exercise 4 Day 99

Worldview & Literary Analysis

Read the following excerpt from the chapter "The Truth" found in *Gifted Mind*.

> One of those who worked closely with the Wright Brothers on their new invention was a man by the name of Marcel Pénot Jr., my grandmother's brother. That's Marcel ... my great-uncle pictured in the photograph on my wall. And that "contraption" he's seated in is an early version of the Wright Brother's [*sic*] airplane, the "Wright Flyer." Orville Wright once said, "If birds can glide for long periods of time, then why can't I?"[1] Marcel Pénot, my grandmother's father ... was a pioneer of France's internal **combustion** engine.
>
> It is precisely this spirit of curiosity and **inquisitiveness** that has driven mankind throughout history — pushing the boundaries of discovery in exploration, medicine, science, and technology. What the Wright Brothers did was simply to dream and then experiment with those dreams. In time, and based on what they learned from their failures, they slowly began discovering and experiencing the previously unknown properties of flight — weight, drag, thrust, and lift — all physical science principles demonstrated all around us in creation. In inventing the world's first successful heavier-than-air flying machine, the Wright Brothers accomplished more than just birthing one of the greatest technologies in all of human history.
>
> They uncovered God's truth.
>
> As a Christian, this truth is everything to me. It is the foundation of knowledge and the basis of all understanding. Some may choose to leave this pursuit of truth to **philosophers** and **theologians**, but not me. While all truth ultimately originates in the person of God, for He Himself *is* the truth, I believe it also has a **fundamental** place in science as well (John 14:6). The goal of science is to explore, investigate, **validate**, understand, and explain knowledge of our human kind, the world, and the universe. We do this so we can take this knowledge and use it for the benefit for all humanity.
>
> I believe God, as Creator, has **embedded** certain truths within everything He has made (Romans 1:18–20). As man discovers and acknowledges these realities, we understand that the universe and all it contains reveals the fingerprints of God — His invisible **attributes**, His eternal power, and divine nature. But that's not the end of the story. What is obvious about God on a macro level (the universe) is equally true on the micro level (the atom). The Creator has brilliantly designed creation in such a way that no matter where we look, we see the undeniable handiwork of amazing intelligence. We have but to open our eyes and minds, and what unfolds before us is the creative, imaginative, powerful, and **awe**-inspiring display of His greatness and glory. It's there, just waiting for us to discover it. Without a Creator, there is no universe or mankind. No God = No Humanity. Without God, there is no **verifiable** reality for us and thus no ultimate truth.[2]

---

1 Endnote from excerpt: http://wrightbrothers.info/biography.php.
2 Damadian, *Gifted Mind*, p. 8–10.

Name_____   Lesson 20 - Exercise 4   Day 99

Respond to the following regarding today's reading excerpt.

1. **What** is the connection between Dr. Damadian and the man in the photo sitting in the "contraption"?
   _____
   _____

2. **Record** Orville Wright's quote about birds.
   _____
   _____

The "spirit of curiosity and inquisitiveness" drove the Wright brothers to "dream and then experiment with those dreams." Have you ever thought of an invention you believe would work? **Write** about it.
_____
_____

3. Besides birthing one of the greatest technologies in all of human history, **what** did the Wright brothers accomplish?
   _____

4. The sentence "They uncovered God's truth" is given its own separate paragraph space. **Why** do you believe the author wrote it that way?
   _____
   _____

5. **What** is the foundation of knowledge and the basis of all understanding?
   _____

6. While many would leave the "pursuit of truth to philosophers and theologians," Dr. Damadian believes this pursuit can involve science as well. **Explain** why.
   _____
   _____
   _____
   _____

7. **What** can we understand as man discovers and acknowledges God's embedded truths?
   _____
   _____

The world looks at scientific discoveries and inventions as the genius of mankind. **How** do you view them?
_____
_____
_____

Read Romans 1:18–20 and **pray** that God keeps your eyes open to see Him in the things He has made!

216   Lesson 20, Day 99   Language Lessons for a Living Education Level 10

Name _____   Lesson 20 - Exercise 5   Day 100

Review

☐ **Update** the Reading List chart with books you have read this week.

☐ **Recite** John 14:6 from memory to your instructor.

Vocabulary Review

Match each word to the correct definition.

a. attributes	c. combustion	e. fundamental	g. philosophers	i. validate
b. awe	d. embedded	f. inquisitiveness	h. theologians	j. verifiable

1. _____ able to be proved true
2. _____ to prove accuracy
3. _____ reverential respect
4. _____ qualities or characteristics
5. _____ chemical process of reaction causing heat
6. _____ those who study God or religion
7. _____ people who seek wisdom or enlightenment
8. _____ foundational, basic, essential
9. _____ tendency to inquire or investigate

Grammar & Punctuation Review

Underline the pronouns. **Circle** any antecedents. **Label** the pronouns as **INT** (interrogative), **RC** (reciprocal), or **DIS** (distributive).

1. Maria and Joanna are challenging each other to eat healthy foods and get fit.
2. There were only two types of cookies at the banquet, but each looked delicious!
3. Whose phone got left outside?
4. **Describe** the difference between a possessive pronoun and a possessive adjective.

_____
_____

Label the underlined pronoun with **PP** (possessive pronoun) or **PA** (possessive adjective). **Circle** any antecedents. Remember, there is not always a written antecedent.

5. The only true hope is in Christ's work on the Cross because <u>His</u> righteousness became <u>mine</u>.

6. After Sarah found <u>her</u> wallet at the grocery store, she had to prove to the manager that it was <u>hers</u>.

Underline the correct pronoun.

7. I never realized how much my mother loved (myself, me).
8. I had enough confidence in (me, myself) that I knew I could conquer my fears.
9. My sister is the one (whom, who) bakes up a storm at Christmastime.
10. God has mercy on (whoever, whomever) He will.

Review

Name _____   Lesson 20 - Exercise 5   Day 100

Communication Review

List the six steps for writing an autobiography.

1. _____   4. _____
2. _____   5. _____
3. _____   6. _____

Describe how you felt filling out the personal questions on Day 98. Was it difficult to come up with answers? If so, why? Did you feel like you were bragging about your abilities and accomplishments? Did you feel like you were putting yourself down by describing your weaknesses?

_____
_____
_____
_____
_____
_____
_____
_____

Worldview & Literary Analysis Review

1. Besides birthing one of the greatest technologies in all of human history, **what** did the Wright brothers accomplish?

   _____

2. **What** is the foundation of knowledge and the basis of all understanding?

   _____

Copy Romans 1:18–20 using the Bible translation of your choice.

_____
_____
_____
_____
_____
_____
_____
_____

Special Feature

Hymn Study: "A Mighty Fortress Is Our God" by Martin Luther (1529)

A mighty fortress is our God, a bulwark never failing;
Our helper He, amid the flood of mortal ills prevailing:
For still our ancient foe doth seek to work us woe;
His craft and pow'r are great, and, armed with cruel hate,
On earth is not his equal.

Did we in our own strength confide, our striving would be losing,
Were not the right Man on our side, the Man of God's own choosing:
Dost ask who that may be? Christ Jesus, it is He;
Lord Sabaoth, His Name, from age to age the same,
And He must win the battle.

And though this world, with devils filled, should threaten to undo us,
We will not fear, for God hath willed His truth to triumph through us;
The Prince of Darkness grim, we tremble not for him;
His rage we can endure, for lo, his doom is sure,
One little word shall fell him.

That word above all earthly pow'rs, no thanks to them, abideth;
The Spirit and the gifts are ours through Him Who with us sideth;
Let goods and kindred go, this mortal life also;
The body they may kill: God's truth abideth still,
His kingdom is forever.

Read the hymn aloud to your instructor and discuss its meaning. **Write** a summary in your own words.

Name _____   Lesson 21 - Exercise 1   Day 101

Study these vocabulary words that are bolded in the excerpt from "The Truth" that you will read on Day 104.

Vocabulary

aspiration	hope of achieving something	**personified**	to represent or embody a certain concept
democracy	government by the will of the people	**political**	of or relating to government
empowerment	power or authority given	**pursuit**	act of following; going after someone or something
exclusive	restricted to a certain person or thing	**quest**	long or arduous search for something specific
genuinely	in a way that is real; truthfully	**subsequent**	coming after something in time
impede	to delay or prevent by obstructing	**tyranny**	harsh, cruel government by a single ruler
inconvenient	causing discomfort, difficulty, or trouble	**vistas**	scenes, views, or panoramas

1. Using the vocabulary words, **fill in** the blanks in the excerpt from *Gifted Mind*.

   "_____ of the truth generates *new* knowledge — understanding that not only opens up new _____ about God, but also has proven to profoundly impact humanity for good as well. This _____ is part of what drives me, propelling my research forward, because truth is critical to every aspect of human life. It can be ignored and denied, but it *cannot* be defeated. Truth, by its very nature, is invincible, and those who dishonor it ultimately dishonor themselves, _____ discovery, and hurt humanity."

2. **Write** a sentence using the words *democracy* and *political*. Use the word *political* as an adjective.

   _____
   _____

☐ **Use** index cards to **write** each vocabulary word from this lesson on one side and the definition on the other. **Check** the box when complete.

☐ **Copy** the Scripture verse on an index card. **Memorize** it by the end of this lesson. You may choose the Bible translation or use the one given. **Check** the box when complete.

So Jesus said to the Jews who had believed him, "If you abide in my word, you are truly my disciples, and you will know the truth, and the truth will set you free." John 8:31–32

Name _____ Lesson 21 - Exercise 2 Day 102

Grammar & Punctuation

Direct Objects

The subject of the sentence is the noun that *performs* the action. A **direct object** is a noun that *receives* the action of the verb and answers the questions "what?" or "whom?" In the examples below, the subject is underlined once, and the verb is underlined twice.

> A **direct object** is a noun that *receives* the action of the verb and answers the questions "what?" or "whom?"
>
> An **indirect object** is a noun that is *affected* by the action of the verb but is not the primary object receiving the action.

> *Examples:* My dog gobbles *food* in a matter of seconds.
> (My dog gobbles what? *Food* "receives" the action.)
> Joy carefully bathed *the baby* in the sink.
> (Joy bathed whom? *The baby* "receives" the action.)

Draw one line under the subject, two lines under the verb, and then **circle** the direct object. Include any modifying words when circling the direct object (*example: the little baby* instead of *baby*).

1. We spent a lot of money at the county fair last weekend.
2. At the tournament, Mitchell threw the ball like a real champ!
3. Weaving in and out of traffic, the police car finally caught the suspect three blocks from the scene of the crime.
4. Chosen last for the team, I wasted no time training to improve.

Write a compound sentence (Day 52) that includes a direct object.

_____

_____

Indirect Objects

An **indirect object** is a noun that is *affected* by the action of the verb but is not the primary object receiving the action. The indirect object *receives* the direct object rather than the action. Indirect objects answer questions like "to whom?" or "for what?" and can be one word or a phrase. An indirect object *only* appears in a sentence that has a direct object. (IO = indirect object, DO = direct object)

>   IO   DO   IO   DO
> *Examples:* My cat brought *me* a dead mouse. | Rasul passed *Trevor* the ball.

How to Find Direct and Indirect Objects
Angela handed Madison the gift.

Step 1:	Find the verb. (*handed*)
Step 2:	Ask "what?" (*handed* what? *The gift* = direct object)
Step 3:	Ask "who or what received it?" (*handed* whom the gift? *Madison* = indirect object)

Grammar & Punctuation Lesson 21, Day 102

Name_____ Lesson 21 - Exercise 2 Day 102

Underline the subject once and the verb twice. Then **underline** the direct objects and any indirect objects (include any modifying words). **Label** them as **IO** or **DO**.

5. After school yesterday, Mom bought us ice cream.
6. The pastor gave the congregation a sermon they will never forget!
7. Sharing the last of her treats, Leah handed Cole an enormous cookie.
8. Jesse bought Maddie a beautiful ring.
9. The hotel worker gave the room a quick cleaning.

Write a sentence that includes a helping verb (Day 17), an indirect object, and a direct object.

_____

_____

Usually, the indirect object comes immediately *after* the verb and *before* the direct object, as you saw in the sentences you just evaluated. However, in some situations, the positions are reversed. In those situations, usually a preposition is involved.

>   **DO**   **IO**
> *Examples:* Mr. Smith presented *diplomas* to *the students*.
>   **DO**   **IO**
>   I gave an *apple* to *Cindy*.

Some grammarians (grammar specialists) disagree on whether an indirect object can be considered as such when it is also the object of the preposition. For our purposes, we stand with the view that even though the indirect object is within a prepositional phrase, it is still considered an indirect object.

Underline the subject once and the verb twice. Then **underline** the direct objects and indirect objects. **Label** them as **IO** or **DO**. **Place** parentheses around the prepositional phrases. (Have your list of prepositions handy!)

10. My aunt and uncle generously bought dinner for me after the play.
11. Not surprisingly, Corbin's coach gave a game ball to him.
12. The king offered protection for his guests when they traveled home.

Write a sentence that contains a gerund phrase (Day 82) and an indirect object that is within a prepositional phrase.

_____

_____

In your own words, **describe** the difference between a direct object and an indirect object.

_____

_____

☐ Using your index cards, **copy** the definitions for direct and indirect objects. Provide an example sentence and label it. **Check** the box when you are done.

Name _____ Lesson 21 - Exercise 3 Day 103

❓ Communication

Autobiography Notes: Memories

Your autobiography is a collection of memories, both pleasant and challenging, that have helped form you into the person you are today. It is important to keep your autobiography in chronological order so the reader understands the flow of events. **Record** some memories from each life stage. These can be brief sentences that you will expand on when you write your rough draft. Not all memories need to be used. This is a "brainstorming" session.

Record memories from ages 0–5.

_____
_____
_____
_____
_____

Record memories from ages 6–10.

_____
_____
_____
_____
_____

Record memories from age 11 until the present.

_____
_____
_____
_____
_____

Based on what you have written in the past couple of lessons, are you beginning to see a theme emerging? **Review** Step 3: "Establish a theme" on Day 98 and record your theme here.

_____
_____

In the back of this book, you will find an Autobiography Rubric that will help you understand the expectations of this assignment. **Study** it now and refer to it often when you begin writing the rough draft on Day 118.

Name _____   Lesson 21 - Exercise 3   Day 103

Wisdom Speaks

Copy the proverb.

> *The purpose in a man's heart is like deep water, but a man of understanding will draw it out.* Proverbs 20:5

_____
_____

Using a dictionary or an online search with a parent's permission, **write** the definitions of the words below.

1. purpose: _____
   _____

2. draw (verb): _____
   _____

Write a sentence about your life using the word *purpose*.

_____
_____

This verse uses the metaphor of a deep well that would require some work and patience to draw water from. A person's motivations, goals, beliefs, attitudes, and feelings can be buried very deep inside their heart and mind. Sometimes the person is trying to discern their own "purpose," and other times a friend, mentor, or parent is trying to discern what is deep inside to help give wise counsel. A person who has wisdom and understanding can pull out the truths hidden in the heart.

Write a paragraph sharing about a time when you or someone in your life had to work at getting to the truth about the motivations, goals, beliefs, attitudes, feelings, and other thoughts buried in your heart.

_____
_____
_____
_____
_____
_____
_____
_____
_____

224 Lesson 21, Day 103   *Language Lessons for a Living Education* Level 10

Worldview & Literary Analysis

Read the following excerpt from the chapter "The Truth," found in *Gifted Mind*.

For me, therein lies the real reward of science. Discovery of God's truth bridges the gap between philosophy and science as well as showing us something greater than the two. **Pursuit** of the truth generates *new* knowledge — understanding that not only opens up new **vistas** about God, but also has proven to profoundly impact humanity for good as well. This **quest** is part of what drives me, propelling my research forward, because truth is critical to every aspect of human life. It can be ignored and denied, but it *cannot* be defeated. Truth, by its very nature, is invincible, and those who dishonor it ultimately dishonor themselves, **impede** discovery, and hurt humanity.

Over a century ago, our 20th president, James Garfield, proclaimed, "The truth shall make you free" (John 8:32). He then quickly added, "But first it will make you miserable." He was right. The truth has a way of being decidedly **inconvenient** at times.

Surprisingly, today it's not freedom from bondage or **tyranny** that most of us in the Western world seek. Rather, unfortunately we seek to break ties from the very God who graciously grants us our freedom to choose. Mankind's ultimate **aspiration** seems to manifest itself through becoming the final authority in all aspects of his own existence. In other words, we want to be in charge, replacing God as supreme authority. Ironically, it's *this* brand of "freedom" that eventually makes slaves of us all.

You've no doubt heard the saying, "Being free comes with a price," and that's true. We typically think of this freedom during holidays, recognizing those who have given their lives so that we in the United States of America could remain free. But it's a fair question to ask, "Can anyone be **genuinely** 'free' apart from the truth of Jesus Christ?" Can we know real freedom apart from the truth of God that exposes the lies of mankind? Jesus unashamedly claimed to be "the way, the TRUTH and the life; no man cometh to the Father, but by me" (John 14:6, emphasis added). That's a very bold and **exclusive** statement, and one not made by any other major religious leader in history.

Jesus' words, quoted by both presidents and Apostles, remind us that he is truth personified, as well as the exclusive expressway to it. When President George Washington rejected kingship following the American Revolution, choosing **democracy** instead, he intentionally transferred **political** power to the "power of the truth." This effectively replaced the British king's power with the unbounded power of the truth. I believe our **subsequent** advancements in science and technology are the fruits of such an **empowerment**. Seemingly miraculous discoveries in these fields have helped create the most extraordinary economic prosperity in human history, so much so that God's *truth* becomes the real "Founding Father" of Western civilization and ultimately, the United States of America.[1]

---
1 Damadian, *Gifted Mind*, p. 10–11.

Name _____ Lesson 21 - Exercise 4   Day 104

Respond to the following regarding today's reading excerpt.

1. **What** is the "real" reward of science? _____
   _____

2. **What** does the pursuit of truth generate?
   _____

Copy this statement about the truth from Dr. Damadian.

> "It can be ignored and denied, but it *cannot* be defeated. Truth, by its very nature, is invincible, and those who dishonor it ultimately dishonor themselves, impede discovery, and hurt humanity."

_____
_____

3. **What** did President Garfield mean when he stated, "The truth shall make you free, but first it will make you miserable"?
   _____
   _____
   _____
   _____

4. According to Dr. Damadian, **what** is often mankind's "ultimate aspiration"?
   _____
   _____

5. **What** happens to people when they replace God as the supreme authority?
   _____

For you, **how** does knowing the Truth (Jesus Himself) set you free?
_____
_____

6. Dr. Damadian states that God's truth becomes the real "Founding Father" of Western civilization. **Describe** what you believe he means by this.
   _____
   _____
   _____
   _____

Name _____   Lesson 21 - Exercise 5   Day 105

Review

☐ **Update** the Reading List chart with books you have read this week.

☐ **Recite** John 8:31–32 from memory to your instructor.

Vocabulary Review

Match each word to the correct definition.

a. aspiration	d. exclusive	g. inconvenient	j. pursuit	m. tyranny
b. democracy	e. genuinely	h. personified	k. quest	n. vistas
c. empowerment	f. impede	i. political	l. subsequent	

1. _____ scenes, views, or panoramas
2. _____ government by will of the people
3. _____ coming after something in time
4. _____ restricted to a person or thing
5. _____ causing discomfort, difficulty, or trouble
6. _____ delay or prevent by obstructing
7. _____ harsh, cruel government by a single ruler
8. _____ act of following; pursuing someone or thing
9. _____ long or arduous search for something specific
10. _____ relating to government
11. _____ represent or embody a concept
12. _____ in a way that is real; truthful
13. _____ power or authority given
14. _____ hope of achieving

Grammar & Punctuation Review

1. **Define** a direct object.
   _____
   _____

2. **Define** an indirect object.
   _____
   _____

Underline the subject once and the verb twice. Then **underline** the direct objects and any indirect objects (include any modifying words). **Label** them as **IO** or **DO**.

3. My dad gave my mother diamond earrings for her birthday this year.
4. The chemist cleaned the lab one last time before going home for the evening.
5. Running frantically back and forth, the squirrel finally snatched the acorn from the middle of the road.
6. Aunt Sue handed her nieces and nephews each a small gift after the recital.

Name _____   Lesson 21 - Exercise 5   Day 105

Communication Review

Write a paragraph describing what it was like to think back over memories from your early childhood to the present. Do you believe your memories to be accurate? Did you need to ask a family member for clarification? Did you remember any negative memories? If so, ask God to help you heal and forgive. What did you enjoy about writing out your memories?

_____
_____
_____
_____
_____
_____
_____
_____
_____

Worldview & Literary Analysis Review

1. **What** is the "real" reward of science?
   _____

2. **What** does the pursuit of truth generate?
   _____

3. According to Dr. Damadian, **what** is often mankind's "ultimate aspiration"?
   _____

4. **What** happens to people when they replace God as the supreme authority?
   _____

President Garfield stated, "The truth shall make you free, but first it will make you miserable." **Write** a paragraph telling whether you agree with this statement. **Back up** your answer with a real-life example.

_____
_____
_____
_____
_____
_____
_____
_____

Special Feature

Lesson 22

Scripture Study: Romans 1:18–25

Summarize each verse using your own words. Stay true to the meaning of the verse. **Have** your instructor read your sentences and **discuss** them with you.

¹⁸ For the wrath of God is revealed from heaven against all ungodliness and unrighteousness of men, who by their unrighteousness suppress the truth.

_____
_____

¹⁹ For what can be known about God is plain to them, because God has shown it to them.

_____
_____

²⁰ For his invisible attributes, namely, his eternal power and divine nature, have been clearly perceived, ever since the creation of the world, in the things that have been made. So they are without excuse.

_____
_____

²¹ For although they knew God, they did not honor him as God or give thanks to him, but they became futile in their thinking, and their foolish hearts were darkened.

_____
_____

²² Claiming to be wise, they became fools,

_____
_____

²³ and exchanged the glory of the immortal God for images resembling mortal man and birds and animals and creeping things.

_____
_____

²⁴ Therefore God gave them up in the lusts of their hearts to impurity, to the dishonoring of their bodies among themselves,

_____
_____

²⁵ because they exchanged the truth about God for a lie and worshiped and served the creature rather than the Creator, who is blessed forever! Amen.

_____
_____

Name _____   Lesson 22 - Exercise 1   Day 106

Study these vocabulary words that are bolded in the excerpt from "The Truth" that you will read on Day 109.

Vocabulary

aerial	existing or happening in the air	**musings**	thoughts or meditations; contemplations
coincidence	occurrence of events happening together by chance	**phenomenal**	remarkable or extraordinary; very great
colossal	a human creation of immense dimensions	**privileged**	special right or advantage possessed by a group or individual
liberate	to set free from restrictions or bonds	**renaissance**	a rebirth or revival; new vigor or interest
masterpiece	a work created by extraordinary skill	**revolution**	radical change, usually in government or social situations
multi-faceted (multifaceted)	having many aspects or sides		

Write a paragraph using at least six of the vocabulary words. Be creative and vary your sentence structure and length.

_____
_____
_____
_____
_____
_____
_____
_____
_____
_____

☐ **Use** index cards to **write** each vocabulary word from this lesson on one side and the definition on the other. **Check** the box when complete.

☐ **Copy** the Scripture verse on an index card. **Memorize** it by the end of this lesson. You may choose the Bible translation or use the one given. **Check** the box when complete.

That their hearts may be encouraged, being knit together in love, to reach all the riches of full assurance of understanding and the knowledge of God's mystery, which is Christ, in whom are hidden all the treasures of wisdom and knowledge. Colossians 2:2–3

Name _____   Lesson 22 - Exercise 2   Day 107

Grammar & Punctuation

Number: Subject-Verb Agreement

Subject nouns and their verbs must agree in number. "Number" in this sense refers to whether the subject is singular (one) or plural (more than one).

Nouns add an -s to form most plurals, but verbs do not. *Example:* Rabbit**s** eat green plants. (verb is plural)

Singular verbs add -s to match their singular nouns. *Example:* The rabbit eat**s** green plants. (verb is singular)

While it is usually easy to spot errors in number, there are a few tricky circumstances. **Study** the chart.

Nine Rules for Subject-Verb Agreement	
1. If the subject is singular, the verb must be singular. If the subject is plural, the verb must be plural.	
	She reads the Bible every day. (singular subject = singular verb) The *students read* the Bible every day. (plural subject = plural verb)
Exception:	When using "they" in a singular way. (This *person is* a great cook. *They are* amazing!)
2. Use a plural verb when the subject is composed of two or more nouns connected by the word *and*.	
	The *teacher* <u>and</u> the *students walk* slowly and quietly down the hall.
3. When there is one subject but multiple verbs, all verbs in the sentence must agree.	
	Vehicles are expensive and *require* a lot of maintenance.
4. When a phrase comes between the subject and the verb, the verb must agree with the subject, not other nouns in the phrase.	
	The *firetruck*, along with other emergency vehicles in our town, *requires* major repairs.
5. Use a singular verb when two or more singular nouns are connected by *or* or *nor*.	
	The *pastor* <u>or</u> the *worship leader needs* to approve the song selection.
6. When a compound subject contains both a singular and plural noun joined by *or* or *nor*, the verb should agree with the subject that is *closest* to it.	
	The *pastor* <u>or</u> the *worship leaders need* to approve the song selections. The *worship leaders* <u>or</u> the *pastor needs* to approve the song selections.
7. The words and phrases *each*, *each one*, *either*, *neither*, *everyone*, *everybody*, *anyone*, *anybody*, *nobody*, *somebody*, *someone*, and *no one* are considered singular and need a singular verb.	
	No one was available to clean after the concert. *Everybody needs* encouragement.
8. Noncount nouns are words that have no specific quantity. They need singular verbs.	
	The *evidence needs* to be made available. *Diabetes is* a terrible problem in the United States.
9. Collective nouns (imply more than one person) are considered singular and need a singular verb.	
	The *choir runs* through their song list every Saturday morning. The *youth group meets* on Tuesday nights.

Name _____ Lesson 22 - Exercise 2 Day 107

Use the Rules for Subject-Verb Agreement chart to **underline** the correct verb.

1. My chess club (are, is) traveling to Canada for an international competition.
2. Although it is getting late in the day, everybody (want, wants) to stay longer.
3. The evangelist and several of the missionaries (speaks, speak) at this conference each year.
4. Neither idea (was, were) plausible, considering the circumstances.
5. Vacations (are, is) fun but also (costs, cost) a lot of money these days.
6. The camp director or the camp counselors (announces, announce) the activities for the day.
7. The camp counselors or the camp director (announces, announce) the activities for the day.
8. My dogs, including the puppy, (eats, eat) an enormous amount of food every day.
9. I firmly believe that no one (are, is) able to comprehend God's love for them.

Use the Subject-Verb Agreement chart to complete the following.

Write a sentence that applies Rule 2.

_____

_____

Write a sentence that applies Rule 3.

_____

_____

Write a sentence that applies Rule 5.

_____

_____

Write a sentence that applies Rule 6.

_____

_____

Communication

Autobiography Notes: Anecdotes

Since your autobiography is the chronological story of your life to date, sharing short stories (anecdotes — see Day 59) will be an important aspect of your writing and will help hold your reader's interest. Storytelling is an art that needs development and practice. **Study** these types of anecdotes.

> **Types of Anecdotes**
> - **Cautionary:** A tale that involves a character flaw or poor judgment and results in negative consequences. The point is to teach a lesson about what not to do. Examples are often seen in myths, parables, and fairy tales.
> - **Humorous:** A funny story used to lighten the mood, create a short break in the main story, and entertain the reader. An example would be a short joke or making fun of a character in a way that adds to the enjoyment of the story.
> - **Inspirational:** A persuasive or emotional appeal. This type aims to create a certain feeling in the reader by telling a story they can relate to and identify with. Often, political speeches and sermons will use these short stories to inspire the audience.
> - **Characterizing:** A story that reveals more about the main character or side character's personality. It may not be part of the main story but gives a glimpse at certain virtues or attributes of the character. An example is the cherry tree story about George Washington.
> - **Reminiscent:** A nostalgic story focused on the more distant past, especially on aspects of the world that have changed, creating a longing for the old days ("Back in my day …" OR "When I was a small child, society was different …").

Note: Anecdote types are not mutually exclusive and may be blended. An inspirational anecdote may also be humorous, and a characterizing anecdote could be reminiscent, and so on.

As you think about anecdotes to "tuck" into your autobiography, consider your theme and choose anecdotes that will enhance your overall story. Excellent storytelling begins with excellent sentence structure and word choice. **Study** the Tips for Better Writing chart.

> **Tips For Better Writing**
> - **Vary your sentences:** Use different sentence types and lengths to add interest.
> - **Avoid repeating words:** Use synonyms — words that are similar — rather than repeating the same word excessively (*example: gatherings* instead of *competitions*).
> - **Be engaging:** Avoid phrases like *once upon a time … when I was … one day I….* Be fresh in how you present your story.
> - **Use good transitions:** When starting a new paragraph, use words and phrases like *in addition to, besides, finally, next, as a result, after that, furthermore, nevertheless, consequently,* etc.
> - **Use vivid imagery:** Insert lively verbs, adjectives, and adverbs.
> - **Grammar and punctuation:** Make sure you abide by the grammar and punctuation rules you know.

Name _____   Lesson 22 - Exercise 3   Day 108

- **Stay focused:** Regularly look back at your thesis or topic sentence and make sure your sentences are relevant and concise.
- **Keep your voice interesting:** The way you come across to your reader through your choice of vocabulary, expression, point of view, and detail all make up your voice.

An anecdote can be one to two paragraphs in length. Remember, it is a short story tucked into a main story. **Have** your instructor read your anecdotes and sign on the line below.

Write a humorous anecdote from your life.

_____
_____
_____
_____
_____
_____
_____
_____
_____

Write a characterizing anecdote from your life.

_____
_____
_____
_____
_____
_____
_____
_____
_____

Write a cautionary anecdote from your life.

_____
_____
_____
_____
_____
_____
_____
_____
_____

Instructor's signature: _____

Name _____ **Lesson 22 - Exercise 4** **Day 109**

Worldview & Literary Analysis

Read the following excerpt from the chapter "The Truth" found in *Gifted Mind*.

As far back as A.D. 1455, Johannes Gutenberg's invention of the printing press helped spark this **revolution** of truth. And what was the first book to roll of [sic] his press? The Holy Bible. Before this time, the common man (those outside the **privileged** circle of priests and clergy) had virtually no access to Scripture and its fascinating truths, including scientific truths. But from the moment God's Word was revealed through Gutenberg's invention, reverence for the truth has been the foundation of Western civilization. I find it more than **coincidence** that the vast majority of mankind's major scientific discoveries were made *after* the Bible "went public" in Western civilization. It ignited the **renaissance** (rebirth) of God's Laws. Remarkably, the **colossal** industrial revolution and economic explosion in the West that followed access to the wisdom of God's Word in Gutenberg's Bible did not occur in Asia where there is no shortage of smart people. It is also interesting that those who made such discoveries either cited Scripture's truths or were inspired by them!

In granting us access to His *truth*, God has gifted us with the ability to make scientific discoveries that reveal things previously known only by Him. Inventions like the MRI simply **liberate** and unveil His truth for the benefit of mankind, just as it was with His revelation of electricity to Faraday, wireless transmission to Armstrong, electric lighting to Edison, and **aerial** transport to the Wright Brothers. We did not *create* these truths, but instead merely *discovered* ways to harness them for our benefit and progress.

Therefore, without robbing inventors of the credit due them, we should nevertheless recognize these **phenomenal** scientific advances for what they actually are: products of God's all-encompassing truth! In Colossians 2:3, Paul acknowledges, *"In [Christ] are hid all the treasures of wisdom and knowledge."* Thanks to Gutenberg, for the first time in history, all mankind was granted expanded access to God's Word, the Bible. It may surprise you to know that many of modern science's founding fathers cited God's Word as the origin of their discoveries, including Isaac Newton, Galileo, Copernicus, Kepler, and Faraday.

Prior to the printing press, Leonardo DaVinci delved into experimental science, optics, anatomy, and hydraulics. But it wasn't until *after* Gutenberg's Bible that he brushstroked such **masterpieces** as "Adoration of the Magi" (1481) and the "Last Supper" (1497).

Nicolaus Copernicus (1543)	Astronomy
Johannes Kepler (1596)	Astronomy
William Gilbert (1600)	Discovered earth's magnetic poles
Galileo Galilei (1613)	Astronomy, invented the telescope
Francis Bacon (1620)	The scientific method for empirical science
Blaise Pascal (1654)	Pascal's triangle, calculating machine, forerunner of the computer
Robert Boyle (1674)	The "Gas Laws," known as "Boyle's Law"
Isaac Newton (1715)	Universal laws of gravitation, the dynamic laws of motion
Michael Faraday (1859)	Major laws of electricity and means of generating it
Louis Pasteur (1866)	Microbial origin of disease

Name _____   Lesson 22 - Exercise 4   Day 109

> A complicated and **multi-faceted** [multifaceted] man, DaVinci's **musings** and experiments made pioneering contributions to the birth of present-day science. He would be followed by the likes of Christopher Columbus, who, upon discovering the new world, credited the truth of Scripture for his feat.[1] History records that many of mankind's great scientific pioneers were motivated by God and *His truth*, including:[2] [See chart on previous page.]

Respond to the following regarding today's reading excerpt.

1. **How** did Gutenberg's invention of the printing press help spark a revolution of truth?

   _____
   _____

2. **What** happened after the Bible "went public"?

   _____
   _____

3. **Fill in** the blanks of this quote from Dr. Damadian.

   "In granting us _____ to His *truth*, God has _____ us with the ability to make scientific discoveries that _____ things previously known only by _____."

Match the invention/discovery to the scientist.

4. _____ Faraday   a. aerial transport
5. _____ Armstrong   b. electricity
6. _____ Wright brothers   c. electric lighting
7. _____ Edison   d. wireless transmission

8. **Finish** the sentence from *Gifted Mind*.

   "We did not *create* these truths, but _____
   _____."

9. **Summarize** Dr. Damadian's view of biblical truth being foundational to true scientific advancement. List some of the scientists who were motivated by God's truth.

   _____
   _____
   _____
   _____
   _____

---

1 Endnote from excerpt: In a letter to Queen Isabella and King Ferdinand in 1502, Columbus wrote, "Fully accomplished were the words of Isaiah, 'He shall gather together the dispersed of Judah from the four corners of the earth.'"
2 Damadian, *Gifted Mind*, p. 11–14.

Name _____   Lesson 22 - Exercise 5   Day 110

Review

☐ **Update** the Reading List chart with books you have read this week.

☐ **Recite** Colossians 2:2–3 from memory to your instructor.

Vocabulary Review

Match each word to the correct definition.

a. aerial	d. liberate	g. musings	j. renaissance
b. coincidence	e. masterpiece	h. phenomenal	k. revolution
c. colossal	f. multi-faceted (multifaceted)	i. privileged	

1. _____ existing or happening in the air
2. _____ remarkable or extraordinary
3. _____ many aspects or sides
4. _____ to set free from restrictions
5. _____ created by extraordinary skill
6. _____ special right or advantage possessed by a group or individual
7. _____ rebirth or revival; new vigor
8. _____ human creation of immense dimensions
9. _____ events happening together by chance
10. _____ thoughts or meditations
11. _____ radical change in government or society

Grammar & Punctuation Review

Use the rules for subject-verb agreement to **underline** the correct verb.

1. The volleyball team (are, is) traveling to France for an international competition.
2. The rooster and all the hens (pecks, peck) the ground in search of small bugs.
3. The furniture (need, needs) to be moved out of the room to install the carpet.
4. His mother or his older sisters usually (picks, pick) him up after soccer practice.
5. A young boy, one of several student volunteers, (are, is) helping serve lunches this week.
6. Often, the town council members or the mayor (have, has) the final say on issues like these.

Review

Name _____ Lesson 22 - Exercise 5 Day 110

Communication Review

List five types of anecdotes and briefly **describe** each one.

1. _____
   _____
2. _____
   _____
3. _____
   _____
4. _____
   _____
5. _____
   _____

Worldview & Literary Analysis Review

1. **How** did Gutenberg's invention of the printing press help spark a revolution of truth?
   _____
   _____

2. **What** happened after the Bible "went public"?
   _____
   _____

Copy the quote from Dr. Damadian.

> "Therefore, without robbing inventors of the credit due them, we should nevertheless recognize these phenomenal scientific advances for what they actually are: products of God's all-encompassing truth!"

_____
_____
_____

3. **List** the five founding fathers of science that Dr. Damadian says cited God's Word as the origin of their discoveries.

   a. _____   d. _____
   b. _____   e. _____
   c. _____

Special Feature

Lesson 23

Biblical Autobiography Excerpt: Psalm 3

Save Me, O My God

A Psalm of David, when he fled from Absalom his son.

¹ O Lord, how many are my foes!
   Many are rising against me;
² many are saying of my soul,
   "There is no salvation for him in God." *Selah*

³ But you, O Lord, are a shield about me,
   my glory, and the lifter of my head.
⁴ I cried aloud to the Lord,
   and he answered me from his holy hill. *Selah*

⁵ I lay down and slept;
   I woke again, for the Lord sustained me.
⁶ I will not be afraid of many thousands of people
   who have set themselves against me all around.

⁷ Arise, O Lord!
   Save me, O my God!
For you strike all my enemies on the cheek;
   you break the teeth of the wicked.

⁸ Salvation belongs to the Lord;
   your blessing be on your people! *Selah*

David wrote this psalm while fleeing from his son, who was trying to kill him! Imagine how he must have felt as he recorded these personal words about his own life.

Summarize what David expressed in the psalm in your own words. **Write** from the first-person point of view.

_____
_____
_____
_____
_____
_____
_____
_____
_____
_____

Name _____   Lesson 23 – Exercise 1   Day 111

Study these vocabulary words that are bolded in the excerpt from "The Truth" that you will read on Day 114.

Vocabulary

atheistic	relating to the denial of the existence of God or gods	**malign**	to speak about in critical manner; to slander or defame
conventional	based on what is generally done or believed	**naturalistic**	based only on natural desire or instinct
implode	collapse violently inward	**override**	to use authority to cancel or reject something
infinite	limitless; impossible to measure or calculate	**peril**	immediate and serious danger
inherent	existing as a natural, inseparable quality of someone or something	**radical**	extremist; very different from other views or actions
intervention	the act of interfering with an outcome or course of events	**seep**	to flow or leak through slowly
juncture	a particular point in time or events	**truth**	true; in accordance with facts and reality

1. **Write** a sentence using the words *intervention* and *peril*. **Use** a complex sentence structure. (Day 52)
   _____
   _____

2. **Write** a short paragraph that includes dialogue (Day 47) by creating a conversation between two people discussing the existence of God and truth. **Use** at least four vocabulary words.
   _____
   _____
   _____
   _____
   _____
   _____

☐ **Use** index cards to **write** each vocabulary word from this lesson on one side and the definition on the other. **Check** the box when complete.

☐ **Copy** the Scripture verse on an index card. **Memorize** it by the end of this lesson. You may choose the Bible translation or use the one given. **Check** the box when complete.

The fool says in his heart, "There is no God." They are corrupt, doing abominable iniquity; there is none who does good. Psalm 53:1

Name _____   Lesson 23 - Exercise 2   Day 112

📝 Grammar & Punctuation

Conjugating Verbs

Have you ever conjugated a verb? The answer is yes! You may or may not be familiar with the term "conjugate." To **conjugate** is to give the different forms of a verb according to voice, mood, tense, number, and person. Verb conjugation tells us six things:

> To **conjugate** is to give the different forms of a verb according to voice, mood, tense, number, and person.

Person	Who or what is performing the action? (the subject "governs" the verb)
Number	Whether the action is performed by one or more than one (subject-verb agreement)
Tense	When the action is happening (past, present, future)
Mood	Whether the action is hypothetical, an order, or a statement (reveals the writer's intention)
Voice	Whether the action is done by or to the subject (active/passive)
Aspect	Whether the action is ongoing or completed

Let's practice conjugating with the verb *pick*.

> Melody *has picked* the flowers.
>   *Has* tells us the action was performed by one person (number).
>   The *-ed* ending tells us the action was performed in the past and was completed (tense/aspect).
>
> Raygan and Melody *have picked* the flowers.
>   *Have* tells us the action was performed by more than one person (number).
>   The *-ed* ending tells us the action was performed in the past and was completed (tense/aspect).
>
> Raygan and Melody *are picking* the flowers.
>   *Are* tells us the action was performed by more than one person (number).
>   *Are* tells us the action is in the present (tense).
>   The *-ing* ending tells us the action is ongoing (aspect).

Note: In some languages, verbs change based on the person's gender. In English, gender does not affect the verb.

☐ Briefly **review** the following lessons. **Check** the box when complete.
  Verb Tense (Day 22)   **Verb Voice** (Day 42)
  Verb Mood (Day 32)   **Subject-Verb Agreement** (number) (Day 107)

The remaining exercises in this lesson relate to the six elements of verb conjugation.

Name _____ Lesson 23 - Exercise 2   Day 112

Person: Underline the subject once and the verb twice (watch for helping verbs). (*Hint:* Compound sentences can have more than one subject and verb.)

1. I have been frightened many times in my life, but God's peace has overcome my fears.
2. Mandy and Josie picked blueberries from the back garden yesterday, but I was not able to help.

Number: Underline the correct verb so the subject and verb agree in number.

3. My father or my uncles frequently (tell, tells) the story of their infamous fishing trip on the Colorado River.
4. The football players and their coach (leaves, leave) the stadium through the rear exit.
5. Melissa, as well as all her siblings, (are, is) happy about being homeschooled.

Tense: Write a sentence for each of the following. (*Hint:* Use the Tense Construction chart from Day 22.)

Write a sentence using the verb *paint* in the past perfect tense.

_____

Write a sentence using the verb *raise* in the present perfect continuous tense.

_____

Mood: On the line, **indicate** whether the verb mood is indicative, imperative, or subjunctive.

6. _____ If only I had listened to the instructor better, this project would have been easier to complete.
7. _____ Josh and Katie take turns cleaning the horse stalls on Saturdays.
8. _____ When you leave the house, please turn the kitchen lights off.

Voice: Write active or passive on the line to indicate the voice of the verb.

9. _____ The volleyball players thanked their coach at the awards banquet last night.
10. _____ Forty pies sold at the bake sale before noon!
11. _____ My best friend Jamie came home from church with us today.
12. _____ Pizza and French fries were the only foods the toddler would eat.

Aspect: On the line, **write** whether the verb expresses completed or ongoing action.

13. _____ Emily had sewn all the squares for her quilting project on her own.
14. _____ Emily was sewing all the squares for her quilting project on her own.
15. _____ The giant fish was flopping like crazy at the bottom of the boat.
16. _____ The giant fish had flopped like crazy at the bottom of the boat.

☐ Using your index cards, **copy** the six elements of verb conjugation. **Check** the box when you are done.

Name _____   Lesson 23 - Exercise 3   Day 113

💬 Communication

Autobiography Notes: Outline

Today you will write a detailed outline for your autobiography. Before you begin writing, let's answer a few more questions that will give you more material to write with.

Write about a future career you would enjoy and why you would be good at that career.

_____
_____
_____
_____

List two good friends of yours and share one brief memory you have with each of them.

_____
_____
_____
_____

Record the details of your education. Are you homeschooled? Part of a private school? When did you start? Is there anything unique about your school situation? What subjects do you enjoy and why? What was the most interesting field trip you have ever taken?

_____
_____
_____
_____

Using the Autobiography Outline Worksheet in the back of this book, **construct** a detailed, chronological outline using the information you have jotted down regarding your autobiography throughout the third quarter. You may be tempted to skip this step and get into writing. However, a well-constructed, detailed outline will organize your thoughts, and the writing process will flow more smoothly. **Study** the outline example for one paragraph and repeat this basic structure for each paragraph of your autobiography. **Refer** to the Autobiography Rubric in the back of this book.

> I. Open with my favorite quote that reflects my life.
>   A. What society was like in my country when I was born (gathered this info from grandmother).
>   B. Details of my birthdate and location, situation my parents were in, other siblings, etc.
>   C. Description of myself with the three adjectives I chose on Day 98.
>   D. Closing sentence linking the quote to my adjectives and giving a hint about my first anecdote.
> II. (second paragraph)

Communication

Name _____ Lesson 23 - Exercise 3 Day 113

Wisdom Speaks

Copy the proverb.

> *Even a child makes himself known by his acts, by whether his conduct is pure and upright.* Proverbs 20:11

_____

_____

Using a dictionary or an online search with a parent's permission, **write** the definitions of the words below.

1. known: _____

_____

2. conduct (noun): _____

_____

Write a sentence using *conduct* as a noun.

_____

_____

A child could tell everyone they are "pure and upright," but their behavior may show otherwise. You are known (generally recognized) by your words *and* your behavior. While we need to make sure our words properly communicate our thoughts and feelings, our behaviors are also a great indicator of who we truly are. Behavior communicates!

Everyone has a standard of personal behavior they live by. This is known as their conduct. Some are known for their poor conduct and some for their good conduct. **Make a list** of the personal standards that are reflected in your conduct. *Examples:* I don't share gossip. I always greet people. I hold doors open for others. I don't interrupt conversations. I don't use my phone when around others.

- _____
- _____
- _____
- _____
- _____
- _____
- _____

Name _____ Lesson 23 - Exercise 4 Day 114

Worldview & Literary Analysis

Read the following excerpt from the chapter "The Truth" found in *Gifted Mind*.

> Similarly, I attribute the invention of the MRI entirely to the Lord's hand in revealing it to me. I credit His specific **intervention** to accomplish its reduction to practice.[1] Of course, one does not have to believe in God in order to discover the things He has made or to apply them to useful or medical purposes. *truth* [*sic*] is truth, no matter who discovers or stumbles upon it. However, the reason it is so important to understand the role of *God's truth* in scientific discovery is because without His truth as the foundation of all knowledge, we limit science to a closed system of natural law alone. In other words, man is all there is, and the physical laws of nature exist without any help from a Divine Being. But this **atheistic** approach **implodes** under its own weight due to both logical and scientific reasons. The universe cannot be **infinite** (as most honest scientists assert) because the laws of science and logic demand a *First Cause* for it. And our vast knowledge concerning man and the universe in which he lives has yet to adequately be explained solely through the **inherent** limitations of natural laws. Human reason requires the existence of an uncaused, Intelligent Being who caused man, the universe, and life to come into existence. Both logic and true science give evidence for this reality.
>
> However, today we find ourselves at a unique **juncture** in history where the approach to science that yielded so many great advancements in the past is held back by a **conventional**, atheistic, and **naturalistic** approach. Further, I believe great damage has been done to our culture by removing God from life's equation. Imagine erasing Monet's signature off of one of his masterpieces, or stripping Van Gogh, Picasso, or Rembrandt of the glory due them? Or simply re-writing [rewriting] history, omitting Galileo or Da Vinci? Tragically, this is exactly what we have done to God by writing Him out of His own creation story.
>
> I believe this is primarily why America is now in great **peril**. I worry that our phenomenal nation is fast losing her soul due to a **radical** departure from *the truths* on which she was founded some 240 years ago. Like the blood that slowly drains from a dying soldier on the battlefield, God's truth is systematically **seeping** from this great country, and she is growing steadily weaker because of it. And unless we do something, we could lose the battle.
>
> Similarly, if we remove Jesus Christ from the thread of scientific discovery, we lose our foundational access to *His truth*, and along with it, its unbounded power. I've observed over my lifetime the tragic and painful transformation that occurs in men's and women's souls throughout Western civilization when they choose to ignore God. I have experienced this firsthand, as "open-minded" scientists who believe in a *closed system* (natural law only) look down on others (Christians who are scientists) viewing *them* as "closed-minded." They **malign** us who believe in an *open system* where God creates laws of nature but also sometimes **overrides** them.[2]

---

1 Endnote from excerpt: *Creation Magazine*, 1994.
2 Damadian, *Gifted Mind*, p. 14–15.

Name _____ Lesson 23 - Exercise 4 Day 114

Respond to the following regarding today's reading excerpt.

1. Dr. Damadian "attribute[s] the invention of the MRI entirely to the Lord's hand." **Why** does he state that "one does not have to believe in God in order to discover the things He has made or to apply them"?
   _____
   _____

2. In your own words, **explain** why it is so important to understand the role of God's truth in scientific discovery.
   _____
   _____
   _____
   _____

   Why do you think a First Cause is necessary when contemplating the origin of the universe?
   _____
   _____
   _____
   _____

3. Both science and logic give evidence for **what** reality?
   _____
   _____

4. **What** does Dr. Damadian believe is holding back scientific advancements?
   _____
   _____

   What are some of the ways that you think God has been "written out" of His own creation story?
   _____
   _____
   _____

   Write a paragraph expressing what you believe are the consequences for a culture whose people choose to ignore God and His truths. Be specific.
   _____
   _____
   _____
   _____
   _____

Name _____ Lesson 23 - Exercise 5 Day 115

Review

☐ **Update** the Reading List chart with books you have read this week.

☐ **Recite** Psalm 53:1 from memory to your instructor.

Vocabulary Review

Match each word to the correct definition.

a. atheistic	d. infinite	g. juncture	j. override	m. seep
b. conventional	e. inherent	h. malign	k. peril	n. truth
c. implode	f. intervention	i. naturalistic	l. radical	

1. _____ collapse violently inward
2. _____ flow or leak through slowly
3. _____ immediate or serious danger
4. _____ limitless; impossible to measure
5. _____ use authority to cancel or reject
6. _____ the act of interfering with outcome
7. _____ existing as a natural, inseparable quality of someone or something
8. _____ based on what is generally done or believed
9. _____ particular point in time or events
10. _____ speak about in critical manner
11. _____ based on natural desire or instinct
12. _____ relating to denial of God's existence
13. _____ true; in accordance with facts
14. _____ extremist; very different from others

Grammar & Punctuation Review

1. **Define** conjugate.

   _____
   _____

Underline the correct verb so the subject and verb agree in number.

2. The fourth-grade students and their teacher (present, presents) a bouquet to the principal each year.
3. Bradley, along with his fishing buddies, (hope, hopes) to have a big catch today.

On the line, **indicate** whether the verb mood is indicative, imperative, or subjunctive.

4. _____ Every year we watch the geese fly south for the winter, and we know what is coming next!
5. _____ Finish your math lesson, and then we can talk about watching a movie.
6. _____ If it were me, I certainly would think twice about that decision.

Review   Lesson 23, Day 115 247

Name _____   Lesson 23 - Exercise 5   Day 115

Write active or passive on the line to indicate the voice of the verb.

7. _____ Thousands of artists assemble each year at the Convention Center for a watercolor art display.

8. _____ The impounded car was sold at an auction for a fraction of its worth.

9. _____ Apples and fish crackers were the favorite snacks in the Sunday school class.

Communication Review

In your own words, **describe** what an outline is and **why** it is important to write one.

_____
_____
_____
_____

Worldview & Literary Analysis Review

1. Both science and logic give evidence for **what** reality?

   _____
   _____

2. **What** does Dr. Damadian believe is holding back scientific advancements?

   _____
   _____

Copy the quote from Dr. Damadian.

> "[I]f we remove Jesus Christ from the thread of scientific discovery, we lose our foundational access to *His truth*, and along with it, its unbounded power. I've observed over my lifetime the tragic and painful transformation that occurs in men's and women's souls throughout Western civilization when they choose to ignore God."

_____
_____
_____
_____
_____
_____
_____

Special Feature

Lesson 24

Picture Study: King David Celebrating the Ark of the Covenant Being Brought into Jerusalem

Imagine yourself in this scene: Your king, David, is the greatest king your nation has known, and the Ark of the Covenant has just been brought into the city. **Describe** what you might hear, see, smell, and feel if you were in the crowd in this painting. **Write** in the present tense from the first-person point of view.

Name _____ Lesson 24 - Exercise 1 Day 116

Study these vocabulary words that are bolded in the excerpt from "The Truth" that you will read on Day 119.

Vocabulary

accountability	acceptance of responsibility for actions	**misapplication**	act of applying something incorrectly or improperly
alternate	another option or choice	**organic**	natural or related to nature
antithesis	contrast between two things; opposites	**presupposition**	believing something is true with no proof
archeology	study of the past through material remains	**primordial**	existing at or from the beginning of time
decadence	deterioration; falling into an inferior state	**status quo**	the current state of things
exempted	freed from obligation or liability	**subscribe**	express agreement with an idea
gargantuan	gigantic; extraordinary in size	**venerate**	to honor or respect a person or thing

Write a short sentence for each of these vocabulary words.

Exempted: _____
_____

Accountability: _____
_____

Status quo: _____
_____

Archeology: _____
_____

☐ **Use** index cards to **write** each vocabulary word from this lesson on one side and the definition on the other. **Check** the box when complete.

☐ **Copy** the Scripture verse on an index card. **Memorize** it by the end of this lesson. You may choose the Bible translation or use the one given. **Check** the box when complete.

For his invisible attributes, namely, his eternal power and divine nature, have been clearly perceived, ever since the creation of the world, in the things that have been made. So they are without excuse. Romans 1:20

Name _____ Lesson 24 - Exercise 2 Day 117

📝 Grammar & Punctuation

Transitive and Intransitive Verbs

A **transitive verb** requires a direct object to receive its action. If you can ask the questions "whom?" or "what?" after the verb, then the verb is transitive. Notice how incomplete these transitive verbs are without a direct object to "act" upon.

> A **transitive verb** requires a direct object to receive its action.
>
> **Intransitive verbs** complete their action without a direct object.

> *Examples:* She *pulled*. | He *borrows*. | We *brought*. | I *pay*. | They'll *raise*.

These transitive verbs need a *who* or a *what*. Let's add them.

> *Examples:* She pulled *the wagon*. | He borrows *money*. | We brought *friends*.
> I pay *taxes*. | They'll raise *the flag*.

Intransitive verbs complete their action without a direct object. Notice how the action of an intransitive verb makes sense *without* a direct object.

> *Examples:* The package *arrived*. | The boy *ran*. | The fish *swam*.
> A bird *chirped*. | A lady *laughed*.

Identify the underlined verb by **writing** transitive or intransitive on the line.

1. _____ Jasper <u>yanked</u> the sheets up over his head since he didn't want to get out of bed this morning.
2. _____ The Thomas family <u>raises</u> turkeys both for their use and for selling.
3. _____ I was so afraid that the mail would not <u>arrive</u> on time.
4. _____ Joel <u>handed</u> the hammer to his father before he even asked for it.
5. _____ Even though the weather was not cooperating, the team still <u>practiced</u>.
6. _____ When I came around the corner very suddenly, my mother <u>jumped</u>!

Write a sentence using an intransitive verb. Include a prepositional phrase. (Day 37)

_____

_____

Write a sentence using a transitive verb. Include an adverb. (Day 72)

_____

_____

Name _____   Lesson 24 - Exercise 2   Day 117

Sometimes, whether a verb is transitive or intransitive can depend on how it is used in a sentence. Verbs that have more than one meaning could be both transitive and intransitive.

> *Examples:* Aaron *walked* through the park. (intransitive use = no direct object)
>   DO
>   Aaron *walked* his dog through the park. (transitive use = has a direct object)

If you are unsure if a verb is transitive or intransitive, remember to ask the question "whom?" or "what?" after the verb. If you get an answer, the verb is transitive.

7. **Write** a sentence using the word *stung* as a transitive verb.

   _____

   _____

8. **Write** a sentence using the word *stung* as an intransitive verb.

   _____

   _____

Since the object of a preposition and a direct object are both nouns, it is easy to confuse the two in a sentence containing an intransitive verb.

> *Example:* The choir *sang* (in the sanctuary).

Sanctuary is not a direct object receiving the action, it is the object of the preposition. Therefore, we know this is an intransitive verb, as it has no direct object.

Study the underlined words and **label** them **DO** for a direct object or **OP** for an object of the preposition. On the line, **write** transitive or intransitive regarding the italicized verb.

9. _____ Our jaws dropped as the eagle *flew* over our heads!
10. _____ Every time I *wash* the car, it seems to rain, and it gets dirty all over again.
11. _____ I *shopped* with my grandmother for the gift I needed for the wedding.
12. _____ The long, black snake *swallowed* the mouse in a matter of minutes.

Review It!

Underline the pronouns and **circle** any antecedents. There may be multiple pronouns per antecedent. (*Hint:* One sentence has a pronoun *as* the antecedent.)

13. The author, who won the award, signed books at the end of the ceremony.
14. Jackson and Juan loved mowing, so they started their own landscaping business.
15. Whenever Mom goes grocery shopping, she can't help but purchase yet another live plant!
16. We left everybody behind and journeyed up the mountain by ourselves.

☐ Using your index cards, **copy** the definitions of transitive and intransitive verbs and include an example of each. **Check** the box when you are done.

Name _____   Lesson 24 - Exercise 3   Day 118

Communication

Autobiography Notes: Rough Draft

Writing is like sculpting. Picture an artist with a lump of clay. The artist has a vision but must first mold and shape, taking off excess clay in some areas and adding extra clay in others. This process can take some time as the artist observes from all angles and adjusts. Finally, finishing touches and details are added until the artist is happy with the creation.

I made several adjustments to the paragraph you just read, molding and shaping it until I was pleased and felt it communicated my thoughts effectively. As you write your autobiography, you will do the same.

The rough draft is like the lump of clay. The outline you wrote is your vision. Start by writing down as much as you can, using the answers to the questions from previous lessons and any other details from your life you wish to include. Mold and shape your "lump" by removing unnecessary words or thoughts and adding more interesting language and transitional words. Whether you are typing your autobiography or writing it by hand, the rough draft is a messy process. Don't be discouraged! With some molding, shaping, and polishing, your final draft will shine.

Review the following charts in the back of this book. They will help you mold and shape your rough draft! **Check** the box next to each chart once reviewed.

- ☐ Paragraph Structure
- ☐ Tips for Better Writing (the chart form)
- ☐ Point of View
- ☐ Autobiography Rubric
- ☐ Building a Better Sentence
- ☐ Five Figures of Speech
- ☐ Transitional Phrases

Today you are "warming up" your lump of clay, getting ready to mold it into a masterpiece. Yes, your life is a masterpiece of God's handiwork! The following exercises will give you more "clay" to work with when writing your rough draft.

Use the Building a Better Sentence chart and **rewrite** the humorous anecdote you wrote on Day 108. **Incorporate** at least one of the five figures of speech.

_____
_____
_____
_____
_____
_____
_____
_____

Communication   Lesson 24, Day 118   253

Name _____ Lesson 24 - Exercise 3 Day 118

Use the Point of View chart to **write** a sentence from the first-person point of view. (Remember, use a sentence that will be included in your autobiography.)

_____
_____

Use vivid imagery (Day 34) to **describe** a location you will mention in your autobiography. This could be your home, a path through the woods, a picnic area, your bedroom, etc.

_____
_____
_____
_____

Transitional words and phrases are used to jump from one thought or place to the next.

> *Example:* My audition did not go very well. <u>Consequently</u>, I decided it was time to give up on being in the choir.

Sometimes they can occur within a paragraph, and sometimes they can be used to transition from one paragraph to the next.

Refer to the Transitional Phrases chart and **incorporate** a transitional phrase into a paragraph about one of your early childhood memories.

_____
_____
_____
_____
_____
_____
_____
_____

In Conclusion

Your concluding paragraph should be a summary of your autobiography. It should look back at the major lessons in your life, obstacles overcome, personality formation, God's hand at work, etc. It could also look forward to the future with hints at the many possible directions your life could go.

It is time to gather all the bits of information about your life you have written throughout this quarter. The **rough draft** is due by the next Communication lesson (Day 123). Your instructor will review it based on the Autobiography Rubric and offer suggestions for improvement. You may type or handwrite your rough draft according to the directions given on Day 93. The **final draft** is due on Day 128.

I hope you are excited to share your story! Remember to reference the Autobiography Rubric, as your instructor will use it for grading purposes. Do your best work as unto the Lord!

Name _____   Lesson 24 - Exercise 4   Day 119

Worldview & Literary Analysis

Read the following excerpt from the chapter "The Truth" found in *Gifted Mind*.

> Of course, all this began when man chose convenience over the Creator, pushing Him out of their new lives in the Garden. In doing so, Adam and Eve (and subsequent generations) **exempted** themselves from God's rule and His laws. Today, we do the same by blindly **subscribing** to a godless theory of human origins. The folly of evolution has officially replaced the Creator as the originator and developer of mankind.
>
> But there is an unintended cause-and-effect consequence to this action. By rejecting His truth, we are not able to exempt ourselves from **accountability** to God or His Laws. *Truth*, like the law of gravity, is still in effect whether we recognize it or not. Even so, with the Creator's natural and supernatural laws eliminated from consideration, not only are we forced to invent an **alternate** theory of origins, but we also unleash a full range of human **decadence** and its devastations (i.e., adultery, fornication, homosexuality, drug and alcohol addiction, and all manner of degradations of human dignity).[1]
>
> Without God as absolute lawgiver and source of morality (right and wrong), we are left with a sliding scale of morality. In other words, what is *good*, *fair*, *right*, or *wrong* now becomes a matter of one's own opinion or worldview. In the same way, without recognizing God as the *giver of truth*, we not only make up our own truths, but are also led to many wrong conclusions in life . . . and in science.
>
> Nowhere is this reality more obvious than with the study of mankind's beginnings. Because men are often content to be what I refer to as "GSQs," or "Guardians of the **Status Quo**," they are either too afraid, too proud, or too unwilling to challenge the blindly accepted belief in evolution. As Darwin speculates:
>
>> Therefore I should infer from analogy that *probably* all the **organic** beings which have ever lived on this earth *have descended from some one* primordial *form* into which life was first breathed[2] (emphasis added).
>
> This speculation, though widely and unquestionably accepted in the scientific and medical community, is founded, not upon science, but rather upon **presupposition**, intellectual bias, and the misunderstanding and **misapplication** of **archeology** and scientific knowledge. It begins with the presupposition that there is no God. This is the foundation upon which evolution is built. So if there is no God, He could not possibly have created the universe or man (because He doesn't exist to create them). Evolution also clings to a built-in bias (prejudice) against all matters of faith, presuming such to be the **antithesis** of science and the scientific method. But nothing could be further from the truth. You rarely hear of the **gargantuan** amount of faith required to convince oneself of evolution.
>
> This then is the lens through which today's mainstream scientific community sees and interprets everything. Consequently, belief in creationism is in the category of "fairy tale" or "myth," while evolution is lovingly perched on the fireplace mantle like an idol, where it is regularly **venerated** and worshiped as unquestionable fact.[3]

1 Endnote from excerpt: Romans 1:18–32 describes in detail the consequences of man's rejection of God as Creator and truth-giver.
2 Endnote from excerpt: Charles Darwin, *The Origin of Species* (New York: Barnes & Noble Classics, 2009), p. 380.
3 Damadian, *Gifted Mind*, p. 16–17.

Name _____ Lesson 24 - Exercise 4 Day 119

Respond to the following regarding today's reading excerpt.

1. **How** are some people today similar to Adam and Eve in their interaction with God?

   _____
   _____
   _____
   _____
   _____
   _____

2. **Summarize** the second paragraph of today's reading excerpt. **Include** a direct quote with the necessary punctuation.

   _____
   _____
   _____
   _____
   _____
   _____

Dr. Damadian expresses that "[w]ithout God as absolute lawgiver … what is *good, fair, right,* or *wrong* now becomes a matter of one's own opinion or worldview." **Explain** why you think this may cause chaos in society.

_____
_____
_____
_____
_____
_____

3. **Give** three reasons why the "Guardians of the Status Quo" blindly accept evolution.

   a. _____
   b. _____
   c. _____

4. **List** three things Dr. Damadian claims evolution is founded upon.

   a. _____
   b. _____
   c. _____

Lesson 24, Day 119

Language Lessons for a Living Education Level 10

Name _____ Lesson 24 - Exercise 5 Day 120

Review

- **Update** the Reading List chart with books you have read this week.
- **Recite** Romans 1:20 from memory to your instructor.

Vocabulary Review

Match each word to the correct definition.

a. accountability	d. archeology	g. gargantuan	j. presupposition	m. subscribe
b. alternate	e. decadence	h. misapplication	k. primordial	n. venerate
c. antithesis	f. exempted	i. organic	l. status quo	

1. _____ express agreement with an idea
2. _____ another option or choice
3. _____ natural or related to nature
4. _____ gigantic; extraordinary size
5. _____ current state of things
6. _____ freed from obligation or liability
7. _____ contrast between things; opposites
8. _____ existing at or from the beginning of time
9. _____ believing something without proof
10. _____ act of applying incorrectly or improperly
11. _____ to honor or respect a person or thing
12. _____ deterioration; falling into inferior state
13. _____ acceptance of responsibility
14. _____ study of past through material remains

Grammar & Punctuation Review

1. **Describe** the difference between a transitive and an intransitive verb.

   _____
   _____

Identify the underlined verb by **writing** transitive or intransitive on the line.

2. _____ Matthew <u>drove</u> his dirt bike to the back of the cornfield, looking for his lost goat.
3. _____ My friend Layla <u>called</u> her mother for a ride home since it was raining.
4. _____ The chili <u>bubbled</u> in the pot on the stove.

Study the underlined words and **label** them **DO** for a direct object or **OP** for an object of the preposition. On the line, **write** transitive or intransitive regarding the italicized verb.

5. _____ Each time I *write* <u>my name</u>, I tend to form my letters slightly differently for some reason.
6. _____ Gabe and Brady *laughed* so hard at the <u>comedian</u> that they started to cry.
7. _____ All I could do was *shake* <u>my head</u> when I realized the mistake I had made.

Review

Name _____ Lesson 24 - Exercise 5 Day 120

8. **Write** a sentence using the word *broke* as a transitive verb.
   _____
   _____

9. **Write** a sentence using the word *broke* as an intransitive verb.
   _____
   _____

Communication Review

1. **Describe** how writing is like sculpting a lump of clay.
   _____
   _____
   _____
   _____
   _____

2. **Tell** how transitional words and phrases are used in writing.
   _____
   _____

3. **Fill in** the blanks about a concluding paragraph in an autobiography.
   Your _____ _____ should be a _____ of your autobiography. It should look back at the major _____ in your life, obstacles overcome, _____ _____, _____ hand at work, etc. It could also look _____ to the future with _____ at the many possible _____ your life could go.

Worldview & Literary Analysis Review

1. **Give** three reasons why the "Guardians of the Status Quo" blindly accept evolution.
   a. _____
   b. _____
   c. _____

Copy the quote from Dr. Damadian.

> "Without God as absolute lawgiver and source of morality (right and wrong), we are left with a sliding scale of morality."

_____
_____

Special Feature

Poem Study: "The Cross" by John Newton

In evil long I took delight,
Unawed by shame or fear,
Till a new object struck my sight,
And stopped my wild career.

I saw One hanging on a tree,
In agonies and blood;
He fixed His languid eyes on me,
As near His cross I stood.

Sure never till my latest breath,
Shall I forget that look!
It seemed to charge me with His death,
Though not a word He spoke.

A second look He gave, which said,
"I freely all forgive;
This blood is for thy ransom paid;
I die that thou mayest live."

Thus while His death my sin displays
In all its blackest hue,
Such is the mystery of grace,
It seals my pardon too!

Study the poem and notice that every other line rhymes. This is called the ABAB pattern. John Newton's poem contains five stanzas. A stanza is a verse in poetry. After studying the poem and thinking deeply about its meaning, **write** a similar poem of your own that contains two stanzas that use the ABAB pattern.

_____
_____
_____
_____
_____
_____
_____
_____

Name _____ Lesson 25 - Exercise 1 Day 121

Study these vocabulary words that are bolded in the excerpt from "The Truth" that you will read on Day 124. This week's vocabulary words have a lot to do with deception.

Vocabulary

adaptation	the adjustment of organisms to their environment	**maxim**	a general truth or rule of conduct
condemned	sentenced to a certain punishment	**mythical**	based on or described in a myth
demise	end or death of someone or something	**obsolete**	no longer useful
dissuading	advising not to do something	**postulate**	a hypothesis assumed to be true
façade	false or artificial front hiding a reality	**pre-eminence** (preeminence)	quality of being better or more important than others
foisted	forced acceptance about something through deceit	**pride**	feeling that one deserves the respect of others
hoax	deception, either malicious or humorous	**random**	no clear plan or purpose
innate	natural, inborn behavior present from birth	**suffice**	to be adequate; meet the need

Write about a criminal who deceives, is caught, and the truth is revealed. Use at least six vocabulary words. Make your story colorful and interesting. **Have** your instructor read your story then sign below. You may add or change suffixes on the vocabulary words.

_____
_____
_____
_____
_____
_____
_____
_____
_____
_____

Instructor's signature: _____

☐ **Create** definition flashcards with the vocabulary words from this lesson. **Write** the word on one side of an index card and the definition on the other side. **Check** the box when complete.

☐ **Memory Verse: Copy** the verse on an index card and **memorize** it by the end of this lesson. You may use the Bible translation of your choice or use the one provided. **Check** the box when complete.

Lesson 25 - Exercise 2   Day 122

Grammar & Punctuation

Plural and Singular Nouns

Singular refers to one (*example: dog*) and **plural** refers to more than one (*example: dogs*). Most nouns are made plural by adding an *s*. However, there are many other ways to form plurals depending on what letters the noun ends with. Some plural nouns are irregular and do not follow a specific rule. Some nouns remain the same in both the singular and plural forms. **Study** the following chart.

> **Singular** refers to one.
> **Plural** refers to more than one.

Rules for Pluralizing Nouns

Regular Nouns		Ends in *s, ch, sh, x,* or *z*		Ends in *f* or *fe*	
add *s*		add *es*		drop *f/fe*, add *ves*	
1 book	2 books	1 box	2 boxes	1 knife	2 knives
1 apple	2 apples	1 church	2 churches	1 leaf	2 leaves
1 battle	2 battles	1 dish	2 dishes	1 life	2 lives

Exceptions: cliff=cliffs, roof=roofs

Ends in vowel + *o*		Ends in consonant + *o*		No change	
add *s*		add *es*		1 fish	2 fish
1 zoo	2 zoos	1 potato	2 potatoes	1 sheep	2 sheep
1 video	2 videos	1 hero	2 heroes	1 aircraft	2 aircraft
1 stereo	2 stereos	1 echo	2 echoes	1 deer	2 deer

Exceptions: piano=pianos, photo=photos

Ends in vowel + *y*		Ends in consonant + *y*		Irregular Nouns	
add *s*		remove *y*, add *ies*		1 species	2 species
1 day	2 days	1 party	2 parties	1 man	2 men
1 key	2 keys	1 baby	2 babies	1 woman	2 women
1 boy	2 boys	1 country	2 countries	1 mouse	2 mice

There are several more irregular plural nouns, along with nouns that do not change form. The following chart shows some common irregular plurals.

Common Irregular Nouns

larva = larvae	ox = oxen	oasis = oases	swine = swine	trout = trout
cactus = cacti	fungus = fungi	stimulus = stimuli	syllabus = syllabi	datum = data
person = people	foot = feet	child = children	goose = geese	focus = foci
bison = bison	crisis = crises	series = series	tuna = tuna	index = indices
diagnosis = diagnoses	analysis = analyses	curriculum = curricula		

Name _____ Lesson 25 - Exercise 2 Day 122

Write the plural form of the singular nouns listed.

1. factor _____
2. rabbit _____
3. wish _____
4. key _____
5. child _____
6. index _____
7. thief _____
8. trucker _____
9. potato _____
10. bison _____
11. larva _____
12. disciple _____
13. radio _____
14. match _____
15. story _____

Semicolons

Semicolons are used to join two main clauses that require a punctuation mark stronger than a comma but weaker than a period. **Study** these three ways to use a semicolon.

> **Semicolons** are used to join two main clauses that require a punctuation mark stronger than a comma but weaker than a period.

When to Use a Semicolon
Before a conjunction in a long compound sentence
The science project called for a long list of ingredients, including 2 cups of baking soda, 1 cup of vinegar, and 3 ounces of food coloring; but I had only 1 cup of baking soda.
Between word groups containing commas (this includes Bible references if a new chapter is given)
The school had several teachers on the committee, including the art teacher, Mrs. Morris; the gym teacher, Mr. Peters; and the English teacher, Mrs. Johnson.
Our pastor spoke on Ephesians 5:15–17, 21; and 6:10.
Between two independent clauses (not joined by a coordinating conjunction)
I ordered chocolate ice cream; chocolate always helps my mood!
We managed to bake several dozen cookies Saturday afternoon; on Sunday, however, we rested from our baking.

Write a sentence containing a semicolon.

_____
_____

☐ Using your index cards, **copy** the rules for pluralizing nouns based on word endings. **Check** the box when you are done.

Name _____   Lesson 25 - Exercise 3   Day 123

💬 Communication

Rough Draft Due

Give your rough draft to your instructor for review using the Autobiography Rubric in the back of this book. **Ask** them to sign below after receiving the rough draft.

Instructor's signature: _____

Cover Page and Artwork

The final draft of your autobiography will feature a cover page attached to the front that includes artwork. The artwork could be a photograph or sketch of yourself, a work of art you admire, a photograph or sketch of a place you love, or another visual. Choose something that you feel best reflects your life story. This could be printed from a computer or hand drawn.

The cover page must also contain your name and a title.

> *Examples:* Natalia Williams: A Life Full of Promise
> Aaron Reynolds: Overcoming Physical Challenges
> Ryan Peters: Dreams Do Come True

Choose a title that best expresses what the reader will find inside. How you arrange the title and artwork is up to you … this is your story!

Write your name and title here.

_____

Final Draft: Due on Day 128

When your instructor has finished reviewing your autobiography, **make the necessary changes** over the next week. If handwriting, you should rewrite the entire paper as neatly as possible. If using a word processor, make the changes and reprint. **Attach** your cover page to the front.

Oral Presentation

On the final lesson of the third quarter (Day 133), you will have an opportunity to share your autobiography in an oral presentation. Presenting orally (verbally) can be intimidating for some students, while others are comfortable with public speaking. The good news is you are already very familiar with the topic. You and your instructor will decide the date, time, and audience. Possible audience: homeschool co-op, family, grandparents, nursing home, youth group, etc. You will receive further instruction on the oral presentation in Lesson 26. **Fill in** the following information.

Oral presentation audience: _____

Date, time, and location of presentation: _____

_____

Note to instructor: Please use the Oral Presentation Rubric in the back of the book as an aid in grading.

Instructor's signature: _____

Wisdom Speaks

Copy the proverb.

> *Whoever goes about slandering reveals secrets; therefore do not associate with a simple babbler.* Proverbs 20:19

_____
_____

Using a dictionary or an online search with a parent's permission, **write** the definitions of the words below.

1. slander (noun): _____
_____

2. associate (verb): _____
_____

Write a complex sentence (Day 52) using the words *slander* and *associate*.
_____
_____

Some things should be revealed, and other things should not. Wisdom will tell you what to share and what not to share. Many people have been very hurt by words. Even if what you share is true, it may be hurtful and even harmful. Sometimes people share things that are not even true with the intent to put another down. The Bible warns us not to do this and advises us to avoid people who behave this way.

Write a dialogue between you and a person who is slandering a common friend. **Think** about how you would respond in a way that defends the friend without starting an argument with the person. Be sure to **use** quotation marks in your dialogue. (Day 47)

_____
_____
_____
_____
_____
_____
_____
_____
_____

Name_____ Lesson 25 - Exercise 4 Day 124

Worldview & Literary Analysis

Read the following excerpt from the chapter "The Truth" found in *Gifted Mind*.

> However, the "dirty little secret" of Darwinian evolution (the supposition that human existence is entirely the result of statistical chance and **random adaptation** over billions of years) is that there is no *scientific evidence* to sustain such a **postulate**! The flimsy **façade** protecting this theory hides the fact that there's actually nothing to see behind the curtain. Evolution is merely the scientific community's "sideshow," with a few **mythical** freaks and some smoke and mirrors thrown in to divert the audience's attention. And like that circus sideshow, people feel cheated and deceived when they finally discover the real truth.
>
> But all the modern-day scientific "carnival barking" cannot hide the fact that evolution is an empty box — a tragic **hoax foisted** upon mankind, distracting and **dissuading** them from the belief mankind (and science) held for thousands of years — that we are creations of a gracious God. I will deal more specifically with this in chapter 9, but **suffice** it to say that the acceptance of evolution as the official version of history and origins effectually marked the beginning of the end for Western civilization, and particularly the **demise** of the unique miracle that is America. As a consequence, the well-being of our very nation now hangs in the balance. The Christian worldview that brought centuries of blessing in all aspects of society is now pushed to the margins, deemed **obsolete**, and thrown into the trash bin. Belief in the Creator is currently under vicious attack, imperiled by selfishness and financial greed, underwritten and justified by the Darwinian deception of "survival of the fittest." In plain English, when the spiritual assets of a country are drained, its bank accounts go to a zero balance. I believe those accounts are being severely depleted, partially due to the removal of God from society.
>
> An old **maxim** warns, "Those who ignore history are **condemned** to repeat it," and I fear that we are now standing on the threshold of repeating the error and chaos of Babel. Genesis 11:1–9 tells the story of a united human race in the generations following the Great Flood. In those days, Scripture records that humanity spoke a single language and soon began migrating from the east to the land of Shinar. Mankind had become skilled in engineering and construction, and had begun building a city whose tower, they said would "reach to heaven." By attempting to construct this ancient high rise, they asserted their man-centered **pre-eminence** [preeminence] over God along with their independence from Him.
>
> That's when God paid their city a visit, and He was not pleased. This supposed *stairway to heaven* was only further leading mankind away from their Maker. Ironically, in building themselves up towards heaven, they were, in reality, digging a grave of their own demise. Instead of seeking truth from God, they desired to *become* gods themselves. Humanity's **innate pride** once again became its downfall (Proverbs 6:18). And so, according to Moses' account, God confused their language, causing them to speak multiple languages. As a result, they could no longer understand each other. This new language barrier halted construction of the tower and God scattered His creation throughout the earth. And we wonder why the world is so confused and chaotic today! All because of man's inherent pride and rejection of his Creator.[1]

---

1 Damadian, *Gifted Mind*, p. 17–19.

Name _____   Lesson 25 - Exercise 4   Day 124

Respond to the following regarding today's reading excerpt.

1. **Summarize** the first paragraph from today's reading excerpt. Be sure to thoroughly understand the bolded vocabulary words.

   _____
   _____
   _____
   _____
   _____
   _____
   _____

2. **Fill in** the blanks of this quote from Dr. Damadian.

   "But all the modern-day scientific '_____ _____' cannot hide the fact that evolution is an empty box — a _____ _____ foisted upon mankind, distracting and _____ them from the belief mankind (_____ _____) held for thousands of years — that we are creations of a _____ _____."

3. **Finish** the following sentence.

   "Belief in the Creator is currently under vicious attack, _____
   _____
   _____"

Draw an analogy between the "stairway to heaven" that mankind attempted to build at Babel and the construction of Darwinian evolution. **Explain** how evolution has led man further from God, slowed true scientific discovery, and created chaos in our world. **Include** quotes from Dr. Damadian and at least one Scripture reference. **Have** your instructor read your analogy and sign below.

_____
_____
_____
_____
_____
_____
_____
_____
_____

Instructor's signature: _____

Name _____   Lesson 25 - Exercise 5   Day 125

Review

☐ **Update** the Reading List chart with books you have read this week.

☐ **Recite** Isaiah 2:11 from memory to your instructor.

Vocabulary Review

Match each word to the correct definition.

a. adaptation	e. façade	i. maxim	m. pre-eminence (preeminence)
b. condemned	f. foisted	j. mythical	n. pride
c. demise	g. hoax	k. obsolete	o. random
d. dissuading	h. innate	l. postulate	p. suffice

1. _____ no longer useful
2. _____ general truth or rule
3. _____ no clear plan or purpose
4. _____ adequate; meet the need
5. _____ natural, inborn behavior
6. _____ deception, malicious or humorous
7. _____ feeling of deserving respect
8. _____ adjustment of organisms to their environment
9. _____ quality of being better or more important than others
10. _____ false or artificial front hiding a reality
11. _____ forced acceptance through deceit
12. _____ advising not to do something
13. _____ sentenced to certain punishment
14. _____ end or death of someone or something
15. _____ based on or described in myth
16. _____ hypothesis assumed to be true

Grammar & Punctuation Review

1. **Describe** the difference between singular and plural.
   _____
   _____

Describe how to pluralize nouns ending in the following.

2. *s, ch, sh, x,* or *z*: _____
3. vowel + *o*: _____
4. *f* or *fe*: _____
5. consonant + *o*: _____
6. vowel + *y*: _____
7. consonant + *y*: _____

Review   Lesson 25, Day 125

Name _____   Lesson 25 - Exercise 5   Day 125

Write the plural form of the singular nouns listed. Watch for irregular nouns and nouns that do not change form.

8. cactus _____   12. focus _____   16. church _____

9. tuna _____   13. person _____   17. fungus _____

10. country _____   14. vehicle _____   18. bison _____

11. potato _____   15. knife _____   19. stereo _____

20. **Write** a sentence containing a semicolon.

_____
_____

Communication Review

1. **Practice** writing dialogue by sharing the conversation (or possible conversation) you had with your instructor about planning your oral presentation.

_____
_____
_____
_____
_____
_____
_____

Copy the proverb.

> *Whoever goes about slandering reveals secrets; therefore do not associate with a simple babbler.*
> Proverbs 20:19

_____
_____

Worldview & Literary Analysis Review

1. **What** does Dr. Damadian call the "dirty little secret" of Darwinian evolution?

_____
_____

2. **How** does Dr. Damadian define Darwinian evolution?

_____
_____

Special Feature

Lesson 26

Scripture Study: Selections on Truth and Wisdom

Study the verses and **write** a short, personal prayer in response to the truth you read.

So teach us to number our days that we may get a heart of wisdom. Psalm 90:12

Behold, you delight in truth in the inward being, and you teach me wisdom in the secret heart. Psalm 51:6

Jesus said to him, "I am the way, and the truth, and the life. No one comes to the Father except through me." John 14:6

When the Spirit of truth comes, he will guide you into all the truth, for he will not speak on his own authority, but whatever he hears he will speak, and he will declare to you the things that are to come. He will glorify me, for he will take what is mine and declare it to you. John 16:13–14

He [Jesus] is the radiance of the glory of God and the exact imprint of his nature, and he upholds the universe by the word of his power. After making purification for sins, he sat down at the right hand of the Majesty on high. Hebrews 1:3

Stand therefore, having fastened on the belt of truth, and having put on the breastplate of righteousness. Ephesians 6:14

Name_____   Lesson 26 - Exercise 1   Day 126

Study these vocabulary words that are bolded in the excerpt from "The Truth" that you will read on Day 129.

Vocabulary

adept	skilled or proficient; an expert at something	**heinous**	shockingly evil or wicked
bigotry	strong, unreasonable beliefs against people with different ideas or beliefs	**indifference**	lack of interest, sympathy, or concern for
devoid	completely without; entirely lacking	**masquerade**	to pretend to be a person or thing one is not
diabolical	extremely evil; associated with the devil	**perpetually**	forever or an indefinite period of time
epiphany	sudden insight or perception of the meaning of something	**profound**	state of having or showing understanding of serious matters
fabricated	invented or made up with intent to deceive	**propaganda**	spreading of ideas or rumor to injure a cause, idea, or person
genocide	the deliberate destruction of a political or racial group		

1. Use the vocabulary list to **fill in** the blanks in this excerpt from *Gifted Mind* found in this lesson's reading assignment.

   "Some historians, both then and now, even believed Hitler's _____ had some religious roots. But the perpetrator of the crime, Adolph Hitler, was actually _____ of any valid religious beliefs. Instead of religion, Germany's _____ dictator justified his _____ crimes through a belief in Darwinian evolution and it's [*sic*] 'survival of the fittest' _____.[1] But you don't hear that taught today in high school history or science class, do you?"

☐ **Use** index cards to **write** each vocabulary word from this lesson on one side and the definition on the other. **Check** the box when complete.

☐ **Copy** the Scripture verse on an index card. **Memorize** it by the end of this lesson. You may choose the Bible translation or use the one given. **Check** the box when complete.

I thank my God always when I remember you in my prayers, because I hear of your love and of the faith that you have toward the Lord Jesus and for all the saints, and I pray that the sharing of your faith may become effective for the full knowledge of every good thing that is in us for the sake of Christ. Philemon 1:4–6

---
[1] Endnote from excerpt: http://www.creationism.org/csshs/v08n3p24.htm.

Name _____ Lesson 26 - Exercise 2 Day 127

Grammar & Punctuation

Possessive Nouns

A **possessive noun** shows ownership or a direct connection and is usually formed by adding *'s*. Often, there is confusion between plural nouns and possessive nouns. An apostrophe is used to designate the ownership shown by a possessive noun but is *not* used to form a plural noun.

> A **possessive noun** shows ownership or a direct connection and is usually formed by adding *'s*.

> *Examples:* There are six *books* needed for the course. (plural noun formed by adding *s*)
> The *book's* binding was coming apart. (possessive noun – shows ownership – formed by adding *'s*)

Singular and Plural Possessive Nouns

Possessive nouns can be singular or plural. To form the singular possessive, add *'s*. Since most plural nouns already end in *s*, the plural possessive is formed by simply adding an apostrophe (').

> *Examples:* Singular possessive: the cat's tail | the boy's bike | the truck's tires
> Plural possessive: the cats' tails | the boys' bike | the trucks' tires

Usually, the object of the possessive comes immediately after it. However, sometimes adjectives are placed between the possessive and its object, or the possessive appears at the end of the sentence.

> *Examples:* Alex's *room* | Alex's really awesome game *room* | The game *room* is Alex's.

Often, possession is implied without mentioning what is being possessed (*example: I visited Amanda's*). This is sometimes the case with business names.

> *Examples:* Big Ed's (restaurant) | Alexander's (jewelry shop) | Hampton's (grocery store)

Place apostrophes where needed to show possession.

1. My cousins house is so stately; the porchs columns are enormous.
2. Even though the leaves had begun to change color, Octobers weather felt very much like summer.
3. When my mother gets home from jogging, I will ask her if I can go to Anikas.
4. Frustratingly, all the pans lids were stored in a separate drawer.
5. The group meets on Mondays at the park, but this Mondays weather looks unsuitable.
6. It was Tarons incredible memory that made him so competitive at Bible quizzings year-end competition.

On Day 97, we studied possessive pronouns and possessive adjectives. These do not require an apostrophe to show possession. Possessive pronouns function as nouns, while possessive adjectives modify (or describe) nouns. *Any* pronoun used to show possession and functioning as an adjective is considered a possessive adjective.

Name _____ Lesson 26 - Exercise 2 Day 127

> *Examples:* Possessive pronoun: Erin's rabbit is larger than *mine*. His work is harder than *yours*.
> Possessive adjective: *His* car is in the driveway. *This* book was left here.

Review the list of possessive pronouns and possessive adjectives found on Day 97.

Underline the possessive pronouns and possessive adjectives and **place** apostrophes where needed.

7. If it wasn't for Christs work on the Cross, salvation would not be yours or mine.
8. Although Andrew wasn't impressed with the restaurants menu, he appreciated his friends generous offer to treat him to dinner.
9. My science project took first place, yet I really felt that Andreas was far better than mine.
10. We went to visit my aunt and uncle in Massachusetts, and when we turned onto their street, I knew instantly which house was theirs.

Additionally, the possessive adjective *whose* is the possessive form of the pronoun *who*.

> *Examples:* Her brother, *whose name* is Eric, plays soccer at college.
> Angelica, *whose dog* I watch, left on vacation.

Note: The possessive adjective *its* does not use an apostrophe. This is to avoid confusion with the contraction *it's* (meaning *it is*).

Place apostrophes where needed to show possession and **underline** any possessive pronouns or possessive adjectives.

11. In my opinion, its far better to have a few quality friends than several mere acquaintances.
12. Grandma Johnsons house has been in our family for generations, yet it doesn't feel like mine.
13. Ellies birthday gift was left on the table by her brother in hopes of surprising his sister.
14. The maintenance man, whose job it was to keep the grass cut, seemed to forget the responsibility was his.
15. All four cats bowls were empty, and their hunger was evident!

Write a sentence using both a possessive pronoun and a possessive adjective. Remember, function is what differentiates a noun from an adjective in a sentence.

_____

_____

Write a sentence containing a plural possessive noun.

_____

_____

Name _____   Lesson 26 - Exercise 3   Day 128

❓ Communication

Final Draft Due

If you have not done so already, turn in the final draft of your autobiography to your instructor for grading.

Autobiography Reflection

To "reflect" means to give serious thought or consideration to something that took place. Many people never take the time or have the opportunity to write an autobiography, so you have had a somewhat unique experience. Today, you will reflect on the writing process and what you learned.

Answer the following questions regarding your autobiography writing experience.

Did you learn anything new about yourself as you asked parents, guardians, grandparents, and others about your life?

_____
_____
_____
_____

Did you find writing about yourself easy or difficult and why?

_____
_____
_____
_____

What do you hope people gain or learn from reading your autobiography?

_____
_____
_____
_____

Would you like to write another autobiography when you are ten years older? If so, what do you hope it would contain?

_____
_____
_____
_____

Communication

Name _____ Lesson 26 - Exercise 3 Day 128

Oral Presentation

An **oral presentation** consists of an individual or group addressing an audience on a particular topic. The word *oral* in this sense means "by word of mouth." You have communicated your life story in writing, and this presentation will give you a chance to practice verbal communication as you convert your autobiography into an oral presentation.

Create an Oral Presentation Plan

When making a presentation, eye contact with your audience is important. Reading directly from your autobiography without looking up will cause a feeling of disconnect with your audience. Since you are quite familiar with your autobiography, you may choose to present without reading the paper at all. However, if you feel you need to read, make sure to look up at the audience from time to time.

Refer to the Oral Presentation Rubric in the back of the book to become familiar with the expectations for this assignment. Also in the back of this book, you will find the Autobiography Oral Presentation Worksheet you may wish to use as an aid in preparing your presentation. **Study** the following tips for getting your presentation together.

Oral Presentation Tips
- In preparation, read through your autobiography several times so it is fresh in your memory.
- When presenting, introduce yourself and explain the assignment you have been given. A strong start to your presentation will make your audience want to hear more.
- Speak in a friendly, confident way, with enough volume in your voice for your audience to easily hear you. Make sure you choose an area with minimal distractions.
- Use hand gestures to avoid appearing "stiff" and change your facial expressions based on the content of your speech (*example:* an excited expression when sharing a thrilling anecdote, a downcast expression when sharing a difficult moment).
- Use visual aids such as a photo of yourself, a favorite childhood toy or book, artwork you created, something you built, etc.
- Conclude strongly. Make a good final impression by summing up your autobiography on a positive note with an optimistic look at your future.
- Thank your audience for listening. You may ask if they have any questions or comments.

The oral presentation is due on or before the next lesson's Communication exercise on Day 133.

Worldview & Literary Analysis

Read the following excerpt from the chapter "The Truth" found in *Gifted Mind*.

In short, we need God. We need Him for life. For salvation and for knowledge. We even need Him for science. Though many may disagree, I maintain that we cannot achieve **profound** goals in science without God. But progress toward achieving those goals is hindered due to the roadblocks of **bigotry** and bias. Young people today are not only denied access to genuine scientific truths regarding God, but are instead persuaded to believe in **fabricated** fairy tales **masquerading** as scientific fact.

The media also plays a role here. Thirty or 40 years ago, the sole determiner of public opinion was the media, with powerful entities such as *The New York Times* leading the way. Even back then, the media carried a built-in suspicion of anything religious. Some historians, both then and now, even believed Hitler's **genocide** had some religious roots. But the perpetrator of the crime, Adolph Hitler, was actually **devoid** of any valid religious beliefs. Instead of religion, Germany's **diabolical** dictator justified his **heinous** crimes through a belief in Darwinian evolution and it's [*sic*] "survival of the fittest" **propaganda**.[1] But you don't hear that taught today in high school history or science class, do you?

Some may think we are out of time, but I still believe there is hope. Though mankind's **indifference** remains consistent from generation to generation, history teaches us that God will always raise up those who are willing to shine the light of truth. We need more people like Henry Morris and Ken Ham, men who demonstrate that mankind can know the genuine truth about God's role in creation while at the same time exposing the falsity of Darwinian evolution.

But God's truth doesn't require that we have a charismatic leader or even a Billy Graham-like figure. Though prominent Christian leaders and spokesmen with large platforms of influence are important, it's *foot soldiers* just like you who will ultimately win the victory in this war for truth. The common Christian with an uncommon commitment to being equipped with God's Word is a far more powerful influence in helping to change our culture. We just need to do more in equipping believers with His glorious truth.

One day, while talking with one of my top scientific executives, Jay Dworkin, about our company, I suddenly realized that we were actually *selling each other* on our own products! This **epiphany** helped me understand that we are *all* in continuous sell mode — selling to each other, to non-believers, to evolutionists, to our spouses, to family members, etc. We're **perpetually** "promoting" — not ourselves, but Him! In everything we do, our principle activity is sales, not in the telemarketing or business sense, but rather in fighting the battle for the minds of this generation. For this to happen, the truth must be presented to them in a language and a format they can understand. Therefore, we have to be trained and **adept** at both demonstrating the *need* for truth as well as the *practical benefits* of it. In other words, when it comes to truth, we have to answer the question for them, "What's in it for me?" And there's nothing wrong with that. Ultimately, though, we want them to go beyond seeing their own benefit to understanding the glory of God in it all. In our efforts to help others know the "what" about God and truth, we have to reach people *where they are* . . . just like our Savior did.[2]

---
1 Endnote from excerpt: http://www.creationism.org/csshs/v08n3p24.htm.
2 Damadian, *Gifted Mind*, p. 19–20.

Name _____   Lesson 26 - Exercise 4   Day 129

Respond to the following regarding today's reading excerpt.

1. The first paragraph from today's reading opens with four short sentences (one of them isn't even a sentence, but rather a fragment!). Sometimes an author will do this for dramatic effect. **What** effect do these quick, bold statements have on your understanding of Dr. Damadian's views?
   _____
   _____
   _____

2. **What** are young people in schools today denied access to?
   _____

3. **What** did Adolph Hitler use to justify his heinous crimes?
   _____
   _____

4. Although our world is far from God, **why** does Dr. Damadian still have hope?
   _____
   _____

Dr. Damadian calls *you* a "foot soldier" who can ultimately win the victory in this war for truth. **List** three ways you can have an influence on the people and culture around you regarding God's truth.
   _____
   _____
   _____

5. One day, while speaking with one of his top scientific executives, Dr. Damadian realized they were "selling each other" on their "own products." **What** did he mean by this?
   _____
   _____
   _____
   _____

Dr. Damadian explains that we must be "trained and adept at both demonstrating the *need* for truth as well as the *practical benefits* of it." **Share** how you are being trained in the truth. **Think** of the courses you are taking in high school, the sermons you hear, what your parents teach you, etc.
   _____
   _____
   _____
   _____
   _____

Name _____ Lesson 26 - Exercise 5 Day 130

Review

☐ **Update** the Reading List chart with books you have read this week.

☐ **Recite** Philemon 1:4–6 from memory to your instructor.

Vocabulary Review

Match each word to the correct definition.

a. adept	d. diabolical	g. genocide	j. masquerade	m. propaganda
b. bigotry	e. epiphany	h. heinous	k. perpetually	
c. devoid	f. fabricated	i. indifference	l. profound	

1. _____ shockingly evil or wicked
2. _____ completely without; lacking
3. _____ invented with intent to deceive
4. _____ skilled; expert at something
5. _____ evil; associated with the devil
6. _____ deliberate destruction of political or racial group
7. _____ strong, unreasonable beliefs against people with different ideas or beliefs
8. _____ spreading of ideas or rumors to injure a cause, idea, or person
9. _____ forever or indefinite period of time
10. _____ lack of interest or concern
11. _____ pretend to be a person or thing
12. _____ state of understanding of serious matters
13. _____ sudden insight or perception

Grammar & Punctuation Review

1. **Define** a possessive noun.
   _____
   _____

Form the singular possessive for these singular nouns.

2. cat _____
3. house _____
4. library _____
5. arrow _____
6. potato _____
7. phone _____

Form the plural possessive for these plural nouns.

8. dogs _____
9. parks _____
10. girls _____

Review Lesson 26, Day 130 277

Name _____   Lesson 26 - Exercise 5   Day 130

Underline any possessive nouns, possessive pronouns, or possessive adjectives (Day 97) and **place** apostrophes where needed in the following paragraph.

11. On Wednesdays, my friends mother takes us to a painting class offered at Jesses. Jesses is an art and craft shop in our town with a large room in the back that the owners offer for art instructors use. My friend, Macie, painted a cute pile of puppies in a basket. She did an amazing job on the puppies fur; her painting looked very realistic! My painting is of a few tiny birds in a nest. The birds nest is the hardest part. The instructor said she really liked mine. I am hoping to finish this week, but Wednesdays weather forecast is calling for an ice storm! If the weather is bad, I may just stay at Macies.

12. **Write** a sentence using both a possessive pronoun and a possessive adjective. Remember, it is the function in the sentence that differentiates a noun from an adjective.

_____
_____

Communication Review

1. **Define** what it means to reflect.

    _____
    _____

2. **Define** an oral presentation.

    _____
    _____

In your own words, **tell** how you feel about your upcoming oral presentation.

_____
_____
_____
_____

Worldview & Literary Analysis Review

1. **What** are young people in schools today denied access to?

    _____
    _____

2. Although our world is far from God, **why** does Dr. Damadian still have hope?

    _____
    _____

Special Feature

Lesson 27

Biblical Autobiography Excerpt: Jesus

Jesus spoke a lot about Himself. He communicated exactly who He was with the whole world. **Study** these words of Jesus regarding Himself then **write** a paragraph expressing who you believe Jesus to be.

Jesus said to them, "Truly, truly, I say to you, before Abraham was, I am." John 8:58

Jesus said to them, "I am the bread of life; whoever comes to me shall not hunger, and whoever believes in me shall never thirst. But I said to you that you have seen me and yet do not believe." John 6:35–36

Again Jesus spoke to them, saying, "I am the light of the world. Whoever follows me will not walk in darkness, but will have the light of life." John 8:12

So Jesus again said to them, "Truly, truly, I say to you, I am the door of the sheep." John 10:7

I am the good shepherd. The good shepherd lays down his life for the sheep. John 10:11

Jesus said to her, "I am the resurrection and the life. Whoever believes in me, though he die, yet shall he live." John 11:25

Jesus said to him, "I am the way, and the truth, and the life. No one comes to the Father except through me." John 14:6

I am the vine; you are the branches. Whoever abides in me and I in him, he it is that bears much fruit, for apart from me you can do nothing. John 15:5

_____
_____
_____
_____
_____
_____
_____
_____
_____
_____

Special Feature

Name _____   Lesson 27 - Exercise 1   Day 131

Study these vocabulary words that are bolded in the excerpt from "The Truth" that you will read on Day 134.

Vocabulary

access	permission or ability to enter or approach	penetrate	to force into or through a thing
apologetics	defending the Christian faith through logic and reason	presentation	providing information to inform, inspire, or persuade
credible	convincing; able to be believed	principle	a guiding rule, idea, or belief
detours	deviations from the direct course or procedure	secular	relating to worldly, temporary things; unreligious in nature
imperative	necessary or required; important		

1. **Write** a sentence using the words *apologetics* and *secular*.

   _____
   _____

Write a paragraph using four of the vocabulary words. Keep your sentences in the active voice (Day 42). **Have** your instructor read your paragraph and sign below.

_____
_____
_____
_____
_____
_____
_____

Instructor's signature: _____

☐ **Use** index cards to **write** each vocabulary word from this lesson on one side and the definition on the other. **Check** the box when complete.

☐ **Copy** the Scripture verse on an index card. **Memorize** it by the end of this lesson. You may choose the Bible translation or use the one given. **Check** the box when complete.

And he made from one man every nation of mankind to live on all the face of the earth, having determined allotted periods and the boundaries of their dwelling place, that they should seek God, and perhaps feel their way toward him and find him. Yet he is actually not far from each one of us. Acts 17:26–27

Name _____ Lesson 27 - Exercise 2   Day 132

Grammar & Punctuation

Forming Possessive Nouns

On Day 122, we learned about singular, plural, and irregular plural nouns. Forming possessives from these nouns depends on whether they already end in an *s*. To show possession, a **singular noun** adds *'s*. A **plural noun** adds an *'s* unless it already ends with an *s*. In that case, add an apostrophe (') only. **Study** the chart.

> A **singular noun** adds *'s* to show possession.
>
> A **plural noun** adds an *'s* to show possession unless it already ends with an *s*. In that case, add an apostrophe (') only.

Examples of Forming Possessives			
Singular	**Singular Possessive**	**Plural**	**Plural Possessive**
video	video's	videos	videos'
child	child's	children	children's
hero	hero's	heroes	heroes'
man	man's	men	men's
goose	goose's	geese	geese's
person	person's	people	people's
key	key's	keys	keys'
tree	tree's	trees	trees'

1. **Write** a sentence using the plural possessive of *hero*.
   _____
   _____

2. **Write** a sentence using the singular possessive of *child*.
   _____
   _____

3. **Write** a sentence using the plural possessive of *person*.
   _____
   _____

Colons

Colons are used after statements to introduce a quotation, explanation, example, or series. A complete independent clause *must* come before a colon, except in expressions such as the time on a clock or a Bible reference.

> **Colons** are used after statements to introduce a quotation, explanation, example, or series.

Name _____ Lesson 27 - Exercise 2   Day 132

When to Use a Colon

After a salutation of a business letter. Dear Senator Lance:

Between a book title and subtitle. *Jesus Unmasked: The Truth Will Shock You* by Todd Friel

Before a series at the end of a sentence. The trip you have won will include the following: airline tickets, hotel accommodation, food vouchers, and guided tours.

Before a long or formal direct quotation if the quotation appears at the end of a sentence. The student quoted the words of Aristotle: "I count him braver who overcomes his desires than him who conquers his enemies; for the hardest victory is over self."

In Bible references and expressions of time. Ephesians 6:10 | 3:00 p.m.

Between two independent clauses not separated by a coordinating conjunction in which the second clause is an explanation of the first. The boys loved the idea of learning about creationism: they chose *Wonders of Creation* to read.

Write a sentence containing a colon.

_____

_____

Review It!

Underline possessive nouns, possessive pronouns, and possessive adjectives. **Label** the possessive adjectives with **PA**. **Place** apostrophes where needed.

4. I brought all my drawing projects to the art fair, but one of the projects covers was missing, and it got ruined.

5. Lydia and Jessie planned their monthly lunch out at Alexanders.

6. Even though the play was the next night, everyones costumes were ready except for mine!

7. The tomatoes rows were marked with little signs to show they were hers.

8. The childrens choir at our church practices on Mondays when their schedules align.

9. *Pilgrims Progress* was a favorite of mine during my teenage years.

10. The boys bedroom was very clean by the time their mother came to inspect it.

11. When examining the tree, we noticed the fungis color had altered from its original bluish hue.

12. **Write** a sentence containing a possessive noun, possessive pronoun, and possessive adjective.

_____

_____

☐ Using your index cards, **copy** the rule for adding *s*, *'s*, or an apostrophe (') to form possessives. **Check** the box when you are done.

Name _____ Lesson 27 - Exercise 3 Day 133

Communication

Oral Presentation Due

You should have completed your oral presentation of your autobiography on or before today. How do you feel it went? Were you nervous or confident or both?

Write about your experience in three paragraphs. The first paragraph should relate how you felt leading up to the presentation and what your preparation was like. The second paragraph should tell how the actual presentation went. The third paragraph should express your opinion about the presentation, how you feel about it, and if you learned anything that will help you in future presentations.

_____
_____
_____
_____
_____
_____
_____
_____
_____
_____
_____
_____
_____
_____
_____
_____
_____
_____
_____
_____
_____
_____
_____
_____
_____
_____
_____
_____
_____
_____

Name _____   Lesson 27 - Exercise 3   Day 133

Wisdom Speaks

Proverbs 25:11–14

> ¹¹ A word fitly spoken
>   is like apples of gold in a setting of silver.
> ¹² Like a gold ring or an ornament of gold
>   is a wise reprover to a listening ear.
> ¹³ Like the cold of snow in the time of harvest
>   is a faithful messenger to those who send him;
>   he refreshes the soul of his masters.
> ¹⁴ Like clouds and wind without rain
>   is a man who boasts of a gift he does not give.

These verses each contain a simile that helps the nugget of wisdom come to life in its meaning. Isn't it wonderful that God's Word gives us clear visual images to reveal these deep truths?

Think deeply about the similes presented and **paraphrase** each verse in this selection from Proverbs. **Remove** the similes and **replace** them with the concepts they represent. **Personalize** each verse by using the pronoun *I*.

> *Example:* When I say something at just the right time, I am bringing beauty and value to the person listening. (*Hint:* Use a thesaurus if you need variety in your word choices.)

Verse 11:
_____
_____

Verse 12:
_____
_____

Verse 13:
_____
_____
_____

Verse 14:
_____
_____

Name _____   Lesson 27 - Exercise 4   Day 134

Worldview & Literary Analysis

Read the following excerpt from the chapter "The Truth" found in *Gifted Mind*.

> In a world of competitive *counter-truths*, we must do our best to reveal why God's truth is **credible**, beneficial, and *better* than other ideas and speculations. This is the fundamental mission of Christian **apologetics** — to "give a defense" (i.e., a logical reason) for *why* we believe.
>
> To effectively reach the **secular** world, we must utilize different methods from those we've used for the past few decades. It's obvious that secularism in all its forms has a stranglehold on the youth of this age; therefore it's **imperative** that we use both *creativity* as well as *credibility* in communicating to the secular world, particularly in our American culture. While I am certain that our great nation would never have arrived at this junction — medically, technologically, and scientifically — without the Lord and His *truth*, nevertheless knowing this is only half the battle. We have to advance, moving forward in helping others realize and embrace that same truth.
>
> So if truth is really on our side, how do we tell others about it? I'm not sure I have all the answers, but I firmly believe it begins in America's pulpits. Believers must be trained and equipped in their churches as well as in their homes. But it can't end there. We must also **penetrate** the circles of the academic, legal, political, and scientific communities. We must inspire Christian young adults to pursue these fields. Only then will our influence be fully realized. That is precisely what I've tried to do in my own world.
>
> For me, my greatest single discovery in life was not a machine or a physical **principle**. My highest purpose was realized when I discovered I could actually know God and serve His will, that I could live for something greater than science, medicine, or myself. When I found out that my life could bring joy to my Maker's heart, *that* began to greatly motivate my work as a scientist: exploring and applying the laws of nature and of nature's God for the benefit of mankind.
>
> Yes, I sincerely believe there's hope. God still opens peoples' [sic] eyes to the truth and Jesus still grants us **access** to that truth we spoke of earlier. Our job is to make it available and clearly demonstrated in word *and* deed. In other words, our **presentation** has to go beyond talk, evidence, and scientific *facts*. It has to show up in the lifestyle and *faith* of those who claim to believe it.
>
> However, despite my fierce commitment to this truth, I must confess that I haven't always held this belief. Faith has not always been the guiding light it is for me today. In reality, my journey towards a godly understanding is a long one, with a few dirt roads and **detours** along the way. Over my many years, I have come to realize that truth is not just something man discovers or accidentally stumbles upon. Rather, I learned that *God* is the seeker and man is the object of His search. And to my surprise, I found out that this amazing God had been chasing me from an early age.[1]

---

1 Damadian, *Gifted Mind*, p. 20–21.

Name _____ Lesson 27 - Exercise 4 Day 134

Respond to the following regarding today's reading excerpt.

On Day 19, you learned that an author often has a "secondary purpose" in writing a biography or autobiography. In these cases, the author uses a life story to promote a cause, belief, or idea. After reading the first chapter of *Gifted Mind*, **what** secondary purpose do you believe Dr. Damadian is promoting in his book? **How** is he trying to influence his readers? Be sure to give details.

_____
_____
_____
_____
_____
_____
_____
_____

1. **What** is "the fundamental mission of Christian apologetics"?
   _____

2. Dr. Damadian changed the world through the invention of the MRI, yet he does not count this as his greatest discovery. **What** does he claim his highest purpose to be?
   _____
   _____
   _____

3. **What** does Dr. Damadian have to say about our "presentation" of the truth?
   _____
   _____

The final paragraph of this first chapter gives a glimpse of what is to come in the rest of the autobiography. **Does** this "teaser" interest you? If so, how? If not, why not?

_____
_____
_____
_____
_____
_____
_____

You may choose to finish reading *Gifted Mind*. It can be purchased at www.masterbooks.com. Ask a parent's permission before using the internet.

Name _____ Lesson 27 - Exercise 5 Day 135

Review

☐ **Update** the Reading List chart with books you have read this week.

☐ **Recite** Acts 17:26–27 from memory to your instructor.

Vocabulary Review

Match each word to the correct definition.

a. access	c. credible	e. imperative	g. presentation	i. secular
b. apologetics	d. detours	f. penetrate	h. principle	

1. _____ guiding rule, idea, or belief
2. _____ convincing; able to be believed
3. _____ force into or through a thing
4. _____ necessary, required, or important
5. _____ relating to worldly, temporary things; unreligious in nature
6. _____ defending the Christian faith through logic and reason
7. _____ permission or ability to enter or approach
8. _____ deviations from course or procedure
9. _____ providing information to persuade

Grammar & Punctuation Review

1. **Record** the rule for forming possessives with singular and plural nouns.

   _____
   _____

Fill in the blanks on the possessives chart.

Singular	Singular Possessive	Plural	Plural Possessive
2.	3.	bananas	4.
country	5.	countries	6.
ox	7.	8.	9.
mouse	10.	11.	12.

13. **Write** a sentence using the plural possessive of *bananas*.

    _____
    _____

Add colons where needed in the following sentences.

14. I enjoyed reading the book *Jesus Unmasked The Truth Will Shock You*.
15. Our pastor read from Ephesians 6 10–12, and the sermon lasted until 12 30.
16. The teacher read the words of Jesus from John 14 6 "I am the way, and the truth, and the life. No one comes to the Father except through me."

Review Lesson 27, Day 135 287

Communication Review

Copy the proverb.

> ¹¹ A word fitly spoken
>   is like apples of gold in a setting of silver.
> ¹² Like a gold ring or an ornament of gold
>   is a wise reprover to a listening ear.
> ¹³ Like the cold of snow in the time of harvest
>   is a faithful messenger to those who send him;
>   he refreshes the soul of his masters.
> ¹⁴ Like clouds and wind without rain
>   is a man who boasts of a gift he does not give. Proverbs 25:11–14

_____
_____
_____
_____
_____
_____
_____
_____
_____
_____

Worldview & Literary Analysis Review

1. **What** is "the fundamental mission of Christian apologetics"?
   _____

2. **What** does Dr. Damadian have to say about our "presentation" of the truth?
   _____
   _____
   _____

Special Feature

Lesson 28

Excerpt Study: *Evidence for the Bible* by Clive Anderson and Brian Edwards

Mount of Olives

1st Summit 2nd Summit 3rd Summit

The Mount of Olives is one of three peaks of a mountain ridge which runs for 3.5 km just east of Old Jerusalem across the Kidron Valley. It is named for the olive groves that once covered its slopes.

King David climbed the Mount of Olives and wept as he fled Jerusalem when his son Absolom rebelled against him (2 Samuel 15:30). A millennium later, Jesus wept over the city as He came down the Mount of Olives on Palm Sunday to the general acclaim of the people (Matthew 21:1–10; Luke 19:41). The Mount of Olives also appears in the prophecies of the return of Christ (Zechariah 14:4).

It was here that Jesus answered His disciple's [sic] questions about the future (Matthew 24:3), and He frequently spent the night on the Mount of Olives (Luke 21:37). Jesus came to the Garden of Gethsemane at the foot of the Mount of Olives on the night of His betrayal (Luke 22:39).

It was therefore appropriate that here on the Mount of Olives Christ took His farewell of the disciples in what is known as His Ascension.

His great commission from this mount to take the gospel to the whole world (Acts 1:8–12) began to be fulfilled on the day of Pentecost when Jews and proselytes from what we know today as Egypt, Libya, Crete, Italy, Turkey, Syria, Iran, Iraq, and Saudi Arabia, became followers of Christ (Acts 2:9–11).[1]

1. **Describe** what King David did when he climbed the Mount of Olives.
   _____
   _____

2. **List** the six ways Jesus interacted with the Mount of Olives.
   a. _____
   b. _____
   c. _____
   d. _____
   e. _____
   f. _____

---
[1] Anderson, Clive, and Brian Edwards. *Evidence for the Bible*. Green Forest, AR: New Leaf Publishing Group, LLC, 2018, p. 141.

Name _____ Lesson 28 - Exercise 1 Day 136

It is prophesied that at the Second Coming, Christ will appear on the Mount of Olives. **Look up** Zechariah 14:4 in the Bible translation of your choice and **summarize** it.

_____
_____
_____
_____

A metaphor is a comparison between two things that are otherwise unrelated. Mountains are frequently used as metaphors relating to life. Reaching the summit is never a straight and easy journey, and neither is life. **Answer** the following question relating mountains to life.

How is reaching a mountain's peak a metaphor for reaching a life goal?

_____
_____
_____

Note: Throughout the fourth quarter, Special Feature days will focus on mountains and what they can teach us about faith.

Vocabulary Study

Match the words found in today's excerpt to the correct definition. If you do not know the meaning of a word, read the excerpt for clues. If you are still uncertain, look it up in a dictionary. (If using an online dictionary, ask a parent's permission.)

3. _____ millennium   a. enthusiastic public praise
4. _____ acclaim   b. rising to an important position or higher level
5. _____ betrayal   c. suitable or proper for a certain situation
6. _____ appropriate   d. period of a thousand years
7. _____ ascension   e. converts from one religion or opinion to another
8. _____ Pentecost   f. act of betraying a person, country, group, etc.
9. _____ proselytes   g. Jewish festival of Shavuoth/Christian festival of descent of the Holy Spirit

☐ **Use** index cards to **write** each vocabulary word from this lesson on one side and the definition on the other. **Check** the box when complete.

☐ **Copy** the Scripture verse on an index card. **Memorize** it by the end of this lesson. You may choose the Bible translation or use the one given. **Check** the box when complete.

"For the mountains may depart and the hills be removed, but my steadfast love shall not depart from you, and my covenant of peace shall not be removed," says the LORD, who has compassion on you. Isaiah 54:10

Name _____   Lesson 28 - Exercise 2   Day 137

Grammar & Punctuation

Compound-Complex Sentences

A **compound-complex sentence** contains at least two independent clauses and at least one dependent clause.

>   **Dependent Clause**   **Independent Clause**   **Independent Clause**
> *Example:* Although Manuel was exhausted, he continued running, and he was able to finish the 5k race.

Underline the clauses and **label** them as **IND** for independent or **DP** for dependent.

1. Despite having studied a lot, Brandon failed his driver's test, and he will need to retake it next month.
2. Leaving the past behind, Sadie and Lilly became close friends again, and they vowed never to let hard feelings come between them.
3. **Write** a compound-complex sentence of your own and label the clauses.

   _____
   _____

Prefix Study

A **prefix** is a letter or group of letters that come before the base (root) word and alter its meaning.

The Greek prefix *a-* has a few different meanings. The prefix *a-* can mean "on," "in," or "at." The meaning associated with "in" can mean "in a state or condition" or "in a manner." *Examples:* **a**shore = at or on the shore/**a**bed = in bed/**a**top = on top. The prefix *a-* can also mean "not" or "without."

> *Examples:* **a**biology = the study of nonliving things | **a**symmetrical = not symmetrical | **a**chromatic = not chromatic; without color

Write a word using the prefix *a-* with the meaning of "on," "in," or "at": _____

Write a word using the prefix *a-* with the meaning of "not" or "without": _____

Sometimes we need contextual clues to figure out which meaning of the prefix *a-* is being used. A **contextual clue** is like a hint that helps you decipher the meaning of a word based on the words around it or how it is used in the sentence.

Use what you know about the prefix *a-* and contextual clues to **define** the following bolded words. If you need help, look up the words in a dictionary or online with your parent's permission.

> My professor claims to be an **atheist**, so I believe his moral standards are **adrift**.

4. atheist: _____
   _____

5. adrift: _____
   _____

Name _____   Lesson 28 – Exercise 2   Day 137

Refer to the Grammar & Punctuation exercises in Lessons 1–3 and **complete** the following.

Match the word to the correct definition.

6. _____ interjection   a. describes a noun or pronoun
7. _____ pronoun   b. joins words or phrases
8. _____ verb   c. names a person, place, or thing
9. _____ noun   d. shows action or state-of-being
10. _____ conjunction   e. takes the place of a noun
11. _____ adverb   f. expresses strong feeling or emotion
12. _____ adjective   g. describes a verb, adjective, or other adverb
13. _____ preposition   h. describes a relationship between nouns or pronouns and other words

14. **List** five common nouns, separated by commas.
_____

15. **List** five proper nouns, separated by commas.
_____

Underline the verb twice and **label** it **AV** for action verb or **LV** for linking verb. There may be more than one verb in each sentence.

16. My lunch looked appetizing for the first time since my long, drawn-out illness.

17. Angela frantically looked through the pages of the book, searching for any clue to the answer.

18. Jesus turned the Pharisees' argument against them every time they appeared to have tricked Him.

19. This English Language Arts course equals a full high school credit in all fifty states.

20. Pets fed the proper amount of food stay thinner and healthier than overfed pets.

21. **Write** a sentence using the word *look* as an action verb.
_____

22. **Write** a sentence using the word *look* as a linking verb. (*Hint:* You may use a suffix such as *-ing, -ed,* etc.)
_____

Name _____   Lesson 28 - Exercise 3   Day 138

💬 Communication

Summarizing

Throughout this course, you have been asked to summarize a paragraph, excerpt, or Scripture portion. Today we will work on the skill of summarizing, which is an important part of effective communication. A **summary** is a restatement of the main ideas of someone else's writing, stated in your own words. A summary should be shorter than the original text. **Study** the Tips for Summarizing chart.

> A **summary** is a restatement of the main ideas of someone else's writing, stated in your own words.

Tips for Summarizing
1. Read through the text two or three times to make sure you have a solid understanding of the main ideas.
2. Create notes about the main ideas from memory using your own words.
3. Check what you have written against the original, making sure you have not strayed from the author's ideas.
4. Look for words or phrases that could be changed without altering the meaning of the original. Many "specialty" words will need to stay the same to convey the proper meaning.
5. The use of a dictionary or thesaurus is helpful for alternative word choices.

Read the following excerpt from *Evidence for the Bible* and **study** the example notes and summary.

Original: When Jesus was asked whether or not it was right to pay taxes to Caesar, He called for a small silver *denarius*, the daily wage of a laborer or legionary (Matthew 20:2, 22:19). In the parable of the Good Samaritan, the merchant paid the landlord "two denarii" (Luke 10:[3]5), which presumably covered board and lodging until his return two or three days later. It was known as the "tribute penny," and was an offense to the Jews because it contained an image of the emperor (Tiberius), which broke the second Commandment, and also because the inscription read *Divus Augustus* — the divine Augustus.[1]

Notes:
- Jesus spoke about a denarius.
- The denarius was a day's wage.
- The denarius was common, but it was offensive to the Jews.
- The Jews were offended by the image and the inscription.

A silver denarius coin

Summary: The denarius was a small coin Jesus spoke about on multiple occasions. It was a common coin, as it was a day's wage for an average worker; however, it was a controversial coin due to the image and inscription on it. The Jews saw this image as a violation of the second commandment, and the inscription declaring the emperor as divine was also offensive.

Reading over the original text a few times shows that this excerpt is not about Jesus, parables, or the Jews. It is about the denarius. Knowing that helps when gathering the main points and deciding what to leave out and what is vital to the true meaning.

---
1 Anderson and Edwards, *Evidence for the Bible*, p. 125.

Communication

Name_____   Lesson 28 - Exercise 3   Day 138

Now it's your turn to practice summarizing. **Read** the following excerpt from *God's Wonderous Machine*, Unit 2, "The Breathtaking Respiratory System," then **create** notes and **write** your summary.

> Breathing is essential to life. Without the air that rushes into your lungs you would cease to exist. The Bible makes many references to breathing. Our Heavenly Father is the giver of life and through His breath He calls all creatures into existence. In Genesis 2:7 it says, "Then the LORD God formed a man from the dust of the ground and breathed into his nostrils the breath of life, and the man became a living being."
>
> These is no evidence here of man being formed from an evolutionary process, but rather being formed from the actual loving hands of God. Job, through all his adversity, knew where his life force came from. In Job 33:4 he states, "The Spirit of God has made me; the breath of the Almighty gives me life." Remember, as Psalm 150:6 states, "Let everything that has breath praise the LORD. Praise the LORD."[1]

After reading through the excerpt two or three times, **create** notes for the main points.

_____
_____
_____
_____
_____
_____
_____
_____

Write your summary and **have** your instructor read it, comparing it to the original.

_____
_____
_____
_____
_____
_____
_____
_____
_____
_____

Instructor's signature: _____

Optional: Teacher's Discretion   ☐ No   ☐ Yes   Due Date: _____

Practice! **Find** your favorite book and choose a passage. In a notebook, **write** a summary using the techniques learned in this exercise.

---

[1] Callentine, Lainna. *God's Wondrous Machine*. Green Forest, AR: Master Books, 2022, p. 88.

Worldview & Literary Analysis

The Summit by Eric Alexander

For the remainder of our Worldview & Literary Analysis exercises, you will read excerpts from the book *The Summit* by Eric Alexander, a mountain climber and outdoor enthusiast whose pursuit of adventure has taught him much about his relationship with God and His truth.

The Summit is an autobiography, just like *Gifted Mind*. Often an autobiography will focus on a certain aspect of the writer's life; in this case, the focus is on Alexander's career as a mountain climber and the impact it had on his view of God, others, and himself.

Read the following "About the Author" section found on page 222 of *The Summit*. You will answer questions on the following page.

About the Author

Eric Alexander is a skier, climber, and mountaineer who has lived in the Vail Valley for 20 years. He is married to Amy Alexander and has twin daughters, Karis and Aralyn. Born in Indiana, Eric moved west with his family at the age of four to Evergreen, Colorado, where he gained his first experiences in the outdoors with his church youth group. His mentors there, with world-class credentials, gave him a passion for the outdoors and for the Lord, which continues today.

With a BA degree in environmental science from the University of Denver, Eric was a member of the school's Alpine Club, Ski Team, and was president of Intervarsity Christian Fellowship on campus. In Vail, Eric has worked for the Vail Ski Patrol (including one year in France), Ski School, Vail Mountaineering, and now his own business. On May 25, 2001, Eric defied the odds and scaled Mt. Everest, guiding his blind friend Erik Weihenmayer to its 29,035-foot summit. He has continued to climb and lead others, particularly those with disabilities, on trips around the world. Eric has climbed the highest point on six of the seven continents, which is a feat in and of itself. However, what makes this accomplishment even more notable is that Eric has led a person with a disability to the summit of each continent's highest peak.

From these experiences he has been able to build a business called Higher Summits, allowing him to share an inspirational message with people all over the world, opening the door to share his faith in Christ and the true meaning of purpose in life.

Eric continues to climb and lead expeditions throughout Europe, Africa, North and South America, the Himalayas, and other mountainous regions of the globe with disabled teens and adults. He is always looking for new mountains to climb, both personally and in the outdoors, while challenging people to overcome the "Everest" in their own lives.[1]

---

1 Alexander, Eric. *The Summit*. Green Forest, AR: New Leaf Publishing Group, LLC, 2010, p. 222.

Name _____   Lesson 28 - Exercise 4   Day 139

Answer the following questions based on this lesson's excerpt from *The Summit*.

1. **What** occurred in his early years that changed the course of Eric Alexander's life?

   _____
   _____

2. **What** impact did Alexander's mentors in Colorado have on him?

   _____
   _____

A mentor is a person who offers guidance and support to another. The person they are offering advice to is called the mentee. **Name** someone who has been a mentor to you. **What** impact has this person had on the direction of your life and your worldview?

_____
_____
_____
_____
_____
_____
_____

3. **What** degree did Alexander earn and from where?

   _____

4. **Ask** a parent or, with permission, use the internet to learn what "BA" stands for regarding a college degree. **Write** it below. (You may already know!)

   _____

5. **List** four businesses Alexander has been employed by.

   a. _____   c. _____
   b. _____   d. _____

6. Alexander's business, Higher Summits, has allowed him to do **what**?

   _____
   _____

Optional: Teacher's Discretion   ☐ No   ☐ Yes   Due Date: _____

With your parent's permission, **use** the internet to **look up** three facts about Mt. Everest that are not given in this lesson's excerpt.

   a. _____
   b. _____
   c. _____

Lesson 28, Day 139   *Language Lessons for a Living Education* Level 10

Name _____   Lesson 28 – Exercise 5   Day 140

Review

☐ **Update** the Reading List chart with books you have read this week.

☐ **Recite** Isaiah 54:10 from memory to your instructor.

Vocabulary Review

Define the following vocabulary words.

1. Acclaim: _____
2. Ascension: _____
3. Proselytes: _____
4. Millennium: _____
5. **Write** a sentence using the vocabulary words *appropriate* and *betrayal*.

   _____
   _____

Grammar & Punctuation Review

Label the underlined clauses as **IND** for independent or **DP** for dependent. On the line, **write** whether the sentence is a compound, complex, or compound-complex sentence.

1. _____ If I hadn't been so busy reading, I would have noticed the rain approaching and closed the windows.

2. _____ I like to pack a lot of clothes when I go camping, but my brother barely brings anything with him.

3. _____ After arriving at our hotel, we unloaded our suitcases, and we all headed straight for the pool.

4. **Explain** what a contextual clue is.

   _____
   _____

Match the words with the prefix *a-* to the correct definition.

5. _____ ashore   a. not balanced or not symmetrical
6. _____ abiology   b. without color
7. _____ asymmetrical   c. at or on the shore
8. _____ achromatic   d. the study of nonliving things

Name _____ Lesson 28 - Exercise 5 Day 140

Communication Review

1. **Define** a summary.
   _____
   _____

Summarize the following paragraph. Remember, a summary should be shorter than the original text.

> The Boykin spaniel is a bird-hunting dog and is the state dog of South Carolina. This breed was developed to provide the ideal dog for duck and turkey hunting in swampy areas of the state. The Boykin spaniel is a small, rugged dog that is compact in size, making it ideal for traveling in boats typically weighed down with hunters and gear.

_____
_____
_____
_____

Worldview & Literary Analysis Review

1. **What** impact did Alexander's mentors in Colorado have on him?
   _____
   _____

2. Alexander's business, Higher Summits, has allowed him to do **what**?
   _____
   _____

3. **Define** a mentor and mentee.
   _____
   _____

Write a paragraph of 4–5 sentences that shares your thoughts on the importance of a mentor/mentee relationship.

_____
_____
_____
_____
_____
_____
_____

Special Feature

Lesson 29

Picture Study: Mountain Range with Beautiful Green Landscape

In a complete paragraph, **describe** a journey from the home at the base of the mountain, up the grassy slope, over the boulders at the base, and finally up the steep rocky terrain to the summit. **Use** vivid adjectives as you **describe** what you see, smell, hear, and feel. **Elaborate** on the feelings that would surface as you stood atop the summit.

Name _____   Lesson 29 - Exercise 1   Day 141

Look up the following mountain terms in a dictionary. **Write** the definition on the first line then **write** a short sentence using the word on the second line. If using an online dictionary, ask a parent's permission.

Summit: _____

_____

Ridge: _____

_____

Pinnacle: _____

_____

Gully: _____

_____

Face: _____

_____

Peak: _____

_____

Slope: _____

_____

Mountaineering: _____

_____

☐ **Use** index cards to **write** each vocabulary word from this lesson on one side and the definition on the other. **Check** the box when complete.

☐ **Copy** the Scripture verse on an index card. **Memorize** it by the end of this lesson. You may choose the Bible translation or use the one given. **Check** the box when complete.

Blessed is the man who remains steadfast under trial, for when he has stood the test he will receive the crown of life, which God has promised to those who love him. James 1:12

Grammar & Punctuation

Parallel Items

You have probably heard of parallel lines in geometry. Grammar has parallel items as well. **Parallelism** in grammar means that two or more phrases or clauses in a sentence have the same grammatical structure. In grammar, it is about balance. Use a noun with a noun, a prepositional phrase with a prepositional phrase, an adjective with an adjective, etc.

> *Verb Form Example:* Mandy enjoys singing, playing the piano, and to hike with her friends. (not parallel)
> Mandy enjoys singing, playing the piano, and hiking with her friends. (parallel)
>
> *Noun Example:* For dessert, I love chocolate cake and to eat ice cream. (not parallel, noun/verb mix)
> For dessert, I love to eat chocolate cake and ice cream. (parallel, both in verb form)

Note: It is not necessary to repeat the word *to* for each item listed in the noun example.

1. **Rewrite** the sentence, making all items parallel.

   > According to the Bible, being a wise steward consists of spending wisely, being generous, and to tithe on your income.

   _____

   _____

Suffix Study

A **suffix** is a letter or group of letters that come after a root word and alter its meaning. The suffixes you are probably familiar with include *-ing* and *-ed*. Other suffixes are less common or a little trickier to use. Knowing the meanings of prefixes and suffixes can help you figure out a word's definition.

The suffixes *-er* and *-or* both mean "one who" or "that which." No rule perfectly covers which one to use in each situation, but the following is a good "rule of thumb": If you can change the word to have the suffix *-ion* at the end, use *-or*. If you can't, use *-er*.

> *Example:* The root word *teach* can't be changed to "teachion," therefore use *-er*: teach**er**
> The root word *conduct* can be changed to "conduction," therefore use *-or*: conduct**or**

Add the proper suffixes, *-er* or *-or*, to the following root words using the "rule of thumb." (*Hint:* Remember, there are exceptions!)

2. doct: _____
3. teach: _____
4. command: _____
5. dictate: _____
6. respect: _____
7. calculate: _____
8. inspect: _____
9. run: _____
10. lecture: _____

Write a sentence using an *-or* and *-er* word. (Use different words than those appearing in this exercise.)

_____

_____

Name _____   Lesson 29 - Exercise 2   Day 142

Refer to the Grammar & Punctuation exercises in Lessons 4–6 and **complete** the following.

Write a sentence with a *to be* helping verb.

_____

_____

Write a sentence with a *to have* helping verb.

_____

_____

Write a sentence with a modal helping verb that shows possibility.

_____

_____

Write a sentence with a modal helping verb that shows intent.

_____

_____

Use the Tense Construction chart (Day 22) to **write** the following sentences.

11. **Write** a sentence using the verb *cough* in the past perfect continuous tense.

_____

12. **Write** a sentence using the verb *topple* in the future simple tense.

_____

Identify whether the underlined clause is independent or dependent by **writing IND** or **DP** above the clause.

13. <u>Since we no longer have a leaky roof,</u> <u>we won't need to keep buckets in the attic to catch the raindrops!</u>

14. <u>I noticed a large swarm of flying insects gathering</u>, and <u>I hoped they wouldn't invade our picnic area</u>.

Underline the conjunction and **write CD** for coordinating, **CL** for correlative, and **SB** for subordinating.

15. Although my grandmother lives in another country, we keep in touch and are very close.

16. We had no sooner started playing video games than there was a power outage, and we couldn't play!

17. Jessica really wanted to play board games with her sister, but she was so tired that it just wasn't possible.

Name_____   Lesson 29 - Exercise 3   Day 143

Communication

Using a Thesaurus

A **thesaurus** is a book that lists synonyms (words that mean the same or almost the same thing). Writers turn to a thesaurus to avoid using the same word repeatedly. Some thesauruses list words in alphabetical order, but many do not. Sometimes antonyms (words that mean the opposite) are listed as well. Thesauruses contain an index in the front to help you find the word you are looking for. A knowledge of synonyms is important when writing essays or stories, as it keeps your writing fresh and interesting instead of monotonous or repetitive.

> A **thesaurus** is a book that lists synonyms (words that mean the same or almost the same thing).

A word of caution: A thesaurus can be overused when the writer chooses words that are too "fancy" or unusual and may not be understood by their audience. You don't want it to be obvious that you used a thesaurus! Excessive repetition and excessive variety can both be distracting to the reader. A balanced approach is best.

Use a thesaurus or online thesaurus with a parent's permission to **list** three synonyms for each of the following words.

believe _____ _____ _____
study   _____ _____ _____
prosper _____ _____ _____
create   _____ _____ _____

1. **Use** a thesaurus to find synonyms for the bolded words and **rewrite** the following paragraph. Sentences may need to be slightly reconstructed, and some bolded words are nouns while others are verbs.

> I often walk down a path in the woods behind my house. It is **often** early in the morning when I enjoy taking my walk. I **enjoy** listening to the sweet sound of the birds flying back and forth in the treetops as I **walk** along, thinking about the upcoming day. Of course, schoolwork is a part of the **upcoming** day, and I **feel** I need the fresh air of my morning **walk** to feel more awake and ready. The **fresh** air reminds me that God has made this a new morning just for me!

_____
_____
_____
_____
_____
_____
_____
_____

Communication

Name _____ Lesson 29 - Exercise 3 Day 143

Wisdom Speaks

Copy the proverb.

> *With patience a ruler may be persuaded, and a soft tongue will break a bone.* Proverbs 25:15

_____
_____

Those in authority are more likely to be convinced by a person who displays patience with respect than by one who boldly debates or argues. A parent, teacher, police officer, mayor, or judge may be persuaded by a well-thought-out respectful appeal.

"A soft tongue" speaks of gentle and respectful speech. There is power in such speech, enough power to break something hard (like a bone!). This is an example of hyperbole and is not meant to be taken literally.

Describe a time you patiently and respectfully stated an opinion or sought permission for something.

_____
_____
_____
_____
_____
_____
_____
_____
_____
_____

Using a thesaurus or an online search with a parent's permission, **write** two synonyms for each word.

2. patience: _____

3. persuade: _____

Based on the synonyms, **restate** the proverb in your own words.

_____
_____
_____
_____
_____

Name _____ Lesson 29 - Exercise 4 Day 144

Worldview & Literary Analysis

The excerpts you will study from *The Summit* will take a little explaining. At the end of each chapter of his book, Eric Alexander offers a feature called *Deadpoint Reflections*. According to Alexander, a "**deadpoint** is a [mountain] climbing move where momentum is used to achieve a higher handhold."

Deadpoint Reflections are aimed at looking back or "reflecting" on lessons learned from the experiences described in each chapter. The excerpts you study will all be taken from these reflections. Each one will look at three elements that relate to mountain climbing and to life: the crux, the hold, and the anchor.

Read the following excerpt from *The Summit* that describes the three elements of *Deadpoint Reflections*.

> I will call the struggle we face the **Crux**. As it pertains to climbing, the crux is the most difficult part of the climb. It will make or break the ascent, and usually is the piece of the puzzle that takes up residence in the back of one's mind begging the question: "Do I have what it takes to overcome this difficulty?" The crux will relate to "the climb" that takes place away from the rock and ice of the mountains, but in the heart and the struggle which is often daily living. 
>
> The **Hold** will be the next portion that will serve as an answer to the crux. The hold is that which keeps you attached to the next piece of the puzzle, what to cling to, and what we need to utilize in order to solve the problem. In climbing, sometimes holds are as small as the edge of a dime and sometimes a truck can be parked on them; either way, they present the path for overcoming the crux.
>
> What is presented is just one hold, and just like in climbing, sometimes we need to be patient and wait for the next one to appear, or search for a better one. I know there are better ones, and more than what I present, but the key is to not lose sight of the anchor. 
>
> The **Anchor** is the support should the hold fail. I can think of no better anchor than a giant monolith of uplifted granite: the Rock. "The Lord is the Rock eternal," and is the one true anchor. This portion will give a scriptural answer to the crux, allowing the reader to look for a solid hold knowing the anchor above is solid.[1]

---

1 Alexander, *The Summit*, p. 11.

Name _____ Lesson 29 - Exercise 4 Day 144

Respond to the following based on this lesson's excerpt from *The Summit*.

1. **Define** a "deadpoint" as it relates to mountain climbing.
   _____
   _____

In your own words, **define** the "crux" as it relates to mountain climbing.
_____
_____

In your own words, **define** the "hold" as it relates to mountain climbing.
_____
_____

In your own words, **define** the "anchor" as it relates to mountain climbing.
_____
_____

Why do you believe Alexander chose to end each chapter of his book with *Deadpoint Reflections*?
_____
_____
_____

Describe the crux as it relates to daily living.
_____
_____
_____

Describe the hold as it relates to daily living.
_____
_____
_____

Describe the anchor as it relates to daily living.
_____
_____
_____

> The mountaintop is not meant to *teach* us anything, it is meant to *make* us something.
> — Oswald Chambers[1]

---

[1] Chambers, Oswald. *My Utmost for His Highest*. New York: Dodd & Mead Co., Inc. 1935.

Name _____   Lesson 29 - Exercise 5   Day 145

Review

- [ ] **Update** the Reading List chart with books you have read this week.
- [ ] **Recite** James 1:12 from memory to your instructor.

Vocabulary Review

Write a paragraph with the following vocabulary words: *summit, ridge, pinnacle, gully, face, peak, slope,* and *mountaineering*.

_____
_____
_____
_____
_____
_____
_____
_____

Grammar & Punctuation Review

1. **Describe** parallelism.
   _____
   _____

2. **Rewrite** the sentence, making all items parallel.

   > When considering a major financial purchase, you should ponder the necessity of the item, the amount you are spending, and being in prayer about if the decision is wise.

   _____
   _____
   _____

3. **Explain** the "rule of thumb" for using the suffixes *-er* and *-or*.
   _____
   _____

Add the proper suffixes, *-er* or *-or*, to the following root words. (*Hint:* Remember, there are exceptions!)

4. liberate: _____
5. manage: _____
6. past: _____
7. instruct: _____
8. build: _____
9. create: _____

Review   Lesson 29, Day 145   307

Name _____   Lesson 29 - Exercise 5   Day 145

Communication Review

1. **Describe** how a thesaurus can be overused.
   _____
   _____

Use a thesaurus or online thesaurus with a parent's permission to **list** three synonyms for each of the following words.

circumstance	_____	_____	_____
mechanical	_____	_____	_____
generous	_____	_____	_____
humility	_____	_____	_____

2. **Describe** a "soft tongue."
   _____
   _____

Worldview & Literary Analysis Review

1. **Define** a deadpoint.
   _____
   _____

Match the mountain climbing term to its meaning.

2. _____ crux   a. the support should the hold fail
3. _____ hold   b. keeps you attached
4. _____ anchor   c. the most difficult part of a climb

Copy the quote by Oswald Chambers. **Use** your best cursive writing if you know how to do so.

> "The mountaintop is not meant to *teach* us anything, it is meant to *make* us something."[1]

_____
_____

Rewrite Oswald Chambers' quote in your own words.
_____
_____

---

[1] Chambers, *My Utmost for His Highest.*

Special Feature

Lesson 30

Hymn Study: "Savior, Lead Me Up the Mountain" (Anonymous)

Savior, lead me up the mountain,
  Where the Lord alone is seen,
Where we hear the voice from heaven,
  Where the air is pure and clean.

Chorus:
Lead me higher up the mountain,
  Give me fellowship with Thee;
In Thy light I see the fountain,
  And the blood it cleanses me.

Higher up where light increases,
  Far above all earthly strife,
Where the strain of effort ceases,
  Where in Christ we reign in Life.

Savior, keep me up the mountain
  Pressing on toward the goal,
Till, as one, we share Thine image,
  And Thy love and grace extol.[1]

Respond to the following questions about the Special Feature hymn.

1. According to the first verse of the hymn, **what** are the benefits of being led up the mountain?
   _____
   _____

2. According to the second verse of the hymn, **what** conditions do we find on top of the mountain?
   _____
   _____

3. According to the third verse of the hymn, **who** keeps us on the mountain, and **what** goals are achieved?
   _____
   _____

Write a paragraph in response to this hymn, assuming the mountain to be figurative (a metaphor). What does the mountain represent to you as a metaphor? How is asking the Savior to lead us up the mountain similar to leading us in life? What is the ultimate goal?

_____
_____
_____
_____
_____
_____
_____
_____

---

[1] https://www.churchinmontereypark.org/Docs/sg/en/hymns/378.htm.

Name _____   Lesson 30 - Exercise 1   Day 146

Write a paragraph in response to this hymn, assuming the mountain to be literal. What is it like climbing a real mountain (or hill) to spend time with the Lord? What are the benefits? Have you spent time with God out in nature? How is it different from being indoors?

_____
_____
_____
_____
_____
_____
_____
_____
_____
_____

Vocabulary Study

Match the words found in the hymn to the correct definition. If you do not know the meaning of a word, read the hymn for clues. If you are still uncertain, look it up in a dictionary. (If using an online dictionary, ask a parent's permission.)

4. _____ fellowship   a. come to an end
5. _____ strain   b. determined attempt
6. _____ strife   c. highly praise
7. _____ effort   d. representation of a person or thing
8. _____ cease   e. force tending to pull or stretch
9. _____ image   f. angry, bitter disagreement
10. _____ extol   g. friendly associations with people who share interests

☐ **Use** index cards to **write** each vocabulary word from this lesson on one side and the definition on the other. **Check** the box when complete.

☐ **Copy** the Scripture verse on an index card. **Memorize** it by the end of this lesson. You may choose the Bible translation or use the one given. **Check** the box when complete.

My sheep hear my voice, and I know them, and they follow me. I give them eternal life, and they will never perish, and no one will snatch them out of my hand. John 10:27–28

Name _____   Lesson 30 – Exercise 2   Day 147

Grammar & Punctuation

Double Negatives

A **double negative** occurs when two negative words are used in the same statement, leading to confusion. Reading a sentence with a double negative can be frustrating as you logically try to work through what the writer or speaker intends. Examples of negative words: *nothing, never, no one, hardly, not, no, nowhere,* and *none*.

> *Examples:* Opal *did not* see *nothing* wrong with the sentence she wrote, yet her mother made her fix it. (incorrect)
> Opal *did not* see *anything* wrong with the sentence she wrote, yet her mother made her fix it. (correct)
> I *can't* go *nowhere* tonight because I didn't finish my school or chores. (incorrect)
> I *can't* go *anywhere* tonight because I didn't finish my school or chores. (correct)
> She *didn't* do *nothing* wrong! (incorrect)
> She *did nothing* wrong! (correct)

Rewrite these double-negative sentences by changing one of the negatives.

1. After realizing how long the practices were, Aaron didn't want nothing to do with playing soccer.

   _____

   _____

2. Clarence searched all over the beach but couldn't find none of the beach glass he piled up yesterday.

   _____

   _____

Note: There is an exception to the double-negative rule: when the word *not* is in front of a *negative adjective*.

> *Example:* It's *not uncommon* to have a drought this time of year.
> (Meaning, it is common to have a drought this time of year — perfectly logical!)

Prefix Study

Use the chart to decipher the meaning of the following words and **match** them to their definitions.

Prefix	Meaning	Examples
ante-	before, preceding	antecedent, antechamber
anti-	opposite, against	antisocial, antidote
com-	with, jointly, completely	competent, committee
de-	down, away	deduct, descend
dis-	negation, removal, expulsion	disband, disadvantage

Name _____   Lesson 30 - Exercise 2   Day 147

3. _____ antechamber   a. having the skill necessary to successfully do something
4. _____ antidote   b. to break up and stop functioning
5. _____ competent   c. subtract or take away from a total
6. _____ deduct   d. medicine given to counteract a poison
7. _____ disband   e. a small room leading to a main one

☐ Using your index cards, **copy** each prefix and its meaning. Give an example of a word not found in this lesson. **Check** the box when you are done.

Refer to the Grammar & Punctuation exercises in Lessons 7–9 and **complete** the following.
On the line, **indicate** whether the verb mood is indicative, imperative, or subjunctive.

8. _____ If I could have stayed all night to help my brother prepare for the wedding, I certainly would have.

9. _____ Keep running even when you feel like your body is screaming for you to stop.

10. _____ Martha Washington was such an amazing and supportive wife, companion, and confidant of George Washington throughout his military career and presidency.

Place parentheses around the prepositional phrases and **underline** the objects of the preposition. There may be more than one in each sentence.

11. The teens at church were so excited about their mission trip to England with a local ministry.

12. According to one study, those eating plant-based diets were less likely to be diagnosed with heart disease.

13. Our trip to Yellowstone was beyond amazing, and the memories from that trip will live in my mind for many years.

14. **Write** a sentence containing a prepositional phrase regarding location. Include two adjectives.
    _____
    _____

15. **Write** a sentence containing a prepositional phrase regarding opposition or exception. Include a helping verb. (Day 17)
    _____
    _____

16. **Rewrite** this passive voice sentence, making it active.

    Our cat was operated on by my dad's friend who is a veterinarian.
    _____
    _____

Lesson 30, Day 147   Language Lessons for a Living Education Level 10

Name _____ Lesson 30 - Exercise 3 Day 148

Communication

The Art of Rhetoric

Rhetoric is the art of persuasive speaking or writing that uses language to motivate, persuade, or inform. Rhetoric comes from a Greek word meaning "speaker." Literary devices, such as figures of speech and purposeful repetition, are forms of rhetoric. Rhetoric should consider the audience and use language that best suits the situation. Sometimes, it can be seen as insincere or lacking meaningful content, but this does not need to be the case.

> **Rhetoric** is the art of persuasive speaking or writing that uses language to motivate, persuade, or inform.

Examples of rhetoric:

- A lawyer presenting an emotional argument to persuade a jury
- A missionary presenting the gospel to a group
- An advertisement steering people toward a certain product
- A politician delivering a "rallying cry" to inspire voters

Modes of Persuasion

The ancient Greek philosopher and scientist Aristotle, in his written work *Rhetoric*, presented ideas for persuading one's audience through both writing and speaking. These ideas have become known as the "modes of persuasion." They are based on three Greek words: ethos, logos, and pathos.

The Greek word **ethos** means "character" or "spirit." This term reflects how you present yourself in writing or speaking. You need to come across in a way that gives the reader confidence you know what you are talking about. Credibility is affected by errors in grammar, structure, and logic.

The Greek word **logos** means "logic" or "rationale." This reflects the need for evidence that backs up your claim and the logical presentation of your argument. It is important to present your claim early in your essay, progress through your main points in the right order, and end with a powerful conclusion.

The Greek word **pathos** means "suffering" or "experience." This is about appealing to your reader's emotions. A persuasive essay or speech should "tug at the heartstrings" of the reader or listener. A persuasive essay can stir the feelings of your audience, which may persuade them toward your opinion.

Describe what types of appeals are likely to persuade *you* to think a certain way. Do emotional appeals usually influence you, or are you more likely to be convinced logically? Does credibility matter to you?

_____
_____
_____
_____
_____
_____
_____

Communication

Name _____ Lesson 30 - Exercise 3 Day 148

Let's practice the modes of persuasion. **Study** the left side of the chart. **Fill in** the right side of the chart with something you feel would help you accomplish your schoolwork, using the left side example as a guide. Your goal is to persuade your parent or instructor!

Mode of Persuasion	Audience: Parent/Instructor	
	Subject: Why I need my own desk to get my schoolwork done.	**Subject:** Why I need _____ to get my schoolwork done.
Ethos	As a tenth-grade homeschool student, I have years of experience working on my education. I have observed how certain factors like noise, visual distractions, and physical space affect my concentration.	
Logos	A proper desk in my room would give me the working environment I need to study efficiently and comfortably. The desk I would like to purchase costs $100. I have $50 of this saved, and I am requesting you consider paying the balance. This is a worthy investment in my education and has a direct impact on my future.	
Pathos	Think about how my surroundings as a student play a major role in my ability to comprehend what I am learning and in my enjoyment of school. With less than two years of homeschooling left, making the most of my remaining time feels very important.	

Have your instructor read your persuasive argument and give you feedback on whether you were able to persuade them or not. **Describe** your instructor's feedback.

_____
_____
_____
_____
_____

Worldview & Literary Analysis

Read the following excerpt from *The Summit*.

Deadpoint Reflections

Crux: Success. Three of my most notable successes in the mountains have come from climbs in which I did not reach the summit. I believe all too often in our culture, standing on top of that proverbial mountain is what defines success more than anything else. We define success by winning, earning, status, achievements, possessions, by having well-behaved children who get good grades, by how we look, and even by being well known or well liked. An accurate measure of success is to look at results based upon the goals we set for ourselves. I pride myself on being a safe climber, and safety is my primary goal on any climb, superseding summits, and not influenced by financial investment or reward.

May of 2007, on a climb of the Maroon Bells with my blind friend Erik, we spent hours driving, then riding a fully loaded tandem bike with a trailer carrying all of our climbing gear to then sleep at the trailhead, hiking miles in to the peak in darkness, and then climbing to 13,500 feet. There we were greeted by funky May weather just shy of the summit. Erik was driven and wanted to continue to push on toward the summit. I wanted it too, but looking through the saddle of the Bell Cord Couloir, I could see the squall coming and he could not. I would need to make a decision and he would have to live with it, not really being able to provide much input. I knew the rugged terrain above would slow us down and though it was still early in the morning, turning around at this moment was the right choice. I could discern that Erik was disappointed and frustrated, questioning my decision. I was disappointed too, and really had no guarantee that this weather wouldn't just blow over. We headed down the steep, snowy trench, and just as we removed our crampons at the bottom of the slope, a loud, thunderous boom filled the air as a crack of light flashed around us. Hail and rain began to fall, and we hustled to get down below the tree line. High on the ridge of this peak, bolts like these are often fatal. We made the right decision, we got down safely, and it was a success as defined by my goal of being safe. We don't always get what we set out for on the first attempt. That is one thing about success — unless we set our sights very low, it does not come easily. One year later we made the summit of this peak by the same route and were able to experience the beauty of this climb again. I think the summit was even sweeter due to the fact that it did not come easily.

The other climb I consider a success is Amadablam [*sic*]; a success because it knit our team together and showed the team's character, communication skills, selflessness, and lack of greed for the summit.

Finally, on a climb of Kilimanjaro, I saw four blind students make the summit while I remained behind at high camp with two others who had become ill. Success for me was doing the thing that was best for everyone else and stuffing my pride, which wanted to say I was responsible for their summit. The truth is that they were the ones who carried out each step courageously.

Hold: We must understand that life is a process that God uses to refine and reshape us. We should set goals and be willing to adjust them as life comes at us, and as God reveals the chart for our course. We need to seek and live by success as God would see it, and as more than an accumulation of trophies meant to impress others. God gives us ambition and puts desires in our hearts, and success is not letting the pursuit of those things rule our lives.

Name _____   Lesson 30 – Exercise 4   Day 149

> **Anchor:** This is what we can hook, clip, and tie ourselves onto, being confident in its security. What would biblically defined and exemplified success look like? What makes a person a successful Christian? "Love the Lord your God with all your heart and with all your soul and with all your mind and with all your strength. The second is this: 'Love your neighbor as yourself.' There is no commandment greater than these" (Mark 12:30–31). Biblical success shows nothing of being perfect; rather it is the humble acceptance of God's grace in admission of sin and failure. That is step one. Step two is living a life of obedience out of love, revealing an effort to emulate godly character. It is a process of relationship, striving, and refining.[1]

Respond to the following based on this lesson's excerpt from *The Summit*.

List some of the accomplishments in your own life that have made you feel successful.

_____
_____
_____

Alexander tells about three climbs he made and evaluates the success of each. Next to each of the listed mountains, **describe** why Alexander believes they were successful climbs.

1. Maroon Bells: _____
   _____
   _____

2. Ama Dablam: _____
   _____
   _____

3. Kilimanjaro: _____
   _____
   _____

The hold teaches us to "hold" our goals loosely because life can change as God charts our course. **List** a goal you have in life and how you can "hold it loosely" and allow God to direct you.

_____
_____
_____

4. Alexander lists two steps that relate to biblical success. **List** them here.

   a. Step 1: _____
   _____

   b. Step 2: _____
   _____

---

1. Alexander, *The Summit*, p. 44–45.

Lesson 30, Day 149   Language Lessons for a Living Education Level 10

Name _____ Lesson 30 - Exercise 5 Day 150

Review

☐ **Update** the Reading List chart with books you have read this week.

☐ **Recite** John 10:27–28 from memory to your instructor.

Vocabulary Review

Use the following vocabulary words in a sentence out loud to your instructor. **Check** the boxes when done.

☐ cease   ☐ extol   ☐ image   ☐ strife
☐ effort   ☐ fellowship   ☐ strain

Write a sentence using three of the vocabulary words.

_____
_____
_____

Grammar & Punctuation Review

1. **Define** a double negative.
   _____
   _____

2. **Rewrite** this sentence by changing one of the negatives.

   After observing her behavior, Erin knew she couldn't never work with anybody like that!

   _____
   _____

Based on your knowledge of the prefixes in the following words, **match** them to their definitions.

3. _____ disembark   a. the capacity to be flattened or reduced by pressure
4. _____ antediluvian   b. leave a plane, ship, or other vehicle
5. _____ compressibility   c. of or belonging to the time before Noah's Flood

Review   Lesson 30, Day 150   317

Name _____   Lesson 30 - Exercise 5   Day 150

Communication Review

1. **Define** rhetoric.
   _____
   _____

2. **Define** the three modes of persuasion and how they came to be known as such.
   _____
   _____
   _____
   _____

Worldview & Literary Analysis Review

1. **Describe** why Alexander believes his climb up Mount Kilimanjaro was a success.
   _____
   _____
   _____
   _____

2. **Fill in** the blanks in Alexander's statements about success from a biblical perspective.

   a. Step 1: "Biblical success shows nothing of being _____; rather it is the _____ acceptance of God's _____ in _____ of sin and _____."

   b. Step 2: "Step two is living a life of _____ out of _____, revealing an effort to _____ godly character. It is a process of _____, _____, and _____."

Special Feature

Lesson 31

Scripture Study: Mountain Bible Verses

Study each verse and **rewrite** it in your own words.

Isaiah 54:10
"For the mountains may depart
and the hills be removed,
but my steadfast love shall not depart from you,
and my covenant of peace shall not be removed,"
says the Lord, who has compassion on you.

Nahum 1:5
The mountains quake before him; the hills melt;
the earth heaves before him,
the world and all who dwell in it.

Psalm 90:2
Before the mountains were brought forth,
or ever you had formed the earth and the world,
from everlasting to everlasting you are God.

Psalm 121:1–2
I lift up my eyes to the hills.
From where does my help come?
My help comes from the Lord,
who made heaven and earth.

Matthew 14:23
And after he had dismissed the crowds,
he went up on the mountain by himself to pray.
When evening came, he was there alone.

Psalm 95:4
In his hand are the depths of the earth;
the heights of the mountains are his also.

Psalm 125:2
As the mountains surround Jerusalem,
so the Lord surrounds his people,
from this time forth and forevermore.

Name _____ Lesson 31 - Exercise 1 Day 151

Psalm 65:5–6

By awesome deeds you answer us with righteousness,
O God of our salvation, the hope
of all the ends of the earth and of the farthest seas;
the one who by his strength established the
mountains, being girded with might.

Isaiah 44:23

*Sing, O heavens, for the L*ORD *has done it;*
shout, O depths of the earth; break forth into singing,
O mountains, O forest, and every tree in it!
*For the L*ORD *has redeemed Jacob,*
and will be glorified in Israel.

Vocabulary Study

Match the words found in today's Special Feature to the correct definition. If you do not know the meaning of a word, read the Scripture verses for clues. If you are still uncertain, look it up in a dictionary. (If using an online dictionary, ask a parent's permission.)

1. _____ steadfast
2. _____ covenant
3. _____ heave
4. _____ dismiss
5. _____ girded
6. _____ redeemed

a. lift with great effort
b. saved or delivered from sin
c. fastened, secured, equipped, and prepared
d. unwavering, faithful, devout loving kindness
e. order or allow to leave; send away
f. an agreement between God and his people

☐ **Use** index cards to **write** each vocabulary word from this lesson on one side and the definition on the other. **Check** the box when complete.

☐ **Copy** the Scripture verse on an index card. **Memorize** it by the end of this lesson. You may choose the Bible translation or use the one given. **Check** the box when complete.

*I lift up my eyes to the hills. From where does my help come? My help comes from the L*ORD*, who made heaven and earth. Psalm 121:1–2*

Name _____   Lesson 31 - Exercise 2   Day 152

Grammar & Punctuation

Tricky Words

Often it can be easy to confuse which word to use because some of them are similar in meaning or spelling. **Study** the easily confused words.

Then indicates a moment in time.	**Than** introduces the second element in a comparison.
Sit means to rest in an upright position.	**Set** means to put or place an object.
Rise means to get up or move upward.	**Raise** means to lift or move higher.
Can means to be able to do something.	**May** means to have permission to do something.
Bring means to move something toward a person or place.	**Take** means to move something away from a person or place.

Underline the correct word based on the above definitions. Some of the verbs may be in a different tense than those listed in the chart.

1. I was getting frustrated with her, but (than, then) I remembered she is much younger (then, than) I am and just doesn't know any better.

2. When Dad came home from work, he (set, sat) down in his big comfortable chair and (sat, set) his hat on the table next to him.

3. When the officials (rise, raise) the flag, the people should (rise, raise) and honor those whom it represents.

4. (Can, May) I please go outside now with Jillian? I know I (may, can) finish my reading tonight after dinner!

5. I (took, brought) the volleyball to practice, and my instructor (took, brought) it with him until next week.

Suffix Study

Use the chart to decipher the meaning of the following words and **match** them to their definitions.

Suffix	Meaning	Examples
-al, -ial	related to, character of	formal, emotional, aerial
-en	become, made of, resemble, to make	earthen, sweeten, fasten
-an, -ian	belonging/relating to; able to be	electrician, Texan, veterinarian

6. _____ axial
7. _____ reptilian
8. _____ woolen
9. _____ theatrical

a. made wholly or partly of wool
b. relating to the theater
c. relating to or having the character of an axis
d. belonging or relating to reptiles

Name _____   Lesson 31 - Exercise 2   Day 152

Write a sentence using two words that include the suffixes from the chart. Use words not used in this lesson.

_____

_____

Refer to the Grammar & Punctuation exercises in Lessons 10–12 and **complete** the following.

Place quotation marks, commas, periods, question marks, and exclamation points where needed in the following sentences.

10. When Mom couldn't find her glasses she told us all Since I can't drive without my glasses we can't leave until they are found

11. The word chicken could be used to describe someone who is a coward or the actual bird that lays eggs

12. In frustration I asked my mother How many times will I need to practice memorizing this list of prepositions before they stick in my mind

13. My little sister Joanna suggested I hope I haven't been talking too much; then she continued to ramble on and on

Write a complex sentence that contains a prepositional phrase. (Day 37)

_____

_____

Write a compound sentence in the active voice. (Day 42)

_____

_____

Underline the adjectives, including articles, in the following sentences.

14. A hot, tropical climate sounds very appealing in the middle of a harsh, cold winter.

15. There were amazing sites to see at our local county fair; farm animals, delicious foods, and handcrafted products were everywhere!

Underline the adverbs. There may be more than one per sentence.

16. I really need to clean my room tomorrow so I am not embarrassed for my grandmother to see it!

17. The scared little mouse quickly crawled inside the end of the log to avoid the quietly creeping cat.

Underline the dependent clauses and **write** adjective, adverb, or noun on the line to label them.

18. _____ Whether I am planning to go to college in the fall or not has become the main topic of discussion each week when Dad and I take our walk.

19. _____ Although I am a great artist, I don't see myself attending college for art.

20. _____ My pastor's wife, who is a sweet and loving person, has become a powerful voice for the plight of the unborn in our culture.

Name _____ **Lesson 31 - Exercise 3** Day 153

Communication

Persuasive Essay

Day 148 introduced the modes of persuasion, and you practiced persuading your parent/instructor. You will expand your skills as a persuader through a five-paragraph essay that aims to urge the reader toward a specific opinion through logic, reasoning, and emotion.

Everyone has experience in persuading others; we do it daily. Whether we are convincing our sibling that they left the milk out, explaining to our parents why we really do need a new phone, or trying to persuade the boy at the park that Noah's Flood truly happened, we are constantly trying to convince others of the accuracy of our opinions. Our writing can include the same passion!

Steps for Writing a Persuasive Essay

1. **Choose a Topic:** Our best persuasive abilities come out when arguing in support of something we are passionate about. This makes the experience of researching and writing more enjoyable.

2. **Research:** Every argument has two sides. Thoroughly researching both sides of an argument will help you develop strong supporting evidence. To convince your reader to agree with you, you must be able to acknowledge the opposing side and present evidence against it. Your research for this essay can include online research with a parent's permission or a search through your home or local library.

3. **Create a Thesis Statement:** One of the most important parts of your essay is your thesis statement. This statement summarizes your argument in a way that is powerful and concise. There should be no doubt about where you stand on the matter. Your thesis statement should include *what* you are arguing for and *how* you plan to convince the reader of your stance. A thesis statement for a persuasive essay must be a **debatable claim**, a statement that people could reasonably have differing opinions about. (For example, "Cigarettes are bad for your health" is not a debatable claim.)

4. **Make an Outline:** Creating a structure for your essay will make the writing process flow logically from one point to the next. It is tempting to skip this step and start writing, but it is worth the effort! Making lists of the major points you want to make, the research you want to incorporate, and the emotional/moral appeals you would like to make will help you when structuring your outline. You may use the Persuasive Essay Outline in the back of this book.

5. **Write it Out:** Start with an *introductory paragraph* that explains your topic and end with your thesis statement. Next, incorporate *ethos* (your credibility and voice). Follow with *logos* (rationale, logical reasoning). Then use the idea of *pathos* (suffering or experience) by "tugging at the heartstrings" of the reader. Finally, end with a *closing paragraph* that restates your thesis statement and ends your argument with a "bang." We will walk through the steps of this essay in greater detail in the next lesson. During the upcoming week, **choose** a topic, **research** your topic, and **develop** your thesis statement. Remember to record the sources of your research using the Citation Notes Worksheet in the back of this book. You will need to cite two research sources.

Persuasive Essay Topic: _____

Name _____   Lesson 31 - Exercise 3   Day 153

Wisdom Speaks

Copy the proverb.

> A man who bears false witness against his neighbor is like a war club, or a sword, or a sharp arrow. Proverbs 25:18

_____
_____

Using a thesaurus or an online search with a parent's permission, **write** two synonyms for each word.

1. bear (as in "to hold"): _____
2. witness: _____

Based on the synonyms, **rewrite** the proverb.

_____
_____

This proverb is a simile. Just as literal clubs, swords, and arrows can injure or kill, lies told about a person can result in major damage to jobs, families, reputations, and more. Even statements that are not quite accurate can cause a great deal of trouble. It is so important that we are sure our words are true and necessary before we speak them.

Describe a time when something false was spoken about you or someone you know. What damage did it cause and what lesson did you learn from it?

_____
_____
_____
_____

Copy the verse.

> So also the tongue is a small member, yet it boasts of great things. How great a forest is set ablaze by such a small fire! And the tongue is a fire, a world of unrighteousness. The tongue is set among our members, staining the whole body, setting on fire the entire course of life, and set on fire by hell. James 3:5–6

_____
_____
_____
_____
_____

Worldview & Literary Analysis

Read the following excerpt from *The Summit*.

Deadpoint Reflections

Crux: Loss. One of the few guarantees we have in life is that it will end. Where and when, we do not know, but death in this life is certain. The crux is coming to peace with this inevitable and unavoidable conclusion for ourselves and for those we love. Losing a friend or a family member for most of us will present some of the hardest and most emotional times of our lives. The more sudden and unexpectedly a life comes to an end, often the more difficult it is to accept, and the younger and healthier the person, the greater the question of why. As we age, we come to expect the certainty of uncertainties as our bodies begin to break down, making us more susceptible to illness and injury. But regardless of our age, one question stands out for us all: What happens when the light goes out?

Hold: Hope. Gradually, like a wound that heals, peace will set in, life will go on, and the acceptance of another's passing will be like the wound that leaves a scar. The grieving process must take place or the wound will be like a picked scab and never heal. The memories will remain as the scar is evidence to, but the pain will fade away. We can believe whatever we like about death and whether or not there is life after it, but true peace does not come from what I believe, it comes from God. I know God has a plan and that plan gives me hope in the midst of death's grip when it unjustly and inexplicably grasps people like my friend's ten-month-old baby, or another person falling asleep at the wheel and crossing the median to claim the sweet young life of a local nurse. I like to think that God is populating heaven with babies, toddlers, children, and people of all ages, so that it has some variety that makes it perfect, like He says it will be. I don't quite know exactly how that will look, but I have hope in His plan and that is what I hold on to.

Anchor: "For God so loved the world that he gave his one and only Son, that whoever believes in him shall not perish but have eternal life" (John 3:16). If we cannot take God at His word and anchor ourselves in this hope, then our faith is in vain. As Thoreau said, "Most men lead lives of quiet desperation because they never truly live." It would seem that to live life fully is a choice, as is living your life for what is eternal.[1]

Respond to the following based on this lesson's excerpt from *The Summit* (continued on next page).

The Bible tells us that it is "appointed unto men once to die" (Hebrews 9:27; KJV). However, there are many views on the afterlife (what happens when our bodies die). Some believe we are "reincarnated" (after death, we come back in a different body or life form). Some believe there is no afterlife; we simply cease to exist. Many believe we become spirits or ghosts that roam the earth, "watching over" our loved ones or seeking vengeance on our enemies. Still others believe in an afterlife that does not include a deity (God or gods) of any sort.

☐ **Look up** 1 Corinthians 15:35–49 to see the good news God's Word gives concerning our bodily death. You may use the Bible translation of your choice. **Check** the box after reading the verses.

---
[1] Alexander, *The Summit*, p. 58–59.

Name _____   Lesson 31 - Exercise 4   Day 154

Write a paragraph that compares the many different afterlife views given in this lesson with the verses from 1 Corinthians 15. Clearly **state** the biblical worldview regarding life after death.

_____
_____
_____
_____
_____

1. This lesson's *Deadpoint Reflections* was based on a story Alexander shared about the tragic death of a good friend in a snowboarding accident. Eric Alexander turned to God's Word to help make sense of a "senseless tragedy." **Describe** what you believe Alexander meant by this statement: "We can believe whatever we like about death and whether or not there is life after it, but true peace does not come from what I believe, it comes from God."

_____
_____
_____
_____

Write about a difficult life experience and how God's Word helped you make sense of something that felt senseless.

_____
_____
_____
_____

God's Word promises to give us a peace that is different from the peace the world offers. Worldly peace is temporary and weak and often involves "masking" or ignoring pain. It offers no hope for eternity.

Copy the following verses.

> *And the peace of God, which surpasses all understanding, will guard your hearts and your minds in Christ Jesus.* Philippians 4:7

_____
_____

> *"I have said these things to you, that in me you may have peace. In the world you will have tribulation. But take heart; I have overcome the world."* John 16:33

_____
_____

Name _____ Lesson 31 - Exercise 5 Day 155

Review

☐ **Update** the Reading List chart with books you have read this week.

☐ **Recite** Psalm 121:1–2 from memory to your instructor.

Vocabulary Review

Write a paragraph using the following vocabulary words: *steadfast, covenant, heave, dismiss, girded,* and *redeemed.*

_____
_____
_____
_____
_____
_____
_____
_____

Grammar & Punctuation Review

Match the tricky word to its definition.

1. _____ then
2. _____ than
3. _____ sit
4. _____ set
5. _____ rise
6. _____ raise
7. _____ can
8. _____ may
9. _____ bring
10. _____ take

a. to put or place an object
b. to move something away from a person or place
c. to have permission to do something
d. indicates a moment in time
e. to be able to do something
f. to rest in an upright position
g. to move something toward a person or place
h. introduces the second element in a comparison
i. to lift or move higher
j. to get up or move upward

Based on your knowledge of the prefixes and suffixes in the following words, **match** them to their definitions.

11. _____ inconsequential
12. _____ anticarcinogen
13. _____ antiquarian

a. substance that inhibits the development of cancer
b. not significant or important
c. dealing with or relating to antiques or rare books

Review

Name _____ Lesson 31 - Exercise 5 Day 155

Communication Review

1. **List** the five steps for writing a persuasive essay.

    a. _____
    b. _____
    c. _____
    d. _____
    e. _____

2. **Define** a debatable claim.

    _____
    _____

Write an example of a debatable claim.

_____
_____

Describe how this proverb is a simile.

> *A man who bears false witness against his neighbor is like a war club, or a sword, or a sharp arrow.* Proverbs 25:18

_____
_____

Worldview & Literary Analysis Review

1. **Fill in** the blanks in this quote from Eric Alexander.

    "We can _____ whatever we like about _____ and whether or not there is _____ after it, but true _____ does not come from what I _____, it comes from _____."

Write a summary of this lesson's hold located in the excerpt from *The Summit*.

_____
_____
_____
_____
_____
_____

Special Feature

Lesson 32

Excerpt Study: *Developing a Heart for God* by Ron Auch

Direct my footsteps according to your word; let no sin rule over me.
[Psalm 119:133; NIV]

Sin cannot rule over the man whose footsteps are directed by the Lord. An amazing thing happens when a man humbles himself before his God in a renewed determination to obey God. The devil flees. The devil must flee because through humility Jesus comes on the scene. So often we have a mental picture of spiritual battle being that of Satan giving one blow after another to Jesus. Then Jesus musters His strength and answers each blow with a counter blow. That is not so! The battle has been won, the devil defeated.

Satan would like to direct our steps away from God. He would like us to take the easy path where he could then rule over us. However, if we will determine to submit ourselves to God, Satan must flee. James puts it this way, "Submit yourselves, then, to God. Resist the devil, and he will flee from you. Come near to God and he will come near to you" (James 4:7–8). The devil will flee from those who submit and resist. When we take one step toward God, we find that He has already taken a hundred toward us.

If we look at James 4:6 we read, "But He gives us more grace. That is why Scripture says: 'God opposes the proud but gives grace to the humble.'" Through submission, we resist the devil. Through pride, we resist God. If we will walk according to the Word of God, no sin will rule over us because our submission to it brings Jesus. When Jesus is present, the devil flees. There is an amazing freedom over sin that can be experienced by anyone willing to humble himself before God. Typically, humbling comes through confessing your sin to someone and asking them for help. The instant we do that, God gives us grace. If we fail in this, we fail in everything.[1]

To climb the mountain of life, our footsteps must be directed by the Lord. Also, we must not forget that we have an enemy on our heels as we scale this mountain! Our sinful nature and Satan's cunning are the mudholes, thorns, and wild beasts that threaten to divert us from the path and cause us to abandon following the Savior up the mountain.

Respond to the following about the excerpt from *Developing a Heart for God*.

1. Sin cannot rule over **what** type of man?

2. **Why** must the devil flee when a man humbles himself?

3. **Where** does Satan want to direct our steps?

4. **What** happens when we "take the easy path"?

---

[1] Auch, Ron. *Developing a Heart for God*. Green Forest, AR: New Leaf Publishing Group, LLC, 2022, p. 218.

Name _____   Lesson 32 - Exercise 1   Day 156

5. **What** happens when we determine to submit ourselves to God?
_____
_____

Why do you think the "easy path" up the mountain of life can look so appealing?
_____
_____
_____

List some of the difficulties you have faced in following Jesus' footsteps.
_____
_____
_____

6. **How** do we get to the point where "no sin will rule over us"?
_____
_____

Write 2–3 sentences using as many of these words from the Special Feature as you can. If you do not know the meaning of a word, read the excerpt for clues. If you are still uncertain, look it up in a dictionary. If using an online dictionary, ask a parent's permission. (*Hint:* You may alter word forms, such as adding *-s, -ed, -ing*, etc.)

confess	direct	Jesus	resist
determine	grace	pride	steps
devil	humble	renew	submit

_____
_____
_____

☐ **Use** index cards to **write** each vocabulary word from this lesson on one side and the definition on the other. **Check** the box when complete.

☐ **Copy** the Scripture verse on an index card. **Memorize** it by the end of this lesson. You may choose the Bible translation or use the one given. **Check** the box when complete.

Submit yourselves therefore to God. Resist the devil, and he will flee from you. Draw near to God, and he will draw near to you. Cleanse your hands, you sinners, and purify your hearts, you double-minded. James 4:7–8

Name _____ Lesson 32 - Exercise 2 Day 157

Grammar & Punctuation

Misplaced or Dangling Modifiers

A **modifier** is a word, phrase, or clause that affects the meaning of a word or an entire sentence. The simplest modifiers are adjectives and adverbs, but noun clauses, prepositional phrases, and adverbial or adjectival clauses are also modifiers. **Misplaced** or **dangling modifiers** occur when the subject they are meant to modify is missing from the sentence or not near enough to be clearly associated.

> A **modifier** is a word, phrase, or clause that affects the meaning of a word or an entire sentence.
> **Misplaced** or **dangling modifiers** occur when the subject they are meant to modify is missing from the sentence or not near enough to be clearly associated.

> *Examples:* The boy wore shoes on his feet that were quite dirty. (Were the shoes dirty or were the boy's feet dirty? This is a misplaced modifier.)
> Walking toward the open field, the wind was chilly. (Was the wind walking toward the open field? This is a dangling modifier since the subject of the modifier is missing.)
> To fix these examples: The boy wore dirty shoes on his feet.
> As I walked toward the open field, the chilly wind hit my face.

Rewrite the sentences by fixing the misplaced or dangling modifiers.

1. Travis saw three large groundhogs mowing the lawn.
   _____
   _____

2. Wanting to sit down and rest, the ground was too hard.
   _____
   _____

Prefix Study

Prefix	Meaning	Examples
en-, em-	to cause to be; put or go into or onto	enable, embrace, encounter
hyper-	beyond; more than normal	hyperactive, hyperbole
in-, il-, im-, ir-	in, on, not	infallible, illegal, impolite
ob-	blocking, against, concealing	obstruct, obscene, obliterate

Use a dictionary or online search with your parent's permission to **find** one word for each of the following prefixes. **Record** their definitions.

En-: _____
Definition: _____

Grammar & Punctuation   Lesson 32, Day 157   331

Name _____   Lesson 32 - Exercise 2   Day 157

Hyper-: _____
Definition: _____
In-: _____
Definition: _____

☐ Use your index cards to **copy** the prefixes from this study. Give two examples for each. **Check** the box when you are done.

Refer to the Grammar & Punctuation exercises in Lessons 13–15 and **complete** the following.
Place commas where necessary.

3. Every Saturday which was the Jewish Sabbath Day was a time of rest from the usual workload and activities.

4. I have always lived in the Northeast so I am familiar with the signs of autumn: cooler temperatures changing leaves and geese flying south.

5. From the beginning of creation God has shown His amazing love and care for His people His commitment to His covenants and the fulfillment of His promises.

6. **Write** a sentence containing a proper adjective and a limiting adjective.
   _____
   _____

7. **Write** a sentence containing coordinate adjectives. (Make sure to use a comma if necessary!)
   _____
   _____

8. **Write** a sentence containing a compound adjective. (*Examples:* short-term, grass-fed, ice-cold, etc.)
   _____
   _____

Underline the adverbs. **Circle** the word or words they modify. There may be more than one adverb per sentence. (*Hint:* Some adverbs may be underlined *and* circled, and some may modify the entire sentence.)

9. After we finished dinner, we quickly cleaned up the kitchen so we could watch a movie.

10. I was carelessly cleaning my bird's cage, and he flew outside!

11. We won't have enough paint to finish the project because Jerod slapped it on the shed so quickly that he used too much.

Write a sentence that contains an adverb of manner.
_____
_____

332   Lesson 32, Day 157   Language Lessons for a Living Education Level 10

Name _____ Lesson 32 - Exercise 3 Day 158

🗨️ Communication

Persuasive Essay Development

In the past week, you have chosen a topic you are passionate about, researched both sides of the debate, and developed a thesis statement (the "crux" of your argument). **Record** your thesis statement.

_____
_____

Use the Persuasive Essay Outline in the back of this book to **create** an outline for a five- to seven-paragraph essay. Base your outline on the following elements:

Introductory paragraph: Introduce your topic by explaining the major elements or circumstances surrounding it. (*Example:* Highlight the main differences between creationism and evolution.) End this paragraph with your thesis statement. (*Example:* Through an unbiased look at the evidence at hand, the truth regarding the likely cause of the creation we see today will become evident.)

Ethos paragraph: Establish your credibility and the credibility of your research sources. (Credibility should be present throughout the essay.) Explain why you are passionate about the topic and the experience you have in relating to it. Mention your sources and explain why the reader should consider their testimony on the subject. Incorporate any quotes or paraphrases from your sources that may be appropriate in this paragraph.

Logos paragraph: Present evidence to back up the claim made in your thesis statement. Remember to present both sides of the argument and use your research to counter the opposing view. You will point to your research in this paragraph. You may need more than one paragraph to thoroughly present your ideas. Refer to Day 28 for tips on incorporating research.

Pathos paragraph: Emphasize your evidence with passion in this paragraph. You have shown credibility through your knowledge, sources, and willingness to be objective (looking at both sides). You have logically presented evidence to convince the reader's mind. Now it is time to appeal to the reader's emotions. Whether your topic stirs up a sense of justice, concern for the oppressed, or meeting a serious need, your reader should be able to "feel" the emotion behind your thesis. Avoid being overly dramatic, however.

Closing paragraph: This is your last chance to influence your reader. Close out your essay with a strong argument using a summary of your main points. Restate your thesis statement somewhere in this paragraph and challenge your reader to come to the same conclusion you have.

☐ *Note:* A persuasive essay does not need to have ethos, pathos, and logos neatly contained in paragraphs as this assignment has shown you. Usually, they are interwoven throughout the essay. However, containing each in its own paragraph will help you focus on the distinct elements of persuasion. **Check** the box when you have completed your outline.

Name _____   **Lesson 32 - Exercise 3**   **Day 158**

☐ Throughout the upcoming week, you will use your outline to write a rough draft of your essay using the Persuasive Essay Writing Worksheet in the back of the book. Before beginning to write your persuasive essay, **review** the Persuasive Essay Rubric found in the back of this book. This will remind you of the main elements you will be graded on. The persuasive essay rough draft is due on Day 163. Be sure to double-space your rough draft. **Check** the box when you have reviewed the rubric.

☐ Since this essay requires at least two researched sources, **review** Citing Sources found in the back of the book under Communication Study Sheets. **Check** the box when you have reviewed citing sources.

In preparation for writing your essay, **review** the following tips.

Tips for Better Writing

- **Vary your sentence structure:** Use different sentence types and lengths to add interest. Consider opening a sentence with a prepositional phrase, a verb phrase, or an infinitive. (Days 77, 82, and 87)
- **Avoid repeating words:** Use synonyms (similar words) rather than using the same words excessively. Use a thesaurus for ideas. (Day 143)
- **Be engaging:** Avoid phrases or clichés like *once upon a time … when I was … at the end of the day … ignorance is bliss*, etc. Instead, be fresh in how you present your information and thoughts.
- **Use quality transitions:** When moving from one idea to another or beginning a new paragraph, use appropriate transitional words and phrases, such as *in addition to, besides, finally, because of, after that, furthermore, nevertheless, consequently, likewise, similarly,* etc.
- **Use vivid imagery:** Insert lively verbs, adjectives, and adverbs without being excessive. Make sure your use of words is appropriate within the context of your topic. A light and fun topic would use different imagery than a serious or "heavy" topic.
- **Stay focused:** Regularly look back at your thesis statement and make sure you are only writing thoughts that reinforce your main point. It is very easy to get off-topic as your mind wanders to different points.
- **Keep your voice interesting:** The way you come across to your reader through your choice of vocabulary, expression, point of view, and detail all make up your voice. Staying consistent in all these elements will make you more believable.
- **Use specific words:** Avoid using generic words like *that, things,* or *stuff*. Whenever possible, give specific details. (*Example of generic words: That* is some of the best *stuff* I have ever eaten. *Example of specific words: These chicken wings* are some of the best *restaurant food* I have ever consumed!)
- **Use accurate words:** Nothing will ruin your credibility more than the inaccurate use of words. If you are unsure if the word you have chosen is appropriate, take the time to look in a dictionary or thesaurus. (*Example of wrong word choice:* The man was *adverse* to attending a church. *Example of correct word choice:* The man was *averse* to attending church. Adverse = unfavorable, hazardous. Averse = opposed.)

Name_____   Lesson 32 - Exercise 4   Day 159

Worldview & Literary Analysis

Read the following excerpt from *The Summit*.

Deadpoint Reflections

Crux: Having confidence in things not seen. I don't know where, but somewhere along the way so many of us lose the faith we had as children. Perhaps it is the reality of having been let down over the years when expectations of people and God were not met. I remember a time a few years ago when I reached down to pick something up off the floor, turning away from the bunk bed which held my four-year-old niece Katie on the upper level. Standing back up and turning toward the bed I was caught off guard when I found her airborne, arms stretched open wide, and zinging at me in the superman position, not doubting for a second that I would catch her. Had I paused to pick up a second toy or to tie my shoe, the event would have had an unhappy ending. As it was, I caught her as my heart raced quickly to 120 BPM [beats per minute]. Most of us struggle to exhibit this kind of faith in anyone, or anything, and never risk a dive off the top bunk, so to speak. The faith my niece had in me and my ability to catch her had been learned over time as we developed a relationship through play and time together. She knew I had the strength to carry her and in this relationship, whether I was watching or not, she knew she could trust me. She then quickly figured as long as I was in the room, I would be able to catch her.

Hold: Faith that is expectant. Is faith in God merely a fire insurance policy? Just like with my niece, it is trust that is built on relationship over time, which leads to understanding when faith can be exercised and certain outcomes can be expected.

It would be wrong to march out and expect God to give us whatever we want all the time, which would look like a spoiled child demanding to have all the toys in a toy store. I see expectant faith the way that a young girl was recently rescued from a Florida swamp. She had been missing for days, and experienced search crews had failed to find even a clue to her whereabouts. A skilled civilian outdoorsman heard the voice of God tell him to go seek her out. Without hesitation or question as to where the voice came from, he used his skills and knowledge of the swamp to go directly to her, giving the Lord the credit for guiding him right to the spot where she was stuck. He left his house fully expecting God to use him to find this little girl; hours after he left he had found her.

Anchor: *And without faith it is impossible to please God, because anyone who comes to him must believe that he exists and that he rewards those who earnestly seek him* (Hebrews 11:6).[1]

Respond to the following based on this lesson's excerpt from *The Summit*.

An anecdote (Day 59) is a short story used by an author to underscore a certain aspect they want to emphasize. Alexander shares an anecdote about his four-year-old niece. In your own words, **explain** how this little story emphasizes the point the author is trying to make.

_____
_____
_____

---

[1] Alexander, *The Summit*, p. 80–81.

Name _____ Lesson 32 - Exercise 4 Day 159

Amazingly, the author's niece didn't even wait to see if he was looking; she simply jumped with a firm belief that he would catch her. In Matthew 18:3b, Jesus states, "[U]nless you turn and become like children, you will never enter the kingdom of heaven." **Relate** this verse to the anecdote from the reading.

_____
_____
_____
_____

Alexander states, "[T]rust … is built on relationship over time …" As we step out and trust God (jump off the bunk bed!), He catches us, and the next time we need Him, our faith reminds us that He is there. **Write** about a time you stepped out in faith with confidence in what God wanted you to do. Often, this means simply obeying His Word, even when the world believes it's foolishness.

_____
_____
_____
_____
_____
_____
_____

Copy this verse about faith.

> *Now faith is the assurance of things hoped for, the conviction of things not seen.* Hebrews 11:1

_____
_____

Based on Psalm 78:17–22 and Matthew 4:7, **how** would you describe the difference between stepping out in faith and tempting God?

_____
_____
_____
_____
_____
_____

Record this lesson's anchor verse.

_____
_____

Name _____   Lesson 32 - Exercise 5   Day 160

Review

☐ **Update** the Reading List chart with books you have read this week.

☐ **Recite** James 4:7–8 from memory to your instructor.

Vocabulary Review

Match each word to the correct definition.

1. _____ humble
2. _____ submit
3. _____ grace
4. _____ renew
5. _____ pride
6. _____ determine

a. yield oneself to an authority
b. too high an opinion of one's worth or ability
c. find out or come to a decision about something
d. having or showing a modest view of one's importance
e. change into something new or better
f. undeserved favor

Grammar & Punctuation Review

Rewrite the sentences by fixing the misplaced or dangling modifiers.

1. Rebecca frantically looked for her book digging through her backpack.
   _____
   _____

2. The clothing store window displayed winter children's coats.
   _____
   _____

3. Walking home last night, the weather was terrible.
   _____
   _____

Based on your knowledge of the prefixes and suffixes in the following words, **match** them to their definitions.

4. _____ obliterate
5. _____ hyperbolic
6. _____ inquest
7. _____ embezzlement

a. judicial inquiry about facts relating to an incident
b. fraudulent taking of property by someone entrusted with it
c. completely destroy or wipe out
d. of or relating to overstatements of truth; going beyond what is true

Name _____ Lesson 32 - Exercise 5 Day 160

Communication Review

List the Tips for Better Writing.

1. _____
2. _____
3. _____
4. _____
5. _____
6. _____
7. _____
8. _____
9. _____

Worldview & Literary Analysis Review

Write a summary of this lesson's crux located in the excerpt from *The Summit*.

_____
_____
_____
_____
_____
_____

1. **Fill in** the blanks of this quote from Eric Alexander.

    "It would be _____ to march out and expect _____ to _____ us whatever we want all the time, which would look like a _____ child _____ to have all the toys in a toy store."

Rewrite the following verse in your own words.

> *Now faith is the assurance of things hoped for, the conviction of things not seen.* Hebrews 11:1

_____
_____

Lesson 32, Day 160   Language Lessons for a Living Education Level 10

Special Feature

Lesson 33

Picture Study: Climbing Team Success

In our journey up the mountain, whether the mountain is an obstacle or representative of our entire life, we do not climb solo. We know that Jesus leads us, but other people are essential as well. They are used as instruments of the Lord in molding and shaping us, challenging us, guiding us, and helping us. As the body of Christ, we need each other. First Corinthians 12:27 states, "Now you are the body of Christ and individually members of it." If we are in Christ, then we are bonded to other believers and responsible for supporting and loving them. Philippians 2:4 tells us, "Let each of you look not only to his own interests, but also to the interests of others." In our climb up the mountain, we must concern ourselves with those around us, helping and encouraging them, while at the same time being humble enough to accept their help as well.

Observe the picture and **write** about the four people. Each one is at a different stage in the climb. **Discuss** their positions (body language) and what it tells you about where they are in their climb and what emotions they may feel. **How** are they relating to each other?

_____
_____
_____
_____
_____
_____
_____
_____

Name _____ Lesson 33 - Exercise 1 Day 161

Study the following verses. **Write** thoughts that correspond to each verse. **Include** specific people and circumstances from your own life, asking the Lord to aid you in applying His Word in a personal way.

> *And let us consider how to stir up one another to love and good works, not neglecting to meet together, as is the habit of some, but encouraging one another, and all the more as you see the Day drawing near.* Hebrews 10:24–25

_____
_____
_____

> *[W]ith all humility and gentleness, with patience, bearing with one another in love.* Ephesians 4:2

_____
_____

> *Iron sharpens iron, and one man sharpens another.* Proverbs 27:17

_____
_____

Vocabulary Study: Mountain Climbing Terms

Match the words to the correct definition. If you cannot discern the meaning, look it up in a dictionary. (If using an online dictionary, ask a parent's permission.)

1. _____ aid climbing   a. first person on a climb
2. _____ free climbing   b. weakened or in pain from a strenuous move
3. _____ bouldering   c. type of climb making use of ropes, bolts, slings, etc.
4. _____ solo   d. climbing close to the ground to safely practice moves
5. _____ pumped   e. type of climb using only hands and feet
6. _____ lead   f. temporary encampment during a climb with little to no shelter
7. _____ bivouac   g. to climb alone with no protection

☐ **Use** index cards to **write** each vocabulary word from this lesson on one side and the definition on the other. **Check** the box when complete.

☐ **Copy** the Scripture verse on an index card. **Memorize** it by the end of this lesson. You may choose the Bible translation or use the one given. **Check** the box when complete.

> *Let each of you look not only to his own interests, but also to the interests of others.* Philippians 2:4

Grammar & Punctuation

Irregular Verbs

Irregular verbs are verbs that do not follow the normal patterns for tense and past participle. While most verbs use the ending *-ed* for the past tense and participle forms, irregular verbs do not. They each have their own unique tense with no set formula for conjugating them. They just need to be memorized!

> **Irregular verbs** are verbs that do not follow the normal patterns for tense and past participle.

	Present Tense	Simple Past Tense	Past Participle
Regular verb	dance	danced	danced
Irregular verb	sing	sang	sung

Fill in the missing verb tenses. If you need help, refer to the Irregular Verbs chart in the back of the book.

Present Tense	Simple Past Tense	Past Participle		Present Tense	Simple Past Tense	Past Participle
arise	1. _____	2. _____		let	11. _____	12. _____
become	3. _____	4. _____		light	13. _____	14. _____
build	5. _____	6. _____		mistake	15. _____	16. _____
draw	7. _____	8. _____		see	17. _____	18. _____
fly	9. _____	10. _____		spill	19. _____	20. _____

Suffix Study

Use the chart to decipher the meaning of the following words and **match** them to their definitions.

Suffix	Meaning	Examples
-tion, -ion, -sion, -ation, -ition	act, result, or state of	million, revelation, decision
-logy, -ology	science of or study of	biology, chronology, etymology
-ant, -ent	belonging to; result of	absorbent, deodorant, contestant
-age	causing an action	postage, baggage, marriage

1. _____ etymology
2. _____ attrition
3. _____ exculpation
4. _____ ensuant
5. _____ abhorrent
6. _____ wreckage

a. following; accompanying as a result of something
b. causing or deserving strong hatred
c. an object that has been badly damaged
d. reduction or weakening as a result of a force
e. the study of the origin of words
f. the act of freeing from guilt or blame

Name_____ Lesson 33 - Exercise 2   Day 16

Refer to the Grammar & Punctuation exercises in Lessons 16–18 and **complete** the following.

Place parentheses around the adjective prepositional phrases and **write** the word or words they modify on the line.

27. The old house on the outskirts of town was listed for sale last I saw. _____

28. When I awoke this morning, I realized that my duffle bag with the stripes got lost when we packed our luggage last night. _____

Place parentheses around the adverb prepositional phrases and **write** the word or words they modify on the line. (*Hint:* Remember to ask *how, when, why, where, to what extent,* or *under what conditions.*)

29. The police officer acted with great courage as he attempted the daring rescue. _____

30. My neighbor's little black colt got loose and ran across our backyard! _____

Identify the underlined participial phrases by **writing** present, past, or perfect on the line. **Circle** the word the participial phrase describes or modifies.

31. _____ A little blue bird <u>perched on the telephone wire</u> was singing at the top of his lungs.

32. _____ The firefighter, <u>having fought the flames all night long</u>, collapsed in the fire engine for a quick nap.

33. _____ The dolphins <u>swimming in the enclosure</u> are being rehabilitated.

Write a sentence containing a gerund phrase.

_____
_____

Identify the underlined infinitive phrase as a noun, adjective, adverb, or prepositional phrase.

34. _____ Many people believe the best pets <u>to own</u> are dogs.

35. _____ <u>To hope in God's plan</u> increases our faith as we see Him working in our lives.

36. _____ <u>To enjoy good health</u>, you must try to eat well and exercise regularly.

37. _____ When we went down south to visit my cousins, we went <u>to the beach</u> every day.

38. **Fix** this split infinitive by rewording the sentence.

Everyone tried to quickly enter the bus before it departed from the station.

_____
_____

Name _____ **Lesson 33 - Exercise 3** **Day 163**

Communication

Persuasive Essay Rough Draft Due

Ask your instructor to read over your persuasive essay rough draft, evaluating it using the Persuasive Essay Rubric in the back of the book, and sign here.

Instructor's signature: _____

Now, **write** your final draft, making any corrections or suggestions your instructor gave you. **Review** the charts below based on whether you are typing or writing your assignment by hand.

Formatting a Final Draft (Typed)
- Set margins to 1 inch on all sides.
- Double space and use a 12-point Times New Roman font.
- Indent the first line of each paragraph 1 inch.
- Create a title page for the front of your essay that includes a title, your name, the name of the course, the assignment (Persuasive Essay), and the date. Center these items.
- Create a works cited page. Center the title, Works Cited, at the top. List resources in alphabetical order. Indent ½ inch for any lines after the first line in each reference. Single space entries. Use 1-inch margins.

Formatting a Final Draft (Handwritten)
- Skip every other line when writing.
- Indent approximately 1 inch for a new paragraph.
- Use your best handwriting.
- Create a title page and works cited page as detailed in the Formatting a Final Draft (Typed) chart. Use approximate measurements for indents and spacing.

Complete your final draft and give it to your instructor for review and grading.

Congratulations, you have completed a persuasive essay!

Name _____   Lesson 33 - Exercise 3   Day 163

Wisdom Speaks

Copy the proverb.

> *Whoever meddles in a quarrel not his own is like one who takes a passing dog by the ears.* Proverbs 26:17

_____

_____

Using a thesaurus or an online search with a parent's permission, **write** two synonyms for each word.

1. meddle: _____

2. quarrel: _____

Rewrite the proverb based on the synonyms.

_____

_____

The Book of Proverbs is full of similes, isn't it? That's what makes proverbs so relatable. The writer uses everyday items to compare the tangible with the intangible. Tangible things can be touched or felt, while intangible things are not perceived through touch, as they do not have a physical presence.

List five tangible things.
- _____
- _____
- _____
- _____
- _____

List five intangible things.
- _____
- _____
- _____
- _____
- _____

In your own words, **describe** some of the dangers of meddling in other people's arguments.

_____

_____

_____

_____

Lesson 33, Day 163   Language Lessons for a Living Education Level 10

Name _____ Lesson 33 - Exercise 4 Day 164

Worldview & Literary Analysis

Read the following excerpt from *The Summit*.

Note: In mountain climbing terms, a belayer would be the person who turns the rope around a cleat or pin to make it hold tight for another climber.

Deadpoint Reflections

Crux: Trust. It should come naturally in marriage, in church, and in support groups, but it doesn't. Most of us at some time or another have been burned by words, actions, and misdeeds of others, and we live guarded lives, never allowing others to have a secure position of trust. When we close this door, we miss out on the fullness of what relationships are meant to be. There is an easy-to-grasp climbing analogy of trust where the lead climber must rely on the steady hand of his belayer and have trust in him and also in the rope that keeps him connected to the rock, should the climber fall. This can be likened to the kind of trust we need to have in marriage or in work, but in a way this trust in climbing is easier because the rope is generally solidly anchored.

So how strong is the trust when the rope is taken away and mistakes are even more serious? Skiing with someone who is blind is like climbing without that rope, and trust really becomes a major factor in the relationship. It really boils down to words: precision in vocalizing exactly what needs to be communicated at just the right moment without a second chance. Most of us in a way similar to these examples have been dropped by our belayers or driven into a tree by our ski guide — we have had trust betrayed. It is with words that we typically blow it. In skiing, that would be saying turn left when I mean right, in life, it usually means just keep your mouth shut, think, think some more, then speak. We come away with an attitude of "In me I trust. I'll get it done in my time, my way, on my own." I have been guilty of this kind of thinking and it reminds me of the Frank Sinatra song, "My Way." To me, that is a sad, lonely, and somewhat desperate song.

Hold: Attentiveness. Be trustworthy. Let your actions match your word, and keep your word. Simple. The fastest way to lose a friend is to be a hypocrite, to gossip about that friend, or even people within your circle. I know because I have made this mistake. I have known some gossips, and yes, they can be friends, but I never let them in close, and I never give them any more information than what I think of the weather forecast. A friendship like this can never go too deep. But there is a certain core of friends that I have observed who never divulge information about others, not even under the guise of "prayer." These are people I can trust and do trust with matters of the heart. This is my wife, and just a small select group of others. A gossip will never earn my trust or my close friendship.

Anchor: The Word. We can take God at His Word. It is what He has given us. If we don't trust this, the Bible, then what is the point of having faith? To meet women at church? For some that is exactly it. "Trust in the LORD with all of your heart and lean not on your own understanding; in all of your ways acknowledge him, and he will make your paths straight" (Proverbs 3:5–6). If you only trust God as far as you can throw Him, you don't trust at all. You have got to trust Him as far as He can throw you. If we approach trust in the Lord like we do human relationships, that is to say with a piece of our heart leaning on our own understanding, we will fail. Maybe you can only give a piece at a time; that is okay, but be determined to give it all. Later, you will gain it all.[1]

---
1 Alexander, *The Summit*, p. 94–95.

Name _____   Lesson 33 - Exercise 4   Day 164

Answer the following questions based on this lesson's excerpt from *The Summit*.

1. To be cynical is to believe that others are motivated purely by their self-interest, causing you to be distrustful of them. According to this lesson's crux, **how** is trust eroded, leaving some people cynical?

   _____
   _____
   _____
   _____
   _____

On Day 64, you learned about the literary device of analogy. Alexander uses the analogy of trusting your belayer when mountain climbing. **How** do you think this relates to relationships with others?

   _____
   _____
   _____

We want to trust others and we want them to trust us, but the truth is, sometimes we let each other down and need to forgive or be forgiven. **What** attitude might we adopt if we refuse to trust others?

   _____
   _____

2. According to this lesson's hold, **what** is the fastest way to lose a friend?

   _____
   _____

3. **Fill in** the blanks of the quote by Alexander.

   "Attentiveness. Be _____. Let your _____ match your _____, and _____ your word. Simple."

List the three people you trust the most.

   _____
   _____
   _____

Why do you trust them?

   _____
   _____
   _____

While there are some humans we may not trust, we can always trust in God and His Word!

Name _____ Lesson 33 - Exercise 5 Day 165

Review

- **Update** the Reading List chart with books you have read this week.
- **Recite** Philippians 2:4 from memory to your instructor.

Vocabulary Review

Write a paragraph using the following vocabulary words: *aid climbing, free climbing, bouldering, solo, pumped, lead,* and *bivouac*. (*Hint:* You may use different suffixes such as *-ed* or *-ing*.)

_____
_____
_____
_____
_____
_____
_____
_____
_____
_____

Grammar & Punctuation Review

Fill in the missing verb tenses. If you need help, refer to the Irregular Verbs chart in the back of the book.

Present Tense	Simple Past Tense	Past Participle
ring	1. _____	2. _____
catch	3. _____	4. _____
know	5. _____	6. _____
go	7. _____	8. _____

Define the meaning of the suffixes.

Suffix	Meaning
-tion, -ion, -sion, -ation, -ition	9. _____
-logy, -ology	10. _____
-ant, -ent	11. _____
-age	12. _____

Lesson 33, Day 165

Name _____   Lesson 33 - Exercise 5   Day 1

Communication Review

1. **Fill in** the blanks.

   Formatting a Final Draft (Typed)

   - Set all _____ to _____ _____ on all sides.
   - _____ space and use a _____-point Times _____ _____ font.
   - _____ the first line of each paragraph 1 inch.
   - Create a _____ page for the front of your essay that includes a title, your _____, the name of the course, the _____, and the _____. Center these items.
   - Create a _____ _____ page. Center the title, Works Cited, at the top. List resources in _____ order. Indent _____ inch for any lines after the first line in each reference. _____ space entries. Use 1-inch _____.

2. **Describe** the difference between tangible and intangible.

   _____
   _____

Worldview & Literary Analysis Review

1. **What** does it mean to be cynical?

   _____
   _____

2. **Describe** a belayer.

   _____
   _____

Write a summary of this lesson's hold located in the excerpt from *The Summit*.

_____
_____
_____
_____
_____
_____
_____
_____

Special Feature

Lesson 34

Poem Study: "The Mountain" by Robert Frost (1874–1963)

Study the selection from the poem "The Mountain."

The mountain held the town as in a shadow
I saw so much before I slept there once:
I noticed that I missed stars in the west,
Where its black body cut into the sky.
Near me it seemed: I felt it like a wall
Behind which I was sheltered from a wind.
And yet between the town and it I found,
When I walked forth at dawn to see new things,
Were fields, a river, and beyond, more fields.
The river at the time was fallen away,
And made a widespread brawl on cobble-stones;
But the signs showed what it had done in spring;
Good grass-land gullied out, and in the grass
Ridges of sand, and driftwood stripped of bark.
I crossed the river and swung round the mountain.

Poetry is a form of literature that focuses on the expression of feelings and ideas through a distinct style and rhythm. Poems often use metaphors and other figures of speech. Prose is a term used for written or spoken language in its ordinary form without the rhythm or structure we would find in a poem.

Rewrite the selection from "The Mountain" using prose. **Use** the first-person point of view (using the pronoun *I*). **Imagine** you are the person experiencing the mountain. **Tell** about what you are feeling and thinking using vivid adjectives with varied sentence structure.

_____
_____
_____
_____
_____
_____
_____
_____
_____
_____
_____
_____
_____

Name _____   Lesson 34 - Exercise 1   Day 1

Vocabulary Study

Match the words found in the poem and in this exercise to the correct definition. If you cannot discern the meaning, look it up in a dictionary. (If using an online dictionary, ask a parent's permission.)

1. _____ prose
2. _____ gullied
3. _____ poetry
4. _____ brawl
5. _____ rhythm
6. _____ metaphor
7. _____ cobble-stones (cobblestones)

a. compares two things otherwise unrelated
b. round stones larger than pebbles
c. repeated pattern of movement or sound
d. written or spoken language in ordinary form
e. made a gully or deep channel
f. rough or noisy fight
g. writing that expresses feelings and ideas through distinct style or rhythm

Write a metaphor having to do with mountains.
_____
_____

Write a sentence using the words *poetry* and *prose*.
_____
_____

Explain why you think the author of the poem chose the word "brawl" to describe the river's interaction with the cobblestones.
_____
_____

☐ **Use** index cards to **write** each vocabulary word from this lesson on one side and the definition on the other. **Check** the box when complete.

☐ **Copy** the Scripture verse on an index card. **Memorize** it by the end of this lesson. You may choose the Bible translation or use the one given. **Check** the box when complete.

It shall come to pass in the latter days that the mountain of the house of the LORD shall be established as the highest of the mountains, and it shall be lifted up above the hills; and peoples shall flow to it.
Micah 4:1

Name_____   Lesson 34 - Exercise 2   Day 167

Grammar & Punctuation

Hyphens

A **hyphen** (-) can be used to join words or parts of words and is often used when a compound adjective comes *before* the word that it modifies. Hyphens also appear in some compound words (mother-in-law) and numbers (twenty-four). Many different situations require hyphens. Here are some of the most common.

> A **hyphen** (-) can be used to join words or parts of words and is often used when a compound adjective comes *before* the word that it modifies.

When to Use a Hyphen
Use hyphens to connect compound modifiers that appear before the noun they modify.
Melody wrote a *mind-bending* riddle that stumped her family.
Use hyphens in certain compound words. If unsure, consult a dictionary.
over-the-top, far-flung, well-to-do, short-term, officer-in-charge
Use a hyphen with spelled-out fractions and compound numbers from twenty-one to ninety-nine.
two-thirds, one-fifth, twenty-two, eighty-seven
Use a hyphen in words with the prefixes ex-, self-, all-, anti-, and mid-.
They interviewed the *ex-president*. College requires *self-discipline*. She was born in the *mid-1970s*.

Write a short sentence that contains two hyphenated words.

_____

_____

Place hyphens where needed in the sentence.

1. At the age of thirty two, my father came to believe in an all knowing Creator while listening to a well known evangelist on the radio.

Prefix Study

Study the prefix chart to complete the following exercise. **Use** different words than those listed in the examples on the chart. If you need help, use a dictionary or online search with your parent's permission.

Prefix	Meaning	Examples
inter-	among, between, together	interview, interstate
multi-, poly-	many, much	multigrain, polytheist, multicolor
semi-	half	semicircle, semiannual
trans-	across, beyond, change, through	transcontinental, transmit

Write a short sentence that uses the prefix *inter-*.

_____

Grammar & Punctuation   Lesson 34, Day 167   351

Name _____   Lesson 34 - Exercise 2   Day 167

Write a short sentence that uses the prefix *multi-* or *poly-*.

_____

Write a short sentence that uses the prefixes *semi-* and *trans-*.

_____

☐ Using your index cards, **record** the four uses for hyphens taught in this lesson. **Check** the box when you are done.

Refer to the Grammar & Punctuation exercises in Lessons 19–21 and **complete** the following.

Underline the pronouns. **Circle** any antecedents. **Label** the pronouns as **SP** (subject), **OP** (object), or **RP** (relative). There may be more than one pronoun per sentence.

2. I decided that I would love to go with her to help at the soup kitchen tomorrow.
3. The rollercoaster, which needed maintenance, was closed for a month.
4. Every time Rachel comes over, she brings us a treat.

Underline the pronouns. **Circle** any antecedents. **Label** the pronouns as **DP** (demonstrative), **IP** (indefinite), **RFP** (reflexive), **SP** (subject), **OP** (object), or **RP** (relative). There may be more than one pronoun per sentence.

5. These are the library books that smell like an old basement!
6. If I allow myself to eat too much pizza, it will likely give me a stomachache.
7. This is by far the best art project anyone has turned in so far.

Underline the correct pronoun.

8. My mother is the only one in our family (who, whom) loves to garden.
9. The Lord will have mercy on (whoever, whomever) He chooses.
10. Tell everyone to let (myself, me) know if they have any questions about the trip.
11. Erika always remembers to tell (myself, me) when important test dates are coming up!

Underline the subject once and the verb twice. There may be multiple subjects and verbs. Then **underline** the direct objects and any indirect objects (include any modifying words). **Label** them as **IO** or **DO**. **Place** parentheses around any prepositional phrases.

12. Before church yesterday, my brother lost his tithe money, and he found it under the couch.
13. During our church service on Sunday, Pastor Eric gave the graduating seniors Bibles with their names on the front.
14. Despite being a cautious spender, I have enjoyed giving my family gifts for Christmas.
15. On account of God's love for him, my cousin has committed his entire life to serving God across the ocean.

Name _____ Lesson 34 - Exercise 3 Day 168

Communication

Persuasion in Advertising

Advertisements use persuasion to convince a consumer to purchase a product or service. They do this by appealing to the customer's needs and desires. The modes of persuasion are important in advertising.

Modes of Persuasion in Advertising	
Ethos	The seller must convince the customer that they are trustworthy and knowledgeable.
Logos	The seller must attempt to back up their claim that their product is superior.
Pathos	The seller must appeal to emotions connected to their product.

Match the advertising slogan with the mode of persuasion it uses.

1. _____ ethos   a. "Trusted by mothers everywhere."
2. _____ logos   b. "Your dog will know you love them."
3. _____ pathos   c. "Teeth are straightened in half the time of traditional braces."

Let's have a little fun with persuasion! Pretend you have invented a new product, tested it, and now you are ready to launch an advertising campaign.

Fill out the details about your product.

Name of product: _____

Product's use/function: _____
_____

Who/what uses your product: _____
_____

Product features: _____
_____

Why your product is appealing: _____
_____

How you can give credibility to your product (celebrity endorsement, statistics, etc.): _____
_____
_____

Communication Lesson 34, Day 168 353

Name_____   Lesson 34 – Exercise 3   Day 168

Write one paragraph that "sells" your product using the modes of persuasion and the information you just wrote down. Be sure to aim your advertisement at your target audience (those most likely to use your product).

_____
_____
_____
_____
_____
_____
_____
_____
_____

Draw an advertisement for your new product. **Include** an advertising slogan. Your slogan should be the most important phrase or sentence you would want your customer to know regarding your product.

Show your drawn advertisement to your instructor or a family member as you read your paragraph advertisement to them. Have you effectively persuaded them to purchase your product? **Write** about their reaction.

_____
_____
_____

Worldview & Literary Analysis

Read the following excerpt from *The Summit*.

Deadpoint Reflections

Crux: Choices. We sometimes get caught in a downward spiral of poor choices. It might be that second, third, or fifth scoop of ice cream, that next beer, the decision to push on for the summit in spite of the building dark clouds, or the seemingly innocent flirtation that makes a spouse jealous, and the choice to let one little lie turn into a stream of bigger ones. It seems at first so benign, but eventually will develop into a cancer that can wreck our families and our lives.

Hold: Develop the discipline to look ahead and see the consequences of each decision, and the fortitude to care enough to carry the right decision through. We must deny ourselves in our selfish desires in order to make the right decision. "I'm already fat and there is nothing I can do about it so why not have a fourth plate of pasta." "I can drive after four beers, so a fifth probably won't matter too much, besides it is a short drive home." Start with one choice at a time, look ahead, see the results and work backward, making this a habit and developing consistency and accountability. Make a plan. If my weakness is ice cream, I shouldn't keep it in the house, and if that is not enough, avoid that aisle at the supermarket or invite someone to help. Knowing the right choice is often easy, it is selecting it that is difficult.

Anchor: Integrity. Don't focus on the wrong behavior and choices to avoid, instead focus on the direction that will steer you away from it. Don't focus on the ice cream, focus on the fruit. Don't focus on the crowd that gets you in trouble, focus on those you wish to emulate for their character and integrity. *Finally, brothers, whatever is true, whatever is noble, whatever is right, whatever is pure, whatever is lovely, whatever is admirable — if anything is excellent or praiseworthy — think about such things* (Philippians 4:8).[1]

Respond to the following based on this lesson's excerpt from *The Summit*.

This lesson's crux involves making poor choices. James 1:14–15 states, "But each person is tempted when he is lured and enticed by his own desire. Then desire when it has conceived gives birth to sin, and sin when it is fully grown brings forth death." **Give** an example of how this verse can play out in everyday life.

___

1 Alexander, *The Summit*, p. 109.

Name _____ Lesson 34 - Exercise 4 Day 16

Bad choices have been around since the beginning, but praise God that His Word is full of answers! **Restate** the following verse in your own words.

> *No temptation has overtaken you that is not common to man. God is faithful, and he will not let you be tempted beyond your ability, but with the temptation he will also provide the way of escape, that you may be able to endure it.* 1 Corinthians 10:13

_____
_____
_____
_____
_____

Write a full paragraph discussing the advice given in this lesson's hold about developing the discipline we need to make good choices.

_____
_____
_____
_____
_____
_____
_____
_____

1. The anchor talks about our focus. **What** does Alexander advise us to focus on?

_____
_____

List some things you could focus on that would steer you away from temptation and toward the right choices.

_____
_____
_____
_____
_____
_____
_____

Name _____ Lesson 34 - Exercise 5 Day 170

Review

☐ **Update** the Reading List chart with books you have read this week.

☐ **Recite** Micah 4:1 from memory to your instructor.

Vocabulary Review

Match each word to the correct definition.

1. _____ prose
2. _____ gullied
3. _____ poetry
4. _____ brawl
5. _____ rhythm
6. _____ metaphor
7. _____ cobble-stones (cobblestones)

a. compares two things otherwise unrelated
b. round stones larger than pebbles
c. repeated pattern of movement or sound
d. written or spoken language in ordinary form
e. made a gully or deep channel
f. rough or noisy fight
g. writing that expresses feelings and ideas through distinct style or rhythm

Grammar & Punctuation Review

1. **List** three uses for hyphens.

    a. _____
    b. _____
    c. _____

Write a short paragraph with words containing the prefixes *inter-*, *multi-*, *poly-*, *semi-*, and *trans-*.

_____
_____
_____
_____
_____
_____
_____
_____
_____

Review

Name _____   Lesson 34 - Exercise 5   Day 170

Communication Review

1. **List** three ways the modes of persuasion influence advertising.
   a. Ethos:_____
   b. Logos: _____
   c. Pathos:_____

2. **List** one example related to advertising (a slogan) for each mode of persuasion.
   a. Ethos:_____
   b. Logos: _____
   c. Pathos:_____

Worldview & Literary Analysis Review

1. **Fill in** the blanks in this quote from Eric Alexander.

   "Develop the _____ to look ahead and see the _____ of each _____, and the fortitude to _____ enough to carry the _____ decision through. We must _____ ourselves in our selfish _____ in order to make the right decision."

Rewrite the following verses in your own words.

> But each person is tempted when he is lured and enticed by his own desire. Then desire when it has conceived gives birth to sin, and sin when it is fully grown brings forth death. James 1:14–15

_____
_____
_____

Write a summary of this lesson's anchor found in the excerpt from *The Summit*.

_____
_____
_____
_____
_____
_____
_____

Special Feature

Lesson 35

Scripture Study: Isaiah 40:9–14

⁹ Go on up to a high mountain,
   O Zion, herald of good news;
lift up your voice with strength,
   O Jerusalem, herald of good news;
   lift it up, fear not;
say to the cities of Judah,
   "Behold your God!"
¹⁰ Behold, the Lord GOD comes with might,
   and his arm rules for him;
behold, his reward is with him,
   and his recompense before him.
¹¹ He will tend his flock like a shepherd;
   he will gather the lambs in his arms;
he will carry them in his bosom,
   and gently lead those that are with young.
¹² Who has measured the waters in the hollow of his hand
   and marked off the heavens with a span,
enclosed the dust of the earth in a measure
   and weighed the mountains in scales
   and the hills in a balance?
¹³ Who has measured the Spirit of the LORD,
   or what man shows him his counsel?
¹⁴ Whom did he consult,
   and who made him understand?
Who taught him the path of justice,
   and taught him knowledge,
   and showed him the way of understanding?

Vocabulary Study

Match the words found in the Scripture study to the correct definition using context clues. If you cannot discern the meaning, look it up in a dictionary. (If using an online dictionary, ask a parent's permission.)

1. _____ Zion
2. _____ herald
3. _____ recompense
4. _____ Judah
5. _____ bosom
6. _____ hollow
7. _____ balance

a. instrument used to determine weight; represents justice
b. represents a holy place, kingdom of heaven, God's people
c. space in the palm with hand curved as a cup
d. a place of secrecy or intimacy
e. an official messenger who proclaims news
f. one of the twelve tribes of Israel
g. give back, repay

Special Feature — Lesson 35, Day 171 — 359

Name _____ Lesson 35 - Exercise 1 Day 171

Respond to the following based on the Scripture portion in today's exercise.

8. According to verse 9, **where** are God's people to go and what are they to proclaim?
   _____
   _____

9. **Fill in** the blanks from verse 10.

   "Behold, the Lord God comes with _____, and his _____ _____ for him; behold, his _____ is with him, and his _____ before him."

10. **Describe** how verse 11 brings comfort to God's people.
    _____
    _____

In the boxes below, **sketch** what you see "pictured" in verse 12.

11. Using complete sentences, **answer** the three questions posed in verses 13 and 14.

    a. _____
    b. _____
    c. _____

☐ **Use** index cards to **write** each vocabulary word from this lesson on one side and the definition on the other. **Check** the box when complete.

☐ **Copy** the Scripture verse on an index card. **Memorize** it by the end of this lesson. You may choose the Bible translation or use the one given. **Check** the box when complete.

Go on up to a high mountain, O Zion, herald of good news; lift up your voice with strength, O Jerusalem, herald of good news; lift it up, fear not; say to the cities of Judah, "Behold your God!" Isaiah 40:9

Name _____ Lesson 35 - Exercise 2 Day 172

Grammar & Punctuation

When to Use a Comma
1. **After an introductory clause or phrase.** *When Dad opened the oven, the smell of cookies wafted out.*
2. **To separate independent clauses.** *Alex went surfing with Jay, and he got a bad sunburn.*
3. **To set off nonrestrictive clauses.** *Nolan, who is amazing at baseball, is my brother's best friend.*
4. **Between all items in a series.** *The movie theater offered popcorn, candy, chips, and soda.*
5. **To set off appositives.** *Mary, the mother of Jesus, is mentioned many times in the Bible.*
6. **To indicate direct address.** *I love your dress, Millie. Millie, I love your dress.*
7. **To set off direct quotations.** *Trent said, "Mom, may I go with Ryan?"*
8. **With dates, addresses, titles, and numbers.** *May 27, 1975	Atlanta, GA	Eric Maddox, MD	12,000*

Write a sentence that demonstrates Rules 1 and 4.

_____

_____

Write a sentence that demonstrates Rules 7 and 8.

_____

_____

Suffix Study

Use the chart to decipher the meaning of the following words and **match** them to their definitions.

Suffix	Meaning	Examples
-ous, -eous, -ious	full of; having qualities of	righteous, vigorous, gracious
-ary, -ery, -ory	group of, state or character of, connected with, involving, place for	archery, mandatory, legendary
-cede, -ceed, -sede	to give control, right, or power to	intercede, succeed, concede

1. _____ contemporary   a. polite, considerate, respectful
2. _____ accessory   b. bold, daring; recklessly brave
3. _____ concede   c. living or occurring at the same period in time
4. _____ audacious   d. a nonessential item added for a benefit
5. _____ courteous   e. admit as true, right, or proper

☐ Using your index cards, **copy** the eight comma rules given in the exercise. **Check** the box when you are done.

Name _____   Lesson 35 - Exercise 2   Day 172

Refer to the Grammar & Punctuation exercises in Lessons 22–24 and **complete** the following.

Use the Rules for Subject-Verb Agreement to **underline** the correct verb.

6. The group of committee members (is, are) due to come up with a decision by the end of the month.
7. The row of maple trees, along with several oak trees, (are, is) being cut down this afternoon.
8. My little nephew and his two sisters (want, wants) to come stay at our house while their parents are out of town.
9. I think the parrot or the canary (sound, sounds) the loudest of all the birds in the pet shop.
10. The baseball team (run, runs) through every drill at Friday practices.

Write a sentence using the verb *hike* in the past perfect tense.

_____
_____

On the line, **write** whether the verb expresses completed or ongoing action.

11. _____ The construction crew had hauled all the drywall sheets to the second floor before lunchtime.
12. _____ The construction crew is hauling all the drywall sheets to the second floor.

Identify the underlined verb by **writing** transitive or intransitive on the line.

13. _____ The check <u>appeared</u> in the mailbox just in time for me to cash it for use on my trip out West.
14. _____ Juan <u>hugged</u> his mother goodnight and thanked her for throwing him such a fun birthday party.

15. **Write** a sentence using the word *run* as a transitive verb.

_____
_____

16. **Write** a sentence using the word *run* as an intransitive verb.

_____
_____

Study the underlined words and **label** them **DO** for direct object or **OP** for object of the preposition. On the line, **write** transitive or intransitive regarding the italicized verb.

17. _____ We were so surprised to see that Melanie *gave* <u>her oral presentation</u> with total confidence!
18. _____ Maddie and her mother *shopped* for <u>her wedding dress</u> at three different bridal shops.
19. _____ The toddler *ate* the <u>cheese stick</u> after shredding it into several long strings.

Name _____ Lesson 35 - Exercise 3 Day 173

Communication

Oral Presentation

Humans communicate in varied ways. *Language Lessons for a Living Education Level 9* introduced five aspects of communication: written, verbal, nonverbal and visual, contextual, and active listening. For this assignment, you will focus on the verbal aspect of communication through an oral presentation. The word *oral* means "by word of mouth." An **oral presentation** consists of communicating verbally to an audience on a particular topic.

> An **oral presentation** consists of communicating verbally to an audience on a particular topic.

The topic for your oral presentation is your persuasive essay. This is good news because you are very familiar with your essay! You and your instructor may choose the audience, place, and time for your presentation. Some ideas for an audience include a homeschool co-op, immediate family, grandparents, Sunday school class, your instructor only, or any group that could benefit from being persuaded by your topic.

Avoid simply reading your persuasive essay to your audience. To learn how to convert a persuasive essay into an oral presentation, refer to the Converting a Persuasive Essay into an Oral Presentation chart found in the back of this book. Also, refer to the Oral Presentation Rubric found in the back of the book. This rubric will be used by your instructor to evaluate your oral presentation. The oral presentation is due by the end of this course. **Have** your instructor sign below once you have established the audience, date, and time. You may use the Persuasive Oral Presentation Worksheet to plan your presentation.

Audience: _____ Date: _____ Time: _____
Instructor's signature: _____

Communication

Name _____   Lesson 35 - Exercise 3   Day 173

Wisdom Speaks

Copy the proverb.

> *Oil and perfume make the heart glad, and the sweetness of a friend comes from his earnest counsel.* Proverbs 27:9

_____
_____
_____

In biblical times, oil was used for healing and to flavor and cook food. Perfume or incense was used to cover foul odors, making for a pleasant atmosphere. Our words can have the same effect on the soul. Wise words of counsel can help heal wounds and add flavor to life. Sweet words can make the "stinky" parts of life much more bearable. Are you being a "sweet" friend to those around you?

Using a thesaurus or an online search with a parent's permission, **write** two synonyms for each word.

1. earnest: _____
2. counsel (as in "advice"): _____

Based on the synonyms, **rewrite** the proverb.

_____
_____

Describe a time when your heart was gladdened by the "earnest counsel" of a friend. How did they make the situation more bearable? How did they add healing and flavor to your life? How grateful are you for good friends?

_____
_____
_____
_____
_____
_____
_____
_____
_____
_____

Name _____ Lesson 35 - Exercise 4 Day 174

Worldview & Literary Analysis

Read the following excerpt from *The Summit*.

Deadpoint Reflections

Crux: Perception. Countless people prejudged our Everest team and especially Erik Weihenmayer. It was hard to hear their uninvited comments stream in from all over the globe, especially when they did not know this team or this blind man personally. These comments ticked me off. Even worse, I got mad at these people for something I have been just as guilty of doing myself: making a judgment based on a perception of my own rather than on evidence and truth. I have judged people before meeting them, cars before driving them, restaurants before tasting their food (sometimes this is just wisdom), cities before visiting them, and cultures before engaging them. I even judged these blind kids before we hit the Inca trail. The crux here is to let people show who they are and what they are capable of before putting a label on them. Recently, I had the opportunity to spend some quality time with someone from my church. This person usually had an unhappy look on his face and would come and go rather quickly. I got the feeling he was arrogant, and self-absorbed, and even looking down on people in general. I had these feelings even though I had never had a conversation with him that lasted longer than a handshake. After our circumstantially forced time together I learned this guy had a great sense of humor, was easy going, his heart for kids was very big, and his heart for the Lord even bigger still. This is a mistake I have made numerous times, and I wonder how many great friendships, opportunities, and experiences I have missed out on because of a wrongly formed perception.

Hold: Take a risk to get to know someone a little better. Take a risk to put your beliefs to the fire and see if they remain standing in truth. Take a risk to believe in someone and their dream and stand by them in it. Turn criticism into fuel for the fire if you are wrongly perceived.

Anchor: Want a better perception of yourself and of others? Understand that you are made in the image of God. *God created man in his own image, in the image of God he created him; male and female he created them. God blessed them and said to them, 'Be fruitful and increase in number; fill the earth and subdue it. Rule over the fish of the sea and the birds of the air and over every living creature that moves on the ground.' Then God said, 'I give you every seed-bearing plant on the face of the whole earth and every tree that has fruit with seed in it. They will be yours for food. And to all the beasts of the earth and all the birds of the air and all the creatures that move on the ground — everything that has the breath of life in it — I give every green plant for food.' And it was so. God saw all that he had made, and it was very good* (Genesis 1:27–31).

Not only did God create us in His own image, He gave us responsibility and work to do. Now if you want to feel good about yourself take into account that He paused, took a look at His creation, and said it was better than bad — it was good, very good even. He liked how He made us. Being made in His image, He has also told us that all things are possible: *I can do everything through him who gives me strength* (Philippians 4:13). Jesus . . . said, *With man this is impossible, but not with God; all things are possible with God* (Mark 10:27). If I perceive an obstacle to be too great, myself too lacking, or someone else too <u>fill in the blank here</u>, I need to anchor myself and realize that I am probably the one who needs a shift of perspective.[1]

---
[1] Alexander, *The Summit*, p. 121–122.

Name _____   Lesson 35 - Exercise 4   Day 174

Respond to the following based on this lesson's excerpt from *The Summit*.

1. **Why** was it hard for Eric Alexander to hear the uninvited comments about his friend?

   _____
   _____
   _____
   _____

Describe a time when you had a perception of someone else that turned out to be false.

   _____
   _____
   _____

In 1 Samuel 16, we are told that man looks at the outward appearance, but God looks at the heart. **What** are some outward appearances that can cause us to misjudge others?

   _____
   _____
   _____

2. **What** had Alexander been "guilty of doing" himself?

   _____
   _____

3. **Fill in** the blanks.

   "The _____ here is to let people _____ who they are and what they are _____ _____ before putting a _____ on them."

This lesson's hold talks about taking risks in getting to know others. Is it easy or difficult for you to get to know a new person? **Explain**.

   _____
   _____
   _____
   _____

The anchor talks about how valuable all human beings are because we are made in the image of God. **How** can this reality influence your perception of others?

   _____
   _____
   _____
   _____

Name _____ Lesson 35 - Exercise 5 Day 175

Review

☐ **Update** the Reading List chart with books you have read this week.

☐ **Recite** Isaiah 40:9 from memory to your instructor.

Vocabulary Review

Write a paragraph using the following vocabulary words: *Zion, herald, recompense, Judah, bosom, hollow,* and *balance.*

_____
_____
_____
_____
_____
_____
_____
_____
_____
_____
_____

Grammar & Punctuation Review

Place commas where necessary in these sentences.

1. I walked in just in time to hear Mike say "Let's grab some ice cream peanuts and whipped cream for our movie night!"
2. To my surprise my friend Marley who loves socializing declined to come to the picnic with me.
3. When I graduate on June 21 2028 I may go to a community college work full-time or join the military.

Use a dictionary or online search with your parent's permission and **list** two examples of words that contain the following suffixes.

4. *-eous*: a. _____ b. _____
5. *-ery*: a. _____ b. _____
6. *-cede*: a. _____ b. _____

Name _____ Lesson 35 - Exercise 5 Day 175

Communication Review

1. **Describe** an oral presentation.

_____
_____

Rewrite the proverb in your own words.

> *Oil and perfume make the heart glad, and the sweetness of a friend comes from his earnest counsel.* Proverbs 27:9

_____
_____

Worldview & Literary Analysis Review

1. **Fill in** the blanks from this lesson's hold.

   "Take a _____ to get to _____ someone a little better. Take a risk to put your _____ to the _____ and see if they remain standing in _____. Take a risk to _____ in someone and their _____ and stand by them in it. Turn _____ into fuel for the fire if you are wrongly _____."

Write a summary of this lesson's anchor found in the excerpt from *The Summit*.

_____
_____
_____
_____

Copy the verse.

> *But the LORD said to Samuel, "Do not look on his appearance or on the height of his stature, because I have rejected him. For the LORD sees not as man sees: man looks on the outward appearance, but the LORD looks on the heart."* 1 Samuel 16:7

_____
_____
_____
_____

Special Feature

Lesson 36

Answers Magazine Excerpt: "Making More of the Mountains"
by Dr. Andrew A. Snelling

Ancient Hills?

The standard evolutionary story, presented at the Great Smoky Mountains National Park visitor centers, is that these rolling hills are very ancient, eroded down to bedrock over hundreds of millions of years. They're not like the Rockies, which rise dramatically and still have sharp edges because—we are told—they are younger and haven't had as much time to wear down.

A creationist sees these hills differently, based on the Bible. Every detail of the landscape makes sense within the Bible's 6,000-year time frame, from the Smokies' broad vistas—row upon row of blue-tinted ridges stretching as far as the eye can see—down to the individual rocks and the microscopic crystals inside them.

I see the same processes at work as other geologists, but I believe they occurred at a much faster pace in the past, especially during two unique events revealed in God's Word—the six-day Creation and the yearlong Flood. The Apostle Peter says the Lord originally made the earth out of water and then "destroyed" it in a global Flood (2 Peter 3:6), forming a new world out of the raw materials, including mountain chains we see today. You just have to know what you're looking for.

Here's a basic geology term—*metamorphic rocks*. You first came across it in a science class that you have possibly forgotten if your teacher didn't connect such terms to reality. Geologists believe that the Appalachian Mountain chain (which includes the Smokies) consists of sandy ocean sediments about ten miles thick that were transformed when Africa's tectonic plate moved northward and rammed into the southeastern edge of North America. That hammer blow "crumpled" up the sediments to form the Appalachians.

The heat and pressure caused by smashing up these rocks changed ("metamorphosed") the mineral compositions of the rocks. It's like the metamorphosis of a caterpillar into a butterfly—the rocks are changed. That's why we call them "metamorphic rocks."

As I drive through these mountains, I envision the massive earth-shaping events that laid down all this sandy material and then reshaped it when continents collided during the Flood.

Like other creation geologists, I believe the original earth was a single supercontinent that broke into tectonic plates during the Flood, and then these pieces moved around rapidly, smashing into each other before slowing down to a crawl in their current locations.

If this is a correct interpretation of the evidence, the earth's great mountain chains resulted from catastrophic forces unleashed during the Flood. Yet each mountain chain has its own special story, depending on its unique circumstances.

The evidence indicates that sediment layers making up the Appalachians formed early in the Flood, and the Appalachian Mountains formed soon after. The powerful currents that circled the globe (from east to west) then shaved several miles of rock material off the top of this chain, exposing the deep layers we see today.

That's what I see when I visit the Smokies! They aren't reminders of God's creation, but of a worldwide judgment that produced "beauty out of ashes" (see Isaiah 61:3).[1]

---

1 Snelling, Andrew A. *Answers Magazine*. www.answersingenesis.org. Accessed Jan 22, 2024. https://answersingenesis.org/geology/plate-tectonics/plate-tectonics/making-more-mountains/.

Name _____   Lesson 36 - Exercise 1   Day 176

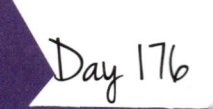

Respond to the following about the article from *Answers Magazine*.

During his trip, Dr. Snelling is in awe of the Great Smoky Mountains. He gives the evolutionist's explanation of how they formed and eroded as well as the biblical explanation. **Summarize** the two different views presented as to the timeline of how the Smoky Mountains formed and eroded.

_____

_____

_____

_____

1. **What** does Dr. Snelling envision as he drives through the mountains?

_____

_____

_____

2. **What** are the Smoky Mountains a reminder of?

_____

_____

Vocabulary Study

Match the words found in today's excerpt to the correct definition using context clues. If you cannot discern the meaning, look it up in a dictionary. (If using an online dictionary, ask a parent's permission.)

3. _____ metamorphic rock   a. massive slabs of rock made of earth's crust and upper mantle
4. _____ geology   b. having caused great and sudden harm
5. _____ tectonic plates   c. air or water moving continuously in a certain direction
6. _____ sediments   d. a solid whose atoms are in a repeating pattern
7. _____ currents   e. any rock changed by intense heat or pressure
8. _____ interpretation   f. study of the earth's structure, composition, and processes
9. _____ catastrophic   g. solid materials that have been redeposited in a new location
10. _____ crystal   h. the explanation of the meaning of something

☐ **Use** index cards to **write** each vocabulary word from this lesson on one side and the definition on the other. **Check** the box when complete.

☐ **Copy** the Scripture verse on an index card. **Memorize** it by the end of this lesson. You may choose the Bible translation or use the one given. **Check** the box when complete.

For they deliberately overlook this fact, that the heavens existed long ago, and the earth was formed out of water and through water by the word of God, and that by means of these the world that then existed was deluged with water and perished. 2 Peter 3:5–6

Name _____ Lesson 36 - Exercise 2 Day 177

Grammar & Punctuation

Commonly Misused Words

The English language contains some words that are confusing because they look and/or sound similar. It is important to learn the meanings of these words to avoid misusing them. **Study** the chart.

	Commonly Misused Words
Affect/Effect	*Affect* is usually a verb. (The dog's barking *affected* my nap.)
	Effect is usually a noun. (I was thrilled with the *effect* our mission trip had.)
Assure/ Ensure/ Insure	*Assure* means to relate that something will happen or is true. (I *assure* you he will be coming soon.)
	Ensure means to guarantee. (The moms *ensured* the safety of the children.)
	Insure means to take out an insurance policy. (My dad *insured* both our cars.)
Complement/ Compliment	A *complement* completes something else. (The color of Liz's dress *complemented* her complexion.)
	A *compliment* is a nice thing to say. (Liz received many *compliments* on her dress.)
Farther/ Further	*Farther* refers to physical distance. (I walked *farther* than Susan.)
	Further refers to metaphorical distance. (Chance was *further* ahead in his studies than his sister.)
Lay/Lie:	To *lay* means to put or place. (Morgan will *lay* out the clothing for his trip.)
	Lie means to recline. (Morgan will *lie* down before packing for his trip.)
	Note: The past tense of *lay* is *laid*, and the past tense of *lie* is *lay*. (Morgan *laid* out his clothing. Morgan *lay* down for his nap.)

Underline the correct word based on the Commonly Misused Words chart.

1. The (further, farther) we got from the campsite in the dark, the more nervous I became.
2. I usually get quite embarrassed when others (complement, compliment) me about my appearance.
3. When I babysit, I always (ensure, assure) the parents that their children are in good hands with me.
4. My father (lie, laid, lay) down and rested knowing our home was (ensured, insured)!

Prefix/Suffix Review

Define the meanings of the prefixes and suffixes. Each one has been defined throughout the fourth quarter Grammar Lessons. Remember, some have multiple meanings.

5. *a-*: _____
6. *-er, -or*: _____
7. *ante-*: _____
8. *anti-*: _____
9. *com-*: _____
10. *-en*: _____
11. *-an, -ian*: _____
12. *en-, em-*: _____
13. *in-, il-, im-, ir-*: _____
14. *-logy, -ology*: _____

Grammar & Punctuation

Name _____   Lesson 36 - Exercise 2   Day 177

15. *de-*: _____   18. *-age*: _____
16. *dis-*: _____   19. *semi-*: _____
17. *-al, -ial*: _____

Write a sentence that uses the suffixes *-ous* and *-eous*.
_____
_____

Refer to the Grammar & Punctuation exercises in Lessons 25–27 and **complete** the following.
Write the plural form of the singular nouns listed.

20. echo: _____   24. aircraft: _____
21. stimulus: _____   25. focus: _____
22. tuna: _____   26. datum: _____
23. stereo: _____   27. train: _____

Write a sentence containing a semicolon.
_____
_____

Place apostrophes where needed to show possession.
28. Last week we ate dinner at Michaels Banquet Hall, and my dads steak was undercooked.
29. When I went to my neighbors coop to feed her chickens this morning, all the chickens water feeders were bone dry.

Underline the possessive pronouns and possessive adjectives and **place** apostrophes where needed.
30. All the mountain climbers gear fit neatly into his backpack, but I couldnt even fit my clothing into mine!
31. When we arrived at my aunt and uncles cabin, I could tell which boat in the lake was theirs.
32. All five houses siding had been scorched by the flames from their neighbors burning home.
33. **Write** a sentence using the plural possessive of *video*.
_____
_____

34. **List** three instances when a colon is used.
   a. _____
   b. _____
   c. _____

Name _____ Lesson 36 - Exercise 3 Day 178

Communication

Etiquette and the Five Aspects of Communication

In the last lesson, we looked at a list of five aspects of communication. Today we will examine each of these and relate them to proper etiquette. **Etiquette** refers to the customary code of polite behavior in society or among members of a particular group. **Study** the chart.

Etiquette and the Five Aspects of Communication
Written Communication: Using written language to express information, ideas, and emotions.
Proper Etiquette: When writing through text, email, or handwritten letters, be courteous by greeting the person. Be clear and concise yet give the details you want to express. Think through what you are saying, considering how your audience will receive your words. Write only what you would be willing to say in person and have read to others.
Verbal Communication: Using spoken language to express information, ideas, and emotions.
Proper Etiquette: Maintain eye contact, giving the person complete attention. Refrain from interrupting and allow the person to express their thoughts. Respect others' time by being concise and not rambling on. Express yourself kindly with well-thought-out words. Speak loud enough to be heard but soft enough to avoid annoying others.
Nonverbal and Visual Communication: Using bodily expression or imagery to convey ideas.
Proper Etiquette: Convey interest and attention with your posture, without slumping or slouching, which makes you look disinterested. A smile and alert countenance show friendliness, while a furrowed brow or frown could express anger. Hand gestures can be used to accentuate a point, but overuse of them can be a distraction. It is not polite to stand too close to someone you are speaking to or in between people who are speaking to each other. Fidgeting, tapping, or shaking your leg incessantly can be distracting and show a lack of concern for those around you. We also communicate through imagery, such as graphics on our clothing, emojis, art, etc. These images we bear should always reflect respect for others and honor God.
Contextual Communication: Proper communication based on the audience or setting. This could be cultural, situational, personal, academic, professional, etc.
Proper Etiquette: Know your surroundings when it comes to communicating. You will communicate differently with a sibling than with a pastor or teacher. There are different levels of respect to be shown to adults in certain fields. What may be an acceptable conversation in a quick meeting on a sidewalk may not be appropriate at a funeral. When speaking with someone from another country or culture, be aware that something unoffensive to you may be offensive to them.
Active Listening: Effectively listening to summarize and restate what another has said.
Proper Etiquette: Give your full attention to the person speaking to you. This may mean minimizing distractions such as phones, TVs, earbuds, or even other people. Focus on their words instead of thinking about what you will say next. "Listen" for nonverbal communication, such as becoming teary-eyed (which may indicate strong emotion). Avoid jumping to conclusions about what another is sharing. Ask questions if you feel you may be misunderstanding or need further details. Paraphrase or restate to show you were listening. ("So you really felt afraid and alone when that happened …")

Name _____ Lesson 36 - Exercise 3 Day 178

Course Self-Evaluation

Throughout this course, you have learned and practiced communicating through many different avenues. You have written a descriptive paragraph, a reflective essay, a definition essay, an autobiography, a biography, a persuasive essay, an advertisement, and several small essays. You have communicated verbally through an oral presentation and learned biblical communication skills through the Wisdom Speaks sections. All these elements have challenged you and helped you grow as a communicator.

Write a paragraph describing the areas you have improved in as a communicator during this course. (Perhaps you are communicating more effectively with friends, writing essays more easily, or speaking publicly with less fear.)

_____
_____
_____
_____
_____
_____
_____
_____
_____

Write a paragraph describing the area of communication that is the biggest challenge for you. (Perhaps it is writing, speaking in front of an audience, or having one-on-one conversations. Whatever the challenge may be, learning, practicing, and asking for the Lord's help will get you to your goals!)

_____
_____
_____
_____
_____
_____
_____
_____
_____

Oral Presentation Due

The oral presentation of your persuasive essay is due today. I hope you enjoyed expressing your opinion and attempting to persuade others. I pray you become an effective communicator of the truth and light of the gospel of Jesus Christ!

Have your instructor sign below when your presentation is complete.

Instructor's signature: _____

Name _____   Lesson 36 - Exercise 4   Day 179

Worldview & Literary Analysis

Read the following excerpt from *The Summit*.

Deadpoint Reflections

Crux: I was going to write something here about quitting, but I lost my motivation; quitting boils down to value. What is the goal worth to you? How bad do you want it? Do you still fight for your wife? How about investing time in your children and their values? Into your fitness, diet, and spiritual well-being, or is it not worth the effort? Is it past failure, obstacles, lack of vision, foresight, funds, confidence? I have to admit, some days I just don't have it. The little blister on my pinky toe takes me out of the race. Usually at that moment I see a double leg amputee run by sweating it out, but grinning ear to ear because he cares. Then I come up with some brilliant excuse — obviously he doesn't have any blisters on his pinky toes. How easy it is to become defensive of that quitting attitude. An unmotivated person with a lack of desire to accomplish a goal will never stand on top of a summit and understand the beauty of effort, the spirit of the fight, the thrill of the victory. This person will understand, however, the want thereof. I believe that quitting is one of the easiest trends to begin, but one of the hardest to end.

Hold: Perseverance: Faith in purpose, stamina, persistence, passion, and risk go down swinging. What makes me want to persevere is not merely seeing the importance of just hanging on; it is letting go of the hold and reaching upward. To stand at the bottom of the cliff looking up, and saying no, not today, is one thing. Being five hundred feet up on the cliff, holding on to edges the size of dimes as tired arms filled with a burn begin to lose their grip and the pain caused by the narrow edge flares up from digging into the tips of the fingers, whose skin is slowly being peeled away and sweat loosens the grip, sending a message to the brain saying move now or fall and lose your progress, is another. Imagine there is no rope. Now, there becomes no choice but to press on. Need necessitates perseverance. In climbing I have a little slogan — "go down swinging." That is to say, I can't just back off out of fear or lack of ability and be lowered down, I have to keep trying, fall though I may. Of course this is done with a rope and partner.

Anchor: *We also rejoice in our sufferings, because we know that suffering produces perseverance; perseverance, character; and character, hope. And hope does not disappoint us, because God has poured out his love into our hearts by the Holy Spirit, whom he has given us* (Romans 5:3–5). Usually this verse reads like this to me in my head: "Why am I suffering, I can't take anymore, I thought I had enough character. Lord, you are disappointing me, though I am thankful for your love, but please, I hope this is it with the character building." *In this world you will have trouble. But take heart! I have overcome the world."* — Jesus Christ (John 16:33).[1]

---

1 Alexander, *The Summit*, p. 156–157.

Name _____   Lesson 36 – Exercise 4   Day 179

Respond to the following based on this lesson's excerpt from *The Summit*.

1. According to Alexander, **what** does quitting boil down to?
   _____

2. **Record** some of the reasons for quitting listed in the crux.
   _____
   _____

In this lesson's crux, Alexander relates what seems to be a fictitious anecdote (perhaps even hyperbole) about a person with serious disabilities who has overcome them to achieve a goal, while Alexander himself is using a minor blister on his toe as an excuse. **Tell** about a person you know who has overcome great difficulty or disabilities and not quit.

_____
_____
_____
_____
_____
_____
_____
_____

Copy the quote by Eric Alexander.

> "An unmotivated person with a lack of desire to accomplish a goal will never stand on top of a summit and understand the beauty of effort, the spirit of the fight, the thrill of the victory."

_____
_____
_____

3. In this lesson's hold, Alexander states, "Need necessitates perseverance." **How** does the mountain climbing story he shares reflect this statement?
   _____
   _____
   _____
   _____
   _____

Name _____   Lesson 36 - Exercise 5   Day 180

Review

☐ **Update** the Reading List chart with books you have read this week.

☐ **Recite** 2 Peter 3:5–6 from memory to your instructor.

Vocabulary Review

Match each word to the correct definition.

1. _____ metamorphic rock   a. massive slabs of rock made of earth's crust and upper mantle
2. _____ geology   b. having caused great and sudden harm
3. _____ tectonic plates   c. air or water moving continuously in a certain direction
4. _____ sediments   d. a solid whose atoms are in a repeating pattern
5. _____ currents   e. any rock changed by intense heat or pressure
6. _____ interpretation   f. study of the earth's structure, composition, and processes
7. _____ catastrophic   g. solid materials that have been redeposited in a new location
8. _____ crystal   h. the explanation of the meaning of something

Grammar & Punctuation Review

Underline the correct word based on the Commonly Misused Words chart.

1. Not everyone agrees, but I feel I will get (farther, further) in life if I pursue a college degree.
2. Sometimes certain personalities really (compliment, complement) each other.
3. God's Word (ensures, assures) me that the sacrifice Christ made when He (laid, lay) down His life for me is sufficient to cover my sins.

Match the prefixes and suffixes to their meanings.

4. _____ a-   a. one who; that which
5. _____ ante-   b. full of; having qualities of
6. _____ com-   c. in a state or condition; in a manner; not; without
7. _____ -er, -or   d. before, preceding
8. _____ -age   e. with, jointly, completely
9. _____ -ious   f. to give control, right, or power to
10. _____ -ceed   g. causing a reaction

Review   Lesson 36, Day 180   377

Name _____   Lesson 36 - Exercise 5   Day 180

Communication Review

1. **Define** etiquette.
   _____
   _____

List the five aspects of communication and give an example of etiquette for each one.

2. _____
   _____

3. _____
   _____

4. _____
   _____

5. _____
   _____

6. _____
   _____

Worldview & Literary Analysis Review

1. According to Alexander, **what** does quitting boil down to?
   _____

Write a summary of this lesson's crux found in the excerpt from *The Summit*.
_____
_____
_____
_____

2. According to Romans 5:3–5, which appears in this lesson's anchor, **why** can we rejoice in sufferings?
   _____
   _____
   _____
   _____
   _____

Assessments & Grading, Teaching Resources

How to Use This Section
The teaching resources in this section provide both required and optional aids and activities. The reading lists, writing prompts, and spelling lists give extra learning opportunities. The templates, rubrics, study sheets, and answer keys are an integral part of this course. Please get familiar with these helpful resources.

Table of Contents

Independent Reading List 381
Recommended Reading Book List 382
Extra! Extra! Another Chance to Communicate! 383
Worksheets 385

- Citation Notes Worksheets
- Historical Narrative Essay Outline
- Historical Narrative Essay Worksheet
- Reflective Essay Outline
- Reflective Essay Worksheet
- Definition Essay Outline
- Definition Essay Worksheet
- Persuasive Essay Outline
- Persuasive Essay Worksheet
- Biography Outline
- Biography Oral Presentation Worksheet
- Autobiography Outline
- Autobiography Oral Presentation Worksheet
- Persuasive Oral Presentation Worksheet

Spelling and Vocabulary 415

- Vocabulary Study Tips
- Spelling List
- Spelling Rules and Exceptions
- Prefixes
- Suffixes
- Root Words

Grammar Study Sheets 429

- The Eight Parts of Speech
- Sentence Basics
- Verbs: Action and Linking
- Helping Verbs
- Modal Helping Verbs
- Verb Tense
- Independent vs. Dependent Clauses
- Conjunctions
- Prepositions
- Quotation Marks
- Quotation Marks and Other Sentence Punctuation
- Punctuating Clauses
- Adjectives
- Adverbs
- Verb Phrases: Infinitives
- Pronouns
- Indirect Objects
- Number: Subject-Verb Agreement
- Conjugating Verbs
- Rules for Pluralizing Nouns
- Semicolons
- Forming Possessive Nouns
- Colons
- Prefix Study
- Tricky Words
- Suffixes
- Irregular Verbs
- Hyphens
- Comma Usage
- Commonly Misused Words

Communication Study Sheets 445
- Biographies and Autobiographies
- Citing Sources
- Finding Items for Citations
- Compiling a Works Cited Page
- Figures of Speech
- Incorporating Quotes, Paraphrases, and Summaries
- Biography Notes
- Transitions
- Anecdotes
- Oral Presentation
- Summarizing
- Formatting a Final Draft
- Tips For Better Writing
- Persuasion in Advertising
- Etiquette and the Five Aspects of Communication

Assessments 455

Rubrics 457
- Historical Narrative Rubric
- Reflective Essay Rubric
- Definition Essay Rubric
- Biography Rubric
- Autobiography Rubric
- Oral Presentation Rubric
- Persuasive Essay Rubric

American Revolutionary War Leaders 465

Exercise Answer Key 467

Review Answer Key 497

Independent Reading List

Your student can keep a record of the books they are reading on the chart below. There are spaces for the title, author, date assigned, date of completion, and a rating scale. Working through a reading list can give your student confidence and a sense of accomplishment. Allow your student to be involved in choosing topics and authors they are interested in, but at the same time, it is good to challenge them to explore a few new topics and authors they may not be familiar with. The rating scale is meant to give the student a voice in how they felt about the book. They can give it a rating based on a scale of 0–10, "0" being a book they would never recommend and "10" being a book they would highly recommend. Let them have some fun with this!

Book Title	Author's Last Name	Date Assigned / Date Completed	Rating 0–10

Recommended Reading Book List

Grades 9–12

- A Good and Faithful Servant
- A Smoother Journey
- Advice for Seekers
- Answers Book for Teens
  - Volume 1
  - Volume 2
- Bible Brainstorms
- Columbus & Cortez, Conquerors for Christ
- Created & Called
- Creation to Babel
- *Dinah Harris Mystery Series:
  - Deadly Disclosures
  - The Shadowed Mind
  - Pieces of Light
  - The Dark Heart
- Evidence for the Bible
- Fruits of Solitude
- G.I. Joe & Lillie
- Gifted Mind
- Great for God
- Hell Is for Real
- Jesus Unmasked
- Life of Series
  - Andrew Jackson
  - John Newton
  - John Knox
  - Luther
  - Sir Isaac Newton
  - Washington
- Nine Things Teens Should Know and Parents Are Afraid to Talk About
- Questions God Asks
- Questions Jesus Asks
- So Noted
- Stressed Out
- The Pilgrim's Progress
- *The Remnant Trilogy:
  - Noah: Man of Destiny
  - Noah: Man of God
  - Noah: Man of Resolve
- Remote Control (download)
- Sky High Faith (download)
- The Priority of Making Disciples
- The Summit
- The Ultimate Proof of Creation
- Unveiling the Kings of Israel
- Will They Stand

*Parents, use discretion when allowing students to read these titles, as they contain mature topics. We advise you to pre-read these titles before giving them to your student.

Extra! Extra! Another Chance to Communicate!

These assignments can be used at the discretion of the instructor for extra writing and communication assignments. They are meant to be lighthearted and personal, drawing the student into the fun of writing, speaking, and listening.

Me or Not Me? That Is the Question!

Would you rather write a biography (a story about someone else's life) or an autobiography (a story about your life)? In a three-paragraph response, **tell** which type of writing you would prefer and why. Don't be shy. Share your opinion!

You Don't Say!

Hyperbole uses exaggeration for emphasis, effect, or impact and is not to be interpreted literally. *I am so thirsty I could drink a swimming pool! This summer, I want to hike until my feet wear off!* **Write** a paragraph about your upcoming summer using hyperbole.

Picture This …

Write a three-paragraph description of an imaginary creature. Make sure to use vivid imagery with adjectives. Start at the head of the creature and work your way down to its feet or tail. Have a friend or family member read your description, then ask them to sketch what you described. See if the imagery in your description created the creature in their mind that you imagined in yours!

A Simile You Can Smile About!

A simile compares two different things using the words *like* or *as*. The Bible uses similes often. *"As a deer pants for flowing streams, so pants my soul for you, O God"* (Psalm 42:1). Many times, people use similes to describe how they feel. *Last night I was so tired, I slept like a log!* **Write** a simile describing how you typically interact with school assignments. See if you can write several of them!

Are You Listening?

The Bible teaches us, "An intelligent heart acquires knowledge, and the ear of the wise seeks knowledge" (Proverbs 18:15). Acquiring knowledge helps us better understand God and others. Learning about other people requires a heart that wants to listen and learn. Effective listening takes practice and a true desire to understand the other person. Think deeply about the above Scripture, then **write** a paragraph describing how you view yourself as a listener and how you might improve.

Do You Mind if I Ask?

We learn about others by asking questions. If you could ask a question of any famous person from world history, whom would you question and what would you ask them? **Write** your answers in a paragraph or two.

Listen Up!

Practice your active listening skills by interviewing a family member about their favorite childhood memory. **Create** a list of five questions. Ask your questions and then try to repeat their answers back to them with as much detail as possible. You can also reverse roles and have your family member ask you questions.

When I Grow Up …

Imagine yourself in a career as an adult. **Write** a narrative three paragraphs in length describing a day of your life in that career. Think of the tasks you would perform, the people you may work with, and your feelings regarding your job. Use the first-person point of view. *I entered the office this morning …*

My Life in Pictures

An autobiography is a written account of your life, but perhaps you would enjoy seeing your life in pictures. **Draw** pictures of your life from the time you were a baby until now. This could be done in comic-book style or a timeline with simple sketches. Think of major events in your life and how God has used them to form who you are today. Share your drawings with your family.

How Did You Do That?

Sometimes you know how to do things that others can't do. Think of something you are great at and how you would communicate the "how" to someone who asked you. In a three-paragraph response, **answer** the question, "How did you do that?"

Hidden in Shadows

Foreshadowing is a literary device used to hint at events yet to come in a story. It can create tension or suspense by giving the reader just enough information to make them curious about what is to come. **Write** a short story that uses foreshadowing. **Have** your instructor read it and offer feedback about the effectiveness of your foreshadowing. Did you give too much of a hint at what was to come? Did you effectively cause the reader to become interested in the mystery?

Who Knows Me Best?

If you were to choose someone you know to write a biography about your life, who would they be? **Write** a paragraph about whom you would choose and why. Then maybe ask them!

The Father of the Constitution

The man called "the Father of the Constitution," James Madison, was homeschooled, as were many of our Founding Fathers and other American heroes. Does this impact your view of homeschooling? **Explain** your answer.

Citation Notes Worksheets

For a Book

Author(s): _____

Title: _____

Publisher and date: _____

Location (page number/numbers): _____

Summary of portion: _____

_____

For a Book

Author(s): _____

Title: _____

Publisher and date: _____

Location (page number/numbers): _____

Summary of portion: _____

_____

For a Book

Author(s): _____

Title: _____

Publisher and date: _____

Location (page number/numbers): _____

Summary of portion: _____

_____

For a Book

Author(s): _____

Title: _____

Publisher and date: _____

Location (page number/numbers): _____

Summary of portion: _____

_____

Note: The publisher and publication date can be found on the title page or copyright page. Record the most recent publication date. "Summary of portion" should include a brief description of the information, quote, paraphrase, or summary you want to use in your writing.

Citation Notes Worksheets

For a Book

Author(s): _____

Title: _____

Publisher and date: _____

Location (page number/numbers): _____

Summary of portion: _____

_____

For a Book

Author(s): _____

Title: _____

Publisher and date: _____

Location (page number/numbers): _____

Summary of portion: _____

_____

For a Book

Author(s): _____

Title: _____

Publisher and date: _____

Location (page number/numbers): _____

Summary of portion: _____

_____

For a Book

Author(s): _____

Title: _____

Publisher and date: _____

Location (page number/numbers): _____

Summary of portion: _____

_____

Citation Notes Worksheets

For a Website

Author(s): _____

Title of article: _____

Blog title: _____

Website name: _____

Date of article or date accessed: _____

URL: _____

Summary of portion: _____

_____

For a Website

Author(s): _____

Title of article: _____

Blog title: _____

Website name: _____

Date of article or date accessed: _____

URL: _____

Summary of portion: _____

_____

For a Website

Author(s): _____

Title of article: _____

Blog title: _____

Website name: _____

Date of article or date accessed: _____

URL: _____

Summary of portion: _____

_____

Note: The item "blog title" is only listed in the case of using a blog entry. "Website name" would not include "www.," which will appear in the URL. The URL appears in the browser and can be copied and pasted into a word processor or written by hand into your notes. If no article date can be found, list the date you accessed the information. "Summary of portion" should include a brief description of the information, quote, paraphrase, or summary you want to use in your writing.

Citation Notes Worksheets

For a Website

Author(s): _____

Title of article: _____

Blog title: _____

Website name: _____

Date of article or date accessed: _____

URL: _____

Summary of portion: _____

_____

For a Website

Author(s): _____

Title of article: _____

Blog title: _____

Website name: _____

Date of article or date accessed: _____

URL: _____

Summary of portion: _____

_____

For a Website

Author(s): _____

Title of article: _____

Blog title: _____

Website name: _____

Date of article or date accessed: _____

URL: _____

Summary of portion: _____

_____

Historical Narrative Essay Outline

Historical Narrative Essay Outline

1. _____
   A. _____
   B. _____
   C. _____
   D. _____
2. _____
   A. _____
   B. _____
   C. _____
   D. _____
3. _____
   A. _____
   B. _____
   C. _____
   D. _____
4. _____
   A. _____
   B. _____
   C. _____
   D. _____
5. _____
   A. _____
   B. _____
   C. _____
   D. _____

This page intentionally left blank.

Historical Narrative Essay Worksheet

Historical Narrative Essay

Topic brainstorm (list possible topics to write about based on the essay type you chose):

___

Essay topic: ___

Research sources/bibliography information (if needed):

___

Writing the First Paragraph

Write a thesis statement.

___

Write an opening sentence to introduce your topic.

___

Write 3–5 sentences that support your opening sentence.

___

Write a concluding sentence (this could be your thesis statement).

___

On the next page, continue writing the next four paragraphs (or more). You've got this. You can be a great writer!

Reflective Essay Outline

Reflective Essay Outline

1. _____
   A. _____
   B. _____
   C. _____
   D. _____
2. _____
   A. _____
   B. _____
   C. _____
   D. _____
3. _____
   A. _____
   B. _____
   C. _____
   D. _____
4. _____
   A. _____
   B. _____
   C. _____
   D. _____
5. _____
   A. _____
   B. _____
   C. _____
   D. _____

This page intentionally left blank.

Reflective Essay Worksheet

Reflective Essay

Topic brainstorm (list possible topics to write about based on the essay type you chose):

_____
_____
_____

Essay topic: _____

Research sources/bibliography information (if needed):

_____
_____
_____

Writing the First Paragraph

Write a thesis statement.
_____
_____

Write an opening sentence to introduce your topic.
_____
_____

Write 3–5 sentences that support your opening sentence.
_____
_____
_____
_____
_____
_____

Write a concluding sentence (this could be your thesis statement).
_____
_____

On the next page, continue writing the next four paragraphs (or more). You've got this. You can be a great writer!

Definition Essay Outline

Definition Essay Outline

1. _____
   A. _____
   B. _____
   C. _____
   D. _____
2. _____
   A. _____
   B. _____
   C. _____
   D. _____
3. _____
   A. _____
   B. _____
   C. _____
   D. _____
4. _____
   A. _____
   B. _____
   C. _____
   D. _____
5. _____
   A. _____
   B. _____
   C. _____
   D. _____

This page intentionally left blank.

Definition Essay Worksheet

Definition Essay

Topic brainstorm (list possible topics to write about based on the essay type you chose):

_____
_____
_____

Essay topic: _____

Research sources/bibliography information (if needed):

_____
_____
_____

Writing the First Paragraph

Write a thesis statement.

_____
_____

Write an opening sentence to introduce your topic.

_____
_____

Write 3–5 sentences that support your opening sentence.

_____
_____
_____
_____
_____

Write a concluding sentence (this could be your thesis statement).

_____
_____

On the next page, continue writing the next four paragraphs (or more). You've got this. You can be a great writer!

Persuasive Essay Outline

Persuasive Essay Outline

1. _____
   A. _____
   B. _____
   C. _____
   D. _____
2. _____
   A. _____
   B. _____
   C. _____
   D. _____
3. _____
   A. _____
   B. _____
   C. _____
   D. _____
4. _____
   A. _____
   B. _____
   C. _____
   D. _____
5. _____
   A. _____
   B. _____
   C. _____
   D. _____

This page intentionally left blank.

Persuasive Essay Worksheet

Persuasive Essay

Topic brainstorm (list possible topics to write about based on the essay type you chose):

_____
_____
_____

Essay topic: _____

Research sources/bibliography information (if needed):

_____
_____
_____

Writing the First Paragraph

Write a thesis statement.
_____
_____

Write an opening sentence to introduce your topic.
_____
_____

Write 3–5 sentences that support your opening sentence.
_____
_____
_____
_____
_____
_____

Write a concluding sentence (this could be your thesis statement).
_____
_____

On the next page, continue writing the next four paragraphs (or more). You've got this. You can be a great writer!

Biography Outline

Biography Outline

1. _____
   A. _____
   B. _____
   C. _____
   D. _____
2. _____
   A. _____
   B. _____
   C. _____
   D. _____
3. _____
   A. _____
   B. _____
   C. _____
   D. _____
4. _____
   A. _____
   B. _____
   C. _____
   D. _____
5. _____
   A. _____
   B. _____
   C. _____
   D. _____
6. _____
   A. _____
   B. _____
   C. _____
   D. _____

7. _____
   A. _____
   B. _____
   C. _____
   D. _____
8. _____
   A. _____
   B. _____
   C. _____
   D. _____
9. _____
   A. _____
   B. _____
   C. _____
   D. _____
10. _____
    A. _____
    B. _____
    C. _____
    D. _____
11. _____
    A. _____
    B. _____
    C. _____
    D. _____
12. _____
    A. _____
    B. _____
    C. _____
    D. _____

Biography Oral Presentation Worksheet

Topic:
_____

Audience:
_____

Date, time, and place:
_____

Visual aids/media:
_____
_____
_____
_____

Opening statement (thesis):
_____
_____
_____

Supporting points:
_____
_____
_____
_____
_____
_____
_____
_____
_____
_____

Conclusion:
_____
_____
_____
_____

This page intentionally left blank.

Autobiography Outline

Autobiography Outline

1. _____
   A. _____
   B. _____
   C. _____
   D. _____
2. _____
   A. _____
   B. _____
   C. _____
   D. _____
3. _____
   A. _____
   B. _____
   C. _____
   D. _____
4. _____
   A. _____
   B. _____
   C. _____
   D. _____
5. _____
   A. _____
   B. _____
   C. _____
   D. _____
6. _____
   A. _____
   B. _____
   C. _____
   D. _____

7. _____
   A. _____
   B. _____
   C. _____
   D. _____
8. _____
   A. _____
   B. _____
   C. _____
   D. _____
9. _____
   A. _____
   B. _____
   C. _____
   D. _____
10. _____
    A. _____
    B. _____
    C. _____
    D. _____
11. _____
    A. _____
    B. _____
    C. _____
    D. _____
12. _____
    A. _____
    B. _____
    C. _____
    D. _____

Autobiography Oral Presentation Worksheet

Topic:

Audience:

Date, time, and place:

Visual aids/media:

Opening statement (thesis):

Supporting points:

Conclusion:

This page intentionally left blank.

Persuasive Oral Presentation Worksheet

Topic:
_____

Audience:
_____

Date, time, and place:
_____

Visual aids/media:
_____
_____
_____
_____

Opening statement (thesis):
_____
_____
_____

Supporting points:
_____
_____
_____
_____
_____
_____
_____
_____
_____
_____

Conclusion:
_____
_____
_____
_____

This page intentionally left blank.

Vocabulary Study Tips

When a student thoroughly understands the meaning of words, they are more likely to use them in the proper context in both writing and speaking. Reading the words in context is especially helpful; that is why the vocabulary words in the course all come from the student reading portions. The following tips can be used to help students remember vocabulary words and their definitions.

Memorization Cards — Write each vocabulary word on an index card. Use separate cards to write the definition for the vocabulary words you chose. Lay out the vocabulary word cards face down. Lay out the definition cards face down. Leave space between the two areas so the words do not get mixed up with the definitions. Flip over a card from the vocabulary word area and then from the definition card area. Decipher whether the word and the definition match. When you get a match, pair them together and set them aside. Do this until the cards are all used up.

Conversation Practice — Challenge yourself to use vocabulary words in everyday conversation. When you use a new vocabulary word in a spoken sentence, it reinforces the word's meaning. Your mind is required to not only understand the meaning of the word but also place the word in the proper context. Ask someone to converse with you over five to ten of your vocabulary words. A conversation about the meaning of words is a great way to help you remember them.

Write, Look, Cover, and Repeat (WLCR) — *Write* the vocabulary word and its definition on an index card, *look* at it thoughtfully as you read it over, *cover* the card, and try to say the word along with its definition. *Repeat* this process until you have it memorized.

Incorporate in Writing — Challenge yourself to incorporate as many new vocabulary words as you can when writing in any of your school subjects. The more you write and speak each word, the more fluent you will become in using them.

Right-brain Flashcards — Write the vocabulary word and its definition on an index card along with a sketch, sticker, or symbol that reminds you of the word. Your brain will associate the word and its meaning with the image you chose. Study the definitions while also looking at the image.

Spelling List

Lesson 1
- amiable
- caravals (caravels)
- charter
- convent
- cultivated
- desponding
- disposition
- eloquent
- endeavouring (endeavoring)
- friar
- hasty
- lamentations
- province
- reproached
- resolutely
- resolution
- toilsome
- tumult

Lesson 2
- adjutant
- anecdote
- ardently
- ascertain
- connexion (connection)
- constitution
- filial
- imprudent
- indulgence
- intercourse
- regiment
- reproof
- requite

Lesson 3
- affable
- aid-de-camp (aide-de-camp)
- approbation
- cultivation
- cumbered
- domestic
- engaged
- halt
- impertinent
- Providence
- suffer
- superintend
- vexation
- vigour (vigor)

Lesson 4
- assail
- cordial
- eloquence
- entrenchment
- garrison
- indulgence
- infantry
- magistrate
- oblige
- opulence
- pecuniary
- repeal
- stores
- unanimity
- unostentatiously

Lesson 5
- animate
- bade
- defray
- frigate
- melancholy
- provincial
- prudent
- riotous
- scantily
- siege
- temperate
- truce
- veneration

Lesson 6
- adhere
- candour (candor)
- convey
- dispersed
- fording
- implore
- imputation
- inoculation
- mortification
- peculiar
- preceding
- presumption
- sundry

Spelling List

Lesson 7
- [ ] avert
- [ ] capitulation
- [ ] disposed
- [ ] flotilla
- [ ] Hessians
- [ ] intelligence
- [ ] marquis
- [ ] obstructions
- [ ] profusion
- [ ] rash
- [ ] redoubt
- [ ] sanguinary
- [ ] surmounting
- [ ] tories

Lesson 8
- [ ] alliance
- [ ] busybodies
- [ ] campaign
- [ ] censure
- [ ] dispersion
- [ ] diverted
- [ ] fidelity
- [ ] idle
- [ ] inclinations
- [ ] insinuations
- [ ] miscreant
- [ ] mutiny
- [ ] procure
- [ ] reconciliation
- [ ] render
- [ ] sentiment
- [ ] specimen

Lesson 9
- [ ] banishment
- [ ] barbarous
- [ ] bayonet
- [ ] consoled
- [ ] conspicuous
- [ ] desertion
- [ ] hostilities
- [ ] imminent
- [ ] impious
- [ ] imprecations
- [ ] infidel
- [ ] profane
- [ ] suppress
- [ ] vice
- [ ] wanton

Lesson 10
- [ ] delusive
- [ ] depraved
- [ ] dissipation
- [ ] feeble
- [ ] feigned
- [ ] indignation
- [ ] ingenuous
- [ ] insolence
- [ ] perilous
- [ ] rectitude
- [ ] sloop of war
- [ ] timid
- [ ] traitor
- [ ] treason
- [ ] vice

Lesson 11
- [ ] abate
- [ ] approbation
- [ ] discharge
- [ ] disperse
- [ ] drolly
- [ ] fortitude
- [ ] homespun
- [ ] ignorant
- [ ] mountaineers
- [ ] musket
- [ ] mutineer
- [ ] powder horn
- [ ] scorn
- [ ] standard
- [ ] stinted
- [ ] trifling
- [ ] vanquished

Lesson 12
- [ ] artillery
- [ ] batteries
- [ ] candid
- [ ] confederation
- [ ] conflagration
- [ ] defrayed
- [ ] desertions
- [ ] effectual
- [ ] eminence
- [ ] fortifications
- [ ] hasty
- [ ] impropriety
- [ ] industrious
- [ ] piety
- [ ] procure
- [ ] rapidity

Spelling List

Lesson 13
- [ ] adjourned
- [ ] bosom
- [ ] compensation
- [ ] delinquency
- [ ] deportment
- [ ] detestation
- [ ] eminent
- [ ] endearing
- [ ] felicity
- [ ] harbinger
- [ ] imbitter (embitter)
- [ ] ingratitude
- [ ] interposition
- [ ] pacific
- [ ] posterity
- [ ] renown
- [ ] sentinels
- [ ] solemn
- [ ] subsistence

Lesson 14
- [ ] agriculture
- [ ] august
- [ ] beseech
- [ ] condescended
- [ ] confounded
- [ ] consolation
- [ ] diffidence
- [ ] dissolution
- [ ] economical
- [ ] haven
- [ ] illustrious
- [ ] minuteness
- [ ] navigation
- [ ] patronage
- [ ] profuse
- [ ] sanguine
- [ ] superseded
- [ ] venerable

Lesson 15
- [ ] adieu
- [ ] agency
- [ ] benediction
- [ ] beneficent
- [ ] benign
- [ ] concourse
- [ ] consecrate
- [ ] conspicuous
- [ ] ferry
- [ ] homage
- [ ] impute
- [ ] judicious
- [ ] meritorious
- [ ] pardon
- [ ] punctuality
- [ ] supplication
- [ ] tenor
- [ ] treaty

Lesson 16
- [ ] ambassador
- [ ] arbiter
- [ ] clamour (clamor)
- [ ] clemency
- [ ] conferred
- [ ] exemplary
- [ ] indigent
- [ ] indispensable
- [ ] insolent
- [ ] insurrection
- [ ] omit
- [ ] perpetual
- [ ] privateer
- [ ] quell
- [ ] restitution
- [ ] tyrant
- [ ] unremitted
- [ ] zeal

Lesson 17
- [ ] ague
- [ ] assent
- [ ] bleed
- [ ] blister of flies
- [ ] calomel
- [ ] convulsed
- [ ] divert
- [ ] expired
- [ ] frank
- [ ] incision
- [ ] intelligibly
- [ ] intered (interred)
- [ ] oration
- [ ] orifice
- [ ] pavilion
- [ ] sal volatile
- [ ] tartar emetic

Lesson 18
- [ ] assiduity
- [ ] canon
- [ ] choler
- [ ] culpable
- [ ] disparagement
- [ ] folio
- [ ] fraternal
- [ ] imbibing
- [ ] inculcated
- [ ] logarithm
- [ ] maxims
- [ ] quires
- [ ] partiality
- [ ] pensive
- [ ] precept
- [ ] solicitude
- [ ] sublime
- [ ] tractable
- [ ] vestryman
- [ ] vitiate

Spelling List

Lesson 19
- [ ] back-story (backstory)
- [ ] contraption
- [ ] embroidery
- [ ] exhilarating
- [ ] furrowed
- [ ] genesis
- [ ] herringbone
- [ ] industry
- [ ] insatiable
- [ ] local
- [ ] MRI
- [ ] perseverance
- [ ] ridicule
- [ ] strategically
- [ ] tweed
- [ ] unique

Lesson 20
- [ ] attributes
- [ ] awe
- [ ] combustion
- [ ] embedded
- [ ] fundamental
- [ ] inquisitiveness
- [ ] philosophers
- [ ] theologians
- [ ] validate
- [ ] verifiable

Lesson 21
- [ ] aspiration
- [ ] democracy
- [ ] empowerment
- [ ] exclusive
- [ ] genuinely
- [ ] impede
- [ ] inconvenient
- [ ] personified
- [ ] political
- [ ] pursuit
- [ ] quest
- [ ] subsequent
- [ ] tyranny
- [ ] vistas

Lesson 22
- [ ] aerial
- [ ] coincidence
- [ ] colossal
- [ ] liberate
- [ ] masterpiece
- [ ] multi-faceted (multifaceted)
- [ ] musings
- [ ] phenomenal
- [ ] privileged
- [ ] renaissance
- [ ] revolution

Lesson 23
- [ ] atheistic
- [ ] conventional
- [ ] implode
- [ ] infinite
- [ ] inherent
- [ ] intervention
- [ ] juncture
- [ ] malign
- [ ] naturalistic
- [ ] override
- [ ] peril
- [ ] radical
- [ ] seep
- [ ] truth

Lesson 24
- [ ] accountability
- [ ] alternate
- [ ] antithesis
- [ ] archeology
- [ ] decadence
- [ ] exempted
- [ ] gargantuan
- [ ] misapplication
- [ ] organic
- [ ] presupposition
- [ ] primordial
- [ ] status quo
- [ ] subscribe
- [ ] venerate

Lesson 25
- [ ] adaptation
- [ ] condemned
- [ ] demise
- [ ] dissuading
- [ ] façade
- [ ] foisted
- [ ] hoax
- [ ] innate
- [ ] maxim
- [ ] mythical
- [ ] obsolete
- [ ] postulate
- [ ] pre-eminence (preeminence)
- [ ] pride
- [ ] random
- [ ] suffice

Spelling List

Lesson 26
- [ ] adept
- [ ] bigotry
- [ ] devoid
- [ ] diabolical
- [ ] epiphany
- [ ] fabricated
- [ ] genocide
- [ ] heinous
- [ ] indifference
- [ ] masquerade
- [ ] perpetually
- [ ] profound
- [ ] propaganda

Lesson 27
- [ ] access
- [ ] apologetics
- [ ] credible
- [ ] detours
- [ ] imperative
- [ ] penetrate
- [ ] presentation
- [ ] principle
- [ ] secular

Lesson 28
- [ ] acclaim
- [ ] appropriate
- [ ] ascension
- [ ] betrayal
- [ ] millennium
- [ ] Pentecost
- [ ] proselytes

Lesson 29
- [ ] face
- [ ] gully
- [ ] mountaineering
- [ ] peak
- [ ] pinnacle
- [ ] ridge
- [ ] slope
- [ ] summit

Lesson 30
- [ ] cease
- [ ] effort
- [ ] extol
- [ ] fellowship
- [ ] image
- [ ] strain
- [ ] strife

Lesson 31
- [ ] covenant
- [ ] dismiss
- [ ] girded
- [ ] heave
- [ ] redeemed
- [ ] steadfast

Lesson 32
- [ ] confess
- [ ] determine
- [ ] devil
- [ ] direct
- [ ] grace
- [ ] humble
- [ ] Jesus
- [ ] pride
- [ ] renew
- [ ] resist
- [ ] steps
- [ ] submit

Lesson 33
- [ ] aid climbing
- [ ] bivouac
- [ ] bouldering
- [ ] free climbing
- [ ] lead
- [ ] pumped
- [ ] solo

Lesson 34
- [ ] brawl
- [ ] cobble-stones (cobblestones)
- [ ] gullied
- [ ] metaphor
- [ ] poetry
- [ ] prose
- [ ] rhythm

Lesson 35
- [ ] balance
- [ ] bosom
- [ ] herald
- [ ] hollow
- [ ] Judah
- [ ] recompense
- [ ] Zion

Lesson 36
- [ ] catastrophic
- [ ] crystal
- [ ] currents
- [ ] geology
- [ ] interpretation
- [ ] metamorphic rock
- [ ] sediments
- [ ] tectonic plates

Spelling Rules and Exceptions

Spelling Rules

Short Vowel Sound

- In order to spell a **short** vowel sound, only one consonant is needed. — *Example:* up
- When we have a short word with one vowel in the middle, it usually has a **short sound**. — *Example:* hat
- We use the consonant blend *ck* only after a single vowel that has the **short sound**. — *Example:* stack
- We use the consonant blend *tch* after a **single vowel** that does not say its name. — *Example:* hatch

Long Vowel Sound

- In order to spell a **long** vowel sound, a second vowel is needed. — *Example:* made
  ⚠ Exceptions: The letters *i* and *o* may say the long sound alone before two consonants. — *Examples:* kind sold
- The second vowel may follow the first one to make a vowel team.
- Remember, in a vowel team, the second vowel is silent and makes the first vowel says its name. — *Example:* maid
- Remember, the silent-e at the end of a word also makes the vowel say its name. — *Example:* made

Vowel Pairs

- When we have a vowel pair, the first vowel is usually long and the second is silent. — *Example:* maid
- Some vowel pairs make a new vowel sound together. — *Example:* boil

Consonant Pairs

- A consonant **blend** forms when two or three consonants are blended together, but you can still hear their individual sounds. — *Example:* scrub
- Some consonants work together to make a new sound. — *Example:* photo

The *gh* Pair

- We only use *gh* at the end of a word or before the letter *t*. The *gh* is either silent or makes the /f/ sound. The letters *gh* are paired with vowels to make one sound: *augh, eigh, igh, ough*. — *Examples:* taught, high, tough

Rarely!

- The letter *s* rarely comes right after the letter *x*.
- The letters *j* and *x* are rarely doubled.
- We rarely end a word in *i, u, j* or *v*.

Soft and Hard *c*

- The letter *c* can make a hard sound /k/ and soft sound /s/.
- When the letter *c* is followed by the vowels *e, i,* or *y*, it usually makes the soft sound. — *Example:* fancy
- The letter *c* also makes a hard sound. — *Example:* cat

Spelling Rules and Exceptions

Letters *c* and *ck*
- Double the letter *c* to keep the vowel sound short in the first syllable of a word. — *Example:* ra**cc**oon
- We use *ck* instead of *cc* when it is followed by the vowels *e, i,* or *y*. — *Example:* lu**ck**y
- Use *ck* when it follows a short vowel. — *Example:* du**ck** ⚠ Exception: yak

Letter *k*
- Use *k* when another consonant is right after the vowel. — *Example:* dri**nk**
- Use *k* instead of *c* if the /k/ sound is followed by the vowels *e, i,* or *y*. — *Example:* fla**k**y
- When the letter *k* comes before *n*, it is silent. — *Example:* **k**night

Letters *g* and *j*
- The /j/ sound is spelled *j, g, ge,* and *dge*.
- When the letter *j* is used, it is usually followed by the vowels *a, o,* or *u*. — *Example:* **j**ump
- When the letter *g* is followed by the vowels *e, i,* or *y*, it usually makes the soft sound /j/. — *Example:* **g**ym
- When the letter *g* follows a short vowel sound, it is usually spelled *dge*. This is to protect the short vowel sound since we rarely double the letter *j*. — *Example:* r**idge**
- The letter *g* also makes the hard sound. — *Example:* yo**g**urt

The /ch/ Sound
- The /ch/ sound is spelled with *ch* and *tch*.
- We use *tch* after a short vowel. — *Example:* ki**tch**en
  ⚠ Exceptions: atta**ch**, ostri**ch**, mu**ch**, ri**ch**, su**ch**, tou**ch**, sandwi**ch**, whi**ch**
- Use *ch* for all other words. — *Example:* **ch**ain

The *qu* Pair
- The letter *q* is always followed by *u*. This pair makes the /kw/ sound and is the only letters that make this sound. The *u* does not act like a vowel in this pair. — *Example:* **qu**een

Silent-e
- Makes the vowel say its name. — *Example:* m**a**d**e**
- Makes the *c* say /s/ and the *g* say /j/. — *Examples:* fa**c**e, a**g**e
- Is added to words that end with the letter *u* or *v*. — *Examples:* cl**ue**, sto**ve**
- Is added to the consonant *l* to form the syllable *le*. — *Example:* puzz**le**
- Is added to show that a word is not plural. — *Example:* dens**e**
- Is added to a very short word to make it longer. — *Example:* ew**e**
- Shows which meaning of a word is used. — *Example:* aid : aid**e**
- Breaks the rules! — *Examples:* com**e**, on**e**, sho**e**, wer**e**, wh**e**re

Spelling Rules and Exceptions

i Before *e*

- *i* before *e* except after *c* or when sounding like *a* as in neighbor or weigh.
  — *Examples:* relief, receipt, vein

i Before *e* Exceptions

- There are many exceptions to the *i before e* rule. — *Examples:* ancient, caffeine, counterfeit, either, feisty, foreign, forfeit, glacier, heifer, heist, leisure, neither, proficient, protein, science, seized, society, sovereign, species, weird
  Hints: The *c* is followed by *i* in some of the exceptions. Notice the *eign* pattern.

Prefixes

Prefixes
A prefix is a group of letters added to the beginning of a word to change the meaning.

- *a-* and *an-* mean: not, without. — *Examples:* atheist, annex
- *a-* means: to, toward. — *Examples:* aside, aback
- *ab(s)-* means: away, from. — *Examples:* abdicate, abstract
- *ad-* means: movement to, change into, addition. — *Example:* advance
- *ante-* means: before, preceding. — *Example:* antecedent
- *anti-* means: opposite, against. — *Example:* antifreeze
- *auto-* means: self. — *Example:* autograph
- *be-* means: cause to be. — *Examples:* becalm, beholden
- *centi-* means: 100. — *Example:* centimeter
- *com-* means: with, jointly, completely. — *Examples:* combat, competent
- *de-* means: down, away. — *Examples:* descend, despair, deduct
- *deca-* and *deci-* mean: 10. — *Examples:* decade, decimal
- *dis-* means: negation, removal, expulsion. — *Examples:* dismount, disbar, disadvantage
- *en-* and *em-* mean: to cause to be, to put into or onto, to go into or onto. — *Examples:* enable, employ
- *extra-* means: outside, beyond. — *Examples:* extracurricular
- *fore-* means: before, earlier. — *Example:* forearm
- *kilo*, *milli-*, and *mille-* mean: 1,000. — *Examples:* kilogram, millimeter, millennium
- *hyper-* means: beyond, more than normal. — *Examples:* hyperactive, hypersensitive
- *in-*, *il-*, *im-*, and *ir-* mean: in, on, not. — *Examples:* infinite, illegal, improper, irregular
- *inter-* means: among, between, in the midst of, together. — *Examples:* interface, interview
- *micro-* means: small. — *Examples:* microphone, microwave
- *multi-* and *poly-* mean: many, much. — *Examples:* multicolor, polygon
- *ob-* means: blocking, against, concealing. — *Examples:* obstruct, obscure, oblique
- *pre-* means: before in time, place, order, or importance. — *Examples:* prelude, precondition, pregame
- *re-* means: again. — *Examples:* repaint, redo, remix
- *semi-* means: half. — *Example:* semicircle
- *sub-* means: below, beneath, at a lower position, secondary, under. — *Examples:* subway, submarine, subsoil
- *super-* means: above, beyond, over. — *Examples:* supernova, supervise
- *trans-* means: across, beyond, change, through. — *Examples:* transact, transplant
- *uni-* means: one. — *Examples:* unicycle, uniform

  (*Hint:* Use the prefix *il-* for words beginning with the letter *l*. Use the prefix *im-* for words beginning with the letter *b*, *m*, or *p*.)

Suffixes

A suffix is letters added to the end of a word to change the meaning.

- A suffix can start with a vowel or a consonant. — *Examples:* -able, -ment
- *-s* and *-es* mean: plural, more than one. — *Example:* kisses
- *-ed* means: past tense. — *Example:* played
- *-ful* means: full of. — *Example:* meaningful
- *-ing* means: action, process. — *Example:* rolling
- *-est* means: superlative (utmost) degree. — *Example:* finest
- *-less* means: without. — *Example:* helpless
- *-al* means: related to, character of. — *Example:* formal
- *-er* means: one who, that which. — *Example:* reader
- *-ness* means: condition, state of. — *Example:* kindness
- *-or* means: one who, that which. — *Example:* operator
- *-en* means: become, made of, resemble, to make. — *Example:* earthen
- *-ial* means: related to, character of. — *Example:* controversial
- *-ment* means: act, process. — *Example:* postponement
- The suffixes *-ion*, *-sion*, *-ation*, and *-ition* also mean: act, result, or state of. They are all a form of the suffix *-tion*. — *Examples:* gumption, million, tension, elevation, addition
- *-able* and *-ible* mean: can be done, fit for. — *Examples:* likable, sensible
- *-an* and *-ian* mean: belonging or relating to, able to be. — *Examples:* electrician, American
- *-ive*, *-ative*, and *-tive* mean: inclined, tending toward an action or having the quality of. — *Examples:* festive, talkative
  Note: In words that end in *-de*, change the *-de* to *s*, then add *-ive*. — *Example:* intrusive
- *-logy* and *-ology* mean: science of or the study of. — *Example:* biology
- *-ance* and *-ence* mean: act or condition of. — *Examples:* importance, excellence
- *-age* means: causing an action. — *Example:* percentage
- *-ant* and *-ent* mean: belonging to, result of. — *Examples:* contestant, absorbent
- *-ic* means: related to. — *Example:* magnetic
- *-ity* and *-ty* mean: state of, condition. — *Examples:* security, loyalty
- *-ize* means: to make, to treat as, to become like. — *Example:* vocalize
- *-ous*, *-eous*, and *-ious* mean: full of, having the qualities of. — *Examples:* rigorous, courteous, gracious
- *-ary*, *-ery*, and *-ory* mean: group of, state or character of, connected with, involving, a place for. — *Examples:* literary, archery, directory
- *-cede*, *-ceed*, and *-sede* mean: to give control, right, or power to. — *Examples:* intercede, succeed, supersede

Suffixes

- **-efy** and **-ify** mean: to make or become. — *Examples:* liquefy, beautify
- **-ize** and **-yze** mean: become or make like, to place in, to cause to become.
  — *Examples:* itemize, paralyze

Consonant Suffixes

- When you add a *consonant* suffix to any word, you just add it. — *Examples:* timeless, thankful (*Hint:* The suffix *-ful* is always spelled with one *l*.)

Root Words

A root word is the base word we add a suffix or prefix to.

- *ject* means: to throw. — *Example:* objection
- *struct* means: to build. — *Example:* construct
- *vis* and *vid* mean: to see. — *Examples:* vision, video
- *jur* and *juris* mean: judge, oath, law. — *Examples:* jury, jurisdiction
- *log* and *logue* mean: word. — *Examples:* apology, dialogue
- *path* means: feeling, suffering, disease. — *Example:* apathetic
- *ast* and *astr* mean: star. — *Examples:* asterisk, astronaut
- *mit* means: to send. — *Example:* transmit
- *audi* and *aud* mean: hear. — *Example:* audience
- *dict* means: to say, tell. — *Example:* diction
- *bene* means: well, in the right way, properly. — *Examples:* benefactor, benefit
- *chron* means: time. — *Examples:* chronicle, chronological
- *hydr* means: water. — *Examples:* hydrate, hydraulic
- *port* means: to carry. — *Examples:* export, report
- *scrib* and *script* mean: write. — *Examples:* prescribe, transcript
- *spect* means: look, see, observe, watch. — *Example:* spectacle
- *therm* means: heat, warm. — *Examples:* thermal, thermos
- *vac* means: empty. — *Example:* vacant
- *rupt* means: break or burst. — *Example:* abrupt
- *terr* means: land. — *Example:* terrarium
- *geo* means: earth, ground, or soil. — *Example:* geography
- *photo* means: light. — *Example:* photography
- *tract* means: pull or drag. — *Example:* retract
- *meter* and *metr* mean: measure. — *Examples:* thermometer, metrics

Grammar Study Sheets

The Eight Parts of Speech

	The Eight Parts of Speech
Noun	names a person, place, or thing
	tree, Jennifer, New York, love
Verb	shows action or state-of-being
	swim, twirl, shout, am, is, were
Adjective	describes a noun or pronoun. Tells what kind, how many, or which one
	blue, kind, ten
Adverb	describes a verb, adjective, or another adverb. Tells when, where, how, or how often.
	slowly, later, above, yesterday
Pronoun	takes the place of a noun
	he, she, it, they, their, him, her
Conjunction	joins words or phrases
	and, yet, although, unless, because, as if
Preposition	describes a relationship between a noun or pronoun and another word that follows
	to, for, with, over, on, between, near, into, at, beneath, in
Interjection	expresses strong feelings or emotions. Often followed by an exclamation point, although sometimes only a comma is needed.
	Hi! Oh no! Yeah! Well,

Sentence Basics

Complete sentence	"Columbus was very attentive to the instructions which he received in the few years that he went to school." (p. 5) (contains a subject, *Columbus*, and a predicate, *was attentive*, and expresses a complete thought)
Sentence fragment	"[U]sing every opportunity to gain a knowledge of geography and navigation." (p. 6) (contains the predicate *using* but no subject and does not express a complete thought)

Grammar Study Sheets

Verbs: Action and Linking

Verb Type	Function	Examples
Action	What the subject is doing or has done	grab, run, shout, walk, play, sing, cook
State-of-being	Explain the state/condition of the subject	am, is, are, was, were, be, being, been
Linking	Explain the state/condition of the subject	be, become, seem, remain, get, appear

Common Linking Verbs	
Permanent linking verbs	be, become, seem (these verbs are never action verbs)
Sensory linking verbs	appear, feel, look, smell, sound, taste
Conditional linking verbs	act, constitute, come, equal, fall, get, go, grow, keep, prove, remain, stay, turn
State-of-being verbs	am, is, are, was, were, be, being, been

Helping Verbs

The Primary Helping Verbs	
The primary helping verbs are *to be*, *to have*, and *to do*. They can appear in the following forms:	
To be:	*am, is, are, was, were, being, been, will be* (notice these are also state-of-being verbs!)
To have:	*has, have, had, having, will have*
To do:	*does, do, did, will do*
	(*Note*: Negative forms are also helping verbs: *don't, haven't, won't, didn't, doesn't, aren't*, etc.)
Examples:	Mikayla *was writing* her essay even though she had a headache. (*was* is the helping verb) Eliana *had been peeling* apples with her mother all afternoon. (*had been* is the helping verb) Jailyn *does swim* much faster than the other girls. (*does* is the helping verb)

Modal Helping Verbs

Modal Helping Verbs	
Full list: *can, could, will, would, shall, should, may, might,* and *must*	
To show possibility:	*may, might, could, must*
To show intent:	*would, should, will, might, shall*
To show ability:	*can, could, may, might*
To show necessity:	*must (have to, have got to)*
Examples:	Despite the rain, I *might walk* to the park with the dog this afternoon. You *must feel* so rejuvenated after that power nap. I *could have been* a professional athlete with a little hard work.

Grammar Study Sheets

Verb Tense

Verb Tenses

	Past	Present	Future
Simple	I *walked* to town.	I *walk* to town.	I *will walk* to town.
Perfect	I *had walked* to town.	I *have walked* to town already.	I *will have walked* to town.
Continuous	I *was walking* to town.	I *am walking* to town.	I *will be walking* to town.
Perfect Continuous	I *had been walking*.	I *have been walking* all day.	I *will have been walking*.

Tense Construction

	Past	Present	Future
Simple	suffix *-ed*	simple verb	*will* + simple verb
Perfect	*had* + suffix *-ed*	*have* + suffix *-ed*	*will have* + suffix *-ed*
Continuous	*was* + suffix *-ing*	*am* + suffix *-ing*	*will be* + suffix *-ing*
Perfect Continuous	*had been* + suffix *-ing*	*have been* + suffix *-ing*	*will have been* + suffix *-ing*

Independent vs. Dependent Clauses

Independent clause	I knew we would be great friends.
Dependent clause	When she first introduced herself.
Independent clause with a dependent clause	I knew we would be great friends when she first introduced herself.

Conjunctions

Three Types of Conjunctions

Coordinating conjunctions	*for, and, nor, but, or, yet, so* (remember them with the acronym FANBOYS) Used to join sentence elements of the same type.
	I want to go to the fair, *but* I'm so tired.
Correlative conjunctions	*either-or, neither-nor, both-and, not only-but also, no sooner-than, rather-than* Used to join equal sentence parts and occur in pairs.
	Either go with Mom *or* stay at home.
Subordinating conjunctions	*after, although, as, because, before, if, once, since, that, unless, until, when, where, while, as if, even though, so that* Used to join dependent clauses to independent clauses.
	I will stay in the car *until* the rain stops.

Grammar Study Sheets

Prepositions

\	Preposition Chart
Location	above, across, against, around, at, behind, below, beneath, beside, between, beyond, by, in, in front of, inside, on, outside, over, past, toward, under, upon, within
Time	after, at, before, between, by, during, for, in, on, past, since, until, till, up to
Association	about, according to, along with, among, around, as for, besides, for, like, of, with
Direction	down, from, into, off, onto, out, out of, through, to, up
Means	by, by means of, with
Cause	because of, due to, in view of, on account of
Opposition or Exception	against, apart from, but, despite, except, except for, in spite of, instead of, without

Quotation Marks

\	When to Use Quotation Marks
Direct Quotations	Quotation marks are used to indicate the exact words of a writer or speaker. Do not use them if you are paraphrasing or summarizing someone else's words.
	Alyssa commented, "I know God has a greater purpose for my life."
Dialogue	Dialogue is a conversation between two or more people and often occurs in books, plays, and movies. Use quotation marks to enclose the words of the speakers and begin a new paragraph whenever the speaker changes.
	"I'm going to run down to the post office to drop off this package," Dad said. "Oh, do you mind," Jesse asked, "if I go with you?"
Titles of Short Works	Use quotation marks to enclose the titles of short works like essays, stories, songs, articles, chapters of a book, individual episodes of radio or television programs, and most poems. Quotation marks are not needed for chapters of the Bible.
	The best chapter in that book was "Overnight Voyage."
Special Words	Sometimes a word, phrase, or expression may need to be set off from the rest of the sentence to emphasize it for purposes like impact, skepticism, a twist of meaning, etc.
	Sometimes "experts" miss the mark. The word "blue" can refer to a color or a mood.

Grammar Study Sheets

Quotation Marks and Other Sentence Punctuation

Rules for Quotation Marks and Other Sentence Punctuation
Commas and periods appear *before* ending quotation marks.
"I want to know God's Word better," Sarah expressed.   David replied, "So do I."
Colons and semicolons appear *after* ending quotation marks.
Maggie answered, "I need all the help I can get"; then she proceeded to ignore my advice.
Question marks and exclamation points may appear inside or outside the quotation marks. If the quotation itself is a question or exclamation, the punctuation goes *inside* the quotation marks. If the quotation did not include these marks originally, the punctuation comes *after* the quotation marks.
"What a beautiful day!" exclaimed Austin.   I can't believe he said, "The tickets are free"!

Punctuating Clauses

Commas and Clauses
Nonessential clauses are set off with commas. One way to determine if a comma is necessary is to ask whether the clause is essential or nonessential to the meaning of the sentence.
I left my sweater, <u>which was a gift from my aunt</u>, in the shopping cart at the grocery store.   The phrase *which was a gift from my aunt* is not essential to the meaning of the sentence. It is an adjective clause that tells us more about *my sweater*.
Use commas to separate two independent clauses connected by a conjunction. These clauses can both stand alone as a sentence and are connected by a conjunction, so a comma is placed after the first clause.
<u>The army set up camp in the dark</u>, yet <u>they did it with perfection</u>.
Three or more short independent clauses need a comma separating them.
<u>The flowers bloomed</u>, <u>the grass grew</u>, and <u>the trees budded</u>.
A comma is needed after a long (five words or more) introductory prepositional phrase.
<u>With a great deal of joy in their hearts</u>, the children opened their presents.
A comma is needed after an introductory adverb clause.
<u>Before I am able to give my honest opinion</u>, I will need to review the entire document.
Use a comma after any introductory element that modifies the sentence.
<u>To put it simply</u>, I really need more time to practice before I am able to teach someone else.

Grammar Study Sheets

Adjectives

Seven Types of Adjectives	
Descriptive Adjective	names a quality of the noun or pronoun that it modifies
	yellow flower, *larger* fish, *soft* rabbit, *sad* expression
Proper Adjective	derived from a proper noun. These include words for nationalities, languages, and ethnicities.
	Spanish architecture, *European* lifestyle, *French* class, *American* diet
Limiting Adjective	restricts the meaning of the word it modifies
	this book, *that* house, *the* car
Interrogative Adjective	used to ask a question
	Whose hat is this? *Which* book belongs to you?
Coordinate Adjective	consists of two or more adjectives separated by a comma instead of a coordinating conjunction
	a *large, sharp* knife; the *warm, scented* fabric; the *constant, monotonous* noise
	To understand if two or more adjectives should be connected by commas, see if the order of the adjectives can be reversed. If they can be reversed, a comma can be used to separate them.
	The boy ate a *crisp, shiny* apple. OR The boy ate a *shiny, crisp* apple. Reversing *crisp* and *shiny* does not change the meaning; therefore, a comma is placed in between. These are coordinate adjectives.
	The boy ate *two shiny* apples. OR The boy ate *shiny two* apples. Reversing *two* and *shiny* does change the meaning; therefore, a comma should not be used. These are *not* coordinate adjectives.
Compound Adjectives	consist of two or more words that function as a single unit. Depending on its position within the sentence, the compound adjective is punctuated with a hyphen. When the compound adjective comes *before* the noun it modifies, use a hyphen. When it *follows* the noun it modifies, do not use a hyphen.
	The item at the museum was a *seventeenth-century* vase. (hyphen used) The vase at the museum was from the *seventeenth century*. (no hyphen)

Determiners as Adjectives	Determiners, like articles (*a, an, the*), numbers, and pronouns, can function as adjectives. Determiners are like limiting adjectives because they restrict the nouns they modify. Determiners functioning as adjectives tell *which one*, *how many*, and *whose*.
	
	    Articles (*a, an, the*)
	    Possessive pronouns (*my, our, your, his, her, its, their*)
	    Relative pronouns (*whose, which, whichever, what, whatever*)
	    Demonstratives (*this, these, that, those*)
	    Indefinite pronouns (*any, each, other, some,* etc.)
	    Cardinal numbers (*one, two, three,* etc.)
	    Ordinal numbers (*first, last, second,* etc.)
	    Possessive proper nouns (*Levi's, John's*)

	John's truck broke down *five* miles from *his* house.

Adverbs

Seven Types of Adverbs	
Adverbs of Manner	An adverb of manner answers the question *how?*
	badly, beautifully, happily, cheerfully, hard, quickly, adequately, healthy, fast, well, better, courageously, etc.
Adverbs of Place	An adverb of place answers the question *where?*
	below, inside, there, up, down, outside, inside, near, far, above, away, etc.
Adverbs of Time	An adverb of time answers the question *when?*
	after, before, during, always, later, early, now, often, yesterday, rarely, recently, sometimes, then, today, tomorrow, usually, never, soon, etc.
Adverbs of Degree	An adverb of degree answers the question *how much?*
	almost, completely, enough, entirely, extremely, hardly, nearly, just, little, much, quite, rather, too, very, etc.
Adverbs of Frequency	An adverb of frequency answers the question *how often?*
	always, never, usually, seldom, sometimes, occasionally, frequently, every now and then, etc.
Interrogative Adverbs	An interrogative adverb introduces a question. They are usually placed at the beginning of the sentence.
	how, when, why, and *where*
Conjunctive Adverbs	Conjunctive adverbs act as transitional words that join and relate to independent clauses.
	accordingly, certainly, finally, nevertheless, moreover, previously, therefore, also, alternatively, consequently, etc.

Verb Phrases: Infinitives

Infinitive Functions	
Infinitive as a noun	*To conquer my fears* was the main reason for the climb. (serves as a subject noun)
Infinitive as an adjective	The teacher gave out several verses *to be memorized*. (describes verses)
Infinitive as an adverb	We work hard *to bring honor to God*. (tells *why*)
Prepositional phrase, *not* an infinitive	After swimming, we went *to the grocery store*. (The word *to* followed by a noun, not a verb, means this is a prepositional phrase, not an infinitive.)

Grammar Study Sheets

Pronouns

Subject (Personal) Pronouns	Object Pronouns	Relative Pronouns
Replace the subject	Object of a verb	Connect relative clauses
I, we, you, he, she, it, they	*me, us, you, her, him, it, them*	*that, what, which, who, whom*
You are my best friend.	Jane gave *me* a ride home.	The cat *that* napped awoke.
He is my uncle.	The bird belongs to *him*.	The man *who* knocked came in.

Demonstrative Pronouns	Indefinite Pronouns	Reflexive Pronouns
Point to or replace antecedent	Non-specific	Ending in *-self* or *-selves*
that, this, these, those	*one, other, none, some,*	*myself, yourself, himself, herself,*
Great *idea*. **That** will work!	*anybody, everybody, no one*	*itself, oneself, themselves,*
He picked up the *book* and said,	*Nobody* seemed to care.	*yourselves, ourselves*
"**This** is for my wife."	*Everybody* was there today.	She took **herself** out of the game.

Interrogative Pronouns	Reciprocal Pronouns	Distributive Pronouns
Introduce questions	Describe mutual relationships	Refer to individuals in a group
who, whose, whom	*each other, one another*	*either, each, neither, any, none*
what, which	Josh and Jen are competing	We all entered the race, but *none* of us won.
What is your name?	with *each other*.	Of the two options, *neither* seemed like
Which one is yours?	My friends love *one another*.	a good choice.

Possessive Pronouns	Possessive (or Pronominal) Adjectives
Designate ownership (possession)	Appear before the noun to modify it
mine, yours, ours, his, hers, theirs, its	*my, your, our, his, her, their, its, whose,* etc.
I believe that letter is *mine*.	The bird flew out of *its* cage.
He didn't know the phone was *hers*.	I would love to visit with *your* mother.

Indirect Objects

	How to Find Direct and Indirect Objects
	Angela handed Madison the gift.
Step 1:	Find the verb. (*handed*)
Step 2:	Ask "what?" (*handed* what? *The gift* = direct object)
Step 3:	Ask "who or what received it?" (*handed* whom the gift? *Madison* = indirect object)

Number: Subject-Verb Agreement

Nine Rules for Subject-Verb Agreement

1. **If the subject is singular, the verb must be singular. If the subject is plural, the verb must be plural.**

	She reads the Bible every day. (singular subject = singular verb) The *students read* the Bible every day. (plural subject = plural verb)
Exception:	When using "they" in a singular way. (This *person is* a great cook. *They are* amazing!)

2. **Use a plural verb when the subject is composed of two or more nouns connected by the word *and*.**

   The *teacher* <u>and</u> the *students walk* slowly and quietly down the hall.

3. **When there is one subject but multiple verbs, all verbs in the sentence must agree.**

   Vehicles are expensive and *require* a lot of maintenance.

4. **When a phrase comes between the subject and the verb, the verb must agree with the subject, not other nouns in the phrase.**

   The *firetruck*, along with other emergency vehicles in our town, *requires* major repairs.

5. **Use a singular verb when two or more singular nouns are connected by *or* or *nor*.**

   The *pastor* <u>or</u> the *worship leader needs* to approve the song selection.

6. **When a compound subject contains both a singular and plural noun joined by *or* or *nor*, the verb should agree with the subject that is *closest* to it.**

   The *pastor* <u>or</u> the *worship leaders need* to approve the song selections.
   The *worship leaders* <u>or</u> the *pastor needs* to approve the song selections.

7. **The words and phrases *each*, *each one*, *either*, *neither*, *everyone*, *everybody*, *anyone*, *anybody*, *nobody*, *somebody*, *someone*, and *no one* are considered singular and need a singular verb.**

   No one was available to clean after the concert.
   Everybody needs encouragement.

8. **Noncount nouns are words that have no specific quantity. They need singular verbs.**

   The *evidence needs* to be made available.
   Diabetes is a terrible problem in the United States.

9. **Collective nouns (imply more than one person) are considered singular and need a singular verb.**

   The *choir runs* through their song list every Saturday morning.
   The *youth group meets* on Tuesday nights.

Conjugating Verbs

Person	Who or what is performing the action? (the subject "governs" the verb)
Number	Whether the action is performed by one or more than one (subject-verb agreement)
Tense	When the action is happening (past, present, future)
Mood	Whether the action is hypothetical, an order, or a statement (reveals the writer's intention)
Voice	Whether the action is done by or to the subject (active/passive)
Aspect	Whether the action is ongoing or completed

Grammar Study Sheets

Rules for Pluralizing Nouns

Regular Nouns		Ends in *s*, *ch*, *sh*, *x*, or *z*		Ends in *f* or *fe*	
add *s*		add *es*		drop *f/fe*, add *ves*	
1 book	2 books	1 box	2 boxes	1 knife	2 knives
1 apple	2 apples	1 church	2 churches	1 leaf	2 leaves
1 battle	2 battles	1 dish	2 dishes	1 life	2 lives

Exceptions: cliff=cliffs, roof=roofs

Ends in vowel + *o*		Ends in consonant + *o*		No change	
add *s*		add *es*		1 fish	2 fish
1 zoo	2 zoos	1 potato	2 potatoes	1 sheep	2 sheep
1 video	2 videos	1 hero	2 heroes	1 aircraft	2 aircraft
1 stereo	2 stereos	1 echo	2 echoes	1 deer	2 deer

Exceptions: piano=pianos, photo=photos

Ends in vowel + *y*		Ends in consonant + *y*		Irregular Nouns	
add *s*		remove *y*, add *ies*		1 species	2 species
1 day	2 days	1 party	2 parties	1 man	2 men
1 key	2 keys	1 baby	2 babies	1 woman	2 women
1 boy	2 boys	1 country	2 countries	1 mouse	2 mice

Common Irregular Nouns

larva = larvae	ox = oxen	oasis = oases	swine = swine	trout = trout
cactus = cacti	fungus = fungi	stimulus = stimuli	syllabus = syllabi	datum = data
person = people	foot = feet	child = children	goose = geese	focus = foci
bison = bison	crisis = crises	series = series	tuna = tuna	index = indices
diagnosis = diagnoses	analysis = analyses	curriculum = curricula		

Grammar Study Sheets

Semicolons

When to Use a Semicolon
Before a conjunction in a long compound sentence
The science project called for a long list of ingredients, including 2 cups of baking soda, 1 cup of vinegar, and 3 ounces of food coloring; but I had only 1 cup of baking soda.
Between word groups containing commas (this includes Bible references if a new chapter is given)
The school had several teachers on the committee, including the art teacher, Mrs. Morris; the gym teacher, Mr. Peters; and the English teacher, Mrs. Johnson.
Our pastor spoke on Ephesians 5:15–17, 21; and 6:10.
Between two independent clauses (not joined by a coordinating conjunction)
I ordered chocolate ice cream; chocolate always helps my mood!
We managed to bake several dozen cookies Saturday afternoon; on Sunday, however, we rested from our baking.

Forming Possessive Nouns

Examples of Forming Possessives			
Singular	**Singular Possessive**	**Plural**	**Plural Possessive**
video	video's	videos	videos'
child	child's	children	children's
hero	hero's	heroes	heroes'
man	man's	men	men's
goose	goose's	geese	geese's
person	person's	people	people's
key	key's	keys	keys'
tree	tree's	trees	trees'

Grammar Study Sheets

Colons

When to Use a Colon
After a salutation of a business letter. Dear Senator Lance:
Between a book title and subtitle. *Jesus Unmasked: The Truth Will Shock You* by Todd Friel
Before a series at the end of a sentence. The trip you have won will include the following: airline tickets, hotel accommodation, food vouchers, and guided tours.
Before a long or formal direct quotation if the quotation appears at the end of a sentence. The student quoted the words of Aristotle: "I count him braver who overcomes his desires than him who conquers his enemies; for the hardest victory is over self."
In Bible references and expressions of time. Ephesians 6:10 | 3:00 p.m.
Between two independent clauses not separated by a coordinating conjunction in which the second clause is an explanation of the first. The boys loved the idea of learning about creationism: they chose *Wonders of Creation* to read.

Prefix Study

Prefix	Meaning	Examples
ante-	before, preceding	antecedent, antechamber
anti-	opposite, against	antisocial, antidote
com-	with, jointly, completely	competent, committee
de-	down, away	deduct, descend
dis-	negation, removal, expulsion	disband, disadvantage
en-, em-	to cause to be; put or go into or onto	enable, embrace, encounter
hyper-	beyond; more than normal	hyperactive, hyperbole
in-, il-, im-, ir-	in, on, not	infallible, illegal, impolite
inter-	among, between, together	interview, interstate
multi-, poly-	many, much	multigrain, polytheist, multicolor
ob-	blocking, against, concealing	obstruct, obscene, obliterate
semi-	half	semicircle, semiannual
trans-	across, beyond, change, through	transcontinental, transmit

Grammar Study Sheets

Tricky Words

Then indicates a moment in time.	**Than** introduces the second element in a comparison.
Sit means to rest in an upright position.	**Set** means to put or place an object.
Rise means to get up or move upward.	**Raise** means to lift or move higher.
Can means to be able to do something.	**May** means to have permission to do something.
Bring means to move something toward a person or place.	**Take** means to move something away from a person or place.

Suffixes

Suffix	Meaning	Examples
-age	causing an action	postage, baggage, marriage
-al, -ial	related to, character of	formal, emotional, aerial
-an, -ian	belonging/relating to; able to be	electrician, Texan, veterinarian
-ant, -ent	belonging to; result of	absorbent, deodorant, contestant
-ary, -ery, -ory	group of, state or character of, connected with, involving, place for	archery, mandatory, legendary
-cede, -ceed, -sede	to give control, right, or power to	intercede, succeed, concede
-en	become, made of, resemble, to make	earthen, sweeten, fasten
-logy, -ology	science of or study of	biology, chronology, etymology
-ous, -eous, -ious	full of; having qualities of	righteous, vigorous, gracious
-tion, -ion, -sion, -ation, -ition	act, result, or state of	million, revelation, decision

Grammar Study Sheets

Irregular Verbs

Present Tense	Simple Past Tense	Past Participle	Present Tense	Simple Past Tense	Past Participle
arise	arose	arisen	fight	fought	fought
awake	awoke	awoken	fly	flew	flown
be	was/were	been	forget	forgot	forgotten
beat	beat	beaten	forgive	forgave	forgiven
become	became	become	go	went	gone
begin	began	begun	have	had	had
break	broke	broken	hold	held	held
bring	brought	brought	keep	kept	kept
build	built	built	know	knew	known
buy	bought	bought	lay	laid	laid
catch	caught	caught	lie	lay	lain
come	came	come	make	made	made
dig	dug	dug	meet	met	met
do	did	done	pay	paid	paid
draw	drew	drawn	ride	rode	ridden
drink	drank	drunk	ring	rang	rung
eat	ate	eaten	say	said	said
fall	fell	fallen	sing	sang	sung

Grammar Study Sheets

Hyphens

When to Use a Hyphen
Use hyphens to connect compound modifiers that appear before the noun they modify.
Melody wrote a *mind-bending* riddle that stumped her family.
Use hyphens in certain compound words. If unsure, consult a dictionary.
over-the-top, far-flung, well-to-do, short-term, officer-in-charge
Use a hyphen with spelled-out fractions and compound numbers from twenty-one to ninety-nine.
two-thirds, one-fifth, twenty-two, eighty-seven
Use a hyphen in words with the prefixes ex-, self-, all-, anti-, and mid-.
They interviewed the *ex-president*. College requires *self-discipline*. She was born in the *mid-1970s*.

Comma Usage

When to Use a Comma
1. After an introductory clause or phrase. *When Dad opened the oven, the smell of cookies wafted out.*
2. To separate independent clauses. *Alex went surfing with Jay, and he got a bad sunburn.*
3. To set off nonrestrictive clauses. *Nolan, who is amazing at baseball, is my brother's best friend.*
4. Between all items in a series. *The movie theater offered popcorn, candy, chips, and soda.*
5. To set off appositives. *Mary, the mother of Jesus, is mentioned many times in the Bible.*
6. To indicate direct address. *I love your dress, Millie. Millie, I love your dress.*
7. To set off direct quotations. *Trent said, "Mom, may I go with Ryan?"*
8. With dates, addresses, titles, and numbers. *May 27, 1975	Atlanta, GA	Eric Maddox, MD	12,000*

Grammar Study Sheets

Commonly Misused Words

	Commonly Misused Words
Affect/Effect	*Affect* is usually a verb. (The dog's barking *affected* my nap.)
	Effect is usually a noun. (I was thrilled with the *effect* our mission trip had.)
Assure/ Ensure/ Insure	*Assure* means to relate that something will happen or is true. (I *assure* you he will be coming soon.)
	Ensure means to guarantee. (The moms *ensured* the safety of the children.)
	Insure means to take out an insurance policy. (My dad *insured* both our cars.)
Complement/ Compliment	A *complement* completes something else. (The color of Liz's dress *complemented* her complexion.)
	A *compliment* is a nice thing to say. (Liz received many *compliments* on her dress.)
Farther/ Further	*Farther* refers to physical distance. (I walked *farther* than Susan.)
	Further refers to metaphorical distance. (Chance was *further* ahead in his studies than his sister.)
Lay/Lie:	To *lay* means to put or place. (Morgan will *lay* out the clothing for his trip.)
	Lie means to recline. (Morgan will *lie* down before packing for his trip.)
	Note: The past tense of *lay* is *laid*, and the past tense of *lie* is *lay*. (Morgan *laid* out his clothing. Morgan *lay* down for his nap.)

Communication Study Sheets

Biographies and Autobiographies

	Differences	
	Biography	**Autobiography**
Authorship	written by someone other than the subject	written by the person the book is about
Point of View	typically written in the third-person point of view (she, her, hers, he, him, his)	typically written in the first-person point of view (I, me, my)
Authorized/ Unauthorized	can be authorized (permission is given by the person the book is about) OR unauthorized (no permission given)	always authorized
Degree of Objectivity	tends to be more objective; the writer gathers research, reviews records, conducts interviews, verifies facts	tends to be less objective, as the author bases content on his or her memories and may be biased

	Similarities
Primary Purpose	The purpose of both is to give an account of the person's life.
Notable Subjects	The people whose stories are told in these forms tend to be those who are known for their accomplishments, and readers find them interesting.
Nonfiction	Both are works of nonfiction, as they represent real events.

Citing Sources

Essay text	In his book, *Unveiling the Kings of Israel*, David Down states, "We do not have to look far for evidence that the Flood happened" (Down 27).
Bibliography entry	Down, David. *Unveiling the Kings of Israel*. Master Books, 2012.

When using a book:	the book's title, the author's name, the publisher, the publication date, and the page number you are referencing
When using a website:	the author's name, the title of the article, the website name, the date of the article, and the URL (The URL is the information in the search bar when you are displaying the researched content. It can be copied and pasted into a word processor or recorded by hand in a notebook.)

Communication Study Sheets

	Citation Not Required
Common knowledge	Information widely available in reference works, such as dates and locations of historical events, biographical facts about famous people, or circumstances surrounding major historical events.
	The attack on Pearl Harbor occurred in Honolulu, Hawaii, on December 7, 1941.
Allusions	Alluding to a well-known passage to create an effect.
	My brother is the *Einstein* in the class. "*To be or not to be*" is the question I was asking!
Passing mentions	Mentioning an author or work in passing when you have not referred to any aspect of it specifically.
	My favorite storybook growing up was *The 10-Minute Bible Journey,* as it really helped me understand the Bible better.

	Three Ways to Incorporate Citable Material
Direct quote	Use the exact words of another person where it fits into your writing.
Paraphrase	Use your own words to retell the information yet include all the important details the source gives.
Summarize	Use your own words to condense a lengthy source so it fits with your topic and space.

Finding Items for Citations

	For a Book
Author	**The primary creator of the work you are citing.** If there is more than one author, record both names in your notes. The author's name is usually found near the title of the book.
Title	**The name of the book you are referencing.** Usually prominently displayed on the cover.
Publisher	**The entity responsible for producing the work.** The name of the publisher is often located on the title page or the copyright page.
Date	**The date this version of the work was published.** It is located on either the title page or the copyright page. Use the most recent date listed.
Location	**The actual page number or numbers you are referencing.**

Communication Study Sheets

For a Website	
Author	**The creator of the web article.** The author's name is usually located near the title. If no author is listed, skip this item and move on to the title.
Title of article	**The name of the article contained within the website.** It is usually in a prominent location.
Website name	**The exact name of the website you are referencing.**
Date of article	**The date the article was written.** If no date is listed, record the date you referenced it.
URL	**The address of any given resource on the Web.** At the top of your browser, click the address bar to select the entire URL. It can be copied into a word processing document or handwritten into your notes.

Compiling a Works Cited Page

Formatting a Works Cited Page in MLA Style
Authors are listed by last name first and placed in alphabetical order.
Books, magazines, and blogs are italicized.
Periods are used after the author's name, a book or article title, and at the very end of the citation.
Commas are used after the publisher, blog title, and any other elements, such as volume numbers.
All lines are double spaced, and any second lines in a single citation are indented ½ inch. Page margins should be one inch.
Dates are listed in the day, month, and year format (27 Oct. 2024). If no date is given for a web source, record the date you accessed the information (Accessed 10 Dec. 2023).
If a source has two authors, list them in alphabetical order separated by the word "and." Only the first author would be listed by last name. (Gabel, Sarah, and Kristen Pratt.)
The URL identifying a web source should be copied and pasted onto the works cited page. Omit the beginning of the URL that reads, "https://."

Figures of Speech

Figures of Speech	
Simile	compares two different things using the words *like* or *as*
	Last night I was so exhausted that I slept like a log.
Metaphor	compares two things without using the words *like* or *as*
	God will turn your heart of stone into a heart of flesh.
Personification	attributes human qualities to something nonhuman
	The wind was screaming in my face as I turned the corner.
Oxymoron	joins two opposite words to create a unique effect and is both true and false at the same time
	There is such sweet sorrow when a friend passes away.
Hyperbole	uses exaggeration for emphasis, effect, or impact and is not to be interpreted literally
	I am so hungry I could eat an elephant!

Communication Study Sheets

Incorporating Quotes, Paraphrases, and Summaries

	Incorporating Research from a Book in MLA Style
Direct Quote	**Use the exact words found in your research.** There are three ways to use a quote:
	1. A quote of four or fewer lines can be set off with quotation marks and included in a sentence. If the author's name is mentioned in the sentence, do not include it in parentheses at the end. If not mentioned, it must be included along with the page number in parentheses at the end of the quote.
	As LaHaye points out, "With his roots deeply entrenched in the Pennsylvania Quaker faith, John Dickinson was anything but a sectarian or unbeliever" (141).
	It is said of Dickinson, "With his roots deeply entrenched in the Pennsylvania Quaker faith, John Dickinson was anything but a sectarian or unbeliever" (LaHaye 141).
	2. A quote of four or more lines can be set in a block quotation apart from the text. The indent should be ½ inch from the left margin, and no quotation marks are needed.
	In his book *Faith of Our Founding Fathers*, Tim LaHaye states: Dickinson was an intellectual activist, yet he refused to sign the Declaration of Independence because no union of government was ready to take the place of the old. He did fight in the war, however, and was later recognized by both Delaware and Pennsylvania, where he served as president of the supreme Executive Council. He founded Dickinson College in Carlisle, Pennsylvania, in 1773. (141)
	3. A full or partial quote can be integrated into your own sentence using quotation marks. The parenthetical citation belongs directly after the quote.
	The idea that "Dickinson was anything but a sectarian or unbeliever" (LaHaye 141) has historical support.
Paraphrase	**Use your own words yet include all the important information the source gives.** Leave out what does not apply to the point you are trying to make.
	Original: "James McHenry was a refined gentleman who studied medicine under the famous Dr. Rush of Philadelphia (a dedicated Christian). He was an ardent patriot with a pronounced hostility toward England (quite typical of the Irish)" (LaHaye 154).
	Paraphrase: James McHenry was a gentleman who studied medicine under the famous Dr. Rush and was also a patriot with hostile feelings toward England (LaHaye 154).
Summary	**Use your own words to condense a lengthy source so it fits with your topic and space.**
	Original: "When war broke out, he volunteered and served with distinction on the medical staff under Washington and Lafayette. Fort McHenry, birthplace of our national anthem, was named in his honor. He said little during the Constitutional Convention, but his presence made Maryland's majority vote favor the strong federal government advocated by Washington, Madison, and Randolph" (LaHaye 154).
	Summary: McHenry volunteered on the medical staff under Washington and Lafayette, and Fort McHenry was named in his honor. Although he did not speak much during the Constitutional Convention, his presence was certainly felt regarding a strong federal government (LaHaye 154).

Communication Study Sheets

Incorporating Research from a Website in MLA Style

When citing a website, list the author's last name in parentheses. If no author is listed, use the article title. No page number or URL is required in-text. These items would only appear on the works cited page. If you use two separate articles written by the same author, both the author's name and article title should be included in the parenthetical citation.

> We do not need to find human and dinosaur tracks together to know that the Bible is true (Ham).

If you include the information's location in your sentence, you do *not* need to do a parenthetical citation, although you would still need the works cited entry.

> In his article "New Dinosaur Tracks Unearthed in Texas' Paluxy River," Ken Ham argues that we do not need to find human and dinosaur tracks in the same place to know the Bible is true.

Additional Notes on MLA Style

All pages in MLA style should be double spaced. If writing by hand, skip every other line.

All punctuation should be placed *after* the parenthetical citation unless it's a question mark or exclamation point that belongs to the quote *or* if using a block quote.

> *Example of question mark within the quoted words:* LaHaye reasons, "This leads a normal person to ask, 'Where did today's scholars get their information?' " (13).

> *Example of an exclamation point as a part of your sentence:* I was astonished to learn that "the religious history of America had been systematically stolen from our nation's texts" (LaHaye 9)!

The first time you refer to a source, use the author's full name. If you mention the source again, use only the person's last name.

> "Tim LaHaye writes …" The next mention would say, "LaHaye writes …"

If you want to add a word or words to a quotation, place brackets around the information you are adding to differentiate it from the person you are quoting.

> LaHaye points out, "Secularism is taught in those same textbooks [which is not surprising], a life and worldview for children and young people that little resembles the one taught in this nation for the first 150 years of its history" (9).

If you want to omit a word or words from a quotation, indicate the deleted information by using ellipses, which are three periods separated by spaces (…) with a space before and after.

> LaHaye points out, "Secularism is taught … a life and worldview … that little resembles the one taught in this nation for the first 150 years of its history" (9).

Communication Study Sheets

Biography Notes

	Signal Verbs
To introduce a fact/statement	states, writes, mentions, adds, points out, notes, comments, finds, observes, discusses, expresses, considers, explores, illustrates
To introduce a claim	claims, argues, posits, reasons, asserts, proposes
To introduce what the author focuses on or excludes	emphasizes, stresses, highlights, focuses on, centers their argument around, overlooks, ignores, downplays, omits, excludes

Topic Outline: Uses Words or Phrases

I. Quote by Washington	II. (Second paragraph topic)
a. Encapsulate lifelong effort	a. (supporting idea/fact)
b. Birthdate and place	b. (supporting idea/fact)
c. Major role in fight for freedom	c. (supporting idea/fact)
d. Quote by Reed from page 19	III. (Third paragraph topic)
e. Thesis statement	a. (supporting idea/fact) … and so on

Transitions

Transitional Words and Phrases Show:

Emphasis	Addition	Contrast	Order
Undoubtedly	Along with	Unlike	Following
Unquestionably	Apart from this	Nevertheless	At this time
Obviously	Moreover	On the other hand	Previously
Particularly/in particular	Furthermore	Nonetheless	First/firstly
Especially	Also	Despite/in spite of	Second/secondly
Clearly	Too	In contrast to	Third/thirdly
Importantly	As well as that	Contrary to	Finally
Absolutely	Besides	Alternatively	Subsequently
Definitely	In addition	Conversely	Above all
Without a doubt	Not only … but also	Even so	Before
Indeed	Additionally	Differing from	First and foremost

Anecdotes

Types of Anecdotes
- **Cautionary:** A tale that involves a character flaw or poor judgment and results in negative consequences. The point is to teach a lesson about what not to do. Examples are often seen in myths, parables, and fairy tales.
- **Humorous:** A funny story used to lighten the mood, create a short break in the main story, and entertain the reader. An example would be a short joke or making fun of a character in a way that adds to the enjoyment of the story.
- **Inspirational:** A persuasive or emotional appeal. This type aims to create a certain feeling in the reader by telling a story they can relate to and identify with. Often, political speeches and sermons will use these short stories to inspire the audience.
- **Characterizing:** A story that reveals more about the main character or side character's personality. It may not be part of the main story but gives a glimpse at certain virtues or attributes of the character. An example is the cherry tree story about George Washington.
- **Reminiscent:** A nostalgic story focused on the more distant past, especially on aspects of the world that have changed, creating a longing for the old days ("Back in my day …" OR "When I was a small child, society was different …").

Oral Presentation

Oral Presentation Tips
- In preparation, read through your autobiography several times so it is fresh in your memory.
- When presenting, introduce yourself and explain the assignment you have been given. A strong start to your presentation will make your audience want to hear more.
- Speak in a friendly, confident way, with enough volume in your voice for your audience to easily hear you. Make sure you choose an area with minimal distractions.
- Use hand gestures to avoid appearing "stiff" and change your facial expressions based on the content of your speech (*example:* an excited expression when sharing a thrilling anecdote, a downcast expression when sharing a difficult moment).
- Use visual aids such as a photo of yourself, a favorite childhood toy or book, artwork you created, something you built, etc.
- Conclude strongly. Make a good final impression by summing up your autobiography on a positive note with an optimistic look at your future.
- Thank your audience for listening. You may ask if they have any questions or comments.

Communication Study Sheets

Summarizing

Tips for Summarizing

1. Read through the text two or three times to make sure you have a solid understanding of the main ideas.
2. Create notes about the main ideas from memory using your own words.
3. Check what you have written against the original, making sure you have not strayed from the author's ideas.
4. Look for words or phrases that could be changed without altering the meaning of the original. Many "specialty" words will need to stay the same to convey the proper meaning.
5. The use of a dictionary or thesaurus is helpful for alternative word choices.

Formatting a Final Draft

Formatting a Final Draft (Typed)

- Set margins to 1 inch on all sides.
- Double space and use a 12-point Times New Roman font.
- Indent the first line of each paragraph 1 inch.
- Create a title page for the front of your essay that includes a title, your name, the name of the course, the assignment (Persuasive Essay), and the date. Center these items.
- Create a works cited page. Center the title, Works Cited, at the top. List resources in alphabetical order. Indent ½ inch for any lines after the first line in each reference. Single space entries. Use 1-inch margins.

Formatting a Final Draft (Handwritten)

- Skip every other line when writing.
- Indent approximately 1 inch for a new paragraph.
- Use your best handwriting.
- Create a title page and works cited page as detailed in the Formatting a Final Draft (Typed) chart. Use approximate measurements for indents and spacing.

Tips For Better Writing

Tips for Better Writing

- **Vary your sentence structure:** Use different sentence types and lengths to add interest. Consider opening a sentence with a prepositional phrase, a verb phrase, or an infinitive. (Days 77, 82, and 87)
- **Avoid repeating words:** Use synonyms (similar words) rather than using the same words excessively. Use a thesaurus for ideas. (Day 143)
- **Be engaging:** Avoid phrases or clichés like *once upon a time … when I was … at the end of the day … ignorance is bliss*, etc. Instead, be fresh in how you present your information and thoughts.
- **Use quality transitions:** When moving from one idea to another or beginning a new paragraph, use appropriate transitional words and phrases, such as *in addition to, besides, finally, because of, after that, furthermore, nevertheless, consequently, likewise, similarly*, etc.
- **Use vivid imagery:** Insert lively verbs, adjectives, and adverbs without being excessive. Make sure your use of words is appropriate within the context of your topic. A light and fun topic would use different imagery than a serious or "heavy" topic.
- **Stay focused:** Regularly look back at your thesis statement and make sure you are only writing thoughts that reinforce your main point. It is very easy to get off-topic as your mind wanders to different points.
- **Keep your voice interesting:** The way you come across to your reader through your choice of vocabulary, expression, point of view, and detail all make up your voice. Staying consistent in all these elements will make you more believable.
- **Use specific words:** Avoid using generic words like *that, things,* or *stuff*. Whenever possible, give specific details. (*Example of generic words: That* is some of the best *stuff* I have ever eaten. *Example of specific words: These chicken wings* are some of the best *restaurant food* I have ever consumed!)
- **Use accurate words:** Nothing will ruin your credibility more than the inaccurate use of words. If you are unsure if the word you have chosen is appropriate, take the time to look in a dictionary or thesaurus. (*Example of wrong word choice:* The man was *adverse* to attending a church. *Example of correct word choice:* The man was *averse* to attending church. Adverse = unfavorable, hazardous. Averse = opposed.)

Persuasion in Advertising

Modes of Persuasion in Advertising	
Ethos	The seller must convince the customer that they are trustworthy and knowledgeable.
Logos	The seller must attempt to back up their claim that their product is superior.
Pathos	The seller must appeal to emotions connected to their product.

Communication Study Sheets

Etiquette and the Five Aspects of Communication

Etiquette and the Five Aspects of Communication
Written Communication: Using written language to express information, ideas, and emotions.
Proper Etiquette: When writing through text, email, or handwritten letters, be courteous by greeting the person. Be clear and concise yet give the details you want to express. Think through what you are saying, considering how your audience will receive your words. Write only what you would be willing to say in person and have read to others.
Verbal Communication: Using spoken language to express information, ideas, and emotions.
Proper Etiquette: Maintain eye contact, giving the person complete attention. Refrain from interrupting and allow the person to express their thoughts. Respect others' time by being concise and not rambling on. Express yourself kindly with well-thought-out words. Speak loud enough to be heard but soft enough to avoid annoying others.
Nonverbal and Visual Communication: Using bodily expression or imagery to convey ideas.
Proper Etiquette: Convey interest and attention with your posture, without slumping or slouching, which makes you look disinterested. A smile and alert countenance show friendliness, while a furrowed brow or frown could express anger. Hand gestures can be used to accentuate a point, but overuse of them can be a distraction. It is not polite to stand too close to someone you are speaking to or in between people who are speaking to each other. Fidgeting, tapping, or shaking your leg incessantly can be distracting and show a lack of concern for those around you. We also communicate through imagery, such as graphics on our clothing, emojis, art, etc. These images we bear should always reflect respect for others and honor God.
Contextual Communication: Proper communication based on the audience or setting. This could be cultural, situational, personal, academic, professional, etc.
Proper Etiquette: Know your surroundings when it comes to communicating. You will communicate differently with a sibling than with a pastor or teacher. There are different levels of respect to be shown to adults in certain fields. What may be an acceptable conversation in a quick meeting on a sidewalk may not be appropriate at a funeral. When speaking with someone from another country or culture, be aware that something unoffensive to you may be offensive to them.
Active Listening: Effectively listening to summarize and restate what another has said.
Proper Etiquette: Give your full attention to the person speaking to you. This may mean minimizing distractions such as phones, TVs, earbuds, or even other people. Focus on their words instead of thinking about what you will say next. "Listen" for nonverbal communication, such as becoming teary-eyed (which may indicate strong emotion). Avoid jumping to conclusions about what another is sharing. Ask questions if you feel you may be misunderstanding or need further details. Paraphrase or restate to show you were listening. ("So you really felt afraid and alone when that happened …")

Assessments

Assessments

We have provided weekly reviews within the curriculum on Day 5 of each week. Each weekly review covers material from the Special Feature, Grammar & Punctuation, Communication, and Worldview Analysis sections. These reviews may be used as quizzes or tests for grading purposes. When completing the weekly review, students may be given access to the study sheets in the back of this book and/or use of the 3x5 index cards recommended for notetaking throughout the course.

Grading Options for This Course

It is always the option of an educator to assess student grades however he or she might deem best. For *Language Lessons,* the teacher may evaluate whether a student has mastered a particular skill or whether the student needs additional experience. A teacher may rank these on a five-point scale as follows:

Skill Mastered				Needs Experience
5 (equals an A)	4 (B)	3 (C)	2 (D)	1 (equals an F)

A — Student shows complete mastery of concepts with no errors.

B — Student shows mastery of concepts with minimal errors.

C — Student shows partial mastery of concepts. Review of some concepts is needed.

D — Student shows minimal understanding of concepts. Review is needed.

F — Student does not show understanding of concepts. Review is needed.

The rubrics on the following pages are included for assistance in grading each of the five essays and the oral presentation. These organizational charts can be very helpful in assessing student performance. Each essay has a slightly different rubric since the essay requirements vary. Most of the rubrics contain four categories, such as structure, expression, word choice, and grammar/punctuation. The student is encouraged to use the rubric while writing their essay and planning their oral presentation as a means of better understanding the standards they will be graded by.

This page intentionally left blank.

Historical Narrative Rubric

	Structure	Expression	Word Choice	Grammar & Punctuation
100%	Paragraphs include topic, supporting, and concluding sentences. Sentences are varied and engaging. The story stays focused on the historical figure and is complete. Plenty of detail given about the figure.	The writer's voice stays in the third person. Creates an interest level that makes the reader want to continue reading and feel emotionally drawn toward the historical figure. The writer has made the story unforgettable.	Great use of synonyms. Lively verbs, adjectives, and adverbs are used. Transition words help flow from one paragraph to another. Creative use of words. Great detail.	The grammar and punctuation are all correct, and words are spelled and used properly.
90%	Paragraphs have good form, and the writer stays focused on the same story. The figure is well presented with good detail.	The expression is understandable, stays in the third person, and the writer does a good job holding the reader's interest and presenting the figure.	Good use of synonyms, verbs, adjectives, and adverbs. Transition words are used, and there is enough detail to paint a mental picture.	There are a few minor errors in grammar, punctuation, or spelling.
80%	Paragraphs lack supporting details and could be more focused. The main point of the story still comes through, and the historical figure is presented satisfactorily.	The writer's voice wanders from the third-person perspective occasionally. Parts of the story come alive, but overall the expression is inconsistent.	Some good use of words, but the transitions from one thought to the next do not flow well. Not enough detail to paint a picture.	The narrative has several errors in grammar, punctuation, or spelling.
70%	Paragraphs are not well developed, and sentences are not varied. Not enough information is presented about the historical figure.	The voice does not stay in the third person and lacks an engaging style. The historical figure is not well presented.	There are some expressive words used, but the overall word choice is lacking in creativity.	Some of the errors cause confusion and ruin the flow of the story.
60%	Paragraphs are not designed well, and sentence structure is weak. The story feels incomplete.	The voice is weak and not believable. The reader does not get a sense of who the historical figure really is.	Lacks interesting words, repeats words, and has no transitional flow from one paragraph to another.	Many errors make the story confusing and difficult to read.

Reflective Essay Rubric

	Structure	**Expression**	**Word Choice**	**Grammar & Punctuation**
100%	Paragraphs include topic, supporting, and concluding sentences that are varied and engaging. Proper transitional words were used to link paragraphs. Topic clearly stated and thoroughly explored. Length requirement met.	The writer's voice stays in the first person and creates interest, making the reader want to continue. The subject is thoroughly reflected on with the use of emotion, humor, or opinion. Shows familiarity with confidence in subject matter. Includes plenty of detail.	Great use of synonyms, verbs, adjectives, and adverbs. Words conveyed emotion, humor, or opinion that the reader could relate to. Words used in context and correctly. Language appropriate for the subject matter presented.	The grammar and punctuation are mostly correct, and words are spelled and used properly.
90%	Paragraphs have good form, and transitions are smooth. Length requirement met. Topic stated and explored adequately.	The expression is understandable, stays in the first person, and is interesting. Subject is reflected on, showing familiarity and good detail.	Good use of synonyms, verbs, adjectives, and adverbs. Words conveyed the writer's opinions well and were used correctly in context.	There are a few minor errors in grammar, punctuation, or spelling.
80%	Paragraphs lack form and could be more focused. A lack of transitional words make the flow feel choppy. The topic is presented and discussed satisfactorily. Length requirement met.	The writer's voice wanders from the first person occasionally. The subject is adequately reflected on with sufficient detail, but not as thoroughly as it could be.	Some good use of words. Overall, lacks the detail needed to thoroughly reflect upon the subject and engage the reader. Some words out of context or not appropriate for subject matter.	The reflection has several errors in grammar, punctuation, or spelling.
70%	Paragraphs are not well developed, and sentences are not varied. Topic is unclear or not sufficiently presented. Insufficient length.	The voice does not stay in the first person and lacks an engaging style. Detail is lacking, so the subject is not thoroughly reflected upon.	There are some expressive words used, but the overall word choice is lacking in creativity. Writer's opinions fail to come through.	Some of the errors cause confusion and ruin the flow of the reflection.
60%	Paragraphs are not designed well, and sentence structure is weak. Topic is not clearly presented. Insufficient length.	The voice does not stay in the first person and is weak or not believable. The subject is not presented well, and little detail is given.	Lacks interesting words. Words used out of context. Language does not hold interest or reflect well on the subject.	Many errors make the reflection confusing and difficult to read.

Definition Essay Rubric

	Structure	Expression	Definition	Word Choice	Grammar & Punctuation
100%	Paragraphs include topic, supporting, and concluding sentences that are varied and engaging. Proper transitional words were used to link paragraphs. Topic or word clearly defined and thoroughly explored. Length requirement met.	The writer's expression creates interest, making the reader want to continue. Shows familiarity with confidence in the subject matter. Communicates using plenty of detail.	A clear initial definition is presented. An extended definition creates support for the thesis in a solid, logical way. Several points are given in support of the thesis. The reader may gain a deeper understanding of the word or phrase chosen.	Great use of synonyms, verbs, adjectives, and adverbs. Words conveyed emotion, humor, or opinion that the reader could relate to. Words used in context and correctly. Language appropriate for the subject matter presented.	The grammar and punctuation are mostly correct, and words are spelled and used properly.
90%	Paragraphs have good form, and transitions are smooth. Length requirement met. Topic defined and explored adequately.	The expression is understandable and is interesting. Shows familiarity with the topic and includes detail.	A clear initial definition is presented. An extended definition creates support for the thesis logically. The reader may gain a deeper understanding of the word or phrase chosen.	Good use of synonyms, verbs, adjectives, and adverbs. Words conveyed the writer's opinions well and were used correctly in context.	There are a few minor errors in grammar, punctuation, or spelling.
80%	Paragraphs lack form and could be more focused. A lack of transitional words make the flow feel choppy. The topic is presented and defined satisfactorily. Length requirement met.	The expression is understandable but not in an interesting way. Lacking the detail needed to create interest.	An initial definition is given, and an extended definition supports the thesis with a few points but feels as though it needs more support. The reader may have only been given a basic understanding of the topic.	Some good use of words. Overall, lacks the detail needed to thoroughly define the subject and engage the reader. Some words are out of context or not appropriate for subject matter.	The reflection has several errors in grammar, punctuation, or spelling.
70%	Paragraphs are not well developed, and sentences are not varied. Topic is unclear or not sufficiently defined. Insufficient length.	The expression is confusing and difficult to understand. The writer does not communicate familiarity with the subject. Detail is lacking.	The initial definition, extended definition, and thesis are all a bit unclear or not thorough enough. Not much support given for the topic. The reader may not have a clear understanding of the topic's definition.	There are some expressive words used, but the overall word choice is lacking in creativity. Writer's opinions fail to come through.	Some of the errors cause confusion and ruin the flow of the reflection.
60%	Paragraphs are not designed well, and sentence structure is weak. Topic is not clearly defined. Insufficient length.	The expression is confusing and difficult to understand. There is no familiarity with the subject. Detail is lacking.	The topic was not defined, and no clear thesis was presented.	Lacks interesting words. Words used out of context. Language does not hold interest or define the topic well.	Many errors make the reflection confusing and difficult to read.

Biography Rubric

	Structure	**Beginning**	**Details**	**Language & Source Use**	**Grammar, Punctuation, & Voice**
100%	Great paragraph construction. Sentences are varied and engaging. Transition words used to link paragraphs. Three research sources used and cited. Length requirement met. Information presented chronologically, causing the writing to flow well. Strong conclusion.	The biography opens with a strong "hook," grabbing the reader's attention. The opening paragraph creates interest and curiosity by presenting facts, quotes, or a literary device that makes the reader want to know more. Strong thesis statement.	Includes details of the subject's childhood, adulthood, education, influences, accomplishments, impact, etc., in a way that gives the reader a well-rounded view. Details presented in a creative way that enhances the story. Fitting anecdotes stay in line with thesis.	Two or more literary devices used well. Language is descriptive and interesting. Storytelling is engaging. Outside sources woven in through direct quotes, paraphrases, or summaries. Signal verbs are varied, and in-text citations are given. Personal opinion/insight given regarding the subject.	The grammar and punctuation are all correct, and words are spelled and used properly, making reading easy and enjoyable. Third-person perspective is maintained throughout, even when sharing personal insight.
90%	Paragraphs have good form, and transitions are smooth. Three research sources used and cited. Length requirement met. Presentation is chronological. Strong conclusion.	The biography opens with a "hook" that grabs attention. The opening paragraph creates interest, and the thesis statement is good.	Includes details about the subject, giving a well-rounded view. Details are presented well, and anecdotes make for a better understanding of the subject.	At least one literary device is used well. Language is interesting, and storytelling is engaging. Sources are used and cited, and some personal insight presented.	There are a few minor errors in grammar, punctuation, or spelling. Overall, these do not interfere with the ease of reading. Third-person perspective maintained.
80%	Paragraphs lack supporting details and could be more focused. Two research sources used and cited. Length requirement met. The story is understandable. Sufficient conclusion.	The biography opens with some interesting information and creates a little interest. The thesis statement is satisfactory.	Some details about the subject are shared, but there are gaps in the story, making it feel incomplete. Anecdotes are shared but stray from the main thesis.	At least one literary device is used well. Language is interesting, and storytelling is engaging. Sources are used and cited, and some personal insight is presented.	Several errors in grammar, punctuation, or spelling cause some confusion when reading. Occasionally moves out of third person.
70%	Paragraphs are not well developed, and sentences are not varied. Less than two research sources and not properly cited. Insufficient length. Information not presented well. Weak conclusion.	The biography opens with information that sparks little interest. The thesis statement is weak or confusing, causing the reader to wonder where the story is headed.	Lacking strong or interesting details about the subject's life. "Who" the subject is doesn't seem to stand out. Anecdotes from their life are weak or nonexistent.	No literary devices are used, and the language is lacking detail and interest. Outside sources are not incorporated well and lack proper citation. Personal insights are not shared.	Errors in grammar and punctuation cause confusion and ruin the flow of the story. Occasionally moves out of third person.
60%	Paragraphs are not designed well, and sentence structure is weak. No research sources. Insufficient length. Insufficient information presented. Weak conclusion.	The beginning of the biography lacks information and does not hook the reader. It leaves the reader unsure of what to expect.	Little detail is shared about the subject, so the biography is incomplete. No anecdotes are presented.	No literary devices are used, and the language is lacking detail and interest. Lacks any outside sources of information. Personal insights are not shared.	Many errors make the story confusing and difficult to follow logically. Third-person perspective not used.

Autobiography Rubric

	Structure	**Sequencing of Events**	**Word Choice**	**Grammar & Punctuation**
100%	Length requirement met, excellent paragraph structure, sentences are interesting and varied, transitional words are used to link thoughts. The writing is double-spaced, a cover sheet is included. The visual presentation is excellent.	Events are in chronological order, creating a great flow to the story. Anecdotes are shared in a way that adds to the overall theme presented. The autobiography is well laid out, making for an enjoyable and interesting read.	Lively verbs, adjectives, and adverbs are used. Imagery creates a visual picture. Figures of speech are incorporated. Enough detail is included to thoroughly understand memories shared. Creative language makes the story very enjoyable.	The grammar and punctuation is nearly perfect. Words are spelled and used properly.
90%	Length requirement met, good paragraph structure, good sentences, transitional words are used. The writing is double-spaced, cover sheet included. The visual presentation is good.	Events are in chronological order, creating a good flow to the story. Anecdotes add to the overall theme. The autobiography is well laid out and enjoyable to read.	Verbs, adjectives, and adverbs are used. Imagery creates a visual picture. At least one figure of speech is used. Details make memories understandable. Creative language makes the story interesting.	There are a few minor errors in grammar, punctuation, or spelling.
80%	Length requirement is nearly met. The paragraph structure is satisfactory. Transitions are often lacking, creating some confusion. No double-spacing, cover sheet is not very interesting. The visual presentation is satisfactory.	Events are not always in chronological order, causing some confusion. Anecdotes are shared but feel unrelated to the overall theme of the story. The layout is good and the story is followable.	Descriptive language and imagery are sometimes used, but overall the language lacks interest. Some parts lack enough detail for the memories shared to be clear. There is some creative language used.	The narrative has several errors in grammar, punctuation, or spelling.
70%	Length requirement is not met, paragraph structure is weak, transitions are lacking, no double-spacing, cover sheet is lacking. The visual presentation is sloppy.	Events are not in chronological order, causing a disjointed feeling. Anecdotes are not included and no obvious theme is presented. The layout causes the story to be uninteresting or confusing.	A lack of creative words and imagery causes the story to be uninteresting and confusing.	Some of the errors cause confusion and ruin the flow of the story.
60%	Length requirement not met, paragraph structure is poor, transitions are lacking, no double-spacing or cover sheet. The visual presentation is very poor.	Events lack chronological order. Anecdotes are not included or not relatable. No theme is present. The layout is poor, and the story is not interesting or understandable.	Little to no use of creative words. No visual pictures are created for the reader. The autobiography is not interesting or understandable.	Many errors make the story confusing and difficult to read.

Oral Presentation Rubric

	Introduction	Content	Delivery	Conclusion
100%	The speaker introduced themselves in a friendly and enthusiastic way. A brief explanation of the speech was given. The introduction got my attention, and I was very interested in hearing more.	The speech was focused on the student's life. The stories and ideas were supported with visual aids and examples. The speech was detailed and captivating.	The speaker was loud enough and spoke convincingly. Eye contact was maintained, and appropriate gestures and expressions were used. I greatly enjoyed listening to the speaker.	The ending was exciting and convincing. The main theme was restated enthusiastically with a positive look to the future. The presentation "wrapped up" well.
90%	The speaker introduced themselves in a friendly way. An explanation of the speech was given. The introduction got my attention.	The speech was focused on the student's life. The stories and ideas were supported with visual aids and examples. The speech was interesting.	The speaker was loud enough and spoke well. Eye contact was present but limited. Appropriate gestures were used. I enjoyed listening to the speaker.	The ending was convincing. The theme was restated with a positive look to the future. The presentation "wrapped up" well.
80%	The speaker introduced themselves and the speech, but lacked enthusiasm. I felt slightly concerned about the direction of the speech.	The speech was fairly focused on the student's life but veered off a few times. Not many visual aids or stories. It lacked detail.	The speaker was not quite loud enough and seemed intimidated. Some eye contact occurred. Gestures were limited. I felt a little uneasy listening.	The ending was slightly dull and lacked "punch." The theme was somewhat restated with no look to the future.
70%	The speaker did not introduce themselves or explain the speech and showed no enthusiasm. I was unclear what the speech would be about.	The speech was not very focused. Stories were not presented well. Lack of visual aids. Uninteresting.	The speaker was too soft-spoken to be heard well. Did not make eye contact or gestures. I was uncomfortable listening.	The ending was abrupt and failed to restate the theme with no mention of the future. It did not feel complete.
60%	The speaker gave no introduction of themselves or the speech. I was not very interested based on this introduction.	The speech lacked focus, stories, visual aids, and details.	The speaker was difficult to hear; did not make eye contact or gestures. It was difficult to listen to.	The ending was abrupt and made no connection to the theme. The speaker failed to "wrap it up."

Persuasive Rubric

	Structure	Ethos	Logos	Pathos	Grammar and Punctuation
100%	Great paragraph construction. Sentences are varied and engaging. Transition words used to link paragraphs. Two research sources used and cited. Length requirement met. Ideas are arranged in a logical way that causes the writing to flow well.	The writer's presentation is believable and credible due to excellent word choice and confident voice. The character (or spirit) of the writing instills confidence. A clear personal opinion is stated.	Strong evidence presented to back up opinion (claim). Main points are progressed through logically, ending with a powerful conclusion. Essay makes great logical sense.	Emotional appeal was made through experience and personal connection. Persuasive wording effectively "pulls at the heartstrings" in a way that makes the reader want to believe the claim.	The grammar and punctuation are mostly correct, and words are spelled and used properly.
90%	Paragraphs have good form and transitions are smooth. Two research sources used and cited. Length requirement met. Ideas are presented logically.	Presentation is believable and credible. A good choice of words creates a sense of confidence. A personal opinion is stated.	Evidence presented to back up opinion. Main points are progressed through logically, ending with a good conclusion.	Emotional appeal was made through experience and personal connection. Persuasive wording effectively "pulls at the heartstrings," making the reader want to believe.	There are a few minor errors in grammar, punctuation, or spelling.
80%	Paragraphs lack supporting details and could be more focused. Two research sources used and cited. Length requirement met. Ideas presented in an understandable way.	Portions of the writing are presented well, but there are inconsistencies that may lead the reader to question the writer's confidence and enthusiasm. Personal opinion is present but not very clear.	Evidence is presented but does not strongly back up opinion. Some points are not logically connected to the claim. The conclusion lacks power.	Emotional appeal was made but not in a very effective or balanced way. Either too much or too little personal connection.	Several errors in grammar, punctuation, or spelling.
70%	Paragraphs are not well developed and sentences are not varied. Less than two research sources. Not properly cited. Insufficient length. Ideas not presented well.	Presentation is not strong. A lack of confidence in voice and poor word choice. Personal opinion is weak or not clearly stated.	A lack of evidence to support claim creates a lack of credibility. The essay does not flow logically. The conclusion is weak.	Emotional appeal was not presented in a way that would pull the reader toward the claim.	Some of the errors cause confusion and ruin the flow of the argument.
60%	Paragraphs are not designed well and sentence structure is weak. No research sources. Insufficient length. No coherent ideas presented.	The presentation is weak. Poor word choice and lack of enthusiasm ruins credibility. No real opinion is stated.	No real evidence presented to back up claim. Writing is illogical and conclusion is lacking.	No emotional appeal was made.	Many errors make the argument confusing and difficult to follow logically.

This page intentionally left blank.

American Revolutionary War Leaders

Refer to this list as you read *Life of Washington*. It will help you keep in mind which side the military leaders are on. You may wish to cut out the bookmark, fold it, and use it as you read along.

American Revolutionary War Leaders

American Generals

Benedict Arnold*

Horatio Gates

Nathanael Greene

William Heath

Henry Knox

Charles Lee

Benjamin Lincoln

Daniel Morgan

Joseph Reed

Friedrich Wilhelm von Steuben

George Washington

Anthony Wayne

Colonel William Prescott

French Leaders on the side of the Americans

Francois Joseph Paul de Grasse

Jean Baptiste de Rochambeau

The Marquis de Lafayette

*Eventually became a traitor, joining the British.

American Revolutionary War Leaders

British Generals

Edward Braddock

John Burgoyne

Sir Guy Carleton

Henry Clinton

Charles Cornwallis

Thomas Gage

William Howe

Sir Banastre Tarleton

This page intentionally left blank.

Answer Key

Quarter 1

Lesson 1, Exercise 1, Day 1, Pages 19–20

1. A biography often includes the individual's place of birth, date of birth, educational background, religious beliefs, professional experience, areas of expertise, impactful life events, and major achievements.
2. Answers will vary. *Example:* As I approached the *convent*, a *friar* came to the front door to greet me.
3. Answers will vary. *Example:* My aunt Joanne has such a cheerful *disposition* that one can't help but be happy in her presence.

Lesson 1, Exercise 2, Day 2, Page 22

1. f
2. e
3. d
4. c
5. b
6. g
7. a
8. h

9. Answers will vary. *Example:* The determined farmer **cultivated** his land yearly. (*determined* is an adjective; *yearly* is an adverb)
10. Answers will vary. *Example:* Well, my bedroom carpet is blue, yet it cannot be seen since my clothing is covering it. (*Well* is an interjection, and *yet* is a conjunction.)
11. S
12. F
13. F
14. S

Lesson 1, Exercise 4, Day 4, Page 26

1. custom, hymn, devout, joyous, feeling, endeavoured, grateful, Ruler, protection, goodness, cheering
2. Answers will vary but could include: Similarities: Both had difficult journeys, both trusted God to see them through, both had trouble with their followers complaining. Differences: Columbus set foot on the land he hoped for, whereas Moses did not enter the Promised Land; Moses had direct encounters with the audible voice of God, but Columbus went by how he felt God was leading him.
3. Jesus Christ
4. Answer should include five of the following: Amerigo Vespucio [Vespucci], John Cabot, Captain (John) Smith, Lord Baltimore, Powhatan, Pocahontas, Rolfe, William Penn, King Charles, the Pilgrims.

Lesson 2, Exercise 2, Day 7, Pages 31–32

1. S
2. P
3. P
4. S
5. P

6. Answers will vary, but students should complete each sentence by showing what the subject did or is.
7. Answers will vary, but students should complete each sentence by showing who or what the action or state of being refers to.
8. "The waters to be crossed were high, and the snow to be waded through, was deep; but persevering resolutely, he arrived at Turtle Creek, where he was told by an Indian trader, that the French commander had died a short time before, and that the French troops had gone into winter quarters." (p. 26)
9. Answers will vary. *Examples:* dog, boy, house, etc.
10. Answers will vary. *Examples:* Greg, New Jersey, Christianity, British, etc.

Lesson 2, Exercise 3, Day 8, Page 34

1. Definitions will vary. *Example*: having, showing, or done with good judgment or sense
2. Definitions will vary. *Example*: the ability to persuade somebody to do or believe something

Language Lessons for a Living Education Level 10

Answer Key

Lesson 2, Exercise 4, Day 9, Pages 35–36

1. To obtain a desired indulgence
2. To escape a deserved punishment or reproof
3. "George Washington says it was so" (p. 20).
4. 10 years old
5. "While I regret the loss of my favourite, *I rejoice in my son, who always speaks the truth*" (p. 24).
6. rejoice, wrongdoing, rejoices, truth
7. To be actively employed
8. Proverbs 22:29 – A person skillful in work will stand before important people, not obscure people.

   Proverbs 16:3 – If a person commits their work to God, He will establish their plans.
9. To return a favor or respond to love
10. One of the adjutant generals of Virginia, with the rank of a major
11. "In this dangerous situation he was saved by the protecting hand of God, and enabled again to get on the raft" (p. 30).

Lesson 3, Exercise 1, Day 11, Pages 39–40

1. Answers will vary. *Example:* God has put His plan in place; the battle belongs to Him, and He will win the war. He will judge the hearts of all people before His throne. I must be quick to answer His call to salvation so I can avoid judgment. When I answer the call, I will be filled with joy.
2. Answers will vary. *Example:* Our happy *domestic* situation was certainly due to the blessing and guidance of *Providence*.
3. Answers should include two of the following definitions: to submit to or be forced to endure; to feel keenly, labor under; to put up with especially as inevitable or unavoidable; to allow especially by reason of indifference; to endure death, pain, or distress; to sustain loss or damage.

Lesson 3, Exercise 2, Day 12, Page 42

1. A fluffy white cat <u>sits</u> (AV) in my neighbor's window every time the sun <u>shines</u> (AV) through.
2. The rope <u>came</u> (LV) loose on the tree branch, and it <u>fell</u> (AV) to the ground with a thud.
3. If you don't <u>keep</u> (LV) calm, your heart will <u>beat</u> (AV) faster and faster.
4. The dinner <u>looked</u> (LV) amazing, and I <u>ate</u> (AV) it with a thankful heart!
5. Mandy <u>looked</u> (AV) through the car's moon roof at the night sky and <u>contemplated</u> (AV) the vastness of the universe.
6. Answers will vary. *Example:* The baby reached out and *felt* the toy dangling overhead.
7. Answers will vary. *Example:* The bird's feathers *felt* smooth to the touch.
8. watched
9. seemed
10. presentation
11. Wow!
12. science
13. she
14. very
15. and

Lesson 3, Exercise 3, Day 13, Page 44

1. Definitions will vary. *Example*: marked by kindness and courtesy[1]
2. Definitions will vary. *Example*: the condition of being sound in body, mind, or spirit[2]

Lesson 3, Exercise 4, Day 14, Pages 45–46

1. "... [T]he courage with which he had acted, and the favourable [favorable] terms he had obtained from so large a force ..." (p. 32).
2. "... [O]rders were received, that officers who had commissions from the king, should be placed above those belonging to the province, without regard to their rank. The feeling of what was due to him as an American, prevented Washington from submitting to this unjust regulation ..." (p. 34).
3. He heard "of the conduct of Washington as an officer, and of his reasons for giving up his commission ..." (p. 34).

---

[1] "Gracious." *Merriam-Webster.com Dictionary*, Merriam-Webster, merriam-webster.com/definition/gracious. Accessed Feb. 16, 2024.

[2] "Health." *Merriam-Webster.com Dictionary*, Merriam-Webster, merriam-webster.com/dictionary/health. Accessed Feb. 16, 2024.

Answer Key

4. "I expected every moment to see him fall;—his duty, his situation, exposed him to every danger; nothing but the superintending care of Providence could have saved him from the fate of all around him" (p. 38).

5. Answers will vary but must relate to Matthew 9:36, "When he saw the crowds, he had compassion for them, because they were harassed and helpless, like sheep without a shepherd."

6. Answers will vary but should include who the student would want to help and how with as much detail as possible.

7. actions, approbation, public, respect, praise, nearest, knew, loved

Lesson 4, Exercise 1, Day 16, Pages 49–50

1. a. He knows when I sit down.
   b. He knows when I rise.
   c. He knows my thoughts.
2. Verse 5: "You hem me in, behind and before, and lay your hand upon me."
3. infantry, stores

Lesson 4, Exercise 2, Day 17, Pages 51–52

1. Micah will be singing the national anthem at the baseball game this weekend.
2. The last brownie in the pan was eaten by my little brother.
3. My mother did call the doctor's office back.
4. I will be sorting through all these photos for hours!
5. I knew I should have gone with my sister on the camping trip.
6. You must believe in the Lord Jesus Christ to be saved, as there is no other way.
7. Isabella might have found the most important clue in the mystery!

Lesson 4, Exercise 4, Day 19, Pages 55–56

1. a. "The Americans had lost a great number of their young men in that war ..." (p. 46).
   b. They "had also contributed their full proportion of money for carrying it on ..." (p. 46).
2. Answers will vary, but students should point out the major reason each man gives to explain his viewpoints.
3. June 1st
4. Answers will vary. The author states, "No doubt many pious American hearts offered such a prayer, with humility and faith and their prayers were granted; for they never would have succeeded in defending their rights, unless the mighty hand of God had upheld and guided them" (p. 50–51).
5. "You can easily distinguish him when Congress goes to prayers—*Mr. Washington is the gentleman who kneels down*" (p. 51).
6. a. "... in defence [defense] of the freedom that is our birth-right ..." (p. 56)
   b. "... for the protection of our property ..." (p. 56)
   c. "... against violence actually offered ..." (p. 57)
7. Answers will vary but should include the following ideas: War is a sorrowful thing. There is "reason to lament that sad disposition of nature 'whence come wars and fightings,' and which can only be restrained by" wisdom from above. When "the hand of oppression ... bind[s] down the liberties ... of a nation," war is often necessary, and the "Ruler of events" can use war to bring about good (p. 59).
8. a. "The firmness of his temper ..." (p. 60)
   b. "... the dignity of his manners ..." (p. 60)
   c. "... the confidence which was felt in his integrity and patriotism ..." (p. 60)

Lesson 5, Exercise 1, Day 21, Page 59

1. His parents "lacked the funds from their candle-making business to pay for his formal education."
2. a. the Newton of his age
   b. Doctor Franklin
3. Answers will vary but should include Franklin's lack of formal (outside the home) education, his ability to teach himself, his drive to learn and create, etc. Students should describe their education and how it may compare.

Answer Key

Lesson 5, Exercise 2, Day 22, Pages 61–62

1. Answers will vary, but the sentence should include *had been laughing*.
2. Answers will vary, but the sentence should include *will fumble*.
3. Answers will vary, but the sentence should include *have scribbled*.
4. Answers will vary, but the sentence should include *will be flowing*.
5. Answers will vary, but the sentence should include *instructed*.
6. Apparently, Justin and Jamie are camping this weekend whether it rains or not.
7. Abigail unloads trucks at the local food pantry every Thursday afternoon.
8. I have been praying about which college to attend this fall, but I feel intimidated.
9. linking
10. action
11. linking
12. Janner could have eaten the entire pizza, but his self-control restrained him.
13. We were passionately singing our hearts out at the Christmas Eve service last night.
14. Amazingly, we will have been living in our home for 20 years this coming April.
15. Aunt Sue should be making the apple pies for the bake sale again this year.

Lesson 5, Exercise 3, Day 23, Pages 63–64

1. Answers will vary, but students should use vivid and interesting language to thoroughly describe an object, place, person, animal, etc. They should have included at least two of the five figures of speech presented in this lesson. The paragraph should include descriptions that appeal to some of the five senses: sight, sound, taste, smell, or touch.
2. Definitions will vary. *Example*: superior in kind, quality, or appearance[1]
3. Definitions will vary. *Example*: suitable, fitting[2]

Lesson 5, Exercise 4, Day 24, Pages 65–66

1. When "he could defend the helpless, or aid in obtaining justice for the oppressed" (p. 61).
2. "When any occurrence raised his anger, he resolutely endeavoured [endeavored] to restrain it, and thus obeyed the Scripture precept given to warm tempers, 'Be ye angry and sin not' " (p. 62).
3. Answers will vary but should be based on 1 Peter 3:15, "… but in your hearts honor Christ the Lord as holy, always being prepared to make a defense to anyone who asks you for a reason for the hope that is in you; yet do it with gentleness and respect." We need to show respect and gentleness to others, even if they do not believe in God or if they worship differently than we do. This is how we show the love of Christ and find the opportunity to share the truth of the gospel with them.
4. "Lord, it is nothing with thee to help, whether with many, or with them that have no power" (p. 67).
5. Many men had left his force, and he was always training new recruits. He needed "patience in his endeavour [endeavor] to have a regular force" (p. 67).
6. She states, "They were not, however, allowed by 'Him who ruleth the winds and the waves,' to succeed, for they were scattered by a violent storm …" (p. 68).
7. "When the war commenced, the Americans thought only of obtaining relief from the oppression of unjust laws; but when they heard that the English had hired foreign troops to assist in subduing them, and had engaged the tomahawk of the Indian against them, they began to think of an entire separation from England, and of declaring themselves to be independent people" (p. 69–70).

---

[1] "Fine." *Merriam-Webster.com Dictionary*, Merriam-Webster, https://www.merriam-webster.com/dictionary/fine. Accessed Mar. 1, 2024.
[2] "Becoming." *Merriam-Webster.com Dictionary*, Merriam-Webster, https://www.merriam-webster.com/dictionary/becoming. Accessed Mar. 1, 2024.

8. Answers will vary, but students should be able to relate the general feelings of modern-day Americans regarding the Founding Fathers and the Declaration of Independence. Distinctions can be made between personal feelings and those of the general population or media.
9. Answers will vary, but students should recognize that Washington did not act on his own and could not be bribed.
10. Wording will vary due to the Bible version chosen but should be similar to the following: "Do nothing from selfish ambition or conceit, but in humility count others more significant than yourselves. Let each of you look not only to his own interests, but also to the interests of others" (Philippians 2:3–4).
11. "On our part the war should be defensive; we should, on all occasions, avoid a general action; nor put any thing to the risk unless compelled by necessity, into which we ought never to be drawn" (p. 77).

Lesson 6, Exercise 1, Day 26, Page 70

1. convey, sundry, candour, imputation, presumption
2. Answers will vary but should be similar to: I will take some of the time I should be sleeping to share several kinds of important matters with Congress. I will be straightforward because that is how an honest man should be. I will share with a sense of freedom in giving useful information without causing anyone to charge me with wrongdoing based on their assumptions.

Lesson 6, Exercise 2, Day 27, Pages 71–72

1. The police officer easily spotted the criminal <u>who was frantically running through the alley in a vain attempt to escape</u>. [DP]
2. <u>Above the tops of trees</u>, I noticed a huge flock of geese approaching, likely wanting to land on the pond. [DP]
3. I have a lot of energy for my schoolwork today <u>since I slept like a log last night</u>! [DP]
4. <u>Unfortunately, we will need to miss church today</u> because four feet of snow fell in our region overnight. [IND]
5. Before I can go to the lake, <u>I really need to get my laundry done or I won't have anything to wear</u>. [IND]
6. My brother is <u>not only</u> my sibling, <u>but also</u> my best friend. [CL] [CL]
7. Fall is one of the most beautiful seasons of the year <u>and</u> I always try to soak up every minute of the beauty before winter sets in. [CD]
8. <u>Until</u> I experienced white water rafting for the first time, I had no idea the adventure I was missing out on. [SB]
9. <u>While</u> sunsets can be stunning, staring at the sun is very bad for your eyes. [SB]
10. The laws in the United States are based on a biblical worldview, <u>yet</u> so many in our country have turned their hearts away from biblical values. [CD]
11. Answers will vary. Refer to this lesson about clauses and check the conjunctions chart to be sure a subordinating conjunction was used along with an action verb.
12. Answers will vary. Check the conjunctions chart to be sure a correlative conjunction was used along with a helping verb.

Answer Key

Lesson 6, Exercise 4, Day 29, Pages 75–76

1. The enemy had taken possession of the city. The "time for which many of the soldiers had agreed to serve was almost spent, and he had but a faint expectation that others would soon be engaged in their places" (p. 77–78).
2. Washington's army was only about 3,000 men, "they were scantily armed, poorly clad, and many of them barefooted." The English army was over twice the number of the Americans, "well armed, well clad and fed, and in high spirits" (p. 79).
3. They "offered fervent and humble prayers to God, who suits his mercies to the necessities of all who honour [honor] him; and beneath the care which he has promised to those who put their trust in him, they slept soundly, though they were unsheltered" (p. 82).
4. Answers will vary, but students should describe a situation in which they needed wisdom beyond themselves and strength to act out what God was leading them to do.
5. "The bright close blaze became as a screening cloud between their enemies and them, while it was as a pillar of fire to light them in the silent preparations …" (p. 85).
6. pious father, children, devout thankfulness, clouds and the winds, Ruler, liberty
7. protecting shield of his Creator was again on every side, to preserve him from the weapons of destruction
8. He meant that God was taking special or distinctive care of Washington.
9. Answers will vary, but students should be able to point out that Congress saw God as the Divine Ruler who was sovereign over the affairs of mankind and that mankind was sinful and needed to pray and repent and seek God's favor.

Lesson 7, Exercise 1, Day 31, Page 80

1. Answers will vary. *Example*: The *sanguinary* events that plagued that period in history would have produced much sadness in the hearts of the people. (*sadness* is an abstract noun)
2. Answers will vary. *Example*: When *surmounting obstructions* in life, it helps to act wisely. (*wisely* is an adverb)

Lesson 7, Exercise 2, Day 32, Pages 81–82

1. subjunctive
2. imperative
3. subjunctive
4. indicative
5. indicative
6. imperative
7. setting, cast
8. most, beautiful, pink
9. sun, horizon, hue, clouds
10. was, was
11. over, on
12. and
13. Answers will vary. *Example*: I will get my grocery shopping done early, but I won't have time to make dinner. (*but* is a conjunction that connects the independent clauses; *grocery* is an adjective; *early* is an adverb)

Lesson 7, Exercise 3, Day 33, Page 84

1. Definitions will vary. *Example*: to prevent from doing, exhibiting, or expressing something[1]
2. Definitions will vary. *Example*: marked by steady dispassionate calmness and self-control[2]

Lesson 7, Exercise 4, Day 34, Pages 85–86

1. "… [H]e proved the patriotism of his feelings by lessening his own force to assist them" (p. 94).
2. "The real advantage of his countrymen, and not the acquirement of fame for himself, was the motive" (p. 94).
3. "… [A] skilful [skillful] retreat was all that the commander could effect, and for his management of this, he received the thanks of Congress" (p. 97).
4. Answers will vary, but students should reword all the important elements of the statement.

---

[1] "Restrain." *Merriam-Webster.com Dictionary*, Merriam-Webster, https://www.merriam-webster.com/dictionary/restrain. Accessed Mar. 1, 2024.
[2] "Cool." *Merriam-Webster.com Dictionary*, Merriam-Webster, https://www.merriam-webster.com/dictionary/cool. Accessed Mar. 1, 2024.

Answer Key

5. Answers will vary, but students should use the information on pages 98–99 to give a complete description of Lafayette's character and motives regarding America and its cause.

6. "… [A] house was soon in flames, which served as a signal to the enemy, who immediately entered the fort, and fired on the retreating troops, and then followed them and attacked them …" (p. 101).

7. Answers will vary, but students should be able to link disobedience with a negative consequence.

8. sanguinary, love, scenes, horror, human passions, struggle for liberty, encouraged, defence

9. Lydia Darrah

Lesson 8, Exercise 1, Day 36, Pages 89–90

1. a. heaven
   b. Sheol (the grave)
   c. wings of the morning
   d. uttermost parts of the sea

2. Wording will vary due to the Bible version chosen but should be similar to the following: "For I am sure that neither death nor life, nor angels nor rulers, nor things present nor things to come, nor powers, nor height nor depth, nor anything else in all creation, will be able to separate us from the love of God in Christ Jesus our Lord" (Romans 8:38–39).

3. Answers will vary. *Example*: In order to successfully finish the exhausting *campaign*, our depleted crew needed to form an *alliance*. (*exhausting* and *depleted* are adjectives)

4. Answers will vary. *Example*: *Busybodies* gather and point out other's faults without any concern for theirs. (*theirs* is a possessive pronoun)

5. Answers will vary. *Example*: George Washington was so respected that the idea of *mutiny* never crossed the mind of the soldiers. (*George Washington* is a proper noun)

Lesson 8, Exercise 2, Day 37, Pages 91–92

1. (Over the hill) and (beyond the next valley) lies a village known (for its cheesemaking).

2. The frightened kitten quickly climbed (up the tree) as the ferocious dog came (around the corner).

3. (Against all odds), the American patriots fought (for the cause) (of freedom) (with great determination).

4. I was hoping we would have time to stop (at the library) (after soccer practice).

5. (Because the forecasted storm) was looming, we cut short our picnic (at the park).

6. (According to the latest polls), fewer Americans are identifying themselves (with a church).

7. Not very many students (in my class) have ever traveled (outside the United States).

8. Sometimes (in the winter), our temperatures drop (below zero).

9. Answers will vary. Refer to the preposition chart.

10. Answers will vary. Refer to the preposition chart.

11. Answers will vary. Refer to the preposition chart.

12. Answers will vary. Refer to the preposition chart.

13. Reese left rehearsal early but was late for her doctor's appointment anyway.

14. We rarely cook broccoli since some family members dislike it.

15. Jonathan not only built his kids an amazing treehouse but also added a climbing net.

16. Answers will vary. The permanent linking verbs are *be, become,* and *seem.*

17. Answers will vary. The sensory linking verbs are *appear, feel, look, smell, sound,* and *taste.*

18. Answers will vary. The conditional linking verbs are *act, constitute, come, equal, fall, get, go, grow, keep, prove, remain, stay,* and *turn.*

Answer Key

Lesson 8, Exercise 4, Day 39, Pages 95–96

1. Imagery
2. Answers will vary, but students should point to the hope that we can have in Christ in the midst of suffering. Suffering can produce character, and character can produce hope. We also know that if we are in Christ, our earthly suffering will pale in comparison to the glory we will experience someday. While this doesn't eliminate suffering, it helps us to endure it.
3. Answers will vary, but students should detail these two contrasting scenes and share their opinion regarding the author fast-forwarding to the second scene.
4. possible, hardships, cheer, prospects, calm, confidence, better days
5. Reed was saying that no amount of money would entice him to submit to the king and turn his back on his country's mission.
6. "My enemies take an ungenerous advantage of me. They know I cannot combat their insinuations, however injurious, without disclosing secrets it is of the utmost importance to conceal" (p. 117).
7. Answers will vary, but students should share details about Washington's need for prayer and the example Jesus gives us for going away to a lonely place to spend time with the Father.

Lesson 9, Exercise 1, Day 41, Pages 99–100

1. Answers should include four of the following: his mother, grandmother, father, his tutors, William Bradford, Samuel Stanhope Smith.
2. Answers will vary, but students should be able to point out four specific people who have been influential in their lives.
3. Answers will vary. *Example*: The brutal attack by the *infidels* resulting in the *banishment* of the people was devastating, yet they held together as a community. (*yet* is a conjunction)
4. hostilities, imminent
5. Answers will vary, but make sure students have used at least one vocabulary word per sentence and have written at least five sentences.

Lesson 9, Exercise 2, Day 42, Pages 101–102

1. The government sold the building.
2. The class was taken to the museum by my teacher.
3. Answers will vary. *Example*: The maintenance crew cut down the giant oak tree in the park.
4. passive
5. passive
6. active
7. passive
8. active
9. active
10. **Simple:** I jumped, I jump, I will jump

    Perfect: I had jumped, I have jumped, I will have jumped

    Continuous: I was jumping, I am jumping, I will be jumping

    Perfect Continuous: I had been jumping, I have been jumping, I will have been jumping

Lesson 9, Exercise 3, Day 43, Page 104

1. Definitions will vary. *Example*: characterized by wisdom; marked by deep understanding, keen discernment, and a capacity for sound judgment[1]
2. Definitions will vary. *Example*: the ability to learn or understand or to deal with new or trying situations[2]
3. Answers will vary but should point to a person's conduct as a way of knowing if they are wise or foolish. James 3:13 reads, "Who is wise and understanding among you? By his good conduct let him show his works in the meekness of wisdom."

---

[1] "Wise." *Merriam-Webster.com Dictionary*, Merriam-Webster, https://www.merriam-webster.com/dictionary/wise. Accessed Mar. 1, 2024.
[2] "Intelligence." *Merriam-Webster.com Dictionary*, Merriam-Webster, https://www.merriam-webster.com/dictionary/intelligence. Accessed Mar. 1, 2024.

Lesson 9, Exercise 4, Day 44, Pages 105–106

1. Providence, conspicuous, infidel, faith, wicked, gratitude
2. Answers will vary, but students should point to the many times God granted Washington wisdom and protection. There were also miraculous weather events, timing in battle situations, and great odds overcome.
3. Answers will vary, but students should recognize Reed's unbiased view, pointing out that she acknowledges that both sides were acting violently and not placing all the blame on one side or people group.
4. Wording will vary due to the Bible version chosen but should be similar to the following: "Pay to all what is owed to them: taxes to whom taxes are owed, revenue to whom revenue is owed, respect to whom respect is owed, honor to whom honor is owed" (Romans 13:7).
5. Answers will vary, but students should point out the major elements of the general order found on pages 129–130 of *Life of Washington*.
6. Answers will vary, but students should give reasons for what their decision would be if they were in this situation and explain their feelings regarding that decision.
7. Answers will vary, but students should show an understanding of the words *distress* and *vexation* and apply their meanings to the question. They should give an opinion on Washington's feelings regarding the troop's conditions.

Quarter 2

Lesson 10, Exercise 1, Day 46, Page 109

1. Answers will vary, but students should condense the biography excerpt of Alexander Hamilton in a way that communicates the main points without copying the original text.

Lesson 10, Exercise 2, Day 47, Page 112

1. My friend Rachel asked, "Will your family be at the homeschool picnic this Saturday?"
2. Just as I was falling asleep, my mom questioned, "Did you finish the dishes?"
3. "Look out!" yelled my dad as the ball whipped past my head.
4. The word "see" could refer to a person's eyesight or to the act of understanding a concept.
5. The chapter "Relevant for Today" contained a lot of interesting information.
6. Answers will vary. *Example*: How many times have I heard her say, "I love you to the moon and back"?
7. Answers will vary. *Example*: I guess I need to leave this one to the "professionals."
8. Answers will vary. *Example*: Ever since I was little, the song "Jesus Loves Me" has been special to me.
9. Be careful playing (in the backyard) because ticks are hiding (under the leaves).
10. (In view) (of the circumstances), let's wait (until Monday).
11. (With no clear-cut directions), assembling the desk was difficult.
12. b. under the bridge
13. b. beside the trees
14. c. For over ten years,

Answer Key

Lesson 10, Exercise 4, Day 49, Pages 115–116

1. Answers will vary, but students should answer based on their response to the use of foreshadowing and its effectiveness.
2. bodily strength, integrity, feeble, hardships, bravery, indulgence, coward, temptations, vice
3. Answers will vary but should be a well-thought-out response to the narrow way versus the broad way and should address the sin nature as the reason why people are drawn down the wrong path.
4. Answers will vary but should be based on the following verses: "But each person is tempted when he is lured and enticed by his own desire. Then desire when it has conceived gives birth to sin, and sin when it is fully grown brings forth death."
5. "But the foundation of those principles was a wrong one; they were placed on what he considered to be the duty he owed to men, and not on that which he owed to God" (p. 144–145).
6. felt for the sad and disgraceful close of life to which this young officer was brought by his departure from the path of rectitude
7. unbounded, wonderful, trifling, directed, by chance, by accident, secret, Divine, smallest, greatest

Lesson 11, Exercise 1, Day 51, Page 120

1. Answers will vary. *Example*: Captain Johnson *discharged* his *musket* in the direction of the approaching enemy. (*Captain Johnson* is a proper noun)
2. Answers will vary. *Example*: The well-prepared *mountaineers* packed many provisions for the long journey, including several *powder horns*. (*well-prepared*, *many*, *long*, and *several* are all adjectives)
3. Answers will vary. *Example*: The general quickly glanced at the *mutineer* with *scorn* in his eyes. (*quickly* is an adverb)

Lesson 11, Exercise 2, Day 52, Page 121

1. simple
2. complex
3. compound

Lesson 11, Exercise 3, Day 53, Page 124

1. Definitions will vary. *Example*: a person who lacks judgment or prudence[1]
2. Definitions will vary. *Example*: a view, judgment, or appraisal formed in the mind about a particular matter[2]

Lesson 11, Exercise 4, Day 54, Pages 125–126

1. He "gave orders that all persons who were found opposing the authority of the king of England, should have their property destroyed, and be treated with the greatest severity" (p. 155).
2. "They sometimes concealed themselves in swamps and wood thickets, from which they rushed out when any opportunity occurred for an attack on the enemies of their country; or when they could defend the helpless families from which those foes were forcing provisions" (p. 157).
3. Answers will vary but should include the following information: They cooked sweet potatoes in ashes, blew the ashes off with their breath, and wiped the potatoes with their clothing. They then sat on a log and ate the potatoes on plates made of bark.
4. "I would rather fight to obtain the blessing of freedom for my country, and feed on roots, than desert the cause, and gain by doing so, all the luxuries that Solomon owned" (p. 158).
5. pay, without clothes, roots, liberty, chance
6. He left "in haste and disorder, leaving nearly two hundred men killed or wounded on the field" (p. 160).
7. "For such was the spirit which animated men who were struggling for freedom that no desertion was feared. They came forth for the defence [defense] of their houses and families, and were ready to return whenever their services were needed" (p. 160).
8. He "wounded the officer with a pistol, and thus saved Colonel Washington, who was engaged defending himself against Tarlton ..." (p. 163).
9. power, disposed, cannot control, determination, not

---

[1] "Fool." *Merriam-Webster.com Dictionary*, Merriam-Webster, https://www.merriam-webster.com/dictionary/fool. Accessed Mar. 6, 2024.
[2] "Opinion." *Merriam-Webster.com Dictionary*, Merriam-Webster, https://www.merriam-webster.com/dictionary/opinion. Accessed Mar. 6, 2024.

Answer Key

10. "… [F]or he was constantly practising [practicing] some severity, either in destroying the property of the faithful Americans, or in punishing them whenever he had an opportunity" (p. 169).

11. Answers will vary but should be similar to: The young man was "taken prisoner, and Tarlton ordered him to be immediately hung by the road side" as an example to others. They placed a sign on his body that read, "such shall be the fate of whoever presumes to cut him down." His brave sister "watched for a time when no one was near" and took the body of her brother and gave him a burial (p. 170).

Lesson 12, Exercise 2, Day 57, Pages 131–132

1. An ice-cold blueberry smoothie on a hot summer afternoon quenches my thirst like nothing else.
2. The smell of sizzling bacon wafted through the entire campground early in the chilly morning.
3. My favorite school subjects are American history, British literature, and creative writing.
4. Yesterday, my pet iguana escaped from its cage and got lost in my bedroom!
5. I crept through the garage quietly, trying not to scare the sleeping dog.
6. I only forget to do my laundry occasionally.
7. After we get the pool cleaned out, we will be able to properly winterize it.
8. The football player, whose contract expired in March, contacted his agent for advice. ADJ
9. While not everybody loves to cook, most people can at least make themselves a sandwich. ADV
10. Alex knew that racing against Jake would not be an easy win. N
11. Once he saw the ball headed his way, he instantly jumped to his feet and ran toward it. ADV
12. Whether I should go on the missions trip to Europe has become a big question in my house. N

Lesson 12, Exercise 4, Day 59, Pages 135–136

1. Because Washington "represented their sufferings so feelingly …" (p. 173).
2. Because Lafayette "moved with so much judgment and quickness …" (p. 175).
3. Answers will vary, but students should discuss Washington's willingness to lose all his possessions rather than bend to the wishes of the enemy and give them a foothold. The author wants the reader to see Washington's commitment, dedication, and self-sacrifice.
4. "… [H]e could trust that the cheering beams of Divine favour [favor] would disperse those clouds, and he became more animated and courageous as others became sad and fearful" (p. 178–179).
5. Answers will vary but should include the following information: He observed Washington controlling his hasty temper. Washington "was as calm as if nothing had occurred to disturb him, and began immediately to form a new plan, without wasting the important moments in useless regrets" (p. 180).
6. "The sacrifice of my property is nothing; and I shall view its destruction with delight, if it shall in any degree contribute to the good of my country" (p. 183).

Lesson 13, Exercise 1, Day 61, Page 140

1. Answers will vary. *Example*: The *eminent* doctor was shocked at the *ingratitude* expressed by the people he was helping. (*at the ingratitude* and *by the people* are both prepositional phrases)
2. Answers will vary. *Example*: The *solemn* procession was moving slowly past the courthouse, knowing their *posterity* would feel the consequences of these mournful events. (*was* is used as a helping verb, assisting the main verb *moving*)

Language Lessons for a Living Education Level 10

Answer Key

Lesson 13, Exercise 2, Day 62, Pages 141–142

1. Next Wednesday, which happens to be the first day of the month, is the day I plan to start my new workout routine.
2. The Constitution describes the executive, legislative, and judicial branches of our government.
3. The church picnic was over, but no one felt like leaving.
4. Behind the parking lot at the school, the teachers set up the field day events.
5. Yesterday was our first day of school, so my mother took us out to the library and then out to lunch.
6. Well, let's just hope for the best in every situation.
7. Usually I wake up early on Sunday mornings, but today I overslept and was late for church!
8. Communicating well helps our relationship with family, our interactions with friends, and our prayer life with the Lord.
9. Mount Everest, the world's tallest mountain, can fit inside the Mariana Trench, the deepest part of the ocean.
10. Answers will vary. *Example*: I left my sweater, which was a gift from my aunt, in the shopping cart at the grocery store.
11. Answers will vary. *Example*: The flowers bloomed, the grass grew, and the trees budded.
12. Answers will vary. *Example*: To put it simply, I really need more time to practice before I am able to teach someone else.
13. The light rain was falling from the gray sky so gently that one could barely notice it.
14. The rough tree bark snagged my favorite green sweater as I walked by.
15. A beam of soft moonlight fell onto my bed through the tiny slit in my curtains.
16. The crisp autumn sky was ablaze with magnificent color, and a chill filled the frosty air.

Lesson 13, Exercise 3, Day 63, Page 144

1. Definitions will vary. *Example*: to damage irreparably; to subject to frustration, failure, or disaster[1]
2. Definitions will vary. *Example*: something by which one is entangled, involved in difficulties, or impeded[2]
3. "A fool's lips walk into a fight, and his mouth invites a beating."
4. "A fool's mouth is his ruin, and his lips are a snare to his soul."

Lesson 13, Exercise 4, Day 64, Pages 145–146

1. "My brave fellows, let no sensation of satisfaction for the triumph you have gained, induce you to insult a fallen enemy;—let no shouting—no clamourous [clamorous] huzzaing, increase their mortification. It is a sufficient satisfaction to us, that we witness their humiliation. Posterity will huzza for us!" (p. 189).
2. Answers will vary, but students should be able to state Jesus' call for us to love in return for hate and pray for our abusers rather than react to abuse with abuse. It is about trusting God to avenge us. However, self-defense is appropriate at times.
3. Congress issued a proclamation for "religiously observing through the United States the 13th day of December, as a day of thanksgiving and prayer" (p. 190).
4. Answers will vary, but students should be able to list specific details about Mrs. Washington's commitment to raising her son in virtue and her trust in his character as an adult. Students should be able to point to Washington's commitment to staying in touch with his mother and his concern for her welfare and feelings. He had always remained simply her son, as they rarely ever spoke of his renown.
5. officers, sufferers, poverty, wretchedness, contempt, remnant, charity, ingratitude, imbitter, future life

---

[1] "Ruin." *Merriam-Webster.com Dictionary*, Merriam-Webster, https://www.merriam-webster.com/dictionary/ruin. Accessed Mar. 6, 2024.
[2] "Snare." *Merriam-Webster.com Dictionary*, Merriam-Webster, https://www.merriam-webster.com/dictionary/snare. Accessed Mar. 6, 2024.

Answer Key

6. "[R]emember, young man, never in future to make a promise, even of a trivial kind, the nature and extent of which you have not duly considered; having made it, let nothing prevent a punctual performance of it, if it be within your power" (p. 202).

Lesson 14, Exercise 1, Day 66, Pages 149–150

1. Answers will vary but should include eight of the following: Bassett "is a man of plain sense," "has modesty enough to hold his tongue," "is a gentlemanly man," "is in high estimation among the Methodists," "freed his slaves and then employed them as hired labor," "is best remembered for his contributions to the life of his chosen church, his generosity toward what he saw as the work of God," had "deep commitment to Christ and His church," "contributed half the cost for building the First Methodist Church in Dover."
2. diffidence, arduous, superseded, rectitude, patronage, sanguine, interposition, Providence

Lesson 14, Exercise 2, Day 67, Page 152

1. The basket contained two chocolate muffins and a large tin of gourmet coffee.
2. I bought a birthday gift for my best friend at the Polish pottery shop in the nearby village.
3. This book has been the best source of encouragement for homeschool families!
4. A biblical worldview is essential to maintaining one's walk with Christ.
5. Answers will vary. *Example*: The British authorities found the man guilty. (*British* is a proper adjective; *the* is a limiting adjective.)
6. Answers will vary. *Example*: The two orange cats fought in the alley. (*Two* and *orange* work together as coordinate adjectives and do not require a comma.)
7. Answers will vary. *Example*: The short-handed staff worked as hard as possible. (*short-handed* is a compound adjective that needs a hyphen since it comes before the noun it modifies.)
8. Answers will vary. *Example*: Whose new Bible was left on the park bench? (*Whose* is an interrogative adjective; *new* and *park* are descriptive adjectives.)

Lesson 14, Exercise 3, Day 68, Page 154

1. Burgess, Stuart, and Andy McIntosh. *Wonders of Creation: Design in a Fallen World*. New Leaf Publishing Group, LLC, 2018.

   Froede, Carl, Jr. *Geology by Design: Interpreting Rocks and Their Catastrophic Record*. New Leaf Publishing Group, LLC, 2017.

   Ham, Ken. "Did an Empire Rule North America Before Europeans Arrived?" Ken Ham Blog, 17 Oct. 2023. answersingenesis.org/blogs/ken-ham/2023/10/17/did-empire-rule-north-america-before-europeans/.

Lesson 14, Exercise 4, Day 69, Pages 155–156

1. "The regularity and minuteness with which he had kept an account of every sum received and expended during eight years, and the faithfulness with which he had, in the midst of his many employments, attended to having the public money used in the most economical and advantageous manner …" (p. 204).
2. "… [T]o the protection of Almighty God, and those who have the superintendence of them to his holy keeping" (p. 205).
3. private citizen, vine, fig-tree, camp, public life, employments, myself, solitary, paths, private life, satisfaction
4. Answers will vary, but students should form a complete paragraph, possibly pointing out some of Washington's feelings toward England, his worldview regarding God's providence, his ability to walk in humility and understanding toward his fellow human beings, and his understanding that England had "devoted their lives to the promotion of the temporal and eternal interests of their fellow beings" (p. 208).
5. "… [T]he tenderest ties of nature were disregarded,—the truths of religion were denied, and the worship of God abolished" (p. 211).
6. Answers will vary, but students should have summarized Reed's direct address to her readers from page 211 of *Life of Washington*.

Language Lessons for a Living Education Level 10

Answer Key

Lesson 15, Exercise 2, Day 72, Page 162

1. The hungry lion ravenously attacked his fresh kill.
2. At Thanksgiving dinner, Aaron ate the pumpkin pie rather greedily.
3. Every child at the piano recital completed their piece beautifully.
4. You need to play outside.
5. I am very excited about this flight to Europe!
6. How do you plan to finish that entire puzzle by yourself?
7. Consequently, there was not enough paint left over to paint the shed.
8. Answers will vary. *Example*: Yesterday, we really enjoyed a walk in the park outside of town. We had never done this before. Young children happily played on the swings, mothers busily chatted on the benches, and older couples slowly strolled along the winding path. It was very pleasant. I really hope we do this often!

Lesson 15, Exercise 3, Day 73, Page 164

1. Definitions will vary. *Example*: lack of good sense or normal prudence and foresight[1]
2. Definitions will vary. *Example*: a condition of humiliating disgrace or disrepute[2]

Lesson 15, Exercise 4, Day 74, Pages 165–166

1. "About ten o'clock I bade adieu to Mount Vernon, to private life, and to domestic felicity, and with a mind oppressed with more anxious and painful sensations than I have words to express, set out for New York,—with the best dispositions to render service to my country in obedience to its call, but with less hope of answering its expectations" (p. 219).
2. ornament, model, improver, friend, protector, benefactor

---

[1] "Folly." *Merriam-Webster.com Dictionary*, Merriam-Webster, https://www.merriam-webster.com/dictionary/folly. Accessed Mar. 8, 2024.
[2] "Shame." *Merriam-Webster.com Dictionary*, Merriam-Webster, https://www.merriam-webster.com/dictionary/shame. Accessed Mar. 8, 2024.

3. Humility
4. "… [A] shout of joy burst from many thousands of grateful and affectionate hearts" (p. 222).
5. "Every step by which they have advanced to the character of an independent nation, seems to have been distinguished by some token of providential agency" (p. 223).
6. a. Everyone needed to account for the money they spent every week (p. 224).
   b. The Sabbath must be kept holy (p. 224).
   c. Everyone needed to be punctual (p. 225).
7. Washington stated that the standard in his home was punctuality. They were going to start on time whether the company was there or not.
8. "He earnestly recommended to Congress to endeavour [endeavor] to form treaties with the Indians" (p. 229). He gathered an army to help defend the frontier against attack and continued to try and form peace treaties (p. 229–231).
9. "… [T]he rich blessing of peace …" (p. 233).
10. "… [T]he Americans increased their trade, and sent large portions of their full harvests to different parts of the world" (p. 233).

Lesson 16, Exercise 1, Day 76, Page 170

1. Answers will vary. *Example*: To firmly establish his authority, the commander *quelled* the *insurrection* with firmness. (*To firmly establish his authority* is an infinitive phrase used to tell why the commander quelled the insurrection.)
2. clamour, unremitted zeal
3. omit, arbiter

Lesson 16, Exercise 2, Day 77, Pages 171–172

1. The first chapter is the very best chapter (in the book). chapter
2. The house (by the field) has been abandoned. house
3. A large black cat (with white paws) keeps sneaking around. cat
4. I can run extremely fast (in my new soccer cleats). run
5. We will tour Alaska (by plane). tour

Answer Key

6. The snake slithered (around the tree). slithered
7. Answers will vary. *Example*: with the wooden cane
8. Answers will vary. *Example*: beside the river
9. Answers will vary. *Example*: on this table
10. Answers will vary. *Example*: with sheer joy
11. Answers will vary. *Example*: in the Bible
12. Answers will vary. *Example*: across the entire lake
13. c
14. h
15. d
16. e
17. b
18. i
19. f
20. a
21. g

Lesson 16, Exercise 4, Day 79, Pages 175–176

1. Strong drink
2. Metaphor
3. They refused to pay a tax on spirits (alcohol) and "treated with violence those who were appointed to collect" the tax (p. 235).
4. a. "The British government had not given up their posts on the south side of the lakes …" (p. 236).
   b. "… [T]he American government had violated the treaty … which had prevented English subjects from recovering debts due to them …" (p. 236).
5. Blessed, peacemakers, sons of God
6. Answers will vary, but students should point out Washington's desire for peace, his concern for the welfare and happiness of the Indians, and his wish that Americans treat the Indians "with kindness and liberality" (p. 237).
7. Answers will vary, but students should point to the loyalty, bravery, and dedication the men showed in trying to free their friend with little to no regard for their own safety. The judge is saying he would like to have friends willing to do that for him.
8. He was elected "vice-president of the American Sunday School Union" (p. 249).
9. He said that most confessed "their career of wickedness [began] by a neglect of the duties of the Sabbath, and a vicious conduct on that day" (p. 250).

Lesson 17, Exercise 1, Day 81, Page 179

1. a. "They speak against you with malicious intent."
   b. They "take your name in vain."
   c. They "hate you."
   d. They "rise up against you."

Lesson 17, Exercise 2, Day 82, Pages 181–182

1. laughing
2. laughed
3. created
4. having created
5. submerging
6. having submerged
7. The (students) sitting by the stage are awaiting their turn to receive their diplomas. present
8. Drenched by the unforeseen thunderstorm, the (hikers) sought shelter under the entrance to a cave. past
9. My (mother), having worked all day in the garden, slumped into her favorite chair and asked for a glass of water. perfect
10. My sister really enjoys reading for hours every day. gerund
11. Having said all that I could to explain my point, I needed to leave the conclusions to those around me. perfect
12. Excited about our trip out West, I worked diligently to book all our overnight stays ahead of time. past
13. Sewing my own clothing has always been something I've longed to learn how to do. gerund
14. Leaning on the shovel, the construction worker sipped some ice water. present

Lesson 17, Exercise 3, Day 83, Page 184

1. Definitions will vary. *Example*: recommendation regarding a decision or course of conduct[1]
2. Definitions will vary. *Example*: the action, practice, or profession of teaching[2]

---

[1] "Advice." *Merriam-Webster.com Dictionary*, Merriam-Webster, https://www.merriam-webster.com/dictionary/advice. Accessed Mar. 11, 2024.
[2] "Instruction." *Merriam-Webster.com Dictionary*, Merriam-Webster, https://www.merriam-webster.com/dictionary/instruction. Accessed Mar. 11, 2024.

Answer Key

Lesson 17, Exercise 4, Day 84, Pages 185–186

1. Foreshadowing
2. Melancholy
3. Answers will vary, but students should summarize in their own words the events from Tobias Lear's account regarding Washington's final days, found on pages 251–252 of *Life of Washington*.
4. Answer should include three of the following: He was "bled," his throat was bathed with sal volatile, his feet soaked in warm water, blister of flies put on his throat, steam of vinegar and hot water, sage tea and vinegar for gargling, calomel and tartar emetic administered, applied blisters to legs.
5. Answers will vary, but students should note that the relationship seemed to be one of trust and respect. Lear and Washington cared for one another, and Washington's coming death was greatly distressing to Lear. Lear says he "aided him all in my power" (p. 256) and felt Washington's gratitude for this. Washington died with his hand held in Lear's and placed on Lear's chest.
6. "His loved wife kneeled beside his bed, with her head resting on the Bible …" (p. 257).
7. Character archetype
8. "I am the resurrection and the life; he that believeth in me, though he were dead, yet shall he live" (p. 259).

Lesson 18, Exercise 1, Day 86, Pages 189–190

1. Gerry did not sign the Constitution because it did not contain a bill of rights.
2. a. Definitions will vary. *Example*: government by the people; especially: rule of the majority[1]
   b. Definitions will vary. *Example*: a state of lawlessness or political disorder due to the absence of governmental authority[2]
3. Answers will vary. Students should discuss Gerry's desire to protect the people from an overreaching government that grows so large it becomes a burden, yet also the need for some level of government to avoid anarchy. The student's opinion regarding these government systems and ideas should also be present in the paragraph. The discussion with the parent/instructor should guide the student according to a biblical worldview regarding government and the sinful nature of man, which can lead to anarchy.
4. Answers will vary. *Example*: The *pensive* man in the black coat sat in the back of the church enjoying the joyous, *fraternal* feelings welling up inside him. (*in the black coat* is a prepositional phrase used as an adjective describing the pensive man)
5. Answers will vary. *Example*: During the long winter months, the *vestryman* spent much time studying the *canon* of his church. (*During the long winter months* is a prepositional phrase used as an adverb to tell when the vestryman spent time.)

---

[1] "Democracy." *Merriam-Webster.com Dictionary*, Merriam-Webster, https://www.merriam-webster.com/dictionary/democracy. Accessed Mar. 11, 2024.
[2] "Anarchy." *Merriam-Webster.com Dictionary*, Merriam-Webster, https://www.merriam-webster.com/dictionary/anarchy. Accessed Mar. 11, 2024.

Lesson 18, Exercise 2, Day 87, Pages 191–192

1. adjective
2. adverb
3. noun
4. noun
5. prepositional phrase
6. adjective
7. adverb
8. Answers will vary. *Example*: *To run a 5k* is my dream.
9. Answers will vary. *Example*: Ryan is the coach *to play for*!
10. Answers will vary. *Example*: I want to use my new skills *to sew a pillow*.
11. Answers will vary. *Example*: My dad quickly picked up the shards of glass off the floor.
12. Answers will vary. *Example*: Melanie promised she would always feed the dog on time.
13. Answers will vary. *Example*: We expected to profit plenty of money for our missions trip.
14. (Over the course) (of three hours), my friend Angela sewed ten Christmas ornaments.
15. (Despite the heat), the exhausted boys completed the treacherous hike up the steep mountain.
16. My Aunt Rachel was the fancy, older lady (with the dog).

Answer Key

Lesson 18, Exercise 4, Day 89, Page 196

1. "Be assured, sir, no occurrence in the course of the war has given me more painful sensations than your information of there being such ideas existing in the army as you have expressed, and I must view with abhorrence, and reprehend with severity" (p. 268–269).

2. Answers will vary. *Example*: It shows that he was a humble man and didn't want to brag about his military victories or his own renown.

3. trials, temptations, industrious, temperate, generous, country, worshipper, imitation

Quarter 3

Lesson 19, Exercise 1, Day 91, Page 200

1. Answers will vary. *Example*: I once worked in the automobile *industry* and enjoyed viewing all the *contraptions* workers would create with spare parts! (*worked, enjoyed viewing*, and *would create* are all action verbs; *once* is an adverb)

2. ridicule, contraption, perseverance, genesis, insatiable, unique

Lesson 19, Exercise 2, Day 92, Pages 201–202

1. When (Eric) got a job and moved into a new apartment, he felt very independent.

2. (Lacie) always loved reading historical fiction. It was her favorite genre by far.

3. The (lumberjack) who[RP] was injured on the job finally recovered enough to return to work today.

4. I[SP] would love to attend the same (university) that[RP] Erica went to.

5. Every time I[SP] visit (Charlene,)[SP] she bakes me[OP] a different type of pie.

6. The (car,) which[RP] had a flat tire, was stuck on the side of the road for over a week.

7. I[SP] would rather go with you[OP] to the concert.

8. What an incredible (idea.)[RP] That[DP] is the best plan anybody[IP] has come up with so far!

9. Kristy told the (nurse) at the office, "Don't blame yourself."[RFP]

10. If (you)[SP] let yourself[RFP] sleep in too late, it will be difficult to fall asleep tonight.

11. I[SP] knew those[DP] were the healthiest-looking (chickens) in the coop.

12. The (horse) found itself[RFP] on the wrong side of that[DP] (fence) once again.

13. verbal, function, noun, adjective, adverb, *to*

Answer Key

Lesson 19, Exercise 3, Day 93, Page 204

1. to cause to come to an end especially gradually: no longer continue[1]
2. to wander from company, restraint, or proper limits[2]

Lesson 19, Exercise 4, Day 94, Page 206

1. "Volumes of books, papers, and research ..."
2. "Each of these pictures forever captures a moment in time, some memorable snapshot of my life, family, and work."
3. Answers will vary, but students could consider the idea that by using *in medias res*, the reader will see his great life experience and his success as a scientist and family man. This will give the reader confidence in Dr. Damadian's opinions. It also helps the reader to relate to the story on an emotional level because most people can look back over their lives and appreciate their accomplishments and families.

Lesson 20, Exercise 1, Day 96, Page 210

1. Answers will vary. *Example*: The *inquisitiveness* of the ancient *philosophers* led to many theories about the purpose of life. (*about the purpose* and *of life* are prepositional phrases)
2. Answers will vary. *Example*: The small group of *theologians* met regularly to study God's Word, and they always left with hearts full of *awe*. (*regularly* is an adverb)
3. Answers will vary. *Example*: I said to the man, "So many of the *fundamental* truths of God's Word are *verifiable* to those with open minds."

Lesson 20, Exercise 2, Day 97, Pages 211-212

1. Which (winter coat) belongs to Olivia? — INT
2. Last summer, (Matthew and Jackson) went camping with each other for the first time. — RC
3. Choosing a winner was difficult because none of the (competitors) made a mistake. — DIS
4. (Eliana) was thrilled because her lost luggage was finally returned after over a week of waiting. — PA
5. When (Jay) met his new coach, he realized the coach's house was just down the street from his! — PA / PP
6. Our first day of summer tradition has always been picnicking with my cousins. It is a favorite tradition of mine. — PA / PA / PA
7. I am one who loves to decorate for the holidays!
8. To whom should I offer my gratitude?
9. The teacher will choose whomever she wishes to lead the group.
10. I couldn't believe that I had allowed myself to fall for that old trick!
11. You should contact me if you have any further questions about the concepts we studied.
12. I felt confident that the class would elect me as president.

Lesson 20, Exercise 4, Day 99, Page 216

1. The man was Dr. Damadian's great-uncle, his grandmother's brother.
2. "If birds can glide for long periods of time, then why can't I?"[3]
3. They uncovered God's truth.
4. Answers will vary, but a possibility is that the author wanted to stress the uncovering of God's truth as a central theme. By letting it stand alone, it shows the importance of the statement. It gives it "punch."
5. God's truth

---

1 "Cease." *Merriam-Webster.com Dictionary*, Merriam-Webster, https://www.merriam-webster.com/dictionary/cease. Accessed Mar. 15, 2024.
2 "Stray." *Merriam-Webster.com Dictionary*, Merriam-Webster, https://www.merriam-webster.com/dictionary/stray. Accessed Mar. 15, 2024.

3 http://wrightbrothers.info/biography.php.

Answer Key

6. If the "goal of science is to explore, investigate, validate, understand, and explain knowledge," and God is the source of all knowledge and is Himself the truth, then the discovery of scientific truths is also a discovery of truth about God. This scientific truth is then used to benefit all humanity.

7. The "universe and all it contains reveals the fingerprints of God — His invisible attributes, His eternal power, and divine nature."

Lesson 21, Exercise 1, Day 101, Page 220

1. Pursuit, vistas, quest, impede
2. Answers will vary. *Example:* In a *democracy*, the people can vote for the candidate of their choice, so *political* advertisements abound during election season. (*political* is used as an adjective that describes the noun *advertisements*)

Lesson 21, Exercise 2, Day 102, Pages 221–222

1. We spent a lot of money at the county fair last weekend.
2. At the tournament, Mitchell threw the ball like a real champ!
3. Weaving in and out of traffic, the police car finally caught the suspect three blocks from the scene of the crime.
4. Chosen last for the team, I wasted no time training to improve.
5. After school yesterday, Mom bought us ice cream. [IO] [DO]
6. The pastor gave the congregation a sermon they will never forget! [IO] [DO]
7. Sharing the last of her treats, Leah handed Cole [IO] an enormous cookie. [DO]
8. Jesse bought Maddie a beautiful ring. [IO] [DO]
9. The hotel worker gave the room a quick cleaning. [IO] [DO]
10. My aunt and uncle generously bought dinner (for me) (after the play). [DO] [IO]
11. Not surprisingly, Corbin's coach gave a game ball (to him). [DO] [IO]
12. The king offered protection (for his guests) when they traveled home. [DO] [IO]

Lesson 21, Exercise 3, Day 103, Page 224

1. something set up as an object or end to be attained[1]
2. to cause to move continuously toward or after a force applied in advance[2]

Lesson 21, Exercise 4, Day 104, Page 226

1. The discovery of God's truth
2. New knowledge
3. Answers will vary. The discovery of the truth shines a light into the darkness, revealing a person's sin and their accountability to God. This can be a miserable discovery, but one that can bring freedom to those who embrace it.
4. "Mankind's ultimate aspiration seems to manifest itself through becoming the final authority in all aspects of his own existence."
5. They become slaves.
6. Answers will vary. *Example*: Since George Washington rejected kingship, he steered control of America from political power (man's power) to the power of the truth (God's power). This open-mindedness regarding truth led the country to great advancements in science and technology. It recognized God as King, and therefore the nation was founded on His truth, establishing it as the real "Founding Father."

---

[1] "Purpose." *Merriam-Webster.com Dictionary*, Merriam-Webster, https://www.merriam-webster.com/dictionary/purpose. Accessed Mar. 19, 2024.
[2] "Draw." *Merriam-Webster.com Dictionary*, Merriam-Webster, https://www.merriam-webster.com/dictionary/draw. Accessed Mar. 19, 2024.

Answer Key

Lesson 22, Exercise 2, Day 107, Page 232

1. My chess club <u>is</u> traveling to Canada for an international competition.
2. Although it is getting late in the day, everybody <u>wants</u> to stay longer.
3. The evangelist and several of the missionaries <u>speak</u> at this conference each year.
4. Neither idea <u>was</u> plausible, considering the circumstances.
5. Vacations <u>are</u> fun but also <u>cost</u> a lot of money these days.
6. The camp director or the camp counselors <u>announce</u> the activities for the day.
7. The camp counselors or the camp director <u>announces</u> the activities for the day.
8. My dogs, including the puppy, <u>eat</u> an enormous amount of food every day.
9. I firmly believe that no one <u>is</u> able to comprehend God's love for them.

Lesson 22, Exercise 4, Day 109, Page 236

1. The Bible was printed, and people had access to "its fascinating truths, including scientific truths."
2. Most of mankind's major scientific discoveries were made.
3. access, gifted, reveal, Him
4. b
5. d
6. a
7. c
8. instead merely *discovered* ways to harness them for our benefit and progress
9. Answers will vary, but the paragraph should be well structured and point to specific ideas from the reading excerpts.

Lesson 23, Exercise 1, Day 111, Page 240

1. Answers will vary. *Example:* Without God's *intervention*, the nation of Israel would have faced great *peril*. (This sentence is a complex sentence.)
2. Answers will vary. The dialogue should be properly written according to the rules given on Day 47. The content of the discussion should include God and truth. The viewpoints could be opposing or in agreement.

Lesson 23, Exercise 2, Day 112, Page 242

1. <u>I have been frightened</u> many times in my life, but God's <u>peace has overcome</u> my fears.
2. <u>Mandy and Josie picked</u> blueberries from the back garden yesterday, but <u>I was</u> not <u>able</u> to help.
3. My father or my uncles frequently <u>tell</u> the story of their infamous fishing trip on the Colorado River.
4. The football players and their coach <u>leave</u> the stadium through the rear exit.
5. Melissa, as well as all her siblings, <u>is</u> happy about being homeschooled.
6. subjunctive
7. indicative
8. imperative
9. active
10. passive
11. active
12. passive
13. completed
14. ongoing
15. ongoing
16. completed

Lesson 23, Exercise 3, Day 113, Page 244

1. generally recognized[1]
2. a mode or standard of personal behavior especially as based on moral principles[2]

Lesson 23, Exercise 4, Day 114, Page 246

1. Because "*truth* is **truth**, no matter who discovers or stumbles upon it."
2. Answers will vary. The text reads, "[T]he reason it is so important to understand the role of *God's truth* in scientific discovery is because without His truth as the foundation of all knowledge, we limit science to a closed system of natural law alone. In other words, man is all there is, and the physical laws of nature exist without any help from a Divine Being."

---

[1] "Known." *Merriam-Webster.com Dictionary*, Merriam-Webster, https://www.merriam-webster.com/dictionary/known. Accessed Mar. 19, 2024.
[2] "Conduct." *Merriam-Webster.com Dictionary*, Merriam-Webster, https://www.merriam-webster.com/dictionary/conduct. Accessed Mar. 19, 2024.

Answer Key

3. An "Intelligent Being … caused man, the universe, and life to come into existence."
4. A "conventional, atheistic, and naturalistic approach" to science.

Lesson 24, Exercise 2, Day 117, Pages 251–252

1. transitive
2. transitive
3. intransitive
4. transitive
5. intransitive
6. intransitive
7. Answers will vary. *Example*: The bee stung the boy on the foot.
8. Answers will vary. *Example*: The cut on my arm stung!
9. Our jaws dropped as the eagle *flew* over our heads! (OP) intransitive
10. Every time I *wash* the car (DO), it seems to rain, and it gets dirty all over again. transitive
11. I *shopped* with my grandmother (OP) for the gift I needed for the wedding. intransitive
12. The long, black snake *swallowed* the mouse (DO) in a matter of minutes. transitive
13. The (author) who won the award, signed books at the end of the ceremony.
14. (Jackson and Juan) loved mowing, so they started their own landscaping business.
15. Whenever (Mom) goes grocery shopping, she can't help but purchase yet another live plant!
16. (We) left everybody behind and journeyed up the mountain by ourselves.

Lesson 24, Exercise 4, Day 119, Page 256

1. Answers will vary. People choose "convenience over the Creator, pushing Him out of their … lives." They take themselves out from under God's rule and choose a godless theory instead.
2. Answers will vary. The paragraph should include all the major points of the second paragraph in the student's own words and include a direct quote from Dr. Damadian's writing.

3. a. They are too afraid.
   b. They are too proud.
   c. They are too unwilling to challenge it.
4. a. Presupposition
   b. Intellectual bias
   c. Misunderstanding and misapplication of archeology and scientific knowledge

Lesson 25, Exercise 2, Day 122, Page 262

1. factors
2. rabbits
3. wishes
4. keys
5. children
6. indices
7. thieves
8. truckers
9. potatoes
10. bison
11. larvae
12. disciples
13. radios
14. matches
15. stories

Lesson 25, Exercise 3, Day 123, Page 264

1. the utterance of false charges or misrepresentations which defame and damage another's reputation[1]
2. to join as a partner, friend, or companion[2]

Lesson 25, Exercise 4, Day 124, Page 266

1. Answers will vary. The paragraph should include all the major points made in the first paragraph and show a good grasp of the vocabulary words.
2. carnival barking, tragic hoax, dissuading, and science, gracious God
3. imperiled by selfishness and financial greed, underwritten and justified by the Darwinian deception of 'survival of the fittest.'

Lesson 26, Exercise 1, Day 126, Page 270

1. genocide, devoid, diabolical, heinous, propaganda

---

[1] "Slander." *Merriam-Webster.com Dictionary*, Merriam-Webster, https://www.merriam-webster.com/dictionary/slander. Accessed Mar. 21, 2024.
[2] "Associate." *Merriam-Webster.com Dictionary*, Merriam-Webster, https://www.merriam-webster.com/dictionary/associate. Accessed Mar. 21, 2024.

Answer Key

Lesson 26, Exercise 2, Day 127, Pages 271–272

1. My cousin's house is so stately; the porch's columns are enormous.
2. Even though the leaves had begun to change color, October's weather felt very much like summer.
3. When my mother gets home from jogging, I will ask her if I can go to Anika's.
4. Frustratingly, all the pans' lids were stored in a separate drawer.
5. The group meets on Mondays at the park, but this Monday's weather looks unsuitable.
6. It was Taron's incredible memory that made him so competitive at Bible quizzing's year-end competition.
7. If it wasn't for Christ's work on the Cross, salvation would not be yours or mine.
8. Although Andrew wasn't impressed with the restaurant's menu, he appreciated his friend's generous offer to treat him to dinner. OR Although Andrew wasn't impressed with the restaurant's menu, he appreciated his friends' generous offer to treat him to dinner.
9. My science project took first place, yet I really felt that Andrea's was far better than mine.
10. We went to visit my aunt and uncle in Massachusetts, and when we turned onto their street, I knew instantly which house was theirs.
11. In my opinion, it's far better to have a few quality friends than several mere acquaintances.
12. Grandma Johnson's house has been in our family for generations, yet it doesn't feel like mine.
13. Ellie's birthday gift was left on the table by her brother in hopes of surprising his sister.
14. The maintenance man, whose job it was to keep the grass cut, seemed to forget the responsibility was his.
15. All four cats' bowls were empty, and their hunger was evident!

Lesson 26, Exercise 4, Day 129, Page 276

1. Answers will vary. By making these statements so short, it makes them stand out as very important, causing the reader to look at each idea individually and give it more attention.

2. "… [G]enuine scientific truths regarding God."
3. A "belief in Darwinian evolution and it's [sic] 'survival of the fittest' propaganda."
4. "… [H]istory teaches us that God will always raise up those who are willing to shine the light of truth."
5. "We're perpetually 'promoting' " ideas about God "to non-believers, to evolutionists, to our spouses, to family members, etc." Our ideas are related to "products" that we essentially "sell" to others, trying to convince them of our beliefs.

Lesson 27, Exercise 1, Day 131, Page 280

1. Answers will vary. *Example*: In a world that is becoming increasingly *secular,* the Church needs students willing to study *apologetics.*

Lesson 27, Exercise 2, Day 132, Pages 281–282

1. Answers will vary. *Example:* A parade was given in the heroes' honor.
2. Answers will vary. *Example:* The child's doctor gave a good report.
3. Answers will vary. *Example:* People's opinions are not to be worshiped.
4. **PA** I brought all my drawing projects to the art fair, but one of the project's covers was missing, and it got ruined.
5. **PA** Lydia and Jessie planned their monthly lunch out at Alexander's.
6. **PA** Even though the play was the next night, everyone's costumes were ready except for mine!
7. The tomatoes' rows were marked with little signs to show they were hers.
8. **PA** The children's choir at our church practices on **PA** Mondays when their schedules align.
9. **PA** *Pilgrim's Progress* was a favorite of mine during my teenage years.
10. **PA** The boys' bedroom was very clean by the time their mother came to inspect it.

11. When examining the tree, we noticed the <u>fungi's</u> (PA) color had altered from <u>its</u> original bluish hue.
12. Answers will vary. *Example: Elijah's* dad brought *his* sleeping bag and labeled it so everyone would know it was *his*.

Lesson 27, Exercise 4, Day 134, Page 286

1. "… [T]o 'give a defense' … for *why* we believe."
2. "My highest purpose was realized when I discovered I could actually know God and serve His will, that I could live for something greater than science, medicine, or myself."
3. "… [O]ur presentation has to go beyond talk, evidence, and scientific *facts*. It has to show up in the lifestyle and *faith* of those who claim to believe it."

Quarter 4

Lesson 28, Exercise 1, Day 136, Pages 289–290

1. He "wept as he fled Jerusalem when his son Absolom rebelled against him."
2. a. He wept over the city on Palm Sunday.
   b. He answered the disciples' questions about the future.
   c. He frequently spent the night there.
   d. He was at the foot of the Mount of Olives the night He was betrayed.
   e. He said His farewell to the disciples at His Ascension.
   f. He gave the great commission on the Mount of Olives.
3. d
4. a
5. f
6. c
7. b
8. g
9. e

Lesson 28, Exercise 2, Day 137, Pages 291–292

1. <u>Despite having studied a lot</u> (DP), <u>Brandon failed his driver's test</u> (IND), and <u>he will need to retake it next month</u> (IND).
2. <u>Leaving the past behind</u> (DP), <u>Sadie and Lilly became close friends again</u> (IND), and <u>they vowed never to let hard feelings come between them</u> (IND).
3. Answers will vary, but the sentence must contain at least two independent clauses and at least one dependent clause.
4. Definitions will vary. *Example:* a person who believes there is no God or gods (without God).
5. Definitions will vary. *Example:* in the state or condition of drifting; having no anchor.
6. f
7. e
8. d
9. c
10. b
11. g
12. a
13. h
14. Answers will vary. A common noun names any person, place, or thing – dog, boy, house, etc.
15. Answers will vary. A proper noun names a specific person, place, or thing – Greg, New Jersey, Christianity, British, etc.
16. My lunch <u>looked</u> (LV) appetizing for the first time since my long, drawn-out illness.
17. Angela frantically <u>looked</u> (AV) through the pages of the book, <u>searching</u> (AV) for any clue to the answer.
18. Jesus <u>turned</u> (AV) the Pharisees' argument against them every time they <u>appeared</u> (LV) to have tricked Him.
19. This English Language Arts course <u>equals</u> (LV) a full high school credit in all fifty states.
20. Pets fed the proper amount of food <u>stay</u> (LV) thinner and healthier than overfed pets.
21. Answers will vary. *Example:* Jay, please look for the broom out on the porch.
22. Answers will vary. *Example:* She looked so excited about the upcoming job opportunity.

Answer Key

Lesson 28, Exercise 4, Day 139, Page 296

1. "Eric moved west with his family at the age of four to Evergreen, Colorado …"
2. Alexander's mentors "gave him a passion for the outdoors and for the Lord, which continues today."
3. Alexander earned a "BA degree in environmental science from the University of Denver …"
4. BA stands for Bachelor of Art.
5. a. Vail Ski Patrol (including one year in France)
   b. Ski School
   c. Vail Mountaineering
   d. His own business
6. Higher Summits has allowed "him to share an inspirational message with people all over the world, opening the door to share his faith in Christ and the true meaning of purpose in life."

Lesson 29, Exercise 2, Day 142, Pages 301–302

1. According to the Bible, being a wise steward consists of spending wisely, being generous, and tithing on your income.
2. doctor
3. teacher
4. commander
5. dictator
6. respecter
7. calculator
8. inspector
9. runner
10. lecturer
11. Answers will vary, but the sentence should include *had been coughing*.
12. Answers will vary, but the sentence should include *will topple*.
13. <u>Since we no longer have a leaky roof</u> [DP], <u>we won't need to keep buckets in the attic to catch the raindrops</u> [IND]!
14. <u>I noticed a large swarm of flying insects gathering</u> [IND], and <u>I hoped they wouldn't invade our picnic area</u> [IND].
15. <u>Although</u> [SB] my grandmother lives in another country, we keep in touch and are very close.
16. We had <u>no sooner</u> [CL] started playing video games <u>than</u> [CL] there was a power outage, and we couldn't play!
17. Jessica really wanted to play board games with her sister, <u>but</u> [CC] she was so tired that it just wasn't possible.

Lesson 29, Exercise 3, Day 143, Pages 303–304

1. Answers will vary. Examples of synonyms found in a thesaurus: often (frequently, repeatedly, constantly), enjoy (love, like, appreciate), upcoming (approaching, impending, forthcoming), walk as a verb (tread, step, wander), feel (sense, perceive, notice), walk as a noun (trip, saunter, stroll), fresh (mint, pristine, virginal).
2. Answers will vary. *Examples:* tolerance, forbearance, long-suffering
3. Answers will vary. *Examples:* convince, satisfy, convert

Lesson 29, Exercise 4, Day 144, Page 306

1. A "deadpoint is a [mountain] climbing move where momentum is used to achieve a higher handhold."

Lesson 30, Exercise 1, Day 146, Pages 309–310

1. The "Lord alone is seen," "we hear the voice from heaven," and "the air is pure and clean."
2. "[L]ight increases," we are "above all earthly strife," we are done straining, and we "reign in Life" with Christ.
3. The Savior keeps us, we share His image, and we extol grace and love.
4. g
5. e
6. f
7. b
8. a
9. d
10. c

Answer Key

Lesson 30, Exercise 2, Day 147, Pages 311–312

1. Answers will vary. *Example:* After realizing how long the practices were, Aaron didn't want anything to do with playing soccer.
2. Answers will vary. *Example:* Clarence searched all over the beach but couldn't find any of the beach glass he piled up yesterday.
3. e
4. d
5. a
6. c
7. b
8. subjunctive
9. imperative
10. indicative
11. The teens (at church) were so excited (about their mission trip) (to England) (with a local ministry).
12. (According to one study), those eating plant-based diets were less likely to be diagnosed (with heart disease).
13. Our trip (to Yellowstone) was (beyond amazing), and the memories (from that trip) will live (in my mind) (for many years).
14. Answers will vary. Refer to the preposition chart.
15. Answers will vary. Refer to the preposition chart.
16. Answers will vary. *Example:* The veterinarian, who is my dad's friend, operated on our cat.

Lesson 30, Exercise 4, Day 149, Page 316

1. Answers will vary. On the first attempt, the climbers had to retreat due to weather, and this was a success because the goal of safety was achieved. On the second attempt, the summit was reached and felt sweeter because it hadn't come easily.
2. Answers will vary. This climb was "a success because it knit our team together and showed the team's character, communication skills, selflessness, and lack of greed for the summit."
3. Answers will vary. This climb was successful because Alexander needed to swallow his pride, as he had to stay back from the summit when the four blind students ascended and reached the summit. He had wanted to take credit for assisting them but had to stay at high camp with two ill climbers.
4. a. Step 1: "Biblical success shows nothing of being perfect; rather it is the humble acceptance of God's grace in admission of sin and failure."

   b. Step 2: "Step two is living a life of obedience out of love, revealing an effort to emulate godly character. It is a process of relationship, striving, and refining."

Lesson 31, Exercise 1, Day 151, Page 320

1. d
2. f
3. a
4. e
5. c
6. b

Answer Key

Lesson 31, Exercise 2, Day 152, Pages 321–322

1. I was getting frustrated with her, but <u>then</u> I remembered she is much younger <u>than</u> I am and just doesn't know any better.
2. When Dad came home from work, he <u>sat</u> down in his big comfortable chair and <u>set</u> his hat on the table next to him.
3. When the officials <u>raise</u> the flag, the people should <u>rise</u> and honor those whom it represents.
4. <u>May</u> I please go outside now with Jillian? I know I <u>can</u> finish my reading tonight after dinner!
5. I <u>brought</u> the volleyball to practice, and my instructor <u>took</u> it with him until next week.
6. c
7. d
8. a
9. b
10. When Mom couldn't find her glasses, she told us all, "Since I can't drive without my glasses, we can't leave until they are found."
11. The word "chicken" could be used to describe someone who is a coward or the actual bird that lays eggs.
12. In frustration, I asked my mother, "How many times will I need to practice memorizing this list of prepositions before they stick in my mind?"
13. My little sister Joanna suggested, "I hope I haven't been talking too much"; then she continued to ramble on and on.
14. <u>A</u> <u>hot</u>, <u>tropical</u> climate sounds very appealing in <u>the</u> middle of <u>a</u> <u>harsh</u>, <u>cold</u> winter.
15. There were <u>amazing</u> sites to see at <u>our</u> <u>local</u> <u>county</u> fair; <u>farm</u> animals, <u>delicious</u> foods, and <u>handcrafted</u> products were everywhere!
16. I <u>really</u> need to clean my room <u>tomorrow</u> so I am <u>not</u> embarrassed for my grandmother to see it!
17. The scared little mouse <u>quickly</u> crawled <u>inside</u> the end of the log to avoid the <u>quietly</u> creeping cat.
18. <u>Whether I am planning to go to college in the fall or not</u> has become the main topic of discussion each week when Dad and I take our walk. noun
19. <u>Although I am a great artist</u>, I don't see myself attending college for art. adverb
20. My pastor's wife, <u>who is a sweet and loving person</u>, has become a powerful voice for the plight of the unborn in our culture. adjective

Lesson 31, Exercise 3, Day 153, Page 324

1. Answers will vary. *Examples*: have, entertain, hold on to
2. Answers will vary. *Examples*: testimony, evidence, proof

Lesson 31, Exercise 4, Day 154, Page 326

1. Answers will vary. Alexander is expressing the idea that people have the right to believe what they want about the afterlife, but ultimately it is not what we believe that matters. The only way to have peace about life after death is in God alone and what His Word states.

Lesson 32, Exercise 1, Day 156, Pages 329–330

1. "Sin cannot rule over the man whose footsteps are directed by the Lord."
2. "The devil must flee because through humility Jesus comes on the scene."
3. "Satan would like to direct our steps away from God."
4. Satan "would like us to take the easy path where he could then rule over us."
5. "[I]f we will determine to submit ourselves to God, Satan must flee."
6. "If we will walk according to the Word of God, no sin will rule over us because our submission to it brings Jesus."

Answer Key

Lesson 32, Exercise 2, Day 157, Pages 331–332

1. Answers will vary. *Example:* While Travis was mowing the lawn, he saw three large groundhogs.
2. Answers will vary. *Example:* Although I wanted to sit down and rest, the ground was too hard.
3. Every Saturday, which was the Jewish Sabbath Day, was a time of rest from the usual workload and activities.
4. I have always lived in the Northeast, so I am familiar with the signs of autumn: cooler temperatures, changing leaves, and geese flying south.
5. From the beginning of creation, God has shown His amazing love and care for His people, His commitment to His covenants, and the fulfillment of His promises.
6. Answers will vary. *Example:* The British authorities found the man guilty. (*British* is a proper adjective; *the* is a limiting adjective)
7. Answers will vary. *Example:* The two orange cats fought in the alley. (*Two* and *orange* work together as coordinate adjectives and do not require a comma.)
8. Answers will vary. *Example:* The short-handed staff worked as hard as possible. (*short-handed* is a compound adjective that needs a hyphen since it comes before the noun it modifies.)
9. After we finished dinner, we quickly cleaned up the kitchen so we could watch a movie.
10. I was carelessly cleaning my bird's cage, and he flew outside!
11. We won't have enough paint to finish the project because Jerod slapped it on the shed so quickly that he used too much.

Lesson 33, Exercise 1, Day 161, Page 340

1. c
2. e
3. d
4. g
5. b
6. a
7. f

Lesson 33, Exercise 2, Day 162, Pages 341–342

1. arose
2. arisen
3. became
4. become
5. build
6. built
7. drew
8. drawn
9. flew
10. flown
11. let
12. let
13. lighted
14. lighted
15. mistook
16. mistaken
17. saw
18. seen
19. spilt/spilled
20. spilt/spilled
21. e
22. d
23. f
24. a
25. b
26. c
27. The old house (on the outskirts) (of town) was listed for sale last I saw. The old house
28. When I awoke this morning, I realized that my duffle bag (with the stripes) got lost when we packed our luggage last night. my duffle bag
29. The police officer acted (with great courage) as he attempted the daring rescue. acted
30. My neighbor's little black colt got loose and ran (across our backyard)! ran
31. A little blue bird perched on the telephone wire was singing at the top of his lungs. past
32. The firefighter, having fought the flames all night long, collapsed in the fire engine for a quick nap. perfect
33. The dolphins swimming in the enclosure are being rehabilitated. present
34. adjective
35. noun
36. adverb
37. prepositional phrase
38. Answers will vary. *Example:* Everyone tried to enter the bus quickly before it departed from the station.

Language Lessons for a Living Education Level 10

Answer Key

Lesson 33, Exercise 3, Day 163, Page 344

1. Answers will vary. *Examples:* interfere, intrude, mess with
2. Answers will vary. *Examples:* dispute, argument, fight

Lesson 33, Exercise 4, Day 164, Page 346

1. "Most of us at some time or another have been burned by words, actions, and misdeeds of others, and we live guarded lives, never allowing others to have a secure position of trust."
2. "The fastest way to lose a friend is to be a hypocrite, to gossip about that friend, or even people within your circle."
3. trustworthy, actions, word, keep

Lesson 34, Exercise 1, Day 166, Page 350

1. d
2. e
3. g
4. f
5. c
6. a
7. b

Lesson 34, Exercise 2, Day 167, Pages 351–352

1. At the age of thirty-two, my father came to believe in an all-knowing Creator while listening to a well-known evangelist on the radio.
2. **SP** I decided that I would love to go with **OP** her to help at the soup kitchen tomorrow.
3. The (rollercoaster,) **RP** which needed maintenance, was closed for a month.
4. Every time (Rachel) comes over, **SP** she brings **OP** us a treat.
5. **DP** These are the (library books) that smell like an old basement!
6. If **SP** I allow **RFP** myself to eat too much (pizza,) **OP** it will likely give **OP** me a stomachache.
7. **DP** This is by far the best (art project) **IP** anyone has turned in so far.
8. My mother is the only one in our family who loves to garden.
9. The Lord will have mercy on whomever He chooses.
10. Tell everyone to let me know if they have any questions about the trip.
11. Erika always remembers to tell me when important test dates are coming up!
12. (Before church yesterday), my brother lost his tithe **DO** money, and he found **DO** it (under the couch).
13. (During our church service) (on Sunday), Pastor Eric gave **IO** the graduating seniors **DO** Bibles (with their names) (on the front).
14. (Despite being a cautious spender), I have enjoyed giving **IO** my family **DO** gifts (for Christmas).
15. (On account) (of God's love) (for him), my cousin has committed **DO** his entire life (to serving God) (across the ocean).

Lesson 34, Exercise 3, Day 168, Page 353

1. a
2. c
3. b

Lesson 34, Exercise 4, Day 169, Page 356

1. "Don't focus on the wrong behavior and choices to avoid, instead focus on the direction that will steer you away from it."

Lesson 35, Exercise 1, Day 171, Pages 359–360

1. b
2. e
3. g
4. f
5. d
6. c
7. a

8. They are to go up to a high mountain and proclaim (herald) the good news.
9. might, arm, rules, reward, recompense
10. Answers will vary. God's people can be comforted knowing He is a loving Shepherd who holds them, protects them in His bosom, and gently leads them.

11. a. Answers will vary. No one is able to measure the Spirit of the Lord, and no one can show Him His counsel.

   b. Answers will vary. The Lord did not consult any man, and no one makes God understand anything.

   c. Answers will vary. No one needed to teach the Lord about justice or show Him how to understand anything.

Lesson 35, Exercise 2, Day 172, Pages 361–362

1. c
2. d
3. e
4. b
5. a

6. The group of committee members <u>is</u> due to come up with a decision by the end of the month.
7. The row of maple trees, along with several oak trees, <u>is</u> being cut down this afternoon.
8. My little nephew and his two sisters <u>want</u> to come stay at our house while their parents are out of town.
9. I think the parrot or the canary <u>sounds</u> the loudest of all the birds in the pet shop.
10. The baseball team <u>runs</u> through every drill at Friday practices.
11. completed
12. ongoing
13. intransitive
14. transitive
15. Answers will vary. *Example:* They run a bookstore together.
16. Answers will vary. *Example:* When he wakes up, John will run.
17. We were so surprised to see that Melanie *gave* <u>her oral presentation</u> with total confidence! transitive
                      DO
18. Maddie and her mother *shopped* for <u>her wedding dress</u> at three different bridal shops. intransitive
                  OP
19. The toddler *ate* the <u>cheese stick</u> after shredding it into several long strings. transitive
         DO

Lesson 35, Exercise 3, Day 173, Page 364

1. Answers will vary. *Examples:* solemn, serious, weighty
2. Answers will vary. *Examples:* advice, guidance, recommendation

Lesson 35, Exercise 4, Day 174, Page 366

1. "It was hard to hear their uninvited comments stream in from all over the globe, especially when they did not know this team or this blind man personally."
2. "[M]aking a judgment based on a perception of my own rather than on evidence and truth."
3. crux, show, capable of, label

Lesson 36, Exercise 1, Day 176, Page 370

1. "As I drive through these mountains, I envision the massive earth-shaping events that laid down all this sandy material and then reshaped it when continents collided during the Flood."
2. "They aren't reminders of God's creation, but of a worldwide judgment that produced 'beauty out of ashes.'"

3. e
4. f
5. a
6. g
7. c
8. h
9. b
10. d

Answer Key

Lesson 36, Exercise 2, Day 177, Pages 371–372

1. The <u>farther</u> we got from the campsite in the dark, the more nervous I became.
2. I usually get quite embarrassed when others <u>compliment</u> me about my appearance.
3. When I babysit, I always <u>assure</u> the parents that their children are in good hands with me.
4. My father <u>lay</u> down and rested knowing our home was <u>insured</u>!
5. in a state or condition; in a manner; not; without
6. one who; that which
7. before, preceding
8. opposite, against
9. with, jointly, completely
10. become, made of, resemble, to make
11. belonging/relating to, able to be
12. to cause to be; put or go into or onto
13. in, on, not
14. science of or study of
15. down, away
16. negation, removal, expulsion
17. related to, character of
18. causing an action
19. half
20. echoes
21. stimuli
22. tuna
23. stereos
24. aircraft
25. foci
26. data
27. trains
28. Last week we ate dinner at Michael's Banquet Hall, and my dad's steak was undercooked.
29. When I went to my neighbor's coop to feed her chickens this morning, all the chickens' water feeders were bone dry.
30. All the mountain climber's gear fit neatly into <u>his</u> backpack, but I couldn't even fit my clothing into <u>mine</u>!
31. When we arrived at <u>my</u> aunt and uncle's cabin, I could tell which boat in the lake was <u>theirs</u>.
32. All five houses' siding had been scorched by the flames from <u>their</u> neighbor's burning home.
33. Answers will vary. *Example:* We made sure that all the videos' content was suitable.
34. Answers should include three of the following: After a salutation of a business letter, between a book title and subtitle, before a series at the end of a sentence, before a long or formal direct quotation if the quotation appears at the end of a sentence, in Bible references and expressions of time, or between two independent clauses not separated by a coordinating conjunction in which the second clause is an explanation of the first.

Lesson 36, Exercise 4, Day 179, Page 376

1. Value
2. Past failure, obstacles, lack of vision, foresight, funds, (lack of) confidence
3. Answers will vary. When you desperately need to accomplish something very important — maybe your life depends on it — you will find a way to persevere. The need is too great not to try your best.

Quarter 1 Reviews

Lesson 1, Exercise 5, Day 5, Pages 27–28

Vocabulary Review

1. d
2. e
3. a
4. f
5. g
6. b
7. c

8. caravals
9. lamentations
10. desponding, reproached
11. tumult

Grammar & Punctuation Review

1. names a person, place, or thing

   Examples will vary: kindness, Mary, Bible, state, etc.

2. shows action or state-of-being

   Examples will vary: speak, run, work, am, is, was, being, etc.

3. describes a noun or pronoun

   Examples will vary: purple, old, shiny, five, heavy, wet, etc.

4. joins words or phrases

   Examples will vary: and, yet, although, because, unless, as if, for, etc.

5. Answers will vary but should contain three of these traits: diligence, confidence, being devout, attentive, committed, resolute, reflective, hopeful.

Communication Review

1. Answers should include four of the following: writing, speaking, gesturing with hands, moving their bodies, making facial expressions, choosing clothing styles, texting, and designing artwork.
2. someone other than the subject (the person the book is about)
3. the person the book is about
4. third-person
5. first-person
6. permission to write it was given by the person the book is about
7. nonfiction

Worldview & Literary Analysis Review

1. Our worldview is our philosophy about life and is the framework through which we understand the world and our relation to it.[1]
2. Answers will vary, but students should describe their beliefs about God and man.
3. Answers will vary, but students should have written a well-thought-out paragraph with examples from the introduction to *Life of Washington*.

---

1 Hodge, Bodie, and Roger Patterson. *World Religions and Cults*, Volume 1. Green Forest, AR: Master Books, 2015, p. 23.

Review Answer Key

Lesson 2, Exercise 5, Day 10, Pages 37–38

Vocabulary Review

1. e
2. d
3. a
4. f
5. c
6. g
7. b

8. Answers will vary. Definitions for vocabulary words are found on Day 6.
9. Answers will vary. Definitions for vocabulary words are found on Day 6.

Grammar & Punctuation Review

1. "The night on which this account was given, **//** was dark and rainy …" (p. 31).
2. Several of my friends and I **//** enjoyed an ice cream cone at the ball game.
3. "By a firm but mild manner, he **//** gained friends among the inhabitants of the forest …" (p. 28).
4. "The spot thus described **//** was soon afterwards the site of the French fort Duquesne" (p. 28).

Communication Review

1. a. Topic sentence – briefly explains what the paragraph is about
   b. Supporting sentences – elaborate on the topic by adding details to explain or support
   c. Concluding sentence – summarizes the topic or presents one final piece of support
2. heart, wise, speech, persuasiveness, lips

Worldview & Literary Analysis Review

1. a. The author needs to be truthful and accurate in presenting the facts for the purpose of educating readers.
   b. The author can create any story they wish using their imagination for the purpose of entertaining readers.
2. a. To obtain a desired indulgence
   b. To escape a deserved punishment or reproof

Lesson 3, Exercise 5, Day 15, Pages 47–48

Vocabulary Review

1. e
2. f
3. g
4. b
5. c
6. a
7. d
8. n
9. m
10. j
11. l
12. i
13. k
14. h

Grammar & Punctuation Review

1. a. what the subject is doing or has done
   b. explains the state or condition of the subject
2. a. permanent
   b. sensory
   c. conditional
   d. state-of-being
3. Juan <u>became</u> (LV) an important part of our family through a foreign exchange program.
4. When the exam <u>was</u> (LV) finally over, I <u>ran</u> (AV) outside for some much-needed fresh air.
5. I will <u>remain</u> (LV) steadfast when the society around me <u>abandons</u> (AV) God's Word.

Communication Review

1. Plagiarism is the practice of taking someone else's work and passing it off as one's own.
2. A citation is a way you let the reader know that certain material in your writing came from another source.
3. The book's title, author's name, publisher, publication date, and page number you are referencing
4. The author's name, title of the article, website name, date of article, and the URL

Worldview & Literary Analysis Review

1. "... [T]he courage with which he had acted, and the favourable [favorable] terms he had obtained from so large a force ..." (p. 32).
2. He heard "of the conduct of Washington as an officer, and of his reasons for giving up his commission ..." (p. 34).

Lesson 4, Exercise 5, Day 20, Pages 57–58

Vocabulary Review

1. e
2. d
3. a
4. h
5. f
6. g
7. b
8. c
9. i
10. n
11. j
12. k
13. m
14. o
15. l

Grammar & Punctuation Review

1. auxiliary
2. a. primary
   b. modal
3. We have been having the best summer weather I can remember.
4. He doesn't think he will be able to come over after the concert tonight.
5. Melanie might compete in the pie-baking contest, but she needs more practice first.
6. Answers will vary, but the sentence should contain one of these verbs: *may, might, could,* or *must.*

Communication Review

1. A historical narrative essay tells a story about a person from history. It is written in the third person (using pronouns like *he, she,* or *they*).
2. Answers will vary. Students should condense their historical narrative essay by placing the most important information from their story into one paragraph.

Worldview & Literary Analysis Review

1. Sometimes a biography will seek to do more than instruct the reader about the life of the subject. The writer may use the subject's character or life events to promote certain ideas.
2. Answers should include two of the following OR any two of the student's choices from the text: Columbus stated he would only accomplish his mission with "the blessing of God" (p. 9); Washington's parents taught him the importance of trusting God's Word when it says to obey one's parents (p. 24); Reed credits "the protecting hand of God" on Washington's life (p. 30).
3. "You can easily distinguish him when Congress goes to prayers—*Mr. Washington is the gentleman who kneels down*" (p. 51).

Review Answer Key

Lesson 5, Exercise 5, Day 25, Pages 67–68

Vocabulary Review

1. e
2. a
3. b
4. f
5. c
6. d
7. g
8. k
9. l
10. m
11. i
12. h
13. j

Grammar & Punctuation Review

1. Verb tense refers to when the action takes place in a sentence — whether it happened in the past, is happening in the present, or will happen in the future.

2. Answers will vary. *Example:* The baby *had been wiggling* on his mother's lap for the entire service.

3. Answers will vary. *Example:* John *will have painted* the entire house by this evening.

4. am + -ing

Communication Review

1. A descriptive paragraph creates a scene that vividly describes a person, place, or thing.
2. Answers will vary. See Day 23 for an example.
3. Answers will vary. See Day 23 for an example.
4. Answers will vary. See Day 23 for an example.
5. Answers will vary. See Day 23 for an example.
6. Answers will vary. See Day 23 for an example.

Worldview & Literary Analysis Review

1. peaceful, comfortable, given up, desire, shrink, duty, others

2. When "he could defend the helpless, or aid in obtaining justice for the oppressed" (p. 61).

3. "When any occurrence raised his anger, he resolutely endeavoured [endeavored] to restrain it, and thus obeyed the Scripture precept given to warm tempers, 'Be ye angry and sin not'" (p. 62).

4. Wording will vary due to the Bible version chosen but should be similar to the following: "Do nothing from selfish ambition or conceit, but in humility count others more significant than yourselves. Let each of you look not only to his own interests, but also to the interests of others" (Philippians 2:3–4).

Lesson 6, Exercise 5, Day 30, Pages 77–78

Vocabulary Review

1. f
2. g
3. b
4. a
5. d
6. c
7. e
8. h
9. j
10. l
11. i
12. m
13. k

Grammar & Punctuation Review

1. An independent clause conveys a complete thought and can stand alone as a sentence.

2. A dependent clause does not contain a complete thought and therefore cannot stand alone as a sentence.

3. <u>The Psalms are my favorite verses to read</u>,[IND] yet <u>I love reading the Gospels as well</u>.[IND]

4. <u>Even though my church is only one block from my house</u>,[DP] <u>my family is occasionally late for services</u>![IND]

5. <u>We are going on a cruise in the spring</u>[IND] or <u>spending a week at my aunt's cabin in Canada</u>.[DP]

6. for, and, nor, but, or, yet, so

7. Answers should include two of the following: either-or, neither-nor, both-and, not only-but also, no sooner-than, rather-than

8. Answers should include four of the following: after, although, as, because, before, if, once, since, that, unless, until, when, where, while, as if, even though, so that

Review Answer Key

Communication Review

1. A citation is required when you quote or paraphrase someone's words or refer to a source substantially.
2. a. common knowledge
   b. allusions
   c. passing mentions
3. a. direct quote
   b. paraphrase
   c. summarize

Worldview & Literary Analysis Review

1. In the midst of things
2. *In medias res* is used to "pull the reader in" by instantly plunging them into the middle of an important or dramatic event in the story.
3. Reed opens with the scene of Columbus and his son standing at the gate of a convent in Spain, weary and begging for bread.

Lesson 7, Exercise 5, Day 35, Pages 87–88

Vocabulary Review

1. g
2. c
3. f
4. b
5. d
6. e
7. a
8. n
9. m
10. h
11. i
12. l
13. j
14. k

Grammar & Punctuation Review

1. a. indicative
   b. imperative
   c. subjunctive
2. The indicative mood expresses a fact.
3. The imperative mood makes a direct request or a demand.
4. The subjunctive mood expresses a condition that is hypothetical, doubtful, wishful, or not factual.
5. subjunctive
6. imperative
7. indicative

Communication Review

1. A reflective essay explores a concept, idea, or observation from the writer's point of view. It is written in the first-person using pronouns like *I, me, we,* and *us*.
2. Answers will vary. Students should condense their reflective essay by placing the most important information from their essay into one paragraph.

Worldview & Literary Analysis Review

1. Imagery is a literary device that uses vivid descriptions to paint a picture in the mind of the reader.
2. The aim is for the reader to feel like they are within the experience being described.
3. "The real advantage of his countrymen, and not the acquirement of fame for himself, was the motive" (p. 94).
4. Lydia Darrah was a woman who gave specific intelligence to Washington which greatly aided his decision-making.

Review Answer Key

Lesson 8, Exercise 5, Day 40, Pages 97–98

Vocabulary Review

1. g
2. c
3. e
4. h
5. d
6. a
7. i
8. f
9. b
10. m
11. q
12. p
13. j
14. o
15. n
16. l
17. k

Grammar & Punctuation Review

1. A preposition is a word that shows a relationship between its object, usually a noun or pronoun, and another word in the sentence.
2. The object of the preposition is the noun or pronoun that follows the preposition.
3. (With renewed enthusiasm), Jason tried climbing (to the top) (of the rock wall) again.
4. (Into the depths) (of the ocean) the submarine plunged and set out (on its maiden voyage).
5. (Without any knowledge) (of edible plants), the lost hikers were (in danger) (of starvation).
6. The moon shone (outside our cabin) and cast a gorgeous glow (on the snow) (around us).
7. Answers will vary but must include a preposition regarding location. See the chart on Day 37.

Communication Review

1. a. Author: The primary creator of the work you are citing.

   b. Title: The name of the book you are referencing.

   c. Publisher: The entity responsible for producing the work.

   e. Date: The date this version of the work was published.

   f. Location: The actual page number or numbers you are referencing.

Worldview & Literary Analysis Review

1. Exposition is a literary device that introduces background information important to the story.
2. It is important to mix it in with other devices like imagery and dialogue. The writer needs to find a balance between giving too little detail and sharing too much detail.
3. Answers will vary, but students should explain their opinion with evidence from the text of *Life of Washington*.

Lesson 9, Exercise 5, Day 45, Pages 107–108

Vocabulary Review

1. c
2. f
3. d
4. g
5. b
6. h
7. a
8. e
9. i
10. n
11. m
12. j
13. o
14. l
15. k

Grammar & Punctuation Review

1. In the active voice, the subject is doing the action.
2. In the passive voice, the action is happening to the subject.
3. passive
4. active
5. passive
6. active
7. Our garbage bins were left lying in the middle of the street by the garbage man.

Language Lessons for a Living Education Level 10

Review Answer Key

Communication Review

1. A definition essay defines a term or an idea, such as a vocabulary word, abstract concept, historical word, technical term, or any idea that can be defined.
2. Answers will vary. Students should condense their definition essay by placing the most important information from their essay into one paragraph.

Worldview & Literary Analysis Review

1. a. She shows that he recognized God as his leader and gave Him the glory in all types of situations.

   b. She shows his concern for his troops showing that he was willing to give up his life for them.

   c. She shows Washington's willingness to bring correction to his troops when needed.

2. Providence, conspicuous, infidel, faith, wicked, gratitude

Quarter 2 Reviews

Lesson 10, Exercise 5, Day 50, Pages 117–118

Vocabulary Review

1. k
2. n
3. d
4. o
5. i
6. e
7. c
8. a
9. b
10. l
11. g
12. h
13. m
14. j
15. f

Grammar & Punctuation Review

1. Jared looked at me and exclaimed, "I could not be happier to call you my brother!"
2. "With all we have going on this week," said Erica, "I don't see us having time to finish our project."
3. Do you remember the song "With My Eyes Looking Up" that we used to sing at church?
4. The word "cool" has so many different meanings.
5. Were you surprised when the announcer said, "The concert is canceled"?

Communication Review

1. a. A quote of four or fewer lines can be set off with quotation marks and included in a sentence.

   b. A quote of four or more lines can be set in a block quotation apart from the text.

   c. A full or partial quote can be integrated into your own sentence using quotation marks.

2. Paraphrasing is using your own words yet including all the important information the source gives.
3. Summarizing is using your own words to condense a lengthy source so it fits with your topic and space.
4. full name, last name

Worldview & Literary Analysis Review

1. Foreshadowing is a literary device used to hint at events yet to come in a story.
2. Answers will vary. Students should write a well-constructed paragraph explaining how a person is drawn into sin and deception.

Review Answer Key

Lesson 11, Exercise 5, Day 55, Pages 127–128

Vocabulary Review

1. b
2. p
3. m
4. j
5. g
6. f
7. c
8. k
9. l
10. e
11. o
12. n
13. a
14. h
15. i
16. q
17. d

Grammar & Punctuation Review

1. a. A compound sentence contains two independent clauses connected by a coordinating conjunction and a comma.

   b. Answers will vary. *Example*: Moses listened to the Lord, and Aaron and Miriam supported him.

2. a. A complex sentence has one independent clause and one dependent clause.

   b. Answers will vary. *Example*: Since I have trouble waking up on time, I really should set an alarm.

3. Answers will vary. *Example*: Yes! I could not be more excited about this job!

Communication Review

1. A signal verb is a verb used to indicate how someone is expressing their ideas.

2. Answers should include six of the following: states, writes, mentions, adds, points out, notes, comments, finds, observes, discusses, expresses, considers, explores, illustrates.

Worldview & Literary Analysis Review

1. a. acts of rebellion

   b. fight, freedom, roots, cause, luxuries, Solomon

2. Answers will vary, but students should have written a paragraph containing the story of either the young lad or Mrs. Heyward and their personal opinion about the person.

Lesson 12, Exercise 5, Day 60, Pages 137–138

Vocabulary Review

1. e
2. p
3. b
4. o
5. i
6. f
7. a
8. j
9. c
10. l
11. n
12. k
13. h
14. g
15. m
16. d

Grammar & Punctuation Review

1. which one, what kind, how many
2. how much, how often, when, why, where, to what extent
3. <u>Suspiciously</u>, the <u>large</u> <u>red</u> fox slithered into <u>the chicken</u> coop for <u>a</u> <u>surprise</u> attack.
4. We must <u>patiently</u> wait until <u>tomorrow</u> to eat <u>those delicious</u> cookies!
5. noun
6. adjective
7. adverb
8. adverb

Review Answer Key

Communication Review

1. a. Begin with a quote either by or about the subject.
   b. Describe their greatest accomplishment.
   c. Relate a fascinating anecdote about them.
   d. Give interesting information about the subject without revealing their name yet.
2. A thesis statement expresses the main idea you are trying to get across about your subject.

Worldview & Literary Analysis Review

1. An anecdote is like a short story within a story that usually focuses on a single character.
2. anecdotes, true, fictional, underscore, trait, emphasize
3. Answers will vary. The paragraph should be well structured and recount any short story from *Life of Washington*.

Lesson 13, Exercise 5, Day 65, Pages 147–148

Vocabulary Review

1. d
2. n
3. i
4. e
5. o
6. f
7. b
8. q
9. p
10. j
11. g
12. l
13. k
14. s
15. c
16. h
17. m
18. a
19. r

Grammar & Punctuation Review

1. The house on the right, the one my aunt used to live in, was just sold to a young family from Texas.
2. In the Rocky Mountains, the cliffs are steep, the trees are huge, and the rivers run clear.
3. Assuming the cloud cover remains, it may be okay that you forgot your sunblock.
4. Over the past three days, we have seen an abundance of much-needed rain in our community.
5. The Bible study group prayed together, for they were of one mind concerning the lost.
6. Answers will vary. *Example*: With an eye for talent, the recruiter formed a team of highly qualified people.

Communication Review

1. An outline is an organizational plan for writing.
2. Roman numerals, paragraph, letters, points
3. a. "A fool's lips walk into a fight, and his mouth invites a beating."
   b. "A fool's mouth is his ruin, and his lips are a snare to his soul."

Worldview & Literary Analysis Review

1. An analogy is a literary device that connects two seemingly unrelated concepts to show their similarities in a way that expands on a thought or idea.
2. comparison, metaphors, meaning, larger point
3. a. Love your enemies.
   b. Do good to those who hate you.
   c. Bless those who curse you.
   d. Pray for those who abuse you.

Review Answer Key

Lesson 14, Exercise 5, Day 70, Pages 157–158

Vocabulary Review

1. l
2. i
3. c
4. q
5. n
6. b
7. o
8. j
9. e
10. r
11. m
12. g
13. a
14. p
15. f
16. d
17. h
18. k

Grammar & Punctuation Review

1. e
2. a
3. d
4. b
5. c
6. f
7. <u>Scuba</u> diving requires <u>a</u> person to have <u>excellent</u> health and <u>good</u> <u>swimming</u> skills.
8. <u>Tropical</u> rainforests are <u>the</u> <u>most</u> <u>biologically</u> diverse <u>terrestrial</u> ecosystems on <u>the</u> planet.
9. <u>Canada's</u> <u>Pacific</u> <u>coast</u> climate is <u>relatively</u> mild, yet <u>the</u> <u>Prairie</u> Provinces have <u>greater</u> <u>weather</u> extremes.

Communication Review

1. A works cited page lists only sources actually referred to and cited in the paper. A bibliography lists all the sources consulted, whether referred to and cited or not.
2. Alexander, Eric. *The Summit*. New Leaf Publishing Group, LLC, 2016.

   Ham, Ken. "Did an Empire Rule North America Before Europeans Arrived?" Ken Ham Blog, 17 Oct. 2023. answersingenesis.org/blogs/ken-ham/2023/10/17/did-empire-rule-north-america-before-europeans/.

Worldview & Literary Analysis Review

1. Authorial intrusion is a literary device in which the author directly addresses the reader by interrupting the story.
2. "Young Americans!" (p. 211)
3. a. The "protection of Almighty God" (p. 205)

   b. "… [T]hose who have the superintendence of them to his holy keeping" (p. 205)
4. a. "… the tenderest ties of nature were disregarded" (p. 211)

   b. "… the truths of religion were denied" (p. 211)

   c. "… the worship of God [was] abolished" (p. 211)

Lesson 15, Exercise 5, Day 75, Pages 167–168

Vocabulary Review

1. a
2. e
3. d
4. l
5. k
6. q
7. o
8. h
9. i
10. f
11. p
12. c
13. g
14. j
15. n b
16. r
17. m
18. b n

Grammar & Punctuation Review

1. d
2. g
3. e
4. c
5. a
6. b
7. f
8. My dog River <u>greedily</u> consumed the plate of chicken scraps I left in his bowl.
9. <u>Yesterday</u> we had a flat tire, and Dad <u>quite</u> <u>easily</u> changed it while we waited in the car.
10. <u>Unfortunately</u>, my average fell <u>below</u> the rest of the class, and I needed to study <u>diligently</u> to make up for it.
11. How <u>often</u> do you read Scripture?

Communication Review

1. A rough draft is the first version of a piece of writing that needs editing and rewriting. A final draft is the final version of a piece of writing that has been edited and rewritten.
2. Answers will vary, but the sentence should be introduced by a transitional word of emphasis found in the chart on Day 73.
3. Answers will vary, but the sentence should be introduced by a transitional word of order found in the chart on Day 73.

Worldview & Literary Analysis Review

1. a. Everyone needed to account for the money they spent every week (p. 224).
   b. The Sabbath must be kept holy (p. 224).
   c. Everyone needed to be punctual (p. 225).
2. Answers will vary, but students should have listed three rules their family abides by.

Lesson 16, Exercise 5, Day 80, Pages 177–178

Vocabulary Review

1. n
2. p
3. q
4. d
5. f
6. g
7. e
8. l
9. m
10. j
11. c
12. r
13. a
14. i
15. k
16. b
17. h
18. o

Grammar & Punctuation Review

1. before, after
2. adjectives, adverbs, after, verb, anywhere
3. The police officer (with the service dog) helped my mother and me. police officer
4. The shed (beside the house) needed to be power washed. shed
5. Put the cat outside, or he will eat the food (on the table). food
6. The student stood up and spoke (with great passion). spoke
7. We usually go Christmas shopping (after Thanksgiving). go
8. I swam (beside the dock), hoping to find my goggles. swam

Communication Review

1. Answers will vary, but the paragraph should be well constructed and thoroughly answer the question.

Worldview & Literary Analysis Review

1. Strong drink
2. habits, political prosperity, morality, indispensable
3. humble, divine, religion, nation

Review Answer Key

Lesson 17, Exercise 5, Day 85, Pages 187–188

Vocabulary Review

1. h
2. l
3. i
4. n
5. o
6. g
7. j
8. b
9. d
10. q
11. e
12. p
13. f
14. k
15. a
16. c
17. m

Grammar & Punctuation Review

1. A verbal phrase functions as a noun, adjective, or adverb and is not a verb.
2. b
3. a
4. c
5. d
6. The women <u>running in the race</u> were running for a cause that was dear to their hearts. present
7. <u>Preparing our property for winter</u> is something my entire family participates in. gerund
8. Erin, <u>thrilled for the chance to participate in the choir</u>, practiced every evening in her bedroom. past
9. The plan, <u>having been thought through for many months</u>, was finally put into place. perfect
10. The rabbit <u>who hopped out of the cage</u> was quickly caught by the little boy. past

Communication Review

1. Answers will vary.

Worldview & Literary Analysis Review

1. An archetype is a literary device that refers to a universal symbol or pattern that recurs in stories and other forms of literature across different cultures and time periods.
2. a. Answers should include two of the following: the hero, the villain, the mother or father figure, the creator, the jester.
   b. Answers should include two of the following: a lost love, an orphan destined for greatness, death/rebirth, a fall from greatness, a quest, light vs. darkness.
   c. Answers should include two of the following: trees (nature or life), fire (destruction or creativity), darkness (evil or despair), a garden (love or fertility), an island (isolation or loneliness).
3. "I am the resurrection and the life; he that believeth in me, though he were dead, yet shall he live" (p. 259).

Lesson 18, Exercise 5, Day 90, Pages 197–198

Vocabulary Review

1. r
2. d
3. t
4. g
5. l
6. s
7. m
8. h
9. c
10. q
11. p
12. b
13. o
14. k
15. n
16. i
17. e
18. a
19. f
20. j

Grammar & Punctuation Review

1. An infinitive is a verbal phrase that can function as a noun, adjective, or adverb.
2. An infinitive consists of the word *to* plus a verb form (*to* + verb).
3. When the word *to* is followed by a noun, not a verb, this means it is a prepositional phrase.
4. noun
5. adverb
6. adjective
7. preposition
8. Answers will vary. *Examples*: The state championships were something I hoped to attend someday. Someday, I hope to attend the state championships.

Communication Review

1. Answers will vary. The response should include that the crowd was cut to the heart, they asked how to be saved, Peter instructed them about salvation, and three thousand souls were saved.

Quarter 3 Reviews

Lesson 19, Exercise 5, Day 95, Pages 207–208

Vocabulary Review

1. i
2. j
3. d
4. h
5. p
6. k
7. g
8. o
9. m
10. l
11. a
12. e
13. c
14. b
15. f
16. n

Grammar & Punctuation Review

1. After hours of studying, (Melody) finally memorized all the books of the Bible, and <u>she</u> felt so accomplished.
2. The (tractor) broke down on the side of the road, and <u>it</u> obviously wasn't going to be moved anytime soon.
3. The (horses) always stay very close to the barn
   SP
   when <u>they</u> hear a thunderstorm coming.

   SP   RP
4. We went to the children's (museum) (that) features antique toys.

   SP   OP
5. When <u>we</u> went to the lake, (Mom) gave <u>me</u> a surprise picnic lunch!

   SP   RFP   IP
6. He gave (himself) permission to enjoy (some) (cookies.)

   DP
7. These (haybales) are soaking wet from all the rain last night.

   IP   RP
8. <u>Everybody</u> will notice (that) (rainbow!)

Communication Review

1. Answers will vary. Writing a biography required research and citation as you scoured sources in search of the person's life details. An autobiography will require some research but *not* the type you would look for in a book or online. Since this account is about *you*, asking parents, relatives, and friends for details, opinions, and quotes will enhance your autobiography and give credibility to it.

2. When Christians write an autobiography, they consider not only what they want others to know about them, but also what they want to communicate about God.

Review Answer Key

Lesson 20, Exercise 5, Day 100, Pages 217–218

Vocabulary Review

1. j
2. i
3. b
4. a
5. c
6. h
7. g
8. e
9. f

Grammar & Punctuation Review

1. (Maria and Joanna) are challenging each other [RC] to eat healthy foods and get fit.
2. There were only two types of (cookies) at the banquet, but each [DP] looked delicious!
3. Whose [INT] phone got left outside?
4. Possessive pronouns show ownership and function as nouns. Possessive adjectives are pronouns functioning as adjectives that show ownership.
5. The only true hope is in (Christ's) work on the Cross because His [PA] righteousness became mine [PP].
6. After (Sarah) found her [PA] wallet at the grocery store, she had to prove to the manager that it was hers [PP].
7. I never realized how much my mother loved me.
8. I had enough confidence in myself that I knew I could conquer my fears.
9. My sister is the one who bakes up a storm at Christmastime.
10. God has mercy on whomever He will.

Communication Review

1. Observe examples.
2. Write down important memories.
3. Establish a theme.
4. Create a detailed outline.
5. Write a rough draft.
6. Write a final draft.

Worldview & Literary Analysis Review

1. They uncovered God's truth.
2. God's truth

Lesson 21, Exercise 5, Day 105, Pages 227–228

Vocabulary Review

1. n
2. b
3. l
4. d
5. g
6. f
7. m
8. j
9. k
10. i
11. h
12. e
13. c
14. a

Grammar & Punctuation Review

1. A direct object is a noun that receives the action of the verb and answers the questions "what?" or "whom?"
2. An indirect object is a noun that is affected by the action of the verb but is not the primary object receiving the action.
3. My dad gave my mother [IO] diamond earrings [DO] for her birthday this year.
4. The chemist cleaned the lab [DO] one last time before going home for the evening.
5. Running frantically back and forth, the squirrel finally snatched the acorn [DO] from the middle of the road.
6. Aunt Sue handed her nieces and nephews [IO] each a small gift [DO] after the recital.

Worldview & Literary Analysis Review

1. The discovery of God's truth
2. New knowledge
3. "Mankind's ultimate aspiration seems to manifest itself through becoming the final authority in all aspects of his own existence."
4. They become slaves.

Review Answer Key

Lesson 22, Exercise 5, Day 110, Pages 237–238

Vocabulary Review

1. a
2. h
3. f
4. d
5. e
6. i
7. j
8. c
9. b
10. g
11. k

Grammar & Punctuation Review

1. The volleyball team <u>is</u> traveling to France for an international competition.
2. The rooster and all the hens <u>peck</u> the ground in search of small bugs.
3. The furniture <u>needs</u> to be moved out of the room to install the carpet.
4. His mother or his older sisters usually <u>pick</u> him up after soccer practice.
5. A young boy, one of several student volunteers, <u>is</u> helping serve lunches this week.
6. Often, the town council members or the mayor <u>has</u> the final say on issues like these.

Communication Review

1. Cautionary: A tale that involves a character flaw or poor judgment and results in negative consequences.
2. Humorous: A funny story used to lighten the mood, create a short break in the main story, and entertain the reader.
3. Inspirational: A persuasive or emotional appeal that aims to create a certain feeling in the reader they can identify with.
4. Characterizing: A story that reveals more about the main character or side character's personality and may not be part of the main story but gives a glimpse at certain virtues or attributes.
5. Reminiscent: A nostalgic story focused on the more distant past, especially on aspects of the world that have changed, creating a longing for the old days.

Worldview & Literary Analysis Review

1. The Bible was printed, and people had access to "its fascinating truths, including scientific truths."
2. Most of mankind's major scientific discoveries were made.
3. a. Isaac Newton   d. Kepler
   b. Galileo   e. Faraday
   c. Copernicus

Lesson 23, Exercise 5, Day 115, Pages 247–248

Vocabulary Review

1. c
2. m
3. k
4. d
5. j
6. f
7. e
8. b
9. g
10. h
11. i
12. a
13. n
14. l

Grammar & Punctuation Review

1. To conjugate is to give the different forms of a verb according to voice, mood, tense, number, and person.
2. The fourth-grade students and their teacher <u>present</u> a bouquet to the principal each year.
3. Bradley, along with his fishing buddies, <u>hopes</u> to have a big catch today.
4. indicative
5. imperative
6. subjunctive
7. active
8. passive
9. passive

Worldview & Literary Analysis Review

1. An "Intelligent Being … caused man, the universe, and life to come into existence."
2. A "conventional, atheistic, and naturalistic approach" to science.

Language Lessons for a Living Education Level 10

Review Answer Key

Lesson 24, Exercise 5, Day 120, Pages 257–258

Vocabulary Review

1. m
2. b
3. i
4. g
5. l
6. f
7. c
8. k
9. j
10. h
11. n
12. e
13. a
14. d

Grammar & Punctuation Review

1. A transitive verb requires a direct object to receive its action, while an intransitive verb completes its action without a direct object.
2. transitive
3. transitive
4. intransitive
5. Each time I *write* <u>my name</u>, I tend to form my letters slightly differently for some reason. (DO above "my name") transitive
6. Gabe and Brady *laughed* so hard at the <u>comedian</u> that they started to cry. (OP above "comedian") intransitive
7. All I could do was *shake* <u>my head</u> when I realized the mistake I had made. (DO above "my head") transitive
8. Answers will vary. *Example*: The boy broke his arm when he fell off his bike.
9. Answers will vary. *Example*: My arm broke when I fell off my bike.

Communication Review

1. Answers will vary. Writing is like sculpting. Picture an artist with a lump of clay. The artist has a vision but must first mold and shape, taking off excess clay in some areas and adding extra clay in others. This process can take some time as the artist observes from all angles and adjusts. Finally, finishing touches and details are added until the artist is happy with the creation.
2. Transitional words and phrases are used to jump from one thought or place to the next.
3. concluding paragraph, summary, lessons, personality formation, God's, forward, hints, directions

Worldview & Literary Analysis Review

1.
   a. They are too afraid.
   b. They are too proud.
   c. They are too unwilling to challenge it.

Lesson 25, Exercise 5, Day 125, Pages 267–268

Vocabulary Review

1. k
2. i
3. o
4. p
5. h
6. g
7. n
8. a
9. m
10. e
11. f
12. d
13. b
14. c
15. j
16. l

Grammar & Punctuation Review

1. Singular refers to one, while plural refers to more than one.
2. add *es*
3. add *s*
4. drop the *f* or *fe* and add *ves*
5. add *es*
6. add *s*
7. remove *y*, add *ies*
8. cacti
9. tuna
10. countries
11. potatoes
12. foci
13. people
14. vehicles
15. knives
16. churches
17. fungi
18. bison
19. stereos
20. Answers will vary. *Example:* We cooked several turkey dinners at the homeless shelter; it was an incredible amount of work! Refer to Day 122 for more examples if needed.

Review Answer Key

Communication Review

1. Answers will vary. This is a short example, but the student's answer should be longer:

   I approached my mother and said, "Mom, I am supposed to present my autobiography in an oral presentation. I'm scared!"

   Mom took one look at me and noticed the apprehension in my voice. She replied, "Honey, I know it can be frightening to speak in front of others, but you have more experience at it than you may think."

Worldview & Literary Analysis Review

1. "… [T]here is no *scientific evidence* to sustain such a postulate!"

2. "… [T]he supposition that human existence is entirely the result of statistical chance and random adaptation over billions of years …"

Lesson 26, Exercise 5, Day 130, Pages 277–278

Vocabulary Review

1. h
2. c
3. f
4. a
5. d
6. g
7. b
8. m
9. k
10. i
11. j
12. l
13. e

Grammar & Punctuation Review

1. A possessive noun shows ownership or a direct connection and is usually formed by adding 's.
2. cat's
3. house's
4. library's
5. arrow's
6. potato's
7. phone's
8. dogs'
9. parks'
10. girls'
11. On Wednesdays, my friend's mother takes us to a painting class offered at Jesse's. Jesse's is an art and craft shop in our town with a large room in the back that the owners offer for art instructors' use. My friend Macie painted a cute pile of puppies in a basket. She did an amazing job on the puppies' fur; her painting looked very realistic! My painting is of a few tiny birds in a nest. The birds' nest is the hardest part. The instructor said she really liked mine. I am hoping to finish this week, but Wednesday's weather forecast is calling for an ice storm! If the weather is bad, I may just stay at Macie's.
12. Answers will vary. *Example*: His office is just down the hall from mine. (*His* is a possessive adjective; *mine* is a possessive pronoun)

Communication Review

1. To "reflect" means to give serious thought or consideration to something that took place.
2. An oral presentation consists of an individual or group addressing an audience on a particular topic.

Worldview & Literary Analysis Review

1. "… [G]enuine scientific truths regarding God."
2. "… [H]istory teaches us that God will always raise up those who are willing to shine the light of truth."

Review Answer Key

Lesson 27, Exercise 5, Day 135, Pages 287–288

Vocabulary Review

1. h
2. c
3. f
4. e
5. i
6. b
7. a
8. d
9. g

Grammar & Punctuation Review

1. To show possession, a singular noun adds 's. A plural noun adds an 's unless it already ends in s. In that case, add an apostrophe (') only.
2. banana
3. banana's
4. bananas'
5. country's
6. countries'
7. ox's
8. oxen
9. oxen's
10. mouse's
11. mice
12. mice's
13. Answers will vary. *Example*: Looking at the cluster hanging from the tree, I noticed the bananas' color seemed odd.
14. I enjoyed reading the book *Jesus Unmasked: The Truth Will Shock You.*
15. Our pastor read from Ephesians 6:10–12, and the sermon lasted until 12:30.
16. The teacher read the words of Jesus from John 14:6: "I am the way, and the truth, and the life. No one comes to the Father except through me."

Worldview & Literary Analysis Review

1. "… [T]o 'give a defense' … for *why* we believe."
2. "… [O]ur presentation has to go beyond talk, evidence, and scientific *facts*. It has to show up in the lifestyle and *faith* of those who claim to believe it."

Quarter 4 Reviews

Lesson 28, Exercise 5, Day 140, Pages 297–298

Vocabulary Review

1. enthusiastic public praise
2. rising to an important position or higher level
3. converts from one religion or opinion to another
4. a period of a thousand years
5. Answers will vary. *Example:* What the officer said about his commander was not *appropriate* and perhaps even an act of *betrayal*.

Grammar & Punctuation Review

1. <u>If I hadn't been so busy reading</u> (DP), <u>I would have noticed the rain approaching and closed the windows</u> (IND). complex
2. <u>I like to pack a lot of clothes when I go camping</u> (IND), but <u>my brother barely brings anything with him</u>. compound
3. <u>After arriving at our hotel</u> (DP), <u>we unloaded our suitcases</u> (IND), and <u>we all headed straight for the pool</u> (IND). compound-complex
4. A contextual clue is like a hint that helps you decipher the meaning of a word based on the words around it or how it is used in the sentence.
5. c
6. d
7. a
8. b

Communication Review

1. A summary is a restatement of the main ideas of someone else's writing, stated in your own words.

Review Answer Key

Worldview & Literary Analysis Review

1. Alexander's mentors "gave him a passion for the outdoors and for the Lord, which continues today."
2. Higher Summits has allowed "him to share an inspirational message with people all over the world, opening the door to share his faith in Christ and the true meaning of purpose in life."
3. A mentor is a person who offers guidance and support to another. The person they are offering advice to is called the mentee.

Lesson 29, Exercise 5, Day 145, Pages 307–308

Grammar & Punctuation Review

1. Parallelism in grammar means that two or more phrases or clauses in a sentence have the same grammatical structure.
2. Answers will vary. Be sure to keep each element parallel. Refer to Day 142 if necessary. *Example:* When considering a major financial purchase, you should ponder the necessity of the item, consider the amount you are spending, and take it to the Lord in prayer.
3. If you can change the word to have the suffix *-ion* at the end, use *-or*. If you can't, use *-er*.
4. liberator
5. manager
6. pastor
7. instructor
8. builder
9. creator

Communication Review

1. A thesaurus can be overused when the writer chooses words that are too "fancy" or unusual and may not be understood by their audience.
2. Answers will vary. "A soft tongue" speaks of gentle and respectful speech. There is power in such speech — enough power to break something hard.

Worldview & Literary Analysis Review

1. A "deadpoint is a [mountain] climbing move where momentum is used to achieve a higher handhold."
2. c
3. b
4. a

Lesson 30, Exercise 5, Day 150, Pages 317–318

Grammar & Punctuation Review

1. A double negative occurs when two negative words are used in the same statement, leading to confusion.
2. Answers will vary. *Example:* After observing her behavior, Erin knew she could never work with anybody like that!
3. b
4. c
5. a

Communication Review

1. Rhetoric is the art of persuasive speaking or writing that uses language to motivate, persuade, or inform.
2. Answers will vary. The three modes of persuasion are ethos (character or spirit), logos (logic or rationale), and pathos (suffering or experience). The ancient Greek philosopher and scientist Aristotle, in his written work *Rhetoric*, presented ideas for persuading one's audience through both writing and speaking. These ideas have become known as the "modes of persuasion."

Worldview & Literary Analysis Review

1. Answers will vary. This climb was successful because Alexander needed to swallow his pride, as he had to stay back from the summit when the four blind students ascended and reached the summit. He had wanted to take credit for assisting them but had to stay at high camp with two ill climbers.
2. a. perfect, humble, grace, admission, failure
   b. obedience, love, emulate, relationship, striving, refining

Review Answer Key

Lesson 31, Exercise 5, Day 155, Pages 327–328

Grammar & Punctuation Review

1. d
2. h
3. f
4. a
5. j
6. i
7. e
8. c
9. g
10. b
11. b
12. a
13. c

Communication Review

1.
   a. Choose a topic
   b. Research
   c. Create a thesis statement
   d. Make an outline
   e. Write it out
2. A debatable claim is a statement that people could reasonably have differing opinions about.

Worldview & Literary Analysis Review

1. believe, death, life, peace, believe, God

Lesson 32, Exercise 5, Day 160, Pages 337–338

Vocabulary Review

1. d
2. a
3. f
4. e
5. b
6. c

Grammar & Punctuation Review

1. Answers will vary. *Example:* Rebecca dug through her backpack, frantically looking for her book.
2. Answers will vary. *Example:* The clothing store window displayed children's winter coats.
3. Answers will vary. *Example:* The weather was terrible when I was walking home last night.
4. c
5. d
6. a
7. b

Communication Review

1. Vary your sentence structure.
2. Avoid repeating words.
3. Be engaging.
4. Use quality transitions.
5. Use vivid imagery.
6. Stay focused.
7. Keep your voice interesting.
8. Use specific words.
9. Use accurate words.

Worldview & Literary Analysis Review

1. wrong, God, give, spoiled, demanding

Lesson 33, Exercise 5, Day 165, Pages 347–348

Grammar & Punctuation Review

1. rang
2. rung
3. caught
4. caught
5. knew
6. known
7. went
8. gone
9. act, result, or state of
10. science of or study of
11. belonging to; result of
12. causing an action

Communication Review

1. margins, 1 inch, Double, 12, New Roman, Indent, title, name, assignment, date, works cited, alphabetical, ½, Single, margins
2. Tangible things can be touched or felt, while intangible things are not perceived through touch, as they do not have a physical presence.

Worldview & Literary Analysis Review

1. To be cynical is to believe that others are motivated purely by their self-interest, causing you to be distrustful of them.
2. In mountain climbing terms, a belayer would be the person who turns the rope around a cleat or pin to make it hold tight for another climber.

Review Answer Key

Lesson 34, Exercise 5, Day 170, Pages 357–358

Vocabulary Review
1. d
2. e
3. g
4. f
5. c
6. a
7. b

Grammar & Punctuation Review
1. Answers should include three of the following: Use hyphens to connect compound modifiers that appear before the noun they modify. Use hyphens in certain compound words. If unsure, consult a dictionary. Use a hyphen with spelled-out fractions and compound numbers from twenty-one to ninety-nine. Use a hyphen in words with the prefixes *ex-*, *self-*, *all-*, *anti-*, and *mid-*.

Communication Review
1. a. The seller must convince the customer that they are trustworthy and knowledgeable.
   b. The seller must attempt to back up their claim that their product is superior.
   c. The seller must appeal to emotions connected to their product.
2. a. Answers will vary. *Example:* "Trusted by mothers everywhere."
   b. Answers will vary. *Example:* "Teeth are straightened in half the time of traditional braces."
   c. Answers will vary. *Example:* "Your dog will know you love them."

Worldview & Literary Analysis Review
1. discipline, consequences, decision, care, right, deny, desires

Lesson 35, Exercise 5, Day 175, Pages 367–368

Grammar & Punctuation Review
1. I walked in just in time to hear Mike say, "Let's grab some ice cream, peanuts, and whipped cream for our movie night!"
2. To my surprise, my friend Marley, who loves socializing, declined to come to the picnic with me.
3. When I graduate on June 21, 2028, I may go to a community college, work full-time, or join the military.
4. Answers will vary. *Examples:* gorgeous, gaseous
5. Answers will vary. *Examples:* fiery, machinery
6. Answers will vary. *Examples:* recede, intercede

Communication Review
1. An oral presentation consists of communicating verbally to an audience on a particular topic.

Worldview & Literary Analysis Review
1. risk, know, beliefs, fire, truth, believe, dream, criticism, perceived

Review Answer Key

Lesson 36, Exercise 5, Day 180, Pages 377–378

Vocabulary Review

1. e
2. f
3. a
4. g
5. c
6. h
7. b
8. d

Grammar & Punctuation Review

1. Not everyone agrees, but I feel I will get <u>further</u> in life if I pursue a college degree.
2. Sometimes certain personalities really <u>complement</u> each other.
3. God's Word <u>assures</u> me that the sacrifice Christ made when He <u>laid</u> down His life for me is sufficient to cover my sins.
4. c
5. d
6. e
7. a
8. g
9. b
10. f

Communication Review

1. Etiquette refers to the customary code of polite behavior in society or among members of a particular group.
2. Written Communication. Answers will vary. Refer to Day 178.
3. Verbal Communication. Answers will vary. Refer to Day 178.
4. Nonverbal and Visual Communication. Answers will vary. Refer to Day 178.
5. Contextual Communication. Answers will vary. Refer to Day 178.
6. Active Listening. Answers will vary. Refer to Day 178.

Worldview & Literary Analysis Review

1. Value
2. Answers will vary but should follow these ideas laid out in Romans 5:3–5: "[B]ecause we know that suffering produces perseverance; perseverance, character; and character, hope. And hope does not disappoint us, because God has poured out his love into our hearts by the Holy Spirit, whom he has given us."

Photo Credits

All photos Shutterstock.com except
AdobeStock.com: pg 249
Dr. Raymond Damadian: pg 209
Generation Word: pg 289
istock.com: pg 29, pg 119, pg 159
Library of Congress: pg 156
New York Digital Library: pg 40, pg 119
Public Domain: pg 24, pg 39, pg 45, pg 54, pg 79, pg 99, pg 109, pg 149, pg 189, pg 324, pg 349,
Wikimedia: pg 359 (CC-BY-SA3.0); pg 186 (CC-BY-SA2.0)

LOGIC
FROM A BIBLICAL PERSPECTIVE

This logic course will both challenge and inspire high school students to be able to defend their faith against atheists and skeptics alike.

978-1-68344-159-5

JASON LISLE

DR. JASON LISLE is a Christian astrophysicist who writes and speaks on various topics relating to science and the defense of the Christian faith. He earned his Ph.D. in astrophysics at the University of Colorado in Boulder.

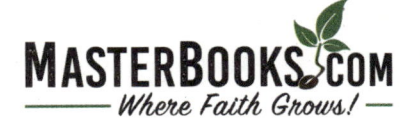

MasterBooks.com — Where Faith Grows!

TO SEE OUR FULL LINE OF FAITH-BUILDING CURRICULUM